Laboratory Manual

Hole's

Human Anatomy
&Physiology

ELEVENTH EDITION

DAVID SHIER
JACKIE BUTLER
RICKI LEWIS

TERRY R. MARTIN
Kishwaukee College

D1451712

Mc Graw Hill **Higher Education**

Boston   Burr Ridge, IL   Dubuque, IA   Madison, WI   New York   San Francisco   St. Louis
Bangkok   Bogotá   Caracas   Kuala Lumpur   Lisbon   London   Madrid   Mexico City
Milan   Montreal   New Delhi   Santiago   Seoul   Singapore   Sydney   Taipei   Toronto

The McGraw·Hill Companies

Higher Education

LABORATORY MANUAL to accompany HOLE'S HUMAN ANATOMY & PHYSIOLOGY
ELEVENTH EDITION

1 2 3 4 5 6 7 8 9 0 QPD/QPD 0 9 8 7 6

ISBN-13 978-0-07-282957-0
ISBN-10 0-07-282957-5

Publisher: *Michelle Watnick*
Developmental Editor: *Fran Schreiber*
Lead Project Manager: *Joyce M. Berendes*
Lead Production Supervisor: *Sandy Ludovissy*
Designer: *Laurie B. Janssen*
(USE) Cover Image: © *Images.com/CORBIS*
Senior Photo Research Coordinator: *John C. Leland*
Photo Research: *Mary Reeg*
Compositor: *Interactive Composition Corporation*
Typeface: *10/12 Garamond Book*
Printer: *Quebecor World Dubuque, IA*

The credits section for this book is on page 509 and is considered an extension of the copyright page.

Some of the laboratory experiments included in this text may be hazardous if materials are handled improperly or if procedures are conducted incorrectly. Safety precautions are necessary when you are working with chemicals, glass test tubes, hot water baths, sharp instruments, and the like, or for any procedures that generally require caution. Your school may have set regulations regarding safety procedures that your instructor will explain to you. Should you have any problems with materials or procedures, please ask your instructor for help.

www.mhhe.com

CONTENTS

Lymphatic System

Digestive System

Respiratory System

Urinary System

Reproductive Systems and Development

Supplemental Frog Laboratory Exercises

*These laboratory exercises are available at www.mhhe.com/shier11 (click on this laboratory manual cover).

PREFACE

This laboratory manual was prepared to be used with the textbook *Hole's Human Anatomy and Physiology*, 11th edition, by David Shier, Jackie Butler, and Ricki Lewis. As with the textbook, the laboratory manual is designed for students with minimal backgrounds in the physical and biological sciences who are pursuing careers in professional health fields.

The laboratory manual contains sixty-four laboratory exercises and reports, which are closely integrated with the chapters of the textbook. (Three of these exercises appear only online.) The exercises are planned to illustrate and review anatomical and physiological facts and principles presented in the textbook and to help students investigate some of these ideas in greater detail.

Often the laboratory exercises are short or are divided into several separate procedures. This allows an instructor to select those exercises or parts of exercises that will best meet the needs of a particular program. Also, exercises requiring a minimal amount of laboratory equipment have been included.

The laboratory exercises include a variety of special features that are designed to stimulate interest in the subject matter, to involve students in the learning process, and to guide them through the planned activities. These special features include the following:

MATERIALS NEEDED

This section lists the laboratory materials that are required to complete the exercise and to perform the demonstrations and learning extensions.

 ## SAFETY

A list of safety guidelines is included inside the front cover. Each lab session that requires special safety guidelines has a safety section following "Materials Needed." Your instructor might require some modifications of these guidelines.

INTRODUCTION

The introduction briefly describes the subject of the exercise or the ideas that will be investigated.

PURPOSE OF THE EXERCISE

The purpose provides a statement about the intent of the exercise—that is, what will be accomplished.

LEARNING OBJECTIVES

The learning objectives list in general terms what a student should be able to do after completing the exercise.

PROCEDURE

The procedure provides a set of detailed instructions for accomplishing the planned laboratory activities. Usually these instructions are presented in outline form so that a student can proceed through the exercise in stepwise fashion. Often the student is referred to particular sections of a textbook for necessary background information or for review of subject matter presented previously.

The procedures include a wide variety of laboratory activities and, from time to time, direct the student to complete various tasks in the laboratory reports.

LABORATORY REPORTS

A laboratory report to be completed by the student immediately follows each exercise. These reports include various types of review activities, spaces for sketches of microscopic objects, tables for recording observations and experimental results, and questions dealing with the analysis of such data.

It is hoped that as a result of these activities, students will develop a better understanding of the structural and functional characteristics of their bodies and will increase their skills in gathering information by observation and experimentation. Some of the exercises also include demonstrations, optional activities, and useful illustrations.

DEMONSTRATIONS

Demonstrations appear in separate boxes. They describe specimens, specialized laboratory equipment, or other materials of interest that an instructor may want to display to enrich the student's laboratory experience.

 ## LEARNING EXTENSIONS

Learning extensions also appear in separate boxes. They encourage students to extend their laboratory experiences. Some of these activities are open-ended in that they suggest the student plan an investigation or experiment and carry it out after receiving approval from the laboratory instructor. Some of the figures are illustrated as line art or in grayscale. This will allow colored pencils to be used as a visual learning activity to distinguish various structures.

THE USE OF ANIMALS IN BIOLOGY EDUCATION*

The National Association of Biology Teachers (NABT) believes that the study of organisms, including nonhuman animals, is essential to the understanding of life on Earth. NABT recommends the prudent and responsible use of animals in the life science classroom. NABT believes that biology teachers should foster a respect for life. Biology teachers also should teach about the interrelationship and interdependency of all things.

Classroom experiences that involve nonhuman animals range from observation to dissection. NABT supports these experiences so long as they are conducted within the long-established guidelines of proper care and use of animals, as developed by the scientific and educational community.

As with any instructional activity, the use of nonhuman animals in the biology classroom must have sound educational objectives. Any use of animals, whether for observation or dissection, must convey substantive knowledge of biology. NABT believes that biology teachers are in the best position to make this determination for their students.

NABT acknowledges that no alternative can substitute for the actual experience of dissection or other use of animals and urges teachers to be aware of the limitations of alternatives. When

---

* Adopted by the Board of Directors in October 1995. This policy supersedes and replaces all previous NABT statements regarding animals in biology education.

the teacher determines that the most effective means to meet the objectives of the class do not require dissection, NABT accepts the use of alternatives to dissection, including models and the various forms of multimedia. The Association encourages teachers to be sensitive to substantive student objections to dissection and to consider providing appropriate lessons for those students where necessary.

To implement this policy, NABT endorses and adopts the "Principles and Guidelines for the Use of Animals in Precollege Education" of the Institute of Laboratory Animals Resources (National Research Council). Copies of the "Principles and Guidelines" may be obtained from the ILAR (2101 Constitution Avenue, NW, Washington, DC 20418; 202 334-2590).

ILLUSTRATIONS

Diagrams from the textbook and diagrams similar to those in the textbook often are used as aids for reviewing subject matter. Other illustrations provide visual instructions for performing steps in procedures or are used to identify parts of instruments or specimens. Micrographs are included to help students identify microscopic structures or to evaluate student understanding of tissues.

In some exercises, the figures include line drawings that are suitable for students to color with colored pencils. This activity may motivate students to observe the illustrations more carefully and help them to locate the special features represented in the figures. Students can check their work by referring to the corresponding full-color illustrations in the textbook.

It should be noted that frequent variations exist in anatomical structures among humans. The illustrations in the textbook and the laboratory manual represent normal (normal means the most common variation) anatomy.

FEATURES OF THIS EDITION

This new edition of the laboratory manual has been made more user-friendly. Many of the changes are a result of evaluations and suggestions from anatomy and physiology students. Many suggestions from users and reviewers of the tenth edition have been incorporated. Some features include the following:

1. To meet the need for clearer and more definite safety guidelines, a revised and updated safety list is located inside the front cover, and safety sections are found in appropriate labs.
2. A section called "Study Skills for Anatomy and Physiology" is located in the front material. This section was written by students enrolled in a Human Anatomy and Physiology course.
3. The "Materials Needed" section is located at the beginning of each laboratory exercise for greater ease in laboratory preparations.
4. New art has been created for the textbook and the lab manual. Additional color has been included for many figures.
5. To clarify whether a figure label refers to a general area or a specific structure, "clue" words in parentheses have been added to some figures to direct students in their answers. The first example is figure 2.1.
6. A list of terms is provided to assist in the labeling of many figures. The first example is figure 12.4.
7. Computer literacy is integrated with relevant laboratory exercises. "Web Quest" activities are found at the end of most exercises. Discover the answers to many scientific questions at www.mhhe.com/shier11 Click on Student Edition and click on Martin Lab Manual, Web Quest. Here you'll find links to help you with your quest.
8. "Critical Thinking Applications" are incorporated within most of the laboratory exercises to enhance valuable critical thinking skills that students will need throughout their lives.
9. A new chemistry lab has been added to this lab manual for the first time. Lori Garrett of Danville Area Community College was the contributing author of this laboratory exercise.
10. The endocrine system lab has been revised. The histology portions have been retained, but experiments on diabetes mellitus have replaced many of the figures to label.
11. A new genetics lab has been added to this lab manual for the first time as requested by many reviewers.
12. The three labs using live frogs have been moved from the lab manual to the Online Learning Center.
13. Two assessment tools (rubrics) for laboratory reports are included in Appendix 2.
14. The *Instructor's Manual for the Laboratory Manual to Accompany Hole's Human Anatomy and Physiology* has been revised and updated. It contains a "Student Safety Contract" and a "Student Informed Consent Form" for possible inclusion in the class. The forms could be adapted for a specific institution based upon school policy. The instructor's manual is found in the Online Learning Center for Hole's Human Anatomy & Physiology, 11th edition, www.mhhe.com/shier11 and www.mhhe.com/biosci/ap/labcentral

REVIEWERS

I would like to express my sincere gratitude to all users of the laboratory manual who provided suggestions for its improvement. I am especially grateful for the contributions of the reviewers who kindly reviewed the manual and examined the manuscript of the new edition. Their thoughtful comments and valuable suggestions are greatly appreciated. They include the following:

Penny P. Antley
University of Louisiana at Lafayette
Joseph Cameron
Hinds Community College
Cara L. Davies
Ohio Northern University
Terrel A. Dent
Mississippi College
Charles J. Dick
Pasco–Hernando Community College
Cecile A. Dolan
NH Community Technical College at Manchester
Terese Dudek
Kishwaukee College
Lori K. Garrett
Danville Area Community College
Brenda Gustin
Corning Community College
Susan K. McGamant-Grigsby
Houston Community College Central

ACKNOWLEDGMENTS

I value all the support and encouragement by the staff at McGraw-Hill Higher Education, including Michael Lange,

Kent Peterson, Michelle Watnick, Fran Schreiber, Kristine Tibbetts, Joyce Berendes, and Darlene Schueller. Special recognition is granted to Colin Wheatley for his insight, confidence, wisdom, warmth, and friendship.

I am grateful for the professional talent of David Shier, Jackie Butler, and Ricki Lewis for all of their coordination efforts and guidance with the laboratory manual. A special thank-you is given to Lori Garrett for her contribution of the chemistry lab and her complete and thorough reviews. The deepest gratitude is extended to John W. Hole, Jr. for his years of dedicated effort in early editions of this classic work and for the opportunity to revise his established laboratory manual.

I am particularly thankful to Dr. Norman Jenkins, retired president of Kishwaukee College, and Dr. David Louis, president of Kishwaukee College, for their support and confidence in my endeavors. I am appreciative for the expertise of J. Womack Photography. The professional reviews of the nursing procedures were provided by Kathy Schnier. I am also grateful to Rebecca Doty, Michele Dukes, Troy Hanke, Jenifer Holtzclaw, Stephen House, Shannon Johnson, Brian Jones, Marissa Kannheiser, Morgan Keen, Angele Myska, Sparkle Neal, Susan Rieger, Robert Stockley, Shatina Thompson, Nancy Valdivia, Marla Van Vickle, Jana Voorhis, Joyce Woo, and DeKalb Clinic Chartered for their special contributions. There have been valuable contributions from my students, who have supplied thoughtful suggestions and assisted in the clarification of details.

To my son Ross, I owe gratitude for his keen eye and creative suggestions. Foremost, I am appreciative to Sherrie Martin, my spouse and best friend, for advice, understanding, and devotion throughout the writing and revising.

Terry R. Martin
Kishwaukee College
21193 Malta Road
Malta, IL 60150

ABOUT THE AUTHOR

This eleventh edition is the fifth revision by Terry R. Martin of Kishwaukee College. Terry's teaching experience of over thirty years, his interest in students and love for college instruction, and his innovative attitude and use of technology-based learning enhance the solid tradition of John Hole's laboratory manual. Among Terry's awards are the 1972 Kishwaukee College Outstanding Educator, 1977 Phi Theta Kappa Outstanding Instructor Award, 1989 Kishwaukee College ICCTA Outstanding Educator Award, 1996 and 2004 Who's Who Among America's Teachers, 1996 Kishwaukee College Faculty Board of Trustees Award of Excellence, and 1998 Continued Excellence Award for Phi Theta Kappa Advisors. Terry's professional memberships include the National Association of Biology Teachers, Illinois Association of Community College Biologists, Human Anatomy and Physiology Society, Chicago Area Anatomy and Physiology Society (founding member), Phi Theta Kappa (honorary member), DeKalb County Prairie Stewards, and Nature Conservancy. In addition to writing many publications, he co-produced with Hassan Rastegar a videotape entitled *Introduction to the Human Cadaver and Prosection,* published by Wm. C. Brown Publishers in 1989. Terry revised the *Laboratory Manual to Accompany Hole's Essentials of Human Anatomy and Physiology,* 9th edition, and authored *Human Anatomy and Physiology Laboratory Manual, Fetal Pig Dissection,* 3rd edition. Terry serves as a Faculty Consultant for the Advanced Placement Biology examination readings. During 1994, Terry was a faculty exchange member in Ireland. He has also been involved in his community, most notably as a Commissioner for Boy Scouts of America. We are pleased to have Terry continue the tradition of John Hole's laboratory manual.

The Editor

TO THE STUDENT

The exercises in this laboratory manual will provide you with opportunities to observe various anatomical parts and to investigate certain physiological phenomena. Such experiences should help you relate specimens, models, microscope slides, and your own body to what you have learned in the lecture and read about in the textbook.

The following list of suggestions may help to make your laboratory activities more effective and profitable.

1. Prepare yourself before attending the laboratory session by reading the assigned exercise and reviewing the related sections of the textbook. It is important to have some understanding of what

will be done in the laboratory before you come to class.

2. Bring your laboratory manual and textbook to each laboratory session. These books are closely integrated and will help you complete most of the exercises.

3. Be on time. During the first few minutes of the laboratory meeting, the instructor often will provide verbal instructions. Make special note of any changes in materials to be used or procedures to be followed. Also listen carefully for information about special techniques to be used and precautions to be taken.

4. Keep your work area clean and your materials neatly arranged so that you can locate needed items quickly. This will enable you to proceed efficiently and will reduce the chances of making mistakes.

5. Pay particular attention to the purpose of the exercise, which states what you are to accomplish in general terms, and to the learning objectives, which list what you should be able to do as a result of the laboratory experience. Then, before you leave the class, review the objectives and make sure that you can meet them.

6. Precisely follow the directions in the procedure and proceed only when you understand them clearly. Do not improvise procedures unless you have the approval of the laboratory instructor. Ask questions if you do not understand exactly what you are supposed to do and why you are doing it.

7. Handle all laboratory materials with care. These materials often are fragile and expensive to replace. Whenever you have questions about the proper treatment of equipment, ask the instructor.

8. Treat all living specimens humanely and try to minimize any discomfort they might experience.

9. Although at times you might work with a laboratory partner or a small group, try to remain independent when you are making observations, drawing conclusions, and completing the activities in the laboratory reports.

10. Record your observations immediately after making them. In most cases, such data can be entered in spaces provided in the laboratory reports.

11. Read the instructions for each section of the laboratory report before you begin to complete it. Think about the questions before you answer them. Your responses should be based on logical reasoning and phrased in clear and concise language.

12. At the end of each laboratory period, clean your work area and the instruments you have used. Return all materials to their proper places and dispose of wastes, including glassware or microscope slides that have become contaminated with human blood or body fluids, as directed by the laboratory instructor. Wash your hands thoroughly before leaving the laboratory.

STUDY SKILLS FOR ANATOMY AND PHYSIOLOGY

My students have found that certain study skills worked well for them while they were enrolled in Human Anatomy and Physiology. Although everyone has his or her own learning style, there are techniques that work well for most students. Using some of the skills listed here could make your course more enjoyable and rewarding.

1. **Time management:** Prepare monthly, weekly, and daily schedules. Include dates of quizzes, exams, and projects on the calendar. On your daily schedule, budget several short study periods. Daily repetition alleviates cramming for exams. Prioritize your time so that you still have time for work and leisure activities. Find an appropriate study atmosphere with minimum distractions.

2. **Note taking:** Look for the main ideas and briefly express them in your own words. Organize, edit, and review your notes soon after the lecture. Add textbook information to your notes as you reorganize them. Underline or highlight with different colors the important points, major headings, and key terms. Study your notes daily, as they provide sequential building blocks of the course content.

3. **Chunking:** Organize information into logical groups or categories. Study and master one chunk of information at a time. For example, study the bones of the upper limb, lower limb, trunk, and head as separate study tasks.

4. **Mnemonic devices:** An *acrostic* is a combination of association and imagery to aid your memory. It is often in the form of a poem, rhyme, or jingle in which the first letter of each word corresponds to the first letters of the words you need to remember. **S**o **L**ong **T**op **P**art, **H**ere **C**omes **T**he **T**humb is an example of such a mnemonic device for remembering the eight carpals in the correct sequence. *Acronyms* are words that are formed by the first letters of the items to remember. *IPMAT* is an example of this type of mnemonic device to help you remember the phases of the cell cycle in the correct sequence. Try to create some of your own.

5. **Note cards/flash cards:** Make your own. Add labels and colors to enhance the material. Keep them with you in your pocket or purse. Study them often and for short periods of time. Concentrate on a small number of cards at one time. Shuffle your cards and have someone quiz you on their content. As you become familiar with the material, you can set aside cards that don't require additional mastery.

6. **Recording and recitation:** An auditory learner can benefit by recording lectures and review sessions with a cassette recorder. Many students listen to the taped sessions as they drive or just before they go to bed. Reading your notes aloud can help also. Explain the material to anyone (even if there are no listeners). Talk about anatomy and physiology in everyday conversations.

7. **Study groups:** Small study groups that meet periodically to review course material and compare notes have helped and encouraged many students. However, keep the group on the task at hand. Work as a team and alternate leaders. This group often becomes a support group.

Best wishes on your anatomy and physiology endeavor.

CORRELATION OF TEXTBOOK CHAPTERS AND LABORATORY EXERCISES

CORRELATION OF TEXTBOOK CHAPTERS AND SUPPLEMENTAL FROG LABORATORY EXERCISES

*These laboratory exercises are available at www.mhhe.com/shier11 (click on this laboratory manual cover).

SCIENTIFIC METHOD AND MEASUREMENTS

MATERIALS NEEDED

Meterstick
Calculator
Human skeleton

Scientific investigation involves a series of logical steps to arrive at explanations for various biological phenomena. This technique, called the *scientific method,* is used in all disciplines of science. It allows scientists to draw logical and reliable conclusions about phenomena.

The scientific method begins with *observations* related to the topic under investigation. This step commonly involves the accumulation of previously acquired information and/or your own observations of the phenomenon. These observations are used to formulate a tentative explanation known as the *hypothesis.* An important attribute of a hypothesis is that it must be testable. The testing of the hypothesis involves performing a carefully controlled *experiment* to obtain data that can be used to support, disprove, or modify the hypothesis. An *analysis of data* is conducted using all of the information collected during the experiment. Data analysis may include organization and presentation of data as tables, graphs, and drawings. From the interpretation of the data analysis, *conclusions* are drawn. (If the data do not support the hypothesis, you must reexamine the experimental design and the data, and if needed, develop a new hypothesis.) The final presentation of the information is made from the conclusions. Results and conclusions are presented to the scientific community for evaluation through peer reviews, presentations at professional meetings, and published articles. If many investigators working independently can validate the hypothesis by arriving at the same conclusions, the explanation becomes a **theory.** A theory that is verified continuously over a period of time and accepted by the scientific community becomes known as a **scientific law** or **principle.** A scientific law serves as the standard explanation for an observation unless it is disproved by new information. The five components of the scientific method are summarized as

Observations
↓
Hypothesis
↓
Experiment
↓
Analysis of data
↓
Conclusions

Metric measurements are characteristic tools of scientific investigations. Because the English system of measurements is often used in the United States, the investigator must make conversions from the English system to the metric system. A reference table for the conversion of English units of measure to metric units for length, mass, volume, time, and temperature is located inside the back cover of the laboratory manual.

PURPOSE OF THE EXERCISE

To become familiar with the scientific method of investigation, to learn how to formulate sound conclusions, and to provide opportunities to use the metric system of measurements.

LEARNING OBJECTIVES

After completing this exercise, you should be able to

1. List in the correct order and describe all steps of the scientific method.
2. Use the scientific method to test the validity of a hypothesis concerning the direct, linear relationship between human height and upper limb length.
3. Make conversions from English measurements to the metric system, and vice versa.
4. Formulate a hypothesis and test it using the scientific method.

PROCEDURE A—USING THE STEPS OF THE SCIENTIFIC METHOD

1. Many people have observed a correlation between the length of the upper and lower limbs and the height (stature) of an individual. For example, a

Figure 1.1 Metric ruler with metric lengths indicated. A meterstick length would be 100 centimeters. (The image size is approximately to scale.)

Metric ruler

Figure 1.2 Measurement of upper limb length.

person who has long upper limbs (the arm, forearm, and hand combined) tends to be tall. Make some visual observations of other people in your class to observe a possible correlation.

2. From such observations, the following hypothesis is formulated: The length of a person's upper limb is equal to 0.4 (40%) of the height of the person. Test this hypothesis by performing the following experiment.

3. In this experiment, use a meterstick (fig. 1.1) to measure an upper limb length of ten subjects. For each measurement, place the meterstick in the axilla (armpit) and record the length in centimeters to the end of the longest finger (fig. 1.2). Obtain the height of each person in centimeters by measuring them without shoes against a wall (fig. 1.3). The height of each person can be calculated by multiplying each individual's height in inches by 2.54 to obtain his/her height in centimeters. Record all your measurements in Part A of Laboratory Report 1.

4. The data collected from all of the measurements can now be analyzed. The expected (predicted) correlation between upper limb length and height is determined using the following equation:

Height × 0.4 = expected upper limb length

The observed (actual) correlation to be used to test the hypothesis is determined by

**Length of upper limb/height
= actual % of height**

5. A graph is an excellent way to display a visual representation of the data. Plot the subjects' data in Part A of the laboratory report. Plot the upper limb length of each subject on the x-axis and the height of each person on the y-axis. A line is already located on the graph that represents a hypothetical relationship of 0.4 (40%) upper limb length compared to height. This is a graphic representation of the original hypothesis.

Figure 1.3 Measurement of height.

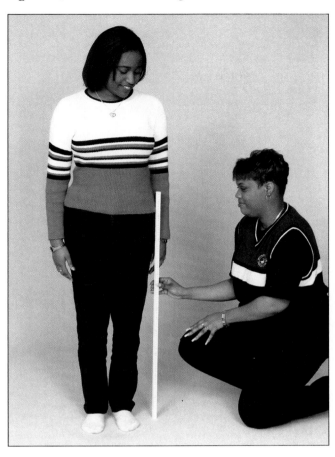

6. Compare the distribution of all of the points (actual height and upper limb length) that you placed on the graph with the distribution of the expected correlation represented by the hypothesis.
7. Complete Part A of the laboratory report.

PROCEDURE B—DESIGN AN EXPERIMENT

 ### Critical Thinking Application

You have probably concluded that there is some correlation of the length of body parts to height. Often when a skeleton is found, it is not complete, especially when paleontologists discover a skeleton. It is occasionally feasible to use the length of a single bone to estimate the height of an individual. Observe human skeletons and locate the radius bone in the forearm. Use your observations to identify a mathematical relationship between the length of the radius and height. Formulate a hypothesis that can be tested. Make measurements, analyze data, and develop a conclusion from your experiment. Complete Part B of the laboratory report.

Web Quest
Examine additional information about the scientific method at
www.mhhe.com/shier11
Click on Student Edition. Click on Martin Lab Manual, Web Quest.

NOTES

SCIENTIFIC METHOD AND MEASUREMENTS

PART A

1. Record measurements for height and the upper limb length of ten subjects. Use a calculator to determine the expected upper limb length and the actual percentage (as a decimal or a percentage) of the height for the ten subjects. Record your results in the following table.

Subject	Height (cm)	Measured Upper Limb Length (cm)	Height × 0.4 = Expected Upper Limb Length (cm)	Actual % of Height = Upper Limb Length (cm)/ Height (cm)
1.				
2.				
3.				
4.				
5.				
6.				
7.				
8.				
9.				
10.				

2. Plot the distribution of data (upper limb length and height) collected for the ten subjects on the following graph. The line located on the graph represents the **expected** 0.4 (40%) ratio of upper limb length to measured height (the original hypothesis). (Note that the x-axis represents upper limb length and the y-axis represents height.) Draw a line of *best fit* through the distribution of points of the plotted data of the ten subjects. Compare the two distributions (expected line and the distribution line drawn for the ten subjects).

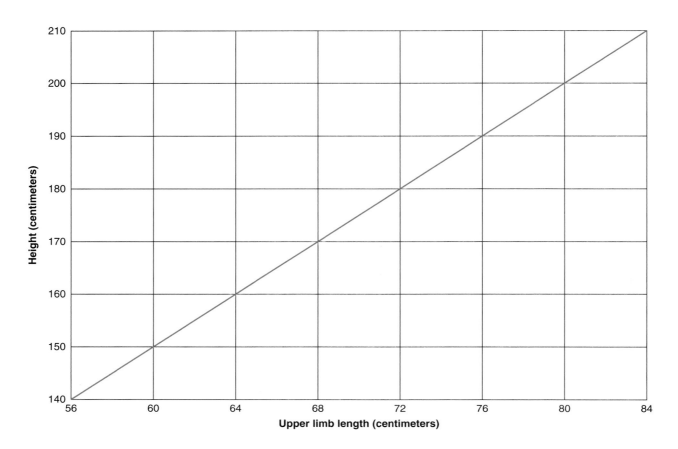

3. Does the distribution of the ten subjects' measured upper limb lengths support or disprove the original hypothesis? _____ Explain your answer.

PART B

1. Describe your observations of a possible correlation between the radius length and height.

2. Write a hypothesis based on your observations.

3. Describe the design of the experiment that you devised to test your hypothesis.

4. Place your analysis of the data in this space in the form of a table and a graph.

5. Based on an analysis of your data, what conclusions can you make? Did these conclusions confirm or refute your original hypothesis?

6. Discuss your results and conclusions with classmates. What common conclusion can the class formulate about the correlation between radius length and height?

LABORATORY EXERCISE 2

BODY ORGANIZATION AND TERMINOLOGY

MATERIALS NEEDED

Textbook
Dissectible human torso model (manikin)
Variety of specimens or models sectioned along various
    planes

For Learning Extension:

Colored pencils

The major features of the human body include certain cavities, a set of membranes associated with these cavities, and a group of organ systems composed of related organs. In order to communicate effectively with each other about the body, scientists have devised names to describe these body features. They also have developed terms to represent the relative positions of body parts, imaginary planes passing through these parts, and body regions.

PURPOSE OF THE EXERCISE

To review the organizational pattern of the human body, to review its organ systems and the organs included in each system, and to become acquainted with the terms used to describe the relative position of body parts, body sections, and body regions.

LEARNING OBJECTIVES

After completing this exercise, you should be able to

1. Locate and name the major body cavities and identify the membranes associated with each cavity.
2. Name the organ systems of the human organism.
3. List the organs included within each system and locate the organs in a dissectible human torso model.
4. Describe the general functions of each system.
5. Define the terms used to describe the relative positions of body parts.
6. Define the terms used to identify body sections and identify the plane along which a particular specimen is cut.
7. Define the terms used to identify body regions.

PROCEDURE A—BODY CAVITIES AND MEMBRANES

1. Review the sections entitled "Body Cavities" and "Thoracic and Abdominopelvic Membranes" in chapter 1 of the textbook.
2. As a review activity, label figures 2.1 and 2.2.
3. Locate the following features on the reference plates near the end of chapter 1 of the textbook and on the dissectible human torso model (fig. 2.3):

body cavities
  cranial cavity
  vertebral canal (spinal cavity)
  thoracic cavity
    mediastinum (region between the lungs)
    pleural cavity
  abdominopelvic cavity
    abdominal cavity
    pelvic cavity
diaphragm
smaller cavities within the head
  oral cavity
  nasal cavity with connected sinuses
  orbital cavity
  middle ear cavity
membranes and cavities
  pleural cavity
    parietal pleura
    visceral pleura
  pericardial cavity
    parietal pericardium (covered by fibrous pericardium)
    visceral pericardium (epicardium)
  peritoneal cavity
    parietal peritoneum
    visceral peritoneum

4. Complete Part A of Laboratory Report 2.

9

Figure 2.1 Label the major body cavities.

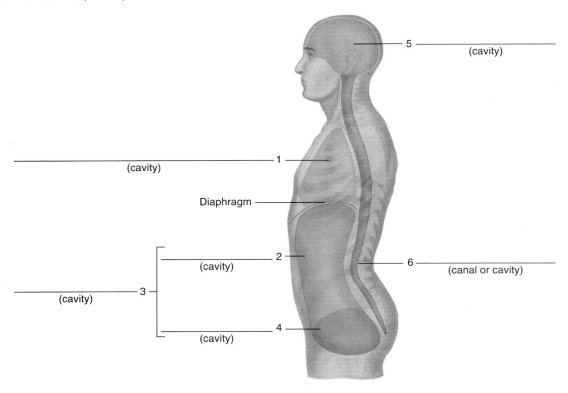

5 _____ (cavity)

1 _____ (cavity)

Diaphragm

2 _____ (cavity)

3 _____ (cavity)
  _____ (cavity)

4 _____ (cavity)

6 _____ (canal or cavity)

Figure 2.2 Label the thoracic membranes and cavities in (*a*) and the abdominopelvic membranes and cavity in (*b*) as shown in these superior views of transverse sections.

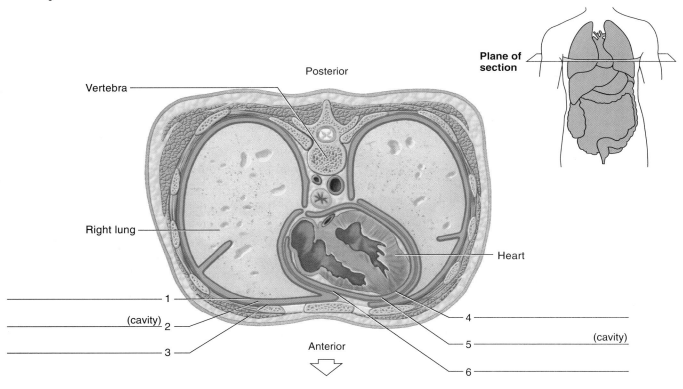

Posterior

Plane of section

Vertebra

Right lung

Heart

1 _____
  _____ (cavity)
2 _____
3 _____

Anterior

4 _____
5 _____ (cavity)
6 _____

(a)

Figure 2.2   *Continued.*

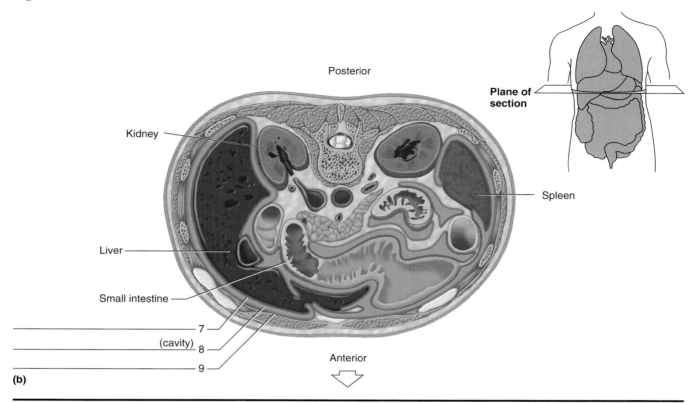

(b)

Figure 2.3   Dissectible human torso model with body cavities, abdominopelvic quadrants, body planes, and major organs indicated.

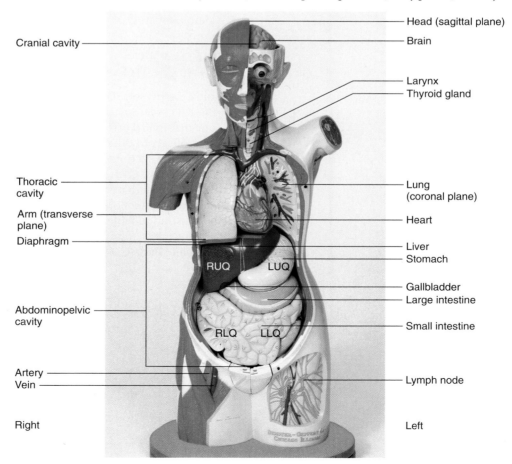

11

PROCEDURE B—ORGAN SYSTEMS

1. Review the section entitled "Organ Systems" in chapter 1 of the textbook.
2. Use the reference plates on pages 29–49 of the textbook and the dissectible human torso model (fig. 2.3) to locate the following organs:

integumentary system
    skin
    accessory organs such as hair and nails

skeletal system
    bones
    ligaments
    cartilages

muscular system
    skeletal muscles
    tendons

nervous system
    brain
    spinal cord
    nerves

endocrine system
    pituitary gland
    thyroid gland
    parathyroid glands
    adrenal glands
    pancreas
    ovaries
    testes
    pineal gland
    thymus

cardiovascular system
    heart
    arteries
    veins

lymphatic system
    lymphatic vessels
    lymph nodes
    thymus
    spleen

digestive system
    mouth
    tongue
    teeth
    salivary glands
    pharynx
    esophagus
    stomach
    liver
    gallbladder
    pancreas
    small intestine
    large intestine

respiratory system
    nasal cavity
    pharynx
    larynx
    trachea
    bronchi
    lungs

urinary system
    kidneys
    ureters
    urinary bladder
    urethra

male reproductive system
    scrotum
    testes
    penis
    urethra

female reproductive system
    ovaries
    uterine tubes (oviducts; fallopian tubes)
    uterus
    vagina

3. Complete Part B of the laboratory report.

PROCEDURE C—RELATIVE POSITIONS, PLANES, SECTIONS, AND REGIONS

1. Study the person standing in anatomical position (fig. 2.4). Anatomical terminology assumes the body is in anatomical position even though a person is often observed differently.
2. Review the section entitled "Anatomical Terminology" in chapter 1 of the textbook.
3. As a review activity, label figures 2.5, 2.6, and 2.7.
4. Examine the sectioned specimens on the demonstration table and identify the plane along which each is cut.
5. Complete Parts C, D, E, and F of the laboratory report.

Figure 2.4 Anatomical position with directional terms indicated. The body is standing erect, face forward, with upper limbs at the sides and palms forward. This results in an anterior view of the body.

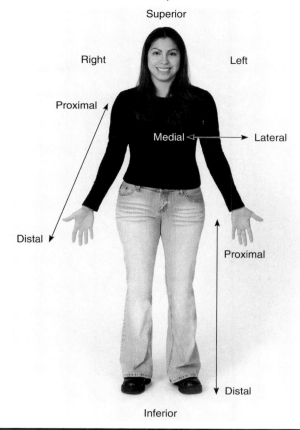

Figure 2.5 Label the planes represented in this illustration.

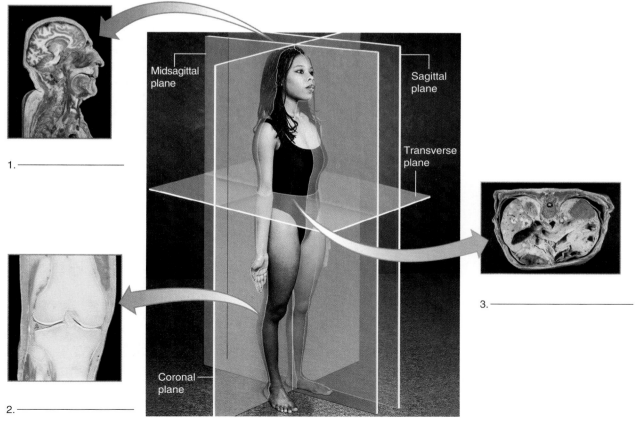

1. _____

2. _____

3. _____

13

Figure 2.6 Label (*a*) the regions and (*b*) the quadrants of the abdominal area.

(a)

(b)

Figure 2.7 Label these diagrams with terms used to describe body regions: (*a*) anterior regions; (*b*) posterior regions.

1 _____
2 _____
3 _____
4 _____
5 _____
6 _____
7 _____
8 _____
9 _____
10 _____
11 _____
12 _____
13 _____
14 _____

(leg) _____
15 _____

16 _____

17 _____
18 _____
19 _____
20 _____
21 _____
22 _____
23 _____
24 _____
25 _____
26 _____

27 _____

28 _____

(a)

Figure 2.7 *Continued.*

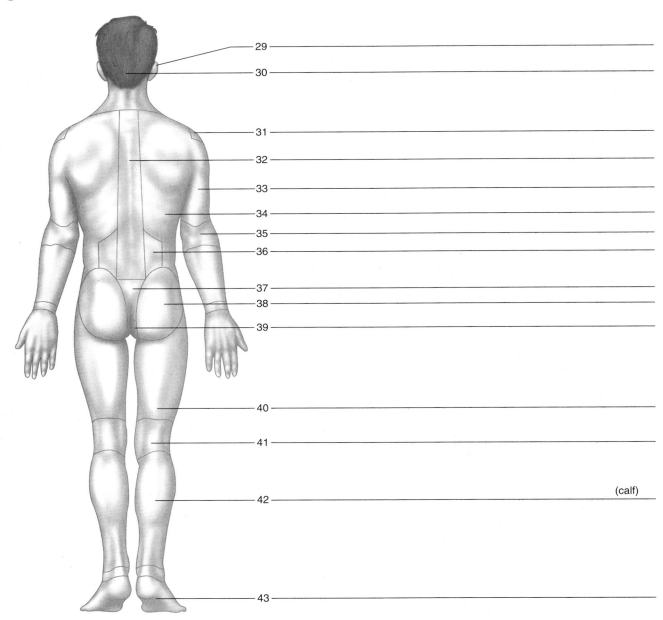

29 _____
30 _____

31 _____
32 _____
33 _____
34 _____
35 _____
36 _____

37 _____
38 _____
39 _____

40 _____

41 _____

(calf)
42 _____

43 _____

(b)

LEARNING EXTENSION

Use different colored pencils to distinguish body regions in figure 2.7.

Web Quest

Identify organs in the three planes of the body from digitized sections of a human body. Search these at

www.mhhe.com/shier11

Click on Student Edition. Click on Martin Lab Manual, Web Quest.

BODY ORGANIZATION AND TERMINOLOGY

PART A

Match the body cavities in column A with the organs contained in the cavities in column B. Place the letter of your choice in the space provided.

Column A	Column B
a. Abdominal cavity	_____ 1. Liver
b. Cranial cavity	_____ 2. Lungs
c. Pelvic cavity	_____ 3. Spleen
d. Thoracic cavity	_____ 4. Stomach
e. Vertebral canal (spinal cavity)	_____ 5. Brain
	_____ 6. Internal reproductive organs
	_____ 7. Gallbladder
	_____ 8. Urinary bladder
	_____ 9. Mediastinum
	_____ 10. Spinal cord
	_____ 11. Heart
	_____ 12. Small intestine

PART B

Match the organ systems in column A with the functions in column B. Place the letter of your choice in the space provided.

Column A	Column B
a. Cardiovascular system	_____ 1. Main system that secretes hormones
b. Digestive system	_____ 2. Provides an outer covering of the body
c. Endocrine system	_____ 3. Produces a new organism
d. Integumentary system	_____ 4. Stimulates muscles to contract and interprets information from sensory units
e. Lymphatic system	
f. Muscular system	_____ 5. Provides a framework for soft tissues and produces blood cells in red marrow
g. Nervous system	
h. Reproductive system	_____ 6. Exchanges gases between air and blood
i. Respiratory system	
j. Skeletal system	_____ 7. Transports excess fluid from tissues to blood
k. Urinary system	

_____ 8. Maintains posture and generates most body heat

_____ 9. Removes liquid and wastes from blood and transports them to the outside

_____ 10. Converts food molecules into forms that are absorbed

_____ 11. Transports nutrients, wastes, and gases throughout the body

PART C

Indicate whether each of the following sentences makes correct or incorrect usage of the word in boldface type (assume that the body is in the anatomical position as observed in fig. 2.4). If the sentence is incorrect, supply a term that will make it correct in the space provided.

1. The mouth is **superior** to the nose.   _____

2. The stomach is **inferior** to the diaphragm.   _____

3. The trachea is **anterior** to the spinal cord.   _____

4. The larynx is **posterior** to the esophagus.   _____

5. The heart is **medial** to the lungs.   _____

6. The kidneys are **inferior** to the adrenal glands.   _____

7. The hand is **proximal** to the elbow.   _____

8. The knee is **proximal** to the ankle.   _____

9. Blood in **deep** blood vessels gives color to the skin.   _____

10. A **peripheral** nerve passes from the spinal cord into the limbs. _____

11. The spleen and gallbladder are **ipsilateral.**   _____

12. The dermis is the **superficial** layer of the skin.   _____

PART D

Match the body regions in column A with the locations in column B. Place the letter of your choice in the space provided.

Column A	Column B
a. Antecubital	_____ 1. Wrist
b. Axillary	_____ 2. Reproductive organs
c. Brachial	_____ 3. Armpit
d. Buccal	_____ 4. Elbow
e. Carpal	_____ 5. Buttocks
f. Cephalic	_____ 6. Back
g. Cervical	_____ 7. Neck
h. Crural	_____ 8. Arm
i. Cubital	_____ 9. Cheek
j. Dorsal	_____ 10. Leg
k. Genital	_____ 11. Head
l. Gluteal	_____ 12. Front of elbow

PART E

Match the body regions in column A with the locations in column B. Place the letter of your choice in the space provided.

Column A	Column B
a. Inguinal	_____ 1. Pelvis
b. Lumbar	_____ 2. Breasts
c. Mammary	_____ 3. Between anus and reproductive organs
d. Occipital	_____ 4. Sole
e. Palmar	_____ 5. Middle of thorax
f. Pectoral	_____ 6. Chest
g. Pedal	_____ 7. Back of knee
h. Pelvic	_____ 8. Foot
i. Perineal	_____ 9. Lower posterior region of head
j. Plantar	_____ 10. Abdominal wall near thigh (groin)
k. Popliteal	_____ 11. Lower back
l. Sternal	_____ 12. Palm

PART F

Critical Thinking Application

State the quadrant of the abdominopelvic cavity where the pain or sound would be located for each of the six common conditions listed. In some cases, there may be more than one correct answer, and pain is sometimes referred to another region. This phenomenon, called *referred pain,* occurs when pain is interpreted as originating from some area other than the parts being stimulated.

1. Stomach ulcer _____

2. Appendicitis _____

3. Bowel sounds _____

4. Gallbladder attack _____

5. Kidney stone in left ureter _____

6. Ruptured spleen _____

NOTES

CHEMISTRY OF LIFE

MATERIALS NEEDED

For pH Tests:

Chopped fresh red cabbage
Beaker (250 mL)
Distilled water
Tap water
Vinegar
Baking soda
Laboratory scoop for measuring
Pipets for measuring
Full-range pH test papers
7 assorted common liquids clearly labeled in closed
    bottles on a tray or in a tub
Droppers labeled for each liquid

For Organic Tests:

Test tubes
Test-tube rack
Test-tube clamps
China marker
Hot plate
Beaker for hot water bath (500 mL)
Pipets for measuring
Benedict's solution
Biuret reagent (or 10% NaOH and 1% $CuSO_4$)
Iodine-potassium-iodide (IKI) solution
Sudan IV dye
Egg albumin
10% glucose solution
Clear carbonated soft drink
10% starch solution
Potatoes for potato water
Distilled water
Vegetable oil
Brown paper
Numbered unknown organic samples

⚠ SAFETY

- Review all safety guidelines inside the front cover of your laboratory manual.
- Clean laboratory surfaces before and after laboratory procedures using soap and water.
- Use extreme caution when working with chemicals.
- Safety goggles must be worn at all times.
- Wear disposable gloves while working with the chemicals.
- Precautions should be taken to prevent chemicals from contacting your skin.
- Do not mix any of the chemicals together unless instructed to do so.
- Clean up any spills immediately and notify the instructor at once.
- Wash your hands before leaving the laboratory.

All the complexities of the human body arise from the organization and interactions of chemicals. All organisms are made of matter, and the most basic unit of all matter is the chemical element. The smallest unit of an element is an atom, and two or more of those can unite to form a molecule. All processes that occur within the body involve chemical reactions—interactions between atoms and molecules. We breathe to supply oxygen to our cells for energy. We eat and drink to bring chemicals into our bodies that our cells need. Water fills and bathes all of our cells and allows an amazing array of reactions to occur, all of which are designed to keep us alive. Chemistry forms the very basis of life and thus forms the foundation of anatomy and physiology.

PURPOSE OF THE EXERCISE

To review the organization of atoms and molecules, types of chemical interactions, and basic categories of organic compounds, and to differentiate between types of organic compounds.

Figure 3.1 The single electron of a hydrogen atom is located in its first shell. The two electrons of a helium atom fill its first shell. Two of the three electrons of a lithium atom are in the first shell, and one is in the second shell.

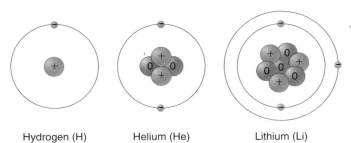

Hydrogen (H)   Helium (He)   Lithium (Li)

LEARNING OBJECTIVES

After completing this exercise, you should be able to

1. Explain and illustrate the basic organization of atoms and molecules.
2. Demonstrate pH values of various substances through testing methods.
3. Predict pH values of some common materials.
4. Perform basic colorimetric tests.
5. Identify categories of organic compounds with simple tests.
6. Determine the organic composition of an unknown solution.

PROCEDURE A—MATTER, MOLECULES, BONDING, AND pH

1. Review the section entitled "Structure of Matter" in chapter 2 of the textbook.
2. Review figures 3.1, 3.2, and 3.3, which show molecular diagrams, formation of an ionic bond, and formation of a covalent bond, respectively.
3. Complete Part A of Laboratory Report 3.

PROCEDURE B—THE pH SCALE

1. Review the section entitled "Acid and Base Concentrations" in chapter 2 of the textbook.
2. Review figure 3.4, which shows the pH scale. Note the range of the scale and the pH value that is considered neutral.
3. **Cabbage water tests.** Many tests can determine a pH value, but among the more interesting are colorimetric tests in which an indicator chemical changes color when it reacts. Many plant pigments, especially anthocyanins (which give plants color, from blue to red), can be used as colorimetric pH indicators. One that works well is the red pigment in red cabbage.
   a. Prepare cabbage water to be used as a general pH indicator. Fill a 250 mL beaker to the 100 mL level with chopped red cabbage. Add water to make

Figure 3.2 Formation of an ionic bond.

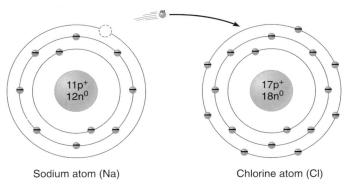

Sodium atom (Na)   Chlorine atom (Cl)

(a) Separate atoms
If a sodium atom loses an electron to a chlorine atom, the sodium atom becomes a sodium ion (Na^+), and the chlorine atom becomes a chloride ion (Cl^-).

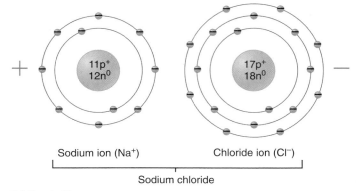

Sodium ion (Na^+)   Chloride ion (Cl^-)

Sodium chloride

(b) Bonded ions
These oppositely charged particles attract electrically and join by an ionic bond.

150 mL. Place the beaker on a hot plate and simmer the mixture until the pigments come out of the cabbage and the water turns deep purple. Allow the water to cool. (You may proceed to step 4 while you wait for this to finish.)
   b. Label three clean test tubes, one for water, one for vinegar, and one for baking soda.
   c. Place 2 mL of cabbage water into each test tube.
   d. To the first test tube, add 2 mL of distilled water and swirl the mixture. Note and record the color in Part B of the laboratory report.
   e. Repeat this procedure for test tube 2, adding 2 mL of vinegar and swirling the mixture. Note and record the results.
   f. Repeat this procedure for test tube 3, adding one laboratory scoop of baking soda. Swirl the mixture. Note and record the results.
4. **Testing with pH paper.** Many commercial pH indicators are available. A very simple one to use is pH paper, which comes in small strips. Be cautious when handling the paper so your skin secretions do not contaminate the strip. Gloves are recommended for this procedure, as well as to protect you from

Figure 3.3 A hydrogen molecule forms when two hydrogen atoms share a pair of electrons and join by a covalent bond.

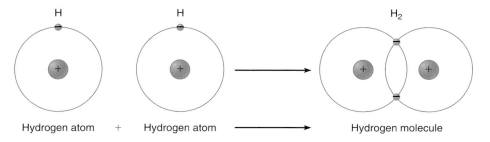

Hydrogen atom   +   Hydrogen atom   Hydrogen molecule

Figure 3.4 As the concentration of hydrogen ions (H^+) increases, a solution becomes more acidic, and the pH value decreases. As the concentration of ions that combine with hydrogen ions (such as hydroxide ions) increases, a solution becomes more basic (alkaline), and the pH value increases. The pH values of some common substances are shown.

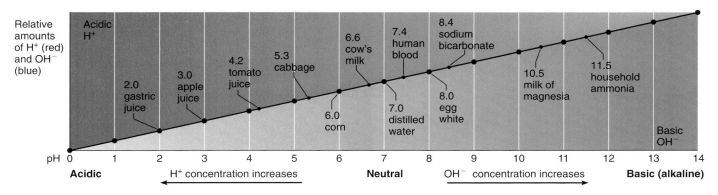

the chemicals you are testing, some of which may be harmful.

a. Test the pH of distilled water by dropping one or two drops of distilled water onto a strip of pH paper and note the color. Compare the color to the color guide on the container. Record the pH value in Part B of the laboratory report.

b. Repeat this procedure for tap water. Record the results.

c. Individually test the various common substances found on your lab table. Record your results.

d. Complete Part B of the laboratory report.

PROCEDURE C—ORGANIC MOLECULES

In this section, you will perform some simple tests to check for the presence of the following categories of organic molecules: protein, sugar, starch, and lipid. Specific color changes will occur if the target compound is present. Please note the original color of the indicator being added so you can tell if the color really changed. For example, Biuret reagent and Benedict's solution are both initially blue, so an end color of blue would indicate no change. Use caution when working with

these chemicals and follow all directions carefully. Carefully label the test tubes and avoid contaminating any of your samples. Also note that only the Benedict's test requires heating and a time delay for accurate results. Do not heat any other tubes. To prepare for the Benedict's test, fill a 500 mL beaker half full with water and place it on the hot plate. Turn the hot plate on and bring the water to a boil. To save time, start the water bath before doing the Biuret test.

1. **Biuret test for protein.** In the presence of protein, Biuret reagent reacts with peptide bonds and changes to violet or purple. A pinkish color indicates that shorter polypeptides are present. The color intensity is proportional to the number of peptide bonds, thus the intensity reflects the length of polypeptides (amount of protein).

a. Label six test tubes as follows: 1W, 1E, 1G, 1D, 1S, and 1P.

b. To each test tube, add 2 mL of one of the samples as follows:

1W—2 mL distilled water

1E—2 mL egg albumin

1G—2 mL 10% glucose solution

1D—2 mL carbonated soft drink

1S—2 mL 10% starch solution

1P—2 mL potato juice

c. To each, add 2 mL of Biuret reagent, swirl the tube to mix it, and note the final color. [*Note:* If Biuret reagent is not available, add 2 mL of 10% NaOH (sodium hydroxide) and about 10 drops of 1% $CuSO_4$ (copper sulfate)]. **Be careful—NaOH is very caustic.**

d. Record your results in Part C of the laboratory report.

e. Mark a "+" on any tubes with positive results and retain them for comparison while testing your unknown sample. Put remaining test tubes aside so they will not get confused with future trials.

2. **Benedict's test for sugar (monosaccharides).** In the presence of a reactive sugar, Benedict's solution changes from its initial blue to a green, yellow, orange, or reddish color, depending on the amount of reactive sugar present. Orange and red indicate greater amounts of sugar.

a. Label six test tubes as follows: 2W, 2E, 2G, 2D, 2S, and 2P.

b. To each test tube, add 2 mL of one of the samples as follows:

2W—2 mL distilled water

2E—2 mL egg albumin

2G—2 mL 10% glucose solution

2D—2 mL carbonated soft drink

2S—2 mL 10% starch solution

2P—2 mL potato juice

c. To each, add 2 mL of Benedict's solution, swirl the tube to mix it, and place all tubes into the boiling water bath for 3 to 5 minutes.

d. Note the final color of each tube after heating and record the results in Part C of the laboratory report.

e. Mark a "+" on any tubes with positive results and retain them for comparison while testing your unknown sample. Put remaining test tubes aside so they will not get confused with future trials.

3. **Iodine test for starch.** In the presence of starch, iodine turns a dark purple or blue-black color. Starch is a long chain formed by many glucose units linked together side by side. This regular organization traps the iodine molecules and produces the dark color.

a. Label six test tubes as follows: 3W, 3E, 3G, 3D, 3S, and 3P.

b. To each test tube, add 2 mL of one of the samples as follows:

3W—2 mL distilled water

3E—2 mL egg albumin

3G—2 mL 10% glucose solution

3D—2 mL carbonated soft drink

3S—2 mL 10% starch solution

3P—2 mL potato juice

c. To each, add 0.5 mL of IKI (iodine solution) and swirl the tube to mix it.

d. Note the final color of each tube and record the results in Part C of the laboratory report.

e. Mark a "+" on any tubes with positive results and retain them for comparison while testing your unknown sample. Put remaining test tubes aside so they will not get confused with future trials.

4. **Tests for lipids.**

a. Label two separate areas of a piece of brown paper as "water" or "oil."

b. Place a drop of water on the area marked "water" and a drop of vegetable oil on the area marked "oil."

c. Let the spots dry several minutes, then record your observations in Part C of the laboratory report. Upon drying, oil leaves a stain (grease spot) on brown paper; water does not leave such a spot.

d. In a test tube, add 2 mL of water and 2 mL of vegetable oil and observe. Shake the tube vigorously then let it sit for 5 minutes and observe again. Record your observations in Part C of the laboratory report.

e. Sudan IV is a dye that is lipid-soluble but not water-soluble. If lipids are present, the Sudan IV will stain them pink or red. Add a small amount of Sudan IV to the test tube that contains the oil and water. Swirl it then let it sit for a few minutes. Record your observations in Part C of the laboratory report.

PROCEDURE D—IDENTIFYING UNKNOWN COMPOUNDS

Now you will apply the knowledge you gained with the tests in the previous section. You will retrieve an unknown sample that contains none, one, or any combination of the following types of organic compounds: protein, sugar, starch, or lipid. You will test your sample using each test from the previous section and record your results in Part D of the laboratory report.

1. Label four test tubes (1, 2, 3, 4).

2. Add 2 mL of your unknown sample to each test tube.

3. **Test for protein.** Add 2 mL of Biuret reagent to tube 1. Swirl the tube and observe the color. Record your observations in Part D of the laboratory report.

4. **Test for sugar.** Add 2 mL of Benedict's solution to tube 2. Swirl the tube and place it in a boiling water bath for 3 to 5 minutes. Record your observations in Part D of the laboratory report.

5. **Test for starch.** Add several drops of iodine solution to tube 3. Swirl the tube and observe the color. Record your observations in Part D of the laboratory report.
6. **Test for lipid.** Add 2 mL of water to tube 4. Swirl the tube and note if there is any separation.
7. Add a small amount of Sudan IV to test tube 4, swirl the tube and record your observations in Part D of the laboratory report.
8. Based on the results of these tests, determine if your unknown sample contains any organic compounds and, if so, what are they? Record and explain your identification in Part D of the laboratory report.

NOTES

Name _____

Date _____

Section _____

CHEMISTRY OF LIFE

PART A

Match the terms in column A with the descriptions in column B. Place the letter of your choice in the space provided.

Column A

a. Atomic number
b. Atomic weight (mass)
c. Base
d. Catalyst (enzyme)
e. Compound
f. Covalent bond
g. Electrolyte
h. Electron
i. Elements
j. Ion
k. Isotopes
l. Nucleus

Column B

_____ 1. The number of protons plus the number of neutrons

_____ 2. A combination of two or more atoms of different elements

_____ 3. A small, negatively charged particle that orbits the nucleus

_____ 4. An atom that has gained or lost electrons, and thus carries an electrical charge

_____ 5. Atoms are held together by sharing electrons

_____ 6. The most fundamental substances of matter

_____ 7. A substance that combines with hydrogen ions

_____ 8. A molecule that influences the rate of chemical reactions but is not consumed in the reaction

_____ 9. Two atoms with the same atomic number but different atomic weights

_____ 10. A substance that releases ions in water

_____ 11. The number of protons in an atom

_____ 12. The area of an atom where protons and neutrons are located

MOLECULES AND BONDING

After reviewing Figures 3.1, 3.2, and 3.3, complete the following:

1. The atomic number of hydrogen is _____ and it has _____ electron(s) in its outer shell.
2. The atomic number of chlorine is _____ and it has _____ electron(s) in its outer shell.
3. Using the style shown in Figure 3.2, draw an atom of hydrogen and one of chlorine, clearly indicating the numbers and positions of the protons, neutrons, and electrons.

Hydrogen   Chlorine

4. Is the hydrogen atom stable? _____

   Is the chlorine atom stable? _____

5. What type of bond is likely to form the compound HCl (hydrochloric acid)? _____

6. Repeat your drawings below, but also show and explain how this bond of HCl would form. Clearly indicate the positions of protons, neutrons, and electrons.

PART B—THE pH SCALE

1. Results from cabbage water test:

Substance	Cabbage Water	Distilled Water	Vinegar	Baking Soda
Color				
Acid, base, or neutral?				

2. Results from pH paper tests:

Substance Tested	Distilled Water	Tap Water	Sample 1:____	Sample 2:____	Sample 3:____	Sample 4:____	Sample 5:____	Sample 6:____	Sample 7:____
pH Value									

3. Are the pH values the same for distilled water and tap water? _____

4. If not, what might explain this difference? _____

   _____

5. Draw the pH scale below, and indicate the following values: 0, 7 (neutral), and 14. Now label the scale with the names and indicate the location of the pH values for each substance you tested.

PART C—TESTING FOR ORGANIC MOLECULES

1. **Biuret test results for protein.** Enter your results from the Biuret test for protein. A color change to purple indicates that protein is present; pink indicates that short polypeptides are present.

Tube	Contents	Color	Protein Present (+) or Absent (−)
1W	Distilled water		
1E	Egg albumin		
1G	Glucose solution		
1D	Soft drink		
1S	Starch solution		
1P	Potato juice		

2. **Benedict's test results for most sugars (monosaccharides).** Enter your results from the Benedict's test for sugars. A color change to green, yellow, orange, or red indicates that sugar is present. Note the color after the mixture has been heated for 3 to 5 minutes.

Tube	Contents	Color	Sugar Present (+) or Absent (−)
2W	Distilled water		
2E	Egg albumin		
2G	Glucose solution		
2D	Soft drink		
2S	Starch solution		
2P	Potato juice		

3. **Iodine test results for starch.** Enter your results from the iodine test for starch. A color change to dark blue or black indicates that starch is present.

Tube	Contents	Color	Starch Present (+) or Absent (−)
3W	Distilled water		
3E	Egg albumin		
3G	Glucose solution		
3D	Soft drink		
3S	Starch solution		
3P	Potato juice		

4. **Lipid test results.** What did you observe when you allowed the drops of oil and water to dry on the brown paper? _____

What did you observe when you mixed the oil and water together? _____

_____

What did you observe when you added the Sudan IV dye? _____

Critical Thinking Application

If a person were on a low-carbohydrate, high-protein diet, which of the six substances tested would the person want to increase?_____
Explain your answer.

_____

_____

_____

_____

PART D—TESTING FOR UNKNOWN ORGANIC COMPOUNDS

1. What is the number of your sample? _____

2. Record the results of your tests on the unknown here:

Test Performed	Results
Biuret test for protein	
Benedict's test for sugars	
Iodine test for starch	
Water test for lipid	
Sudan IV test for lipid	

3. Based on these results, what organic compound(s) does your unknown sample contain? _____

   _____

4. Explain your answer. _____

   _____

   _____

CARE AND USE
OF THE MICROSCOPE

MATERIALS NEEDED

Compound light microscope
Lens paper
Microscope slides
Coverslips
Transparent plastic millimeter ruler
Slide of three colored threads
Medicine dropper
Dissecting needle (needle probe)
Specimen examples for wet mounts
Methylene blue (dilute) or iodine-potassium-iodide stain

For Demonstrations:

Micrometer scale
Stereomicroscope (dissecting microscope)

Because the human eye cannot perceive objects less than 0.1 mm in diameter, a microscope is an essential tool for the study of small structures such as cells. The microscope usually used for this purpose is the *compound light microscope.* It is called compound because it uses two sets of lenses: an eyepiece or ocular lens system and an objective lens system. The eyepiece lens system magnifies, or compounds, the image reaching it after the image is magnified by the objective lens system. Such an instrument can magnify images of small objects up to about one thousand times.

PURPOSE OF THE EXERCISE

To become familiar with the major parts of a compound light microscope and their functions and to make use of the microscope to observe small objects.

LEARNING OBJECTIVES

After completing this exercise, you should be able to

1. Locate and identify the major parts of a compound light microscope.
2. Describe the functions of these parts.
3. Calculate the total magnification produced by various combinations of eyepiece and objective lenses.
4. Prepare a simple microscope slide.
5. Make proper use of the microscope to observe small objects.

PROCEDURE A—MICROSCOPE BASICS

1. Familiarize yourself with the following list of rules for care of the microscope:
   a. Keep the microscope under its *dustcover* and in a cabinet when it is not being used.
   b. Handle the microscope with great care. It is an expensive and delicate instrument. To move it or carry it, hold it by its *arm* with one hand and support its *base* with the other hand (fig. 4.1).
   c. Always store the microscope with the scanning or lowest power objective in place. Always start with this objective when using the microscope.
   d. To clean the lenses, rub them gently with *lens paper* or a high-quality cotton swab. If the lenses need additional cleaning, follow the directions in the "Lens-Cleaning Technique" section that follows.
   e. If the microscope has a substage lamp, be sure the electric cord does not hang off the laboratory table where someone might trip over it. The bulb life can be extended if the lamp is cool before the microscope is moved.
   f. Never drag the microscope across the laboratory table after you have placed it.
   g. Never remove parts of the microscope or try to disassemble the eyepiece or objective lenses.
   h. If your microscope is not functioning properly, report the problem to your laboratory instructor immediately.

LENS-CLEANING TECHNIQUE

1. Moisten one end of a high-quality cotton swab with one drop of Kodak lens cleaner. Keep the other end dry.
2. Clean the optical surface with the wet end. Dry it with the other end, using a circular motion.
3. Use a hand aspirator to remove lingering dust particles.
4. Start with the scanning objective and work upward in magnification, using a new cotton swab for each objective.
5. When cleaning the eyepiece, do not open the lens unless it is absolutely necessary.
6. Use alcohol for difficult cleaning, and only as a last resort use xylene. Regular use of xylene will destroy lens coatings.

Figure 4.1 Major parts of a compound light microscope with a monocular body and a mechanical stage. Some microscopes are equipped with a binocular body.

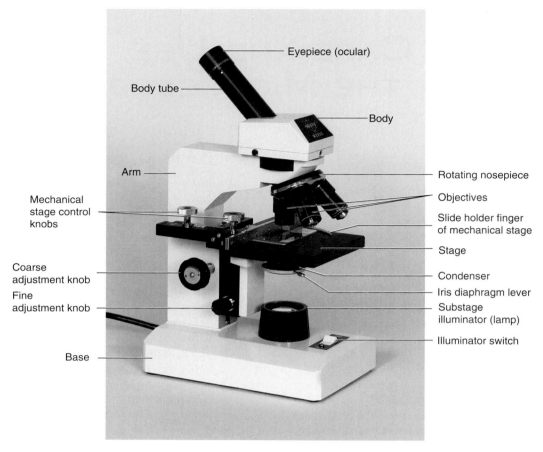

2. Observe a compound light microscope and study figure 4.1 to learn the names of its major parts. Note that the lens system of a compound microscope includes three parts—the condenser, objective lens, and eyepiece or ocular.

Light enters this system from a *substage illuminator (lamp)* or *mirror* and is concentrated and focused by a *condenser* onto a microscope slide or specimen placed on the *stage.* The condenser, which contains a set of lenses, usually is kept in its highest position possible.

The *iris diaphragm,* which is located between the light source and the condenser, can be used to increase or decrease the intensity of the light entering the condenser. Locate the lever that operates the iris diaphragm beneath the stage and move it back and forth. Note how this movement causes the size of the opening in the diaphragm to change. (Some microscopes have a revolving plate called a disc diaphragm beneath the stage instead of an iris diaphragm. Disc diaphragms have different-sized holes to admit varying amounts of light.) Which way do you move the diaphragm to increase the light intensity? _____ Which way to decrease it? _____

After light passes through a specimen mounted on a microscope slide, it enters an *objective lens system.* This lens projects the light upward into the *body tube,* where it produces a magnified image of the object being viewed.

The *eyepiece (ocular) lens* system then magnifies this image to produce another image, which is seen by the eye. Typically, the eyepiece lens magnifies the image ten times (10×). Look for the number in the metal of the eyepiece that indicates its power (fig. 4.2). What is the eyepiece power of your microscope? _____

The objective lenses are mounted in a rotating *nosepiece* so that different magnifications can be achieved by rotating any one of several objective lenses into position above the specimen. Commonly, this set of lenses includes a scanning objective (4×), a low-power objective (10×), and a high-power objective, also called a high-dry-power objective (about 40×). Sometimes an oil immersion objective (about 100×) is present. Look for the number printed on each objective that indicates its power. What are the objective lens powers of your microscope? _____

To calculate the *total magnification* achieved when using a particular objective, multiply the

Figure 4.2 The powers of this 10× eyepiece (*a*) and this 40× objective (*b*) are marked in the metal. DIN is an international optical standard on quality optics. The 0.65 on the 40× objective is the numerical aperture, which is a measure of the light-gathering capabilities.

(a)

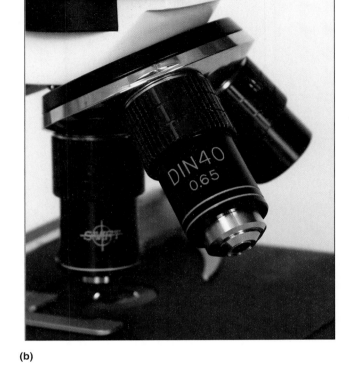

(b)

power of the eyepiece by the power of the objective used. Thus, the 10× eyepiece and the 40× objective produce a total magnification of 10 × 40, or 400×.

3. Complete Part A of Laboratory Report 4.
4. Turn on the substage illuminator and look through the eyepiece. You will see a lighted circular area called the *field of view.*

You can measure the diameter of this field of view by focusing the lenses on the millimeter scale of a transparent plastic ruler. To do this, follow these steps:

a. Place the ruler on the microscope stage in the spring clamp of a slide holder finger on a mechanical stage or under the stage (slide) clips. (*Note:* If your microscope is equipped with a mechanical stage, it may be necessary to use a short section cut from a transparent plastic ruler. The section should be several millimeters long and can be mounted on a microscope slide for viewing.)

b. Center the millimeter scale in the beam of light coming up through the condenser and rotate the scanning objective into position.

c. While you watch from the side to prevent the lens from touching anything, lower the objective until it is as close to the ruler as possible, using the *coarse adjustment knob* and then using the *fine adjustment knob* (fig. 4.3).

(*Note:* The adjustment knobs on some microscopes move the stage upward and downward for focusing.)

d. Look into the eyepiece and use the coarse adjustment knob to raise the objective lens until the lines of the millimeter scale come into sharp focus.

e. Adjust the light intensity by moving the *iris diaphragm lever* so that the field of view is brightly illuminated but comfortable to your eye. At the same time, take care not to overilluminate the field because transparent objects tend to disappear in very bright light.

f. Position the millimeter ruler so that its scale crosses the greatest diameter of the field of view. Also, move the ruler so that one of the millimeter marks is against the edge of the field of view.

g. Measure the distance across the field of view in millimeters.

5. Complete Part B of the laboratory report.
6. Most microscopes are designed to be *parfocal.* This means that when a specimen is in focus with a lower-power objective, it will be in focus (or nearly so) when a higher-power objective is rotated into position. Always center the specimen in the field of view before changing to higher objectives.

Rotate the low-power objective into position, and then look at the millimeter scale of the

33

Figure 4.3 When you focus using a particular objective, you can prevent it from touching the specimen by watching from the side.

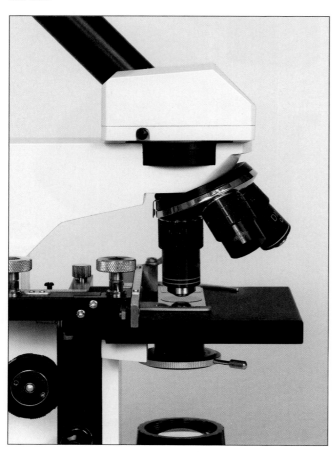

transparent plastic ruler. If you need to move the low-power objective to sharpen the focus, use the *fine adjustment knob.*

Adjust the iris diaphragm so that the field of view is properly illuminated. Once again, adjust the millimeter ruler so that the scale crosses the field of view through its greatest diameter, and position the ruler so that a millimeter mark is against one edge of the field.

Try to measure the distance across the field of view in millimeters.

7. Rotate the high-power objective into position while you watch from the side, and then observe the millimeter scale on the plastic ruler. All focusing using high-power magnification should be done only with the fine adjustment knob. If you use the coarse adjustment knob with the high-power objective, you can accidently force the objective into the coverslip and result in breaking the slide. This is because the *working distance* (the distance from the objective lens to the slide on the stage) is much shorter when using higher magnifications.

Adjust the iris diaphragm for proper illumination. Usually more illumination when using

higher magnifications will help you to view the objects more clearly. Try to measure the distance across the field of view in millimeters.

8. Locate the numeral 4 (or 9) on the plastic ruler and focus on it using the scanning objective. Note how the number appears in the field of view. Move the plastic ruler to the right and note which way the image moves. Slide the ruler away from you and again note how the image moves.

9. Examine the slide of the three colored threads using the low-power objective and then the high-power objective. Focus on the location where the three threads cross. By using the fine adjustment knob, determine the order from top to bottom by noting which color is in focus at different depths. The other colored threads will still be visible, but they will be blurred. Be sure to notice whether the stage or the body tube moves up and down with the adjustment knobs of the microscope that is being used for this depth determination. The vertical depth of the specimen that is clearly in focus is called the *depth of field (focus).* Whenever specimens are examined, continue to use the fine adjustment focusing knob to determine relative depths of structures that are clearly in focus within cells, giving a three-dimensional perspective. It should be noted that the depth of field is less at higher magnifications.

 Critical Thinking Application

What was the sequence of the three colored threads from top to bottom? Explain how you came to that conclusion.

_____

_____

_____

10. Complete Parts C and D of the laboratory report.

DEMONSTRATION

A compound light microscope is sometimes equipped with a micrometer scale mounted in the eyepiece. Such a scale is subdivided into fifty to one hundred equal divisions (fig. 4.4). These arbitrary divisions can be calibrated against the known divisions of a micrometer slide placed on the microscope stage. Once the values of the divisions are known, the length and width of a microscopic object can be measured by superimposing the scale over the magnified image of the object.

Observe the micrometer scale in the eyepiece of the demonstration microscope. Focus the low-power objective on the millimeter scale of a micrometer slide (or a plastic ruler) and measure the distance between the divisions on the micrometer scale in the eyepiece. What is the distance between the finest divisions of the scale in micrometers? _____

Figure 4.4 The divisions of a micrometer scale in an eyepiece can be calibrated against the known divisions of a micrometer slide. (Courtesy of Swift Instruments, Inc., San Jose, California)

Micrometer in eyepiece

Arbitrary divisions

Lines 0.01 mm apart

Micrometer slide

ULTRA LITE

PROCEDURE B—SLIDE PREPARATION

1. Prepare several temporary *wet mounts* using any small, transparent objects of interest, and examine the specimens using the low-power objective and then a high-power objective to observe their details. To prepare a wet mount, follow these steps (fig. 4.5):
   a. Obtain a precleaned microscope slide.

   b. Place a tiny, thin piece of the specimen you want to observe in the center of the slide, and use a medicine dropper to put a drop of water over it. Consult with your instructor if a drop of stain might enhance the image of any cellular structures of your specimen. If the specimen is solid, you might want to tease some of it apart with dissecting needles. In any case, the specimen must be thin enough so that light can

Figure 4.5 Steps in the preparation of a wet mount.

1 Obtain a precleaned microscope slide.

2 Place the specimen in the center of the slide and add drop of water to specimen.

Specimen

Needle probe

Paper

3 Slowly lower coverslip to avoid bubbles.

4 Remove excess water with absorbent paper.

pass through it. Why is it necessary for the specimen to be so thin?

_____

_____

c. Cover the specimen with a coverslip. Try to avoid trapping bubbles of air beneath the coverslip by slowly lowering it at an angle into the drop of water.
d. Remove any excess water from the edge of the coverslip with absorbent paper. If your microscope has an inclination joint, do not tilt the microscope while observing wet mounts because the fluid will flow.
e. Place the slide under the stage (slide) clips or in the slide holder on a mechanical stage, and position the slide so that the specimen is centered in the light beam passing up through the condenser.
f. Focus on the specimen using the scanning objective first. Next focus using the low-power objective, and then examine it with the high-power objective.
2. If an oil immersion objective is available, use it to examine the specimen. To use the oil immersion objective, follow these steps:

a. Center the object you want to study under the high-power field of view.
b. Rotate the high-power objective away from the microscope slide, place a small drop of immersion oil on the coverslip, and swing the oil immersion objective into position. To achieve sharp focus, use the fine adjustment knob only.
c. You will need to open the iris diaphragm more fully for proper illumination. More light is needed because the oil immersion objective covers a very small lighted area of the microscope slide.
d. Because the oil immersion objective must be very close to the coverslip to achieve sharp focus, care must be taken to avoid breaking the coverslip or damaging the objective lens. For this reason, never lower the objective when you are looking into the eyepiece. Instead, always raise the objective to achieve focus, or prevent the objective from touching the coverslip by watching the microscope slide and coverslip from the side if the objective needs to be lowered.
3. When you have finished working with the microscope, remove the microscope slide from the stage and wipe any oil from the objective lens with lens paper or a high-quality cotton swab. Swing the

Figure 4.6 A stereomicroscope, which is also called a dissecting microscope.

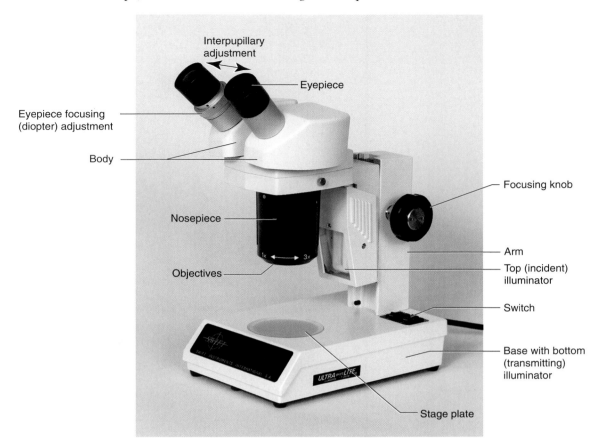

scanning objective or the low-power objective into position. Wrap the electric cord around the base of the microscope and replace the dustcover.

4. Complete Part E of the laboratory report.

DEMONSTRATION

A stereomicroscope (dissecting microscope) (fig. 4.6) is useful for observing the details of relatively large, opaque specimens. Although this type of microscope achieves less magnification than a compound microscope, it has the advantage of producing a three-dimensional image rather than the flat, two-dimensional image of the compound light microscope. In addition, the image produced by the stereomicroscope is positioned in the same manner as the specimen, rather than being reversed and inverted as it is by the compound light microscope.

Observe the stereomicroscope. Note that the eyepieces can be pushed apart or together to fit the distance between your eyes. Focus the microscope on the end of your finger. Which way does the image move when you move your finger to the right? _____

When you move it away? _____

If the instrument has more than one objective, change the magnification to higher power. Use the instrument to examine various small, opaque objects available in the laboratory.

Web Quest

Explore additional explanations on proper microscope use at

www.mhhe.com/shier11

Click on Student Edition. Click on Martin Lab Manual, Web Quest.

NOTES

Name _____

Date _____

Section _____

CARE AND USE
OF THE MICROSCOPE

PART A

Complete the following:

1. What total magnification will be achieved if the 10× eyepiece and the 10× objective are used? _____
2. What total magnification will be achieved if the 10× eyepiece and the 100× objective are used? _____

PART B

Complete the following:

1. Sketch the millimeter scale as it appears under the scanning objective magnification. (The circle represents the field of view through the microscope.)
2. What is the diameter of the scanning field of view in millimeters? _____
3. Microscopic objects often are measured in *micrometers.* A micrometer equals 1/1,000 of a millimeter and is symbolized by µm. What is the diameter of the scanning power field of view in micrometers? _____
4. If a circular object or specimen extends halfway across the scanning field, what is its diameter in millimeters? _____
5. What is its diameter in micrometers? _____

PART C

Complete the following:

1. Sketch the millimeter scale as it appears using the low-power objective.

2. What do you estimate the diameter of this field of view to be in millimeters? _____
3. How does the diameter of the scanning power field of view compare with that of the low-power field?
_____
4. Why is it more difficult to measure the diameter of the high-power field of view than the low-power field?
_____
_____
5. What change occurred in the light intensity of the field of view when you exchanged the low-power objective for the high-power objective? _____

6. Sketch the numeral 4 (or 9) as it appears through the scanning objective of the compound microscope.

7. What has the lens system done to the image of the numeral? (Is it right side up, upside down, or what?) _____

8. When you moved the ruler to the right, which way did the image move? _____

9. When you moved the ruler away from you, which way did the image move? _____

PART D

Match the names of the microscope parts in column A with the descriptions in column B. Place the letter of your choice in the space provided.

Column A	Column B
a. Adjustment knob	_____ 1. Increases or decreases the light intensity
b. Arm	_____ 2. Platform that supports a microscope slide
c. Condenser	_____ 3. Concentrates light onto the specimen
d. Eyepiece (ocular)	_____ 4. Causes objective lens (or stage) to move upward or downward
e. Field of view	
f. Iris diaphragm	_____ 5. After light passes through the specimen, it next enters this lens system
g. Nosepiece	
h. Objective lens system	_____ 6. Holds a microscope slide in position
i. Stage	_____ 7. Contains a lens at the top of the body tube
j. Stage (slide) clip	_____ 8. Serves as a handle for carrying the microscope
	_____ 9. Part to which the objective lenses are attached
	_____ 10. Circular area seen through the eyepiece

PART E

Prepare sketches of the objects you observed using the microscope. For each sketch, include the name of the object, the magnification you used to observe it, and its estimated dimensions in millimeters and micrometers.

LABORATORY EXERCISE 5

CELL STRUCTURE AND FUNCTION

MATERIALS NEEDED

Textbook
Animal cell model
Clean microscope slides
Coverslips
Flat toothpicks
Medicine dropper
Methylene blue (dilute) or iodine-potassium-iodide stain
Prepared microscope slides of human tissues
Compound light microscope

For Learning Extensions:

Single-edged razor blade
Plant materials such as leaves, soft stems, fruits, onion
    peel, and vegetables
Cultures of *Amoeba* and *Paramecium*

 SAFETY

- Review all the safety guidelines inside the front cover.
- Clean laboratory surfaces before and after laboratory procedures.
- Wear disposable gloves for the wet-mount procedures of the cells lining the inside of the cheek.
- Work only with your own materials when preparing the slide of cheek cells. Observe the same precautions as with all body fluids.
- Dispose of laboratory gloves, slides, coverslips, and toothpicks as instructed.
- Precautions should be taken to prevent cellular stains from contacting your clothes and skin.
- Wash your hands before leaving the laboratory.

Cells are the "building blocks" from which all parts of the human body are formed. They account for the shape, organization, and construction of the body and are responsible for carrying on its life processes. Under the light microscope, with a properly applied stain to make structures visible, the **cell (plasma) membrane,** the **cytoplasm,** and a **nucleus** are easily seen. The cytoplasm is composed of a clear fluid, the *cytosol,* and numerous *cytoplasmic organelles* suspended in the cytosol.

PURPOSE OF THE EXERCISE

To review the structure and functions of major cellular components and to observe examples of human cells.

LEARNING OBJECTIVES

After completing this exercise, you should be able to

1. Name and locate the components of a cell on a model or diagram and describe the general functions of these components.
2. Prepare a wet mount of cells lining the inside of the cheek, stain the cells, and identify the major components of these cells.
3. Locate cells on prepared slides of human tissues and identify their major components.
4. Identify major cellular components in a transmission electron micrograph.

PROCEDURE

1. Review the section entitled "A Composite Cell" in chapter 3 of the textbook.
2. Observe the animal cell model and identify its structures.
3. As a review activity, label figure 5.1 and study figure 5.2.
4. Complete Part A of Laboratory Report 5.
5. Prepare a wet mount of cells lining the inside of the cheek. To do this, follow these steps:
   a. Gently scrape (force is not necessary and should be avoided) the inner lining of your cheek with the broad end of a flat toothpick.
   b. Stir the toothpick in a drop of water on a clean microscope slide and dispose of the toothpick as directed by your instructor.
   c. Cover the drop with a coverslip.
   d. Observe the cheek cells by using the microscope. Compare your image with figure 5.3. To report what you observe, sketch a single cell in the space provided in Part B of the laboratory report.
6. Prepare a second wet mount of cheek cells, but this time, add a drop of dilute methylene blue or iodine-potassium-iodide stain to the cells. Cover the liquid with a coverslip and observe the cells with the microscope. Add to your sketch any additional structures you observe in the stained cells.
7. Answer the questions in Part B of the laboratory report.

Figure 5.1 Label the structures of this composite cell. The structures are not drawn to scale.

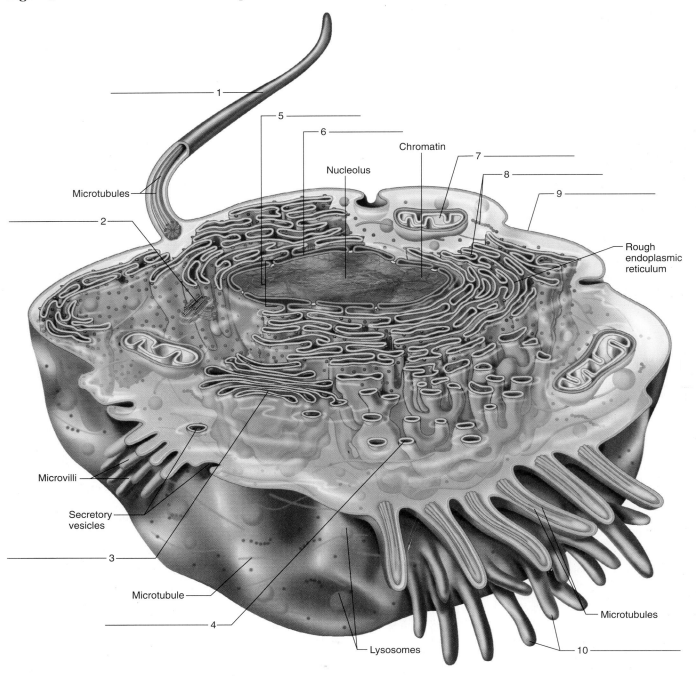

Microtubules

1

2

5

6

Nucleolus

Chromatin

7

8

9

Rough endoplasmic reticulum

Microvilli

Secretory vesicles

3

Microtubule

4

Lysosomes

Microtubules

10

8. Using the microscope, observe each of the prepared slides of human tissues. To report what you observe, sketch a single cell of each type in the space provided in Part C of the laboratory report.

9. Answer the questions in Part C of the laboratory report.

10. Study figure 5.4 *a–c*. These electron micrographs represent extremely thin slices of

cells. Note that each micrograph contains a section of a nucleus and some cytoplasm. Compare the organelles shown in these micrographs with the organelles included in the electron micrographs in chapter 3 of the textbook.

11. Complete Parts D and E of the laboratory report.

Figure 5.2 Structures of the cell membrane.

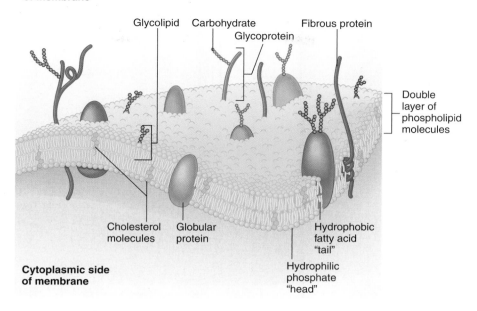

Extracellular side of membrane

Glycolipid   Carbohydrate   Fibrous protein

Glycoprotein

Double layer of phospholipid molecules

Cholesterol molecules   Globular protein   Hydrophobic fatty acid "tail"

Cytoplasmic side of membrane

Hydrophilic phosphate "head"

Figure 5.3 Stained cell lining the inside of the cheek as viewed through the compound light microscope using the high-power objective (400×).

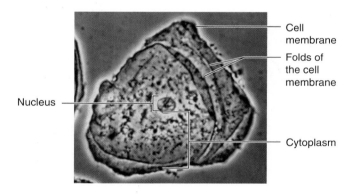

Cell membrane

Folds of the cell membrane

Nucleus

Cytoplasm

Critical Thinking Application

The cells lining the inside of the cheek are frequently removed for making observations of basic cell structure. The cells are from stratified squamous epithelium. Explain why these cells are used instead of outer body surface tissue.

_____

_____

_____

Figure 5.4 Transmission electron micrographs of cellular components. All of the views are only portions of a cell. Magnifications: (*a*) 26,000×; (*b*)10,000×; (*c*) 30,000×. Identify the numbered cellular structures, using the terms provided.

(a)   Cytoplasm   Nucleus

(b)   Nucleus   Cytoplasm

Terms:
Cell membrane
Centrioles
Chromatin
Chromatin
Endoplasmic reticulum
Golgi apparatus
Mitochondria
Mitochondrion (cross section)
Nuclear envelope
Nuclear envelope
Nucleolus
Ribosomes

Nucleus   Cytoplasm

(c)

LEARNING EXTENSION

Investigate the microscopic structure of various plant materials. To do this, prepare very tiny, thin slices of plant specimens, using a single-edged razor blade. (*Take care not to injure yourself with the blade.*) Keep the slices in a container of water until you are ready to observe them. To observe a specimen, place it into a drop of water on a clean microscope slide and cover it with a coverslip. Use the microscope and view the specimen using low- and high-power magnifications. Observe near the edges where your section of tissue is most likely to be one cell thick. Add a drop of dilute methylene blue or iodine-potassium-iodide stain, and note if any additional structures become visible. How are the microscopic structures of the plant specimens similar to the human tissues you observed?

_____

How are they different?

_____

LEARNING EXTENSION

Prepare a wet mount of the *Amoeba* and *Paramecium* by putting a drop of culture on a clean glass slide. Gently cover with a clean coverslip. Observe the movements of the *Amoeba* with pseudopodia and the *Paramecium* with cilia. Try to locate cellular components such as the cell membrane, nuclear envelope, nucleus, mitochondria, and contractile vacuoles. Describe the movement of the *Amoeba*.

_____

_____

Describe the movement of the *Paramecium*.

_____

_____

Web Quest

Review cell structure and function at
www.mhhe.com/shier11
Click on Student Edition. Click on Martin Lab Manual, Web Quest.

NOTES

CELL STRUCTURE AND FUNCTION

PART A

Match the cellular components in column A with the descriptions in column B. Place the letter of your choice in the space provided.

Column A

a. Chromatin
b. Cytoplasm
c. Endoplasmic reticulum
d. Golgi apparatus
e. Lysosome
f. Microtubule
g. Mitochondrion
h. Nuclear envelope
i. Nucleolus
j. Nucleus
k. Ribosome
l. Vesicle (vacuole)

Column B

_____ 1. Loosely coiled fibers containing protein and DNA within nucleus

_____ 2. Location of the energy release from food molecules

_____ 3. Small RNA-containing particles for the synthesis of proteins

_____ 4. Membranous sac formed by the pinching off of pieces of cell membrane

_____ 5. Dense body of RNA within the nucleus

_____ 6. Slender tubes that provide movement in cilia and flagella

_____ 7. Organelles composed of membrane-bound sacs, canals, and vesicles

_____ 8. Occupies space between cell membrane and nucleus

_____ 9. Flattened membranous sacs that package a secretion

_____ 10. Membranous sac that contains digestive enzymes

_____ 11. Separates nuclear contents from cytoplasm

_____ 12. Spherical organelle that contains chromatin and nucleolus

PART B

Complete the following:

1. Sketch a single cheek cell that has been stained. Label the cellular components you recognize. (The circle represents the field of view through the microscope.)

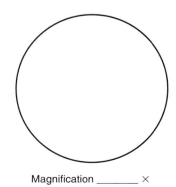

Magnification _____ ×

2. After comparing the wet mount and the stained cheek cells, state the advantage that was gained by staining cells.

_____

_____

3. Are the stained cheek cells nearly the same size and shape? _____ Propose an explanation for your

answer. _____

_____

PART C

Complete the following:

1. Sketch a single cell of each kind you observed in the prepared slides of human tissues. Name the tissue, indicate the magnification used, and label the cellular components you recognize.

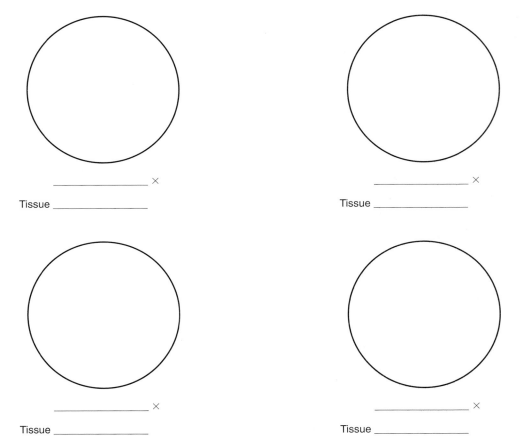

_____ ×

Tissue _____

_____ ×

Tissue _____

_____ ×

Tissue _____

_____ ×

Tissue _____

2. What do the various kinds of cells in these tissues have in common? _____

_____

3. What are the main differences you observed among these cells? _____

_____

PART D

Identify the structures indicated by the arrows in figure 5.4.

1. _____   7. _____
2. _____   8. _____
3. _____   9. _____
4. _____   10. _____
5. _____   11. _____
6. _____   12. _____

PART E

Answer the following questions after observing the transmission electron micrographs in figure 5.4.

1. What cellular structures were visible in the transmission electron micrographs that were not apparent in the cells you observed using the microscope? _____

_____

2. Before they can be observed by using a transmission electron microscope, cells are sliced into very thin sections. What disadvantage does this procedure present in the study of cellular parts? _____

_____

Notes

MOVEMENTS THROUGH CELL MEMBRANES

MATERIALS NEEDED

For Procedure A—Diffusion:

Textbook
Petri dish
White paper
Forceps
Potassium permanganate crystals
Millimeter ruler (thin and transparent)

For Procedure B—Osmosis:

Textbook
Thistle tube
Molasses (or Karo dark corn syrup)
Selectively permeable (semipermeable) membrane
    (presoaked dialysis tubing of 1 5/16″ or greater
    diameter)
Ring stand and clamp
Beaker
Rubber band
Millimeter ruler

*For Procedure C—Hypertonic, Hypotonic,
and Isotonic Solutions:*

Textbook
Test tubes
Marking pen
Test-tube rack
10 mL graduated cylinder
Medicine dropper
Uncoagulated animal blood
Distilled water
0.9% NaCl (aqueous solution)
3.0% NaCl (aqueous solution)
Clean microscope slides
Coverslips
Compound light microscope

For Procedure D—Filtration:

Textbook
Glass funnel
Filter paper
Ring stand and ring
Beaker
Powdered charcoal or ground black pepper
1% glucose (aqueous solution)
1% starch (aqueous solution)
Test tubes
10 mL graduated cylinder
Water bath (boiling water)
Benedict's solution

Iodine-potassium-iodide solution
Medicine dropper

For Alternative Osmosis Activity:

Fresh chicken egg
Beaker
Laboratory balance
Spoon
Vinegar
Corn syrup (Karo)

SAFETY

- Clean laboratory surfaces before and after laboratory procedures.
- Wear disposable gloves when handling chemicals and animal blood.
- Wear safety glasses when using chemicals.
- Dispose of laboratory gloves and blood-contaminated items as instructed.
- Wash your hands before leaving the laboratory.

A cell membrane functions as a gateway through which chemical substances and small particles may enter or leave a cell. These substances move through the membrane by physical processes such as diffusion, osmosis, and filtration, or by physiological processes such as active transport, phagocytosis, or pinocytosis.

PURPOSE OF THE EXERCISE

To demonstrate some of the physical processes by which substances move through cell membranes.

LEARNING OBJECTIVES

After completing this exercise, you should be able to

1. Define *diffusion* and identify examples of diffusion.
2. Define *osmosis* and identify examples of osmosis.
3. Distinguish among hypertonic, hypotonic, and isotonic solutions and observe the effects of these solutions on animal cells.
4. Define *filtration* and identify examples of filtration.

PROCEDURE A—DIFFUSION

1. Review the section entitled "Diffusion" in chapter 3 of the textbook.
2. To demonstrate diffusion, follow these steps:
   a. Place a petri dish half filled with water on a piece of white paper that has a millimeter ruler positioned on the paper. Wait until the water surface is still. Allow approximately 3 minutes. *Note:* The petri dish should remain level. A second millimeter ruler may be needed as a shim under the petri dish.
   b. Using forceps, place one crystal of potassium permanganate near the center of the petri dish and near the millimeter ruler (fig. 6.1).

Figure 6.1 To demonstrate diffusion, place one crystal of potassium permanganate in the center of a petri dish containing water. Place the crystal near the millimeter ruler (positioned under the petri dish).

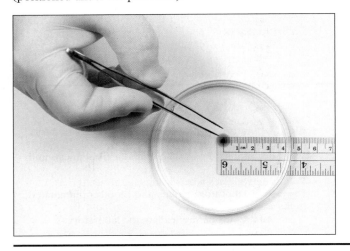

   c. Measure the radius of the purple circle at 1-minute intervals for 10 minutes.
3. Complete Part A of Laboratory Report 6.

 LEARNING EXTENSION

Repeat the demonstration of diffusion using a petri dish filled with ice-cold water and a second dish filled with very hot water. At the same moment, add a crystal of potassium permanganate to each dish and observe the circle as before. What difference do you note in the rate of diffusion in the two dishes? How do you explain this difference?

_____

_____

_____

PROCEDURE B—OSMOSIS

1. Review the section entitled "Osmosis" in chapter 3 of the textbook.
2. To demonstrate osmosis, refer to figure 6.2 as you follow these steps:
   a. One person plugs the tube end of a thistle tube with a finger.
   b. Another person then fills the bulb with molasses until it is about to overflow at the top of the bulb. Note that air remains trapped in the stem.
   c. Cover the bulb opening with a single-thickness piece of moist selectively permeable (semipermeable) membrane. Dialysis tubing that has been soaked for 30 minutes can easily be cut open because it becomes pliable.

Figure 6.2 (*a*) Fill the bulb of the thistle tube with molasses; (*b*) tightly secure a piece of selectively permeable (semipermeable) membrane over the bulb opening; and (*c*) immerse the bulb in a beaker of water. *Note:* These procedures require the participation of two people.

d. Tightly secure the membrane in place with several wrappings of a rubber band.

e. Immerse the bulb end of the tube in a beaker of water. If leaks are noted, repeat the procedures.

f. Support the upright portion of the tube with a clamp on a ring stand. Folded paper under the clamp will protect the thistle tube stem from breakage.

g. Mark the meniscus level of the molasses in the tube. *Note:* The best results will occur if the mark of the molasses is a short distance up the stem of the thistle tube when the experiment starts.

h. Measure the level changes after 10 minutes and 30 minutes.

3. Complete Part B of the laboratory report.

ALTERNATIVE PROCEDURE

Eggshell membranes possess selectively permeable properties. To demonstrate osmosis using a natural membrane, soak a fresh chicken egg in vinegar for about 24 hours to remove the shell. Use a spoon to carefully handle the delicate egg. Place the egg in a hypertonic solution (corn syrup) for about 24 hours. Remove the egg, rinse it, and using a laboratory balance, weigh the egg to establish a baseline weight. Place the egg in a hypotonic solution (distilled water). Remove the egg and weigh it every 15 minutes for an elapsed time of 75 minutes. Explain any weight changes that were noted during this experiment.

_____

_____

_____

_____

_____

_____

PROCEDURE C—HYPERTONIC, HYPOTONIC, AND ISOTONIC SOLUTIONS

1. Review the section entitled "Osmosis" in chapter 3 of the textbook.

2. To demonstrate the effect of hypertonic, hypotonic, and isotonic solutions on animal cells, follow these steps:

a. Place three test tubes in a rack and mark them as *tube 1, tube 2,* and *tube 3.* (*Note:* One set of tubes can be used to supply test samples for the entire class.)

b. Using 10 mL graduated cylinders, add 3 mL of distilled water to tube 1; add 3 mL of 0.9% NaCl to tube 2; and add 3 mL of 3.0% NaCl to tube 3.

c. Place three drops of fresh, uncoagulated animal blood into each of the tubes and gently mix the blood with the solutions. Wait 5 minutes.

d. Using three separate medicine droppers, remove a drop from each tube and place the drops on three separate microscope slides marked *1, 2,* and *3.*

e. Cover the drops with coverslips and observe the blood cells, using the high power of the microscope.

3. Complete Part C of the laboratory report.

ALTERNATIVE PROCEDURE

Various substitutes for blood can be used for Procedure C. Onion, cucumber, or cells lining the inside of the cheek represent three possible options.

PROCEDURE D—FILTRATION

1. Review the section entitled "Filtration" in chapter 3 of the textbook.

2. To demonstrate filtration, follow these steps:

a. Place a glass funnel in the ring of a ring stand over an empty beaker. Fold a piece of filter paper in half and then in half again. Open one thickness of the filter paper to form a cone, wet the cone, and place it in the funnel. The filter paper is used to demonstrate how movement across membranes is limited by the size of the molecules, but it does not represent a working model of biological membranes.

b. Prepare a mixture of 5 cc (approximately 1 teaspoon) powdered charcoal (or ground black pepper) and equal amounts of 1% glucose solution and 1% starch solution in a beaker. Pour some of the mixture into the funnel until it nearly reaches the top of the filter-paper cone. Care should be taken to prevent the mixture from spilling over the top of the filter paper. Collect the filtrate in the beaker below the funnel (fig. 6.3).

c. Test some of the filtrate in the beaker for the presence of glucose. To do this, place 1 mL of filtrate in a clean test tube and add 1 mL of Benedict's solution. Place the test tube in a water bath of boiling water for 2 minutes and then allow the liquid to cool slowly. If the color of the solution changes to green, yellow, or red, glucose is present (fig. 6.4).

d. Test some of the filtrate in the beaker for the presence of starch. To do this, place a few drops of filtrate in a test tube and add one drop of iodine-potassium-iodide solution. If the color of the solution changes to blue-black, starch is present.

e. Observe any charcoal in the filtrate.

3. Complete Part D of the laboratory report.

Figure 6.3 Apparatus used to illustrate filtration.

Ring stand

Mixture

Filter paper

Ring

Filtrate

Figure 6.4 Heat the filtrate and Benedict's solution in a boiling water bath for 2 minutes.

Water bath

Filtrate and
Benedict's
solution

Hot plate

Name _____

Date _____

Section _____

MOVEMENTS THROUGH CELL MEMBRANES

PART A

Complete the following:

1. Enter data for changes in the movement of the potassium permanganate.

Elapsed Time	Radius of Purple Circle in Millimeters
Initial	_____
1 minute	_____
2 minutes	_____
3 minutes	_____
4 minutes	_____
5 minutes	_____
6 minutes	_____
7 minutes	_____
8 minutes	_____
9 minutes	_____
10 minutes	_____

2. Prepare a graph that illustrates the diffusion distance of potassium permanganate in 10 minutes.

3. Explain your graph. _____

_____

4. Briefly define *diffusion*. _____

_____

Critical Thinking Application

By answering yes or no, indicate which of the following provides an example of diffusion.

1. A perfume bottle is opened, and soon the odor can be sensed in all parts of the room. _____
2. A sugar cube is dropped into a cup of hot water, and, without being stirred, all of the liquid becomes sweet tasting. _____
3. Water molecules move from a faucet through a garden hose when the faucet is turned on. _____
4. A person blows air molecules into a balloon by exhaling forcefully. _____
5. A crystal of blue copper sulfate is placed in a test tube of water. The next day, the solid is gone, but the water is evenly colored._____

PART B

Complete the following:

1. What was the change in the level of molasses in 10 minutes? _____
2. What was the change in the level of molasses in 30 minutes? _____
3. How do you explain this change? _____

_____

4. Briefly define *osmosis*. _____

_____

Critical Thinking Application

By answering yes or no, indicate which of the following involves osmosis.

1. A fresh potato is peeled, weighed, and soaked in a strong salt solution. The next day, it is discovered that the potato has lost weight. _____
2. Garden grass wilts after being exposed to dry chemical fertilizer. _____
3. Air molecules escape from a punctured tire as a result of high pressure inside. _____
4. Plant seeds soaked in water swell and become several times as large as before soaking. _____
5. When the bulb of a thistle tube filled with water is sealed by a selectively permeable membrane and submerged in a beaker of molasses, the water level in the tube falls. _____

PART C

Complete the following:

1. In the spaces, sketch a few blood cells from each of the test tubes, and indicate the magnification.

Tube 1
(distilled water)

_____×

Tube 2
(0.9% NaCl)

_____×

Tube 3
(3.0% NaCl)

_____×

2. Based on your results, which tube contained a solution that was hypertonic to the blood cells? _____
   Give the reason for your answer. _____
   _____

3. Which tube contained a solution that was hypotonic to the blood cells? _____
   Give the reason for your answer. _____
   _____

4. Which tube contained a solution that was isotonic to the blood cells? _____
   Give the reason for your answer. _____
   _____

PART D

Complete the following:

1. Which of the substances in the mixture you prepared passed through the filter paper into the filtrate? _____
   _____

2. What evidence do you have for your answer to question 1?_____
   _____
   _____

3. What force was responsible for the movement of substances through the filter paper? _____
   _____

4. What substances did not pass through the filter paper? _____
   _____

5. What factor prevented these substances from passing through? _____
   _____
   _____

6. Briefly define *filtration.* _____
   _____
   _____

Critical Thinking Application

By answering yes or no, indicate which of the following involves filtration.

1. Oxygen molecules move into a cell and carbon dioxide molecules leave a cell because of differences in the concentrations of these substances on either side of the cell membrane. _____

2. Blood pressure forces water molecules from the blood outward through the thin wall of a blood capillary. _____

3. Urine is forced from the urinary bladder through the tubular urethra by muscular contractions. _____

4. Air molecules enter the lungs through the airways when air pressure is greater outside these organs than inside. _____

5. Coffee is made using a coffeemaker (not instant). _____

LABORATORY EXERCISE 7

CELL CYCLE

MATERIALS NEEDED

Textbook
Models of animal mitosis
Microscope slides of whitefish mitosis (blastula)
Compound light microscope

For Demonstration:

Microscope slide of human chromosomes from
  leukocytes in mitosis
Oil immersion objective

The cell cycle consists of the series of changes a cell undergoes from the time it is formed until it divides. Typically, a newly formed cell grows to a certain size and then divides to form two new cells (*daughter cells*). This cell division process involves two major steps: (1) division of the cell's nuclear parts, which is called *mitosis* (karyokinesis) and (2) division of the cell's cytoplasm (*cytokinesis*). Before the cell divides, it must synthesize biochemicals and other contents. This period of preparation is called *interphase*. The extensive period of interphase is divided into three phases. The S phase, when DNA synthesis occurs, is between two gap phases (G_1 and G_2), when cell growth occurs and cytoplasmic organelles duplicate. Eventually, some specialized cells cease further cell division, but remain alive.

PURPOSE OF THE EXERCISE

To review the stages in the cell cycle and to observe cells in various stages of their life cycles.

LEARNING OBJECTIVES

After completing this exercise, you should be able to

1. Describe the cell cycle.
2. Identify the stages in the life cycle of a particular cell.
3. Arrange into a correct sequence a set of models or drawings of cells in various stages of their life cycles.

PROCEDURE

1. Review the section entitled "The Cell Cycle" in chapter 3 of the textbook.
2. As a review activity, study the various stages of the cell's life cycle represented in figure 7.1 and label the structures indicated in figure 7.2.
3. Observe the animal mitosis models and review the major events in a cell's life cycle represented by each of them. Be sure you can arrange these models in correct sequence if their positions are changed. The acronym IPMAT can help you arrange the correct order of phases in the cell cycle. This includes interphase followed by the four phases of mitosis. Cytokinesis overlaps anaphase and telophase.
4. Complete Part A of Laboratory Report 7.
5. Obtain a slide of the whitefish mitosis (blastula).
   a. Examine the slide using the high-power objective of a microscope. The tissue on this slide was obtained from a developing embryo (blastula) of a fish, and many of the embryonic cells are undergoing mitosis. Note that the chromosomes of these dividing cells are darkly stained (fig. 7.3).
   b. Search the tissue for cells in various stages of cell division. Note that there are several sections on the slide. If you cannot locate different stages in one section, examine the cells of another section since the stages occur randomly on the slide.
   c. Each time you locate a cell in a different stage, sketch it in an appropriate circle in Part B of the laboratory report.

 Critical Thinking Application

Which stage (phase) of the cell cycle was the most numerous in the blastula?_____

Explain your answer._____
_____
_____

6. Complete Parts C, D, and E of the laboratory report.

Figure 7.1 The cell cycle: interphase, mitosis, and cytokinesis.

Early Interphase
of daughter cells—
a time of normal cell
growth and function.

Restriction
checkpoint

Late Interphase
Cell has passed the
restriction checkpoint
and completed DNA
replication, as well as
replication of centrioles
and mitochondria, and
synthesis of extra
membrane.

Nuclear
envelope

Chromatin
fibers

Centrioles

Aster

Microtubules

Prophase
Chromosomes condense and
become visible. Nuclear
envelope and nucleolus
disperse. Spindle apparatus
forms.

Cleavage
furrow

Centromere

Spindle fiber

Late Prophase

Sister
chromatids

Chromosomes

Nuclear
envelopes

Telophase and Cytokinesis
Nuclear envelopes begin to
reassemble around two daughter
nuclei. Chromosomes decondense.
Spindle disappears. Division of
the cytoplasm into two cells.

Anaphase
Sister chromatids separate to
opposite poles of cell. Events
begin which lead to cytokinesis.

Metaphase
Chromosomes align along
equator, or metaphase plate,
of cell.

Mitosis

Cytokinesis

G_1 phase

S phase ─── Interphase

G_2 phase

Figure 7.2 Label the structures indicated in the dividing cell.

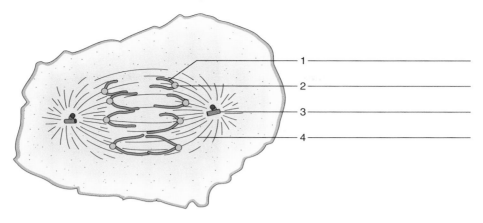

1 _____
2 _____
3 _____
4 _____

Figure 7.3 Cell in prophase (250× micrograph enlarged to 1,000×).

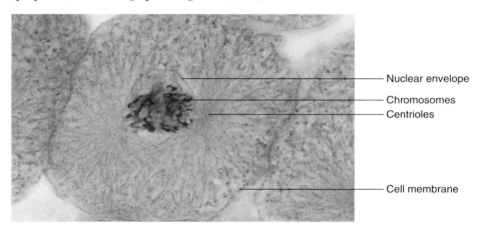

Nuclear envelope

Chromosomes

Centrioles

Cell membrane

DEMONSTRATION

Using the oil immersion objective of a microscope, see if you can locate some human chromosomes by examining a prepared slide of human chromosomes from leukocytes. The cells on this slide were cultured in a special medium and were stimulated to undergo mitosis. The mitotic process was arrested in metaphase by exposing the cells to a chemical called colchicine, and the cells were caused to swell osmotically. As a result of this treatment, the chromosomes were spread apart. A complement of human chromosomes should be visible when they are magnified about 1,000×. Note that each chromosome is double-stranded and consists of two chromatids joined by a common centromere (fig. 7.4).

Web Quest

Review the phases of the cell cycle and the events during each phase. Search these at www.mhhe.com/shier11
Click on Student Edition. Click on Martin Lab Manual, Web Quest.

Figure 7.4 (*a*) A complement of human chromosomes (2,700×). (*b*) A *karyotype* can be constructed by arranging the homologous chromosome pairs together in a chart. The completed karyotype indicates a normal male.

(a)

(b)

Name _____

Date _____

Section _____

CELL CYCLE

PART A

Complete the table.

Stage	Major Events Occurring
Interphase **(G_1, S, and G_2)**	
Mitosis (karyokinesis) Prophase	
Metaphase	
Anaphase	
Telophase	
Cytoplasmic division **(cytokinesis)**	

PART B

Sketch an interphase cell and cells in different stages of mitosis to illustrate the whitefish cell's life cycle. Label the major cellular structures represented in the sketches and indicate cytokinesis locations. (The circles represent fields of view through the microscope.)

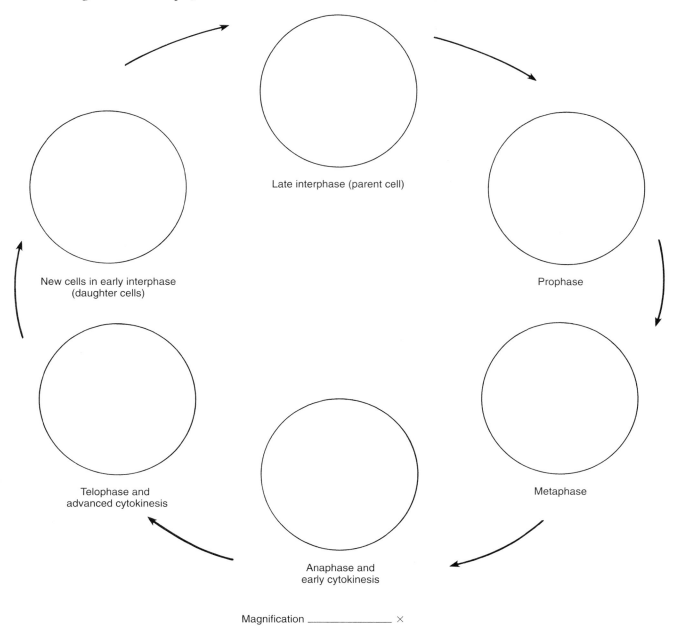

Late interphase (parent cell)

New cells in early interphase
(daughter cells)

Prophase

Telophase and
advanced cytokinesis

Metaphase

Anaphase and
early cytokinesis

Magnification _____ ×

PART C

Complete the following:

1. In what ways are the new cells (daughter cells), which result from a cell cycle, similar? _____

    _____

    _____

2. How do the new cells differ slightly? _____

    _____

    _____

Figure 7.5 Identify the mitotic stage of the cell in each of these micrographs of the whitefish blastula (250×).

(a)

(b)

(c)

(d)

3. Distinguish between mitosis (karyokinesis) and cytoplasmic division (cytokinesis). _____

_____

_____

PART D

Identify the mitotic stage represented by each of the micrographs in figure 7.5(*a–d*).

a. _____   c. _____

b. _____   d. _____

PART E

Identify the structures indicated by numbers in figure 7.5.

1. _____   4. _____

2. _____   5. _____

3. _____   6. _____

NOTES

EPITHELIAL TISSUES

MATERIALS NEEDED

Textbook
Compound light microscope
Prepared slides of the following epithelial tissues:
    Simple squamous epithelium (lung)
    Simple cuboidal epithelium (kidney)
    Simple columnar epithelium (small intestine)
    Pseudostratified (ciliated) columnar epithelium
        (trachea)
    Stratified squamous epithelium (esophagus)
    Transitional epithelium (urinary bladder)

For Learning Extension:

Colored pencils

A tissue is composed of a layer or group of cells—cells that are similar in size, shape, and function. Within the human body, there are four major types of tissues: (1) epithelial, which cover the body's external and internal surfaces; (2) connective, which bind and support parts; (3) muscle, which make movement possible; and (4) nervous, which conduct impulses from one part of the body to another and help to control and coordinate body activities.

Epithelial tissues are tightly packed single (simple) to multiple (stratified) layers of cells that provide protective barriers. The underside of this tissue layer contains a basement membrane layer to which the epithelial cells anchor. The cells readily divide, lack blood vessels, and have little extracellular matrix between them. Epithelial cells always have a free (apical) surface that is exposed to the outside or to an open space internally. Many shapes of the cells exist that are used to name and identify the variations. Many of the prepared slides contain more than the tissue to be studied, so be certain that your view matches the correct tissue. Also be aware that stained colors of all tissues might vary.

PURPOSE OF THE EXERCISE

To review the characteristics of epithelial tissues and to observe examples.

LEARNING OBJECTIVES

After completing this exercise, you should be able to

1. Describe the general characteristics of epithelial tissues.
2. List six types of epithelial tissues.
3. Describe the special characteristics of each type of epithelial tissue.
4. Indicate a location and function of each type of epithelial tissue.
5. Identify examples of epithelial tissues.

PROCEDURE

1. Review the section entitled "Epithelial Tissues" in chapter 5 of the textbook.
2. Complete Part A of Laboratory Report 8.
3. Use the microscope to observe the prepared slides of types of epithelial tissues. As you observe each tissue, look for its special distinguishing features as described in the textbook, such as cell size, shape, and arrangement. Compare your prepared slides of epithelial tissues to the micrographs in figure 8.1.
4. Complete Part B of the laboratory report.
5. Test your ability to recognize each type of epithelial tissue. To do this, have a laboratory partner select one of the prepared slides, cover its label, and focus the microscope on the tissue. Then see if you can correctly identify the tissue.

Web Quest

Identify tissues from micrographs and examine the structural components of tissues. Search these at

www.mhhe.com/shier11

Click on Student Edition. Click on Martin Lab Manual, Web Quest.

Figure 8.1 Micrographs of epithelial tissues. *Note:* The brackets to the right of each micrograph indicate the tissue.

(a) Simple squamous epithelium (side view) (1,100×)

(b) Simple cuboidal epithelium (800×)

(c) Simple columnar epithelium (650×)

(d) Pseudostratified columnar epithelium with cilia (1,500×)

(e) Stratified squamous epithelium (370×)

(f) Transitional epithelium (unstretched) (190×)

EPITHELIAL TISSUES

PART A

Match the tissues in column A with the characteristics in column B. Place the letter of your choice in the space provided. (Some answers may be used more than once.)

Column A

a. Simple columnar epithelium
b. Simple cuboidal epithelium
c. Simple squamous epithelium
d. Pseudostratified columnar epithelium
e. Stratified squamous epithelium
f. Transitional epithelium

Column B

_____ 1. Consists of several layers of cube-shaped, elongated, and irregular cells

_____ 2. Commonly possesses cilia that move dust and mucus out of the airways

_____ 3. Single layer of flattened cells

_____ 4. Nuclei located at different levels within cells

_____ 5. Forms walls of capillaries and air sacs of lungs

_____ 6. Forms linings of trachea and bronchi

_____ 7. Younger cells cuboidal, older cells flattened

_____ 8. Forms inner lining of urinary bladder

_____ 9. Lines kidney tubules and ducts of salivary glands

_____ 10. Forms lining of stomach and intestines

_____ 11. Nuclei located near basement membrane

_____ 12. Forms lining of oral cavity, anal canal, and vagina

PART B

In the space that follows, sketch a few cells of each type of epithelium you observed. For each sketch, label the major characteristics, indicate the magnification used, write an example of a location in the body, and provide a function.

<table>
<tr>
<td>

Simple squamous epithelium (____×)

Location: _____

Function: _____

</td>
<td>

Simple cuboidal epithelium (____×)

Location: _____

Function: _____

</td>
</tr>
<tr>
<td>

Simple columnar epithelium (____×)

Location: _____

Function: _____

</td>
<td>

Pseudostratified columnar epithelium with cilia (____×)

Location: _____

Function: _____

</td>
</tr>
<tr>
<td>

Stratified squamous epithelium (____×)

Location: _____

Function: _____

</td>
<td>

Transitional epithelium (____×)

Location: _____

Function: _____

</td>
</tr>
</table>

Critical Thinking Application

As a result of your observations of epithelial tissues, which one(s) provide(s) the best protection? Explain your answer.

_____

_____

_____

_____

LEARNING EXTENSION

Use colored pencils to differentiate various cellular structures in Part B. Select a different color for a nucleus, cytoplasm, cell membrane, basement membrane, goblet cell, and cilia whenever visible.

CONNECTIVE TISSUES

MATERIALS NEEDED

Textbook
Compound light microscope
Prepared slides of the following:
Loose (areolar) connective tissue
Adipose tissue
Dense connective tissue (regular type)
Elastic connective tissue
Reticular connective tissue
Hyaline cartilage
Elastic cartilage
Fibrocartilage
Bone (compact, ground, cross section)
Blood (human smear)

For Learning Extension:

Colored pencils

Connective tissues contain a variety of cell types and occur in all regions of the body. They bind structures together, provide support and protection, fill spaces, store fat, and produce blood cells.

Connective tissue cells are often widely scattered in an abundance of extracellular matrix. The matrix consists of fibers and a ground substance of various densities and consistencies. Many of the prepared slides contain more than the tissue to be studied, so be certain that your view matches the correct tissue. Additional study of bone and blood will be found in Laboratory Exercises 12 and 37.

PURPOSE OF THE EXERCISE

To review the characteristics of connective tissues and to observe examples of the major types.

LEARNING OBJECTIVES

After completing this exercise, you should be able to

1. Describe the general characteristics of connective tissues.

2. List the major types of connective tissues.
3. Describe the special characteristics of each of the major types of connective tissue.
4. Indicate a location and function of each type of connective tissue.
5. Identify the major types of connective tissues on microscope slides.

PROCEDURE

1. Review the section entitled "Connective Tissues" in chapter 5 of the textbook.
2. Complete Part A of Laboratory Report 9.
3. Use a microscope to observe the prepared slides of various connective tissues. As you observe each tissue, look for its special distinguishing features as described in the textbook. Compare your prepared slides of connective tissues to the micrographs in figure 9.1.
4. Complete Part B of the laboratory report.
5. Test your ability to recognize each of these connective tissues by having a laboratory partner select a slide, cover its label, and focus the microscope on this tissue. Then see if you correctly identify the tissue.

Web Quest

Identify tissues from micrographs and examine the structural components of tissues. Search these at
www.mhhe.com/shier11
Click on Student Edition. Click on Martin Lab Manual, Web Quest.

Figure 9.1 Micrographs of connective tissues.

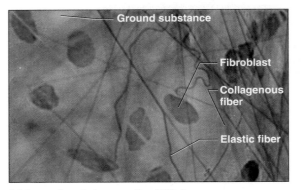

(a) Loose (areolar) connective (400×)

(b) Adipose (265×)

(c) Dense connective (regular) (1,000×)

(d) Elastic connective (680×)

(e) Reticular connective (1,000×)

(f) Hyaline cartilage (500×)

Figure 9.1 *Continued.*

Extracellular matrix

Elastic fibers

Chondrocyte in lacuna

Nucleus

(g) Elastic cartilage (1,200×)

Collagenous fibers

Extracellular matrix

Nucleus of chondrocyte in lacuna

(h) Fibrocartilage (1,800×)

Central canal

Lacuna

Osteon

(i) Bone (100×)

Location of extracellular matrix (plasma)

Red blood cell

White blood cells

Platelets

(j) Blood (1,200×)

Notes

CONNECTIVE TISSUES

PART A

Match the tissues in column A with the characteristics in column B. Place the letter of your choice in the space provided. (Some answers may be used more than once.)

Column A

a. Adipose tissue
b. Blood
c. Bone
d. Dense connective tissue
e. Elastic cartilage
f. Elastic connective tissue
g. Fibrocartilage
h. Hyaline cartilage
i. Loose (areolar) connective tissue
j. Reticular connective tissue

Column B

_____ 1. Forms framework of outer ear

_____ 2. Functions as heat insulator beneath skin

_____ 3. Contains large amounts of fluid and lacks fibers

_____ 4. Cells arranged around central canal

_____ 5. Binds skin to underlying organs

_____ 6. Main tissue of tendons and ligaments

_____ 7. Provides stored energy supply in fat vacuoles

_____ 8. Forms the flexible part of the nasal septum

_____ 9. Pads between vertebrae that are shock absorbers

_____ 10. Matrix contains collagen fibers and mineral salts

_____ 11. Occurs in ligament attachments between vertebrae and artery walls

_____ 12. Forms supporting tissue in walls of liver and spleen

PART B

In the space that follows, sketch a small section of each of the types of connective tissues you observed. For each sketch, label the major characteristics, indicate the magnification used, write an example of a location in the body, and provide a function.

Loose (areolar) connective tissue (____×)

Location: _____

Function: _____

Adipose tissue (____×)

Location: _____

Function: _____

Dense connective tissue (____×)

Location: _____

Function: _____

Elastic connective tissue (____×)

Location: _____

Function: _____

Reticular connective tissue (____×)

Location: _____

Function: _____

Hyaline cartilage (____×)

Location: _____

Function: _____

Elastic cartilage (____×)

Location: _____
Function: _____

Fibrocartilage (____×)

Location: _____
Function: _____

Bone (____×)

Location: _____
Function: _____

Blood (____×)

Location: _____
Function: _____

Critical Thinking Application

Abdominal impact injuries often involve the spleen. Explain the structural tissue characteristics that make the spleen so vulnerable to serious injury.

_____

_____

_____

_____

LEARNING EXTENSION

Use colored pencils to differentiate various cellular structures in Part B. Select a different color for the cells, fibers, and ground substance whenever visible.

NOTES

MUSCLE AND NERVOUS TISSUES

MATERIALS NEEDED

Textbook
Compound light microscope
Prepared slides of the following:
    Skeletal muscle tissue
    Smooth muscle tissue
    Cardiac muscle tissue
    Nervous tissue (spinal cord smear and/or cerebellum)

For Learning Extension:

Colored pencils

Muscle tissues are characterized by the presence of elongated cells or muscle fibers that can contract in response to specific stimuli. As they shorten, these fibers pull at their attached ends and cause body parts to move. The three types of muscle tissues are skeletal, smooth, and cardiac.

Nervous tissues occur in the brain, spinal cord, and peripheral nerves. They consist of neurons (nerve cells), which are the impulse-conducting cells of the nervous system, and neuroglial cells, which perform supportive and protective functions.

PURPOSE OF THE EXERCISE

To review the characteristics of muscle and nervous tissues and to observe examples of these tissues.

LEARNING OBJECTIVES

After completing this exercise, you should be able to

1. List the three types of muscle tissues.
2. Describe the general characteristics of muscle tissues.
3. Describe the special characteristics of each type of muscle tissue.
4. Indicate a location and function of each type of muscle tissue.
5. Identify examples of muscle tissues.
6. Describe the general characteristics of nervous tissues.
7. Identify nervous tissue.

PROCEDURE

1. Review the sections entitled "Muscle Tissues" and "Nervous Tissue" in chapter 5 of the textbook.
2. Complete Part A of Laboratory Report 10.
3. Using the microscope, observe each of the types of muscle tissues on the prepared slides. Look for the special features of each type, as described in the textbook. Compare your prepared slides of muscle tissues to the micrographs in figure 10.1 and the muscle tissue characteristics in table 10.1.
4. Observe the prepared slide of nervous tissue and identify neurons (nerve cells), neuron processes, and neuroglial cells. Compare your prepared slide of nervous tissue to the micrograph in figure 10.1.
5. Complete Part B of the laboratory report.
6. Test your ability to recognize each of these muscle and nervous tissues by having your laboratory partner select a slide, cover its label, and focus the microscope on this tissue. Then see if you correctly identify the tissue.

Web Quest

Identify tissues from micrographs, and examine the structural components of tissues. Search these at

www.mhhe.com/shier11

Click on Student Edition. Click on Martin Lab Manual, Web Quest.

Figure 10.1 Micrographs of muscle and nervous tissues.

(a) Skeletal muscle (700×)

(b) Smooth muscle (900×)

(c) Cardiac muscle (400×)

(d) Nervous tissue (300×)

Table 10.1 Muscle Tissue Characteristics

Characteristic	Skeletal Muscle	Cardiac Muscle	Smooth Muscle
Appearance of cells	Unbranched and relatively parallel	Branched and connected in complex networks	Spindle-shaped
Striations	Present and obvious	Present but faint	Absent
Nucleus	Multinucleated	Uninucleated (usually)	Uninucleated
Intercalated discs	Absent	Present	Absent
Control	Voluntary	Involuntary	Involuntary

MUSCLE AND NERVOUS TISSUES

PART A

Match the tissues in column A with the characteristics in column B. Place the letter of your choice in the space provided. (Some answers may be used more than once.)

Column A

a. Cardiac muscle
b. Nervous tissue
c. Skeletal muscle
d. Smooth muscle

Column B

_____ 1. Coordinates, regulates, and integrates body functions

_____ 2. Contains intercalated discs

_____ 3. Muscle that lacks striations

_____ 4. Striated and involuntary

_____ 5. Striated and voluntary

_____ 6. Contains neurons and neuroglial cells

_____ 7. Muscle attached to bones

_____ 8. Muscle that composes heart

_____ 9. Moves food through the digestive tract

_____ 10. Transmits impulses along cytoplasmic extensions

PART B

In the space that follows, sketch a few cells or fibers of each of the three types of muscle tissues and of nervous tissue as they appear through the microscope. For each sketch, label the major structures of the cells or fibers, indicate the magnification used, write an example of a location in the body, and provide a function.

Skeletal muscle tissue (____×)	Smooth muscle tissue (____×)
Location: _____	Location: _____
Function: _____	Function: _____
Cardiac muscle tissue (____×)	Nervous tissue (____×)
Location: _____	Location: _____
Function: _____	Function: _____

LEARNING EXTENSION

Use colored pencils to differentiate various cellular structures in Part B.

INTEGUMENTARY SYSTEM

MATERIALS NEEDED

Textbook
Skin model
Hand magnifier or dissecting microscope
Forceps
Microscope slide and coverslip
Compound light microscope
Prepared microscope slide of human scalp or axilla
Prepared slide of heavily pigmented human skin
Prepared slide of thick skin (plantar or palmar)

For Learning Extension:

Tattoo slide

The integumentary system includes the skin, hair, nails, sebaceous glands, and sweat glands. These organs provide a protective covering for deeper tissues, aid in regulating body temperature, retard water loss, house sensory receptors, synthesize various chemicals, and excrete small quantities of wastes.

The skin consists of two distinct layers. The outer layer, the epidermis, consists of stratified squamous epithelium. The inner layer, the dermis, consists of a thicker layer of dense connective tissue. Beneath the dermis is the subcutaneous layer (not considered a true layer of the skin), which is composed of adipose and loose connective tissues.

PURPOSE OF THE EXERCISE

To observe the organs and tissues of the integumentary system and to review the functions of these parts.

LEARNING OBJECTIVES

After completing this exercise, you should be able to

1. Name the organs of the integumentary system.
2. Describe the major functions of these organs.
3. Distinguish among epidermis, dermis, and the subcutaneous layer.
4. Identify the layers of the skin, a hair follicle, an arrector pili muscle, a sebaceous gland, and a sweat gland on a microscope slide, diagram, or model.

PROCEDURE

1. Review the sections entitled "Skin and Its Tissues" and "Accessory Structures of the Skin" in chapter 6 of the textbook.
2. As a review activity, label figures 11.1, 11.2, and 11.3. Locate as many of these structures as possible on a skin model.
3. Complete Part A of Laboratory Report 11.
4. Use the hand magnifier or dissecting microscope and proceed as follows:
   a. Observe the skin, hair, and nails on your hand.
   b. Compare the type and distribution of hairs on the front and back of your forearm.
5. Use low-power magnification of the compound light microscope and proceed as follows:
   a. Pull out a single hair with forceps and mount it on a microscope slide under a coverslip.
   b. Observe the root and shaft of the hair and note the scalelike parts that make up the shaft.
6. Complete Part B of the laboratory report.
7. As vertical sections of human skin are observed, remember that the lenses of the microscope invert and reverse images. It is important to orient the position of the epidermis, dermis, and subcutaneous (hypodermis) layers using scan magnification before continuing with additional observations. Compare all of your skin observations to figure 11.4. Use low-power magnification of the compound light microscope and proceed as follows:
   a. Observe the prepared slide of human scalp or axilla.
   b. Locate the epidermis, dermis, and subcutaneous layer, a hair follicle, an arrector pili muscle, a sebaceous gland, and a sweat gland.
   c. Focus on the epidermis with high power and locate the stratum corneum and stratum basale (stratum germinativum). Note how the shapes of the cells in these two layers differ.
   d. Observe the dense connective tissue (irregular type) that makes up the bulk of the dermis.
   e. Observe the adipose tissue that composes most of the subcutaneous layer.

Figure 11.1 Label this vertical section of the skin.

4
Pore
Sweat
5
6
Dermal papilla
Tactile (Meissner's) corpuscle
7
Lamellated (Pacinian) corpuscle
8
Hair root
9
10
Nerve cell process
11

1
2
3

Figure 11.2 Label the epidermal layers in this section of thick skin from the palm of the hand.

1
2
3
4
5
Basement membrane

Dermis

Figure 11.3 Label the features associated with this hair follicle.

3

4

5

6

1

2

Hair papilla

8. Observe the prepared slide of heavily pigmented human skin with low-power magnification. Note that the pigment is most abundant in the epidermis. Focus on this region with the high-power objective. The pigment-producing cells, or melanocytes, are located among the deeper layers of epidermal cells. Differences in skin color are primarily due to the amount of pigment (melanin) produced by these cells. The number of melanocytes in the skin is about the same for members of all racial groups.

Critical Thinking Application

Explain the advantage for melanin granules of being located in the deep layer of the epidermis.

_____

_____

_____

_____

9. Observe the prepared slide of thick skin from the palm of a hand or the sole of a foot. Locate the stratum lucidum. Note how the stratum corneum compares to your observation of human scalp.
10. Complete Part C of the laboratory report.
11. Using low-power magnification, locate a hair follicle that has been sectioned longitudinally through its bulblike base. Also locate a sebaceous gland close to the follicle and find a sweat gland (fig. 11.4). Observe the detailed structure of these parts with high-power magnification.
12. Complete Parts D and E of the laboratory report.

Figure 11.4 Features of human skin are indicated in these micrographs. Magnifications: (*a*) 290×; (*b*) 30× micrograph enlarged to 280×; (*c*) 45×; (*d*) 110×.

Stratum corneum
Stratum granulosum
Stratum spinosum
Stratum basale
Melanin
Dermal papilla
Basement membrane
Epidermis
Dermis

(a)

Epidermis
Dermis
Sweat (eccrine) gland

(b)

Dense connective tissue
Hair follicle
Region of cell division
Hair papilla
Adipose cell

(c)

Figure 11.4 *Continued.*

Pore

Duct of eccrine
sweat gland

Sebaceous
gland

Eccrine sweat
gland

(d)

 LEARNING EXTENSION

Observe a vertical section of human skin through a tattoo, using low-power magnification. Note the location of the dispersed ink granules within the upper portion of the dermis. From a thin vertical section of a tattoo, it is not possible to determine the figure or word of the entire tattoo as seen on the surface of the skin. Compare this to the location of melanin granules found in heavily pigmented skin. Suggest reasons why a tattoo is permanent and a suntan is not.

_____
_____
_____

Web Quest

Identify skin layers from micrographs and review the functions of the skin structures. Search these at
www.mhhe.com/shier11
Click on Student Edition. Click on Martin Lab Manual, Web Quest.

Notes

INTEGUMENTARY SYSTEM

PART A

Match the structures in column A with the description and functions in column B. Place the letter of your choice in the space provided.

Column A		Column B
a.	Apocrine sweat gland	_____ 1. An oily secretion that helps to waterproof body surface
b.	Arrector pili muscle	_____ 2. Outermost layer of epidermis
c.	Dermis	_____ 3. Become active at puberty
d.	Eccrine sweat gland	_____ 4. Epidermal pigment
e.	Epidermis	_____ 5. Inner layer of skin
f.	Hair follicle	_____ 6. Responds to elevated body temperature
g.	Keratin	_____ 7. General name of entire superficial layer of the skin
h.	Melanin	_____ 8. Gland that secretes an oily substance
i.	Sebaceous gland	_____ 9. Hard protein of nails and hair
j.	Sebum	_____ 10. Cell division and deepest layer of epidermis
k.	Stratum basale	_____ 11. Tubelike part that contains the root of the hair
l.	Stratum corneum	_____ 12. Causes hair to stand on end and goose bumps to appear

PART B

Complete the following:

1. How does the skin of your palm differ from that on the back (posterior) of your hand? _____

_____

_____

2. Describe the differences you observed in the type and distribution of hair on the front (anterior) and back (posterior) of your forearm. _____

_____

3. Explain how a hair is formed. _____

_____

4. What cells produce the pigment in hair? _____

PART C

Complete the following:

1. Distinguish among epidermis, dermis, and subcutaneous layer._____

_____

_____

2. How do the cells of stratum corneum and stratum basale differ?_____

_____

_____

3. State the specific location of melanin observed in heavily pigmented skin. _____

_____

4. What special qualities does the connective tissue of the dermis have? _____

_____

PART D

Complete the following:

1. What part of the hair extends from the hair papilla to the body surface? _____
2. In which layer of skin are sebaceous glands found?_____
3. How are sebaceous glands associated with hair follicles? _____

_____

4. In which layer of skin are sweat glands usually located? _____

PART E

Sketch and label a vertical section of human skin, using the scanning objective.

LABORATORY EXERCISE 12

BONE STRUCTURE AND CLASSIFICATION

MATERIALS NEEDED

Textbook
Prepared microscope slide of ground compact bone
Human bone specimens including long, short, flat,
    irregular, and sesamoid types
Human long bone, sectioned longitudinally
Fresh animal bones, sectioned longitudinally and
    transversely
Compound light microscope
Dissecting microscope

For Demonstration:

Fresh chicken bones (radius and ulna from wings)
Vinegar or dilute hydrochloric acid

⚠ SAFETY

- Wear disposable gloves for handling fresh bones and
  for the demonstration of a bone soaked in vinegar or
  dilute hydrochloric acid.
- Wash your hands before leaving the laboratory.

A bone represents an organ of the skeletal system. As such, it is composed of a variety of tissues including bone tissue, cartilage, dense connective tissue, blood, and nervous tissue. Bones are not only very much alive, but also multifunctional. They support and protect softer tissues, provide points of attachment for muscles, house blood-producing cells, and store inorganic salts.

Although bones of the skeleton vary greatly in size and shape, they have much in common structurally and functionally.

PURPOSE OF THE EXERCISE

To review the way bones are classified and to examine the structure of a long bone.

LEARNING OBJECTIVES

After completing this exercise, you should be able to

1. Name five groups of bones based on their shapes and give an example for each group.

2. Locate and name the major structures of a long bone.
3. Describe the functions of various structures of a bone.
4. Distinguish between compact and spongy bone.

PROCEDURE

1. Review the section entitled "Connective Tissues" in chapter 5 of the textbook and the section entitled "Bone Structure" in chapter 7 of the textbook.
2. As a review activity, label figures 12.1 and 12.2.
3. Reexamine the microscopic structure of bone tissue by observing a prepared microscope slide of ground compact bone. Use figure 12.3 of bone tissue to locate the following features:

   osteon (Haversian system)
   central canal (Haversian canal)
   lamella
   lacuna (small chamber for an osteocyte)
   bone extracellular matrix (collagen and calcium
       phosphate)
   canaliculus

 ## Critical Thinking Application

Explain how bone cells embedded in a solid ground substance obtain nutrients and eliminate wastes.

_____

_____

_____

_____

4. Observe the individual bone specimens and arrange them into groups, according to the following shapes:

   long   **irregular**
   short   **sesamoid (round)**
   flat

5. Complete Part A of Laboratory Report 12.

91

Figure 12.1 Label the major structures of this long bone (femur).

Epiphyseal plates

1 _____

Space occupied by red marrow

2 _____

3 _____

4 _____

5 _____

6 _____

7 _____

8 _____

9 _____

6. Examine the sectioned long bones and locate the following:

   epiphysis (proximal and distal)

   epiphyseal plate

   articular cartilage

   diaphysis

   periosteum

   compact bone

   spongy bone

   trabeculae

   medullary cavity

   endosteum

   yellow marrow

   red marrow

7. Use the dissecting microscope to observe the compact bone and spongy bone of the sectioned specimens. Also examine the marrow in the medullary cavity and the spaces within the spongy bone of the fresh specimen.

8. Complete Parts B and C of the laboratory report.

DEMONSTRATION

Examine a fresh chicken bone and a chicken bone that has been soaked for several days in vinegar or overnight in dilute hydrochloric acid. Wear disposable gloves for handling these bones. This acid treatment removes the inorganic salts from the bone extracellular matrix. Rinse the bones in water and note the texture and flexibility of each (fig. 12.4*a*). Based on your observations, what quality of the fresh bone seems to be due to the inorganic salts that were removed by the acid treatment?

_____

_____

Examine the specimen of chicken bone that has been exposed to high temperature (baked at 121°C/250°F for 2 hours). This treatment removes the protein and other organic substances from the bone extracellular matrix (fig.12.4*b*). What quality of the fresh bone seems to be due to these organic materials?

_____

_____

Figure 12.2 Label the features associated with the microscopic structure of bone.

Trabeculae

Bone extracellular
matrix

Lacuna
(space)

Figure 12.3 Micrograph of ground compact bone tissue (160×).

Osteon

Lamella

Central
canal

Osteocyte
in lacuna

Bone extracellular
matrix

Canaliculus

Figure 12.4 Results of fresh chicken bone demonstration: (*a*) soaked in vinegar; (*b*) baked in oven.

(a)

(b)

Name _____

Date _____

Section _____

BONE STRUCTURE AND CLASSIFICATION

PART A

Complete the following statements. (*Note:* Questions 1–6 pertain to bone classification by shape.)

1. A bone that is platelike is classified as a(an) _____ bone.
2. The bones of the wrist are examples of _____ bones.
3. The bone of the thigh is an example of a(an) _____ bone.
4. Vertebrae are examples of _____ bones.
5. The patella (kneecap) is an example of a large _____ bone.
6. The bones of the skull that form a protective covering of the brain are examples of _____ bones.
7. Distinguish between the epiphysis and the diaphysis of a long bone. _____
   _____
8. Describe where cartilage is found on the surface of a long bone. _____
   _____
9. Describe where dense connective tissue is found on the surface of a long bone. _____
   _____
10. Distinguish between the periosteum and the endosteum. _____
    _____
    _____

PART B

Complete the following:

1. What structural differences did you note between compact bone and spongy bone? _____
   _____
   _____
   _____
2. How are these structural differences related to the locations and functions of these two types of bone? _____
   _____
   _____
3. From your observations, how does the marrow in the medullary cavity compare with the marrow in the spaces of the spongy bone? _____
   _____
   _____

PART C

Identify the structures indicated in figure 12.5.

Figure 12.5 Identify the structures indicated in (*a*) the unsectioned long bone (fifth metatarsal) and (*b*) the partially sectioned long bone, using the terms provided.

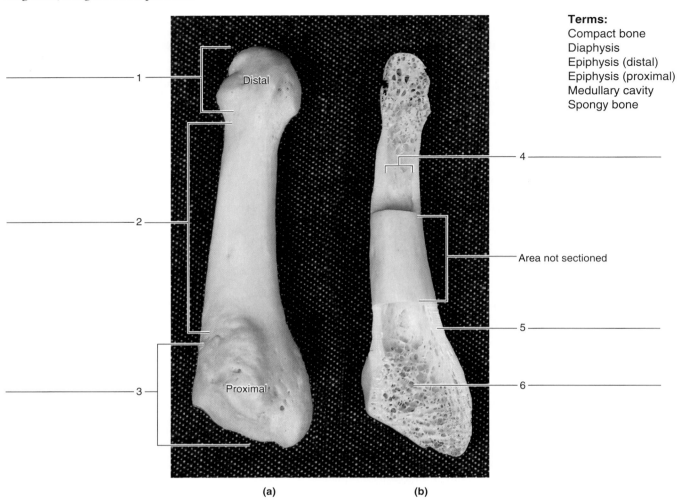

Terms:
Compact bone
Diaphysis
Epiphysis (distal)
Epiphysis (proximal)
Medullary cavity
Spongy bone

Distal

Proximal

Area not sectioned

(a)   (b)

ORGANIZATION OF THE SKELETON

MATERIALS NEEDED

Textbook
Articulated human skeleton

For Learning Extension:
Colored pencils

For Demonstration:
Radiographs (X rays) of skeletal structures

The skeleton can be divided into two major portions: (1) the axial skeleton, which consists of the bones and cartilages of the head, neck, and trunk, and (2) the appendicular skeleton, which consists of the bones of the limbs and those that anchor the limbs to the axial skeleton.

PURPOSE OF THE EXERCISE

To review the organization of the skeleton, the major bones of the skeleton, and the terms used to describe skeletal structures.

LEARNING OBJECTIVES

After completing this exercise, you should be able to

1. Distinguish between the axial skeleton and the appendicular skeleton.
2. Locate and name the major bones of the human skeleton.
3. Define the terms used to describe skeletal structures and locate examples of such structures on the human skeleton.

PROCEDURE

1. Review the section entitled "Skeletal Organization" in chapter 7 of the textbook. (Note that pronunciations of the names for major skeletal structures are included within the narrative of chapter 7.)
2. As a review activity, label figure 13.1.
3. Examine the human skeleton and locate the following parts. As you locate the following bones, note the number of each in the skeleton. Palpate as many of the corresponding bones in your own skeleton as possible.

axial skeleton
  skull

cranium	(8)
face	(14)
middle ear bone	(6)
hyoid bone	(1)

  vertebral column

vertebra	(24)
sacrum	(1)
coccyx	(1)

  thoracic cage

rib	(24)
sternum	(1)

appendicular skeleton
  pectoral girdle

scapula	(2)
clavicle	(2)

  upper limbs

humerus	(2)
radius	(2)
ulna	(2)
carpal	(16)
metacarpal	(10)
phalanx	(28)

  pelvic girdle

coxa (hipbone; pelvic bone; innominate)	(2)

  lower limbs

femur	(2)
tibia	(2)
fibula	(2)
patella	(2)
tarsal	(14)
metatarsal	(10)
phalanx	(28)

Total	**206 bones**

Figure 13.1 Label the major bones of the skeleton: (*a*) anterior view; (*b*) posterior view.

Hyoid bone

(a)

Figure 13.1 Continued.

(b)

LEARNING EXTENSION

Use colored pencils to distinguish the individual bones in figure 13.1.

4. Study table 7.4 in chapter 7 of the textbook. Locate an example of each of the following features (bone markings) on the bone listed, noting the size, shape, and location in the human skeleton:

condyle—occipital
crest—coxa (hipbone)
epicondyle—femur
facet—vertebra
fontanel—skull
foramen—vertebra
fossa—humerus
fovea—femur
head—humerus
linea—femur
meatus—temporal
process—temporal
sinus—frontal
spine—scapula
suture—skull
trochanter—femur
tubercle—humerus
tuberosity—tibia

Critical Thinking Application

Locate and name the largest foramen in the skull.

_____

_____

Locate and name the largest foramen in the skeleton.

_____

_____

5. Complete Parts A, B, C, and D of Laboratory Report 13.

DEMONSTRATION

Images on radiographs (X rays) are produced by allowing X rays from an X-ray tube to pass through a body part and to expose photographic film that is positioned on the opposite side of the part. The image that appears on the film after it is developed reveals the presence of parts with different densities. Bone, for example, is very dense tissue and is a good absorber of X rays. Thus, bone generally appears light on the film. Air-filled spaces, on the other hand, absorb almost no X rays and appear as dark areas on the film. Liquids and soft tissues absorb intermediate quantities of X rays, so they usually appear in various shades of gray.

Examine the available radiographs (X rays) of skeletal structures by holding each film in front of a light source. Identify as many of the bones and features as you can.

Name _____

Date _____

Section _____

ORGANIZATION OF THE SKELETON

PART A

Complete the following statements:

1. The extra bones that sometimes develop between the flat bones of the skull are called _____.

2. Small bones occurring in some tendons are called _____ bones.

3. The cranium and facial bones compose the _____.

4. The _____ bone supports the tongue.

5. The _____ at the inferior end of the sacrum is composed of several fused vertebrae.

6. Most ribs are attached anteriorly to the _____.

7. The thoracic cage is composed of _____ pairs of ribs.

8. The scapulae and clavicles together form the _____.

9. The humerus, radius, and _____ articulate to form the elbow joint.

10. The wrist is composed of eight bones called _____.

11. The coxae (hipbones) are attached posteriorly to the _____.

12. The pelvic girdle (coxae), sacrum, and coccyx together form the _____.

13. The _____ covers the anterior surface of the knee.

14. The bones that articulate with the distal ends of the tibia and fibula are called _____.

15. All finger and toe bones are called _____ .

PART B

Match the terms in column A with the definitions in column B. Place the letter of your choice in the space provided.

Column A	Column B
a. Condyle	_____ 1. Small, nearly flat articular surface
b. Crest	_____ 2. Deep depression
c. Facet	_____ 3. Rounded process
d. Fontanel	_____ 4. Opening or passageway
e. Foramen	_____ 5. Interlocking line of union
f. Fossa	_____ 6. Narrow, ridgelike projection
g. Suture	_____ 7. Soft region between bones of skull

PART C

Match the terms in column A with the definitions in column B. Place the letter of your choice in the space provided.

Column A	Column B
a. Fovea	_____ 1. Tubelike passageway
b. Head	_____ 2. Tiny pit or depression
c. Meatus	_____ 3. Small, knoblike process
d. Sinus	_____ 4. Thornlike projection
e. Spine	_____ 5. Rounded enlargement at end of bone
f. Trochanter	_____ 6. Air-filled cavity within bone
g. Tubercle	_____ 7. Relatively large process

PART D

Identify the bones indicated in figure 13.2.

Figure 13.2 Identify the bones in this random arrangement, using the terms provided.

Terms:

Clavicle	Patella	Sternum
Coxa (hipbone)	Radius	Tibia
Femur	Rib	Ulna
Fibula	Sacrum	
Humerus	Scapula	

SKULL

MATERIALS NEEDED

Textbook
Human skull, articulated
Human skull, disarticulated (Beauchene)
Human skull, sagittal section

For Learning Extension:

Colored pencils

For Demonstration:

Fetal skull

A human skull consists of twenty-two bones that, except for the lower jaw, are firmly interlocked along sutures. Eight of these immovable bones make up the braincase, or cranium, and thirteen more immovable bones and the mandible form the facial skeleton.

PURPOSE OF THE EXERCISE

To examine the structure of the human skull and to identify the bones and major features of the skull.

LEARNING OBJECTIVES

After completing this exercise, you should be able to

1. Distinguish between the cranium and the facial skeleton.
2. Locate and name the bones of the skull and their major features.
3. Locate and name the major sutures of the cranium.
4. Locate and name the sinuses of the skull.

PROCEDURE

1. Review the section entitled "Skull" in chapter 7 of the textbook.
2. As a review activity, label figures 14.1, 14.2, 14.3, 14.4, and 14.5.
3. Examine the **cranial bones** of the articulated human skull and the sectioned skull. Also observe the corresponding disarticulated bones. Locate the following bones and features in the laboratory specimens and, at the same time, palpate as many of these bones and features in your own skull as possible.

frontal bone	**(1)**
supraorbital foramen	
frontal sinus	
parietal bone	**(2)**
sagittal suture	
coronal suture	
occipital bone	**(1)**
lambdoid suture	
foramen magnum	
occipital condyle	
temporal bone	**(2)**
squamous suture	
external acoustic meatus	
mandibular fossa	
mastoid process	
styloid process	
carotid canal	
jugular foramen	
internal acoustic meatus	
zygomatic process	
sphenoid bone	**(1)**
sella turcica	
greater and lesser wings	
sphenoidal sinus	
ethmoid bone	**(1)**
cribriform plate	
perpendicular plate	
superior nasal concha	
middle nasal concha	
ethmoidal sinus	
crista galli	

4. Complete Parts A and B of Laboratory Report 14.

Figure 14.1 Label the anterior bones and features of the skull. (If the line lacks the word *bone*, label the particular feature of that bone.)

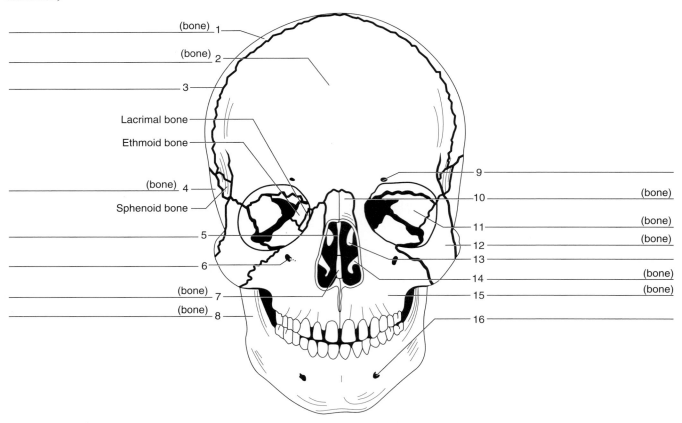

(bone) 1
(bone) 2
3
Lacrimal bone
Ethmoid bone
(bone) 4
Sphenoid bone
5
6
(bone) 7
(bone) 8

9
10 (bone)
11 (bone)
12 (bone)
13
14 (bone)
15 (bone)
16

Figure 14.2 Label the lateral bones and features of the skull.

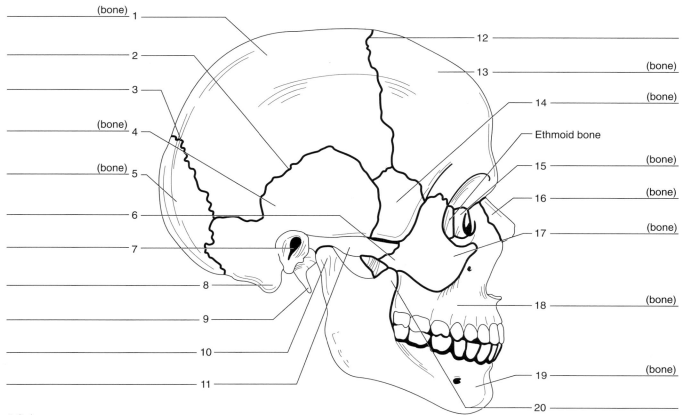

(bone) 1
2
3
(bone) 4
(bone) 5
6
7
8
9
10
11

12
13 (bone)
14 (bone)
Ethmoid bone
15 (bone)
16 (bone)
17 (bone)
18 (bone)
19 (bone)
20

104

Figure 14.3 Label the inferior bones and features of the skull.

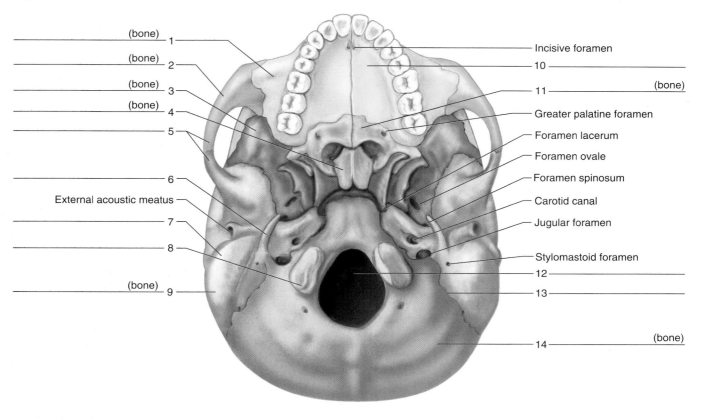

_____ (bone) 1
_____ (bone) 2
_____ (bone) 3
_____ (bone) 4
_____ 5
_____ 6
External acoustic meatus 7
_____ 8
_____ (bone) 9

Incisive foramen
10 _____
11 _____ (bone)
Greater palatine foramen
Foramen lacerum
Foramen ovale
Foramen spinosum
Carotid canal
Jugular foramen
Stylomastoid foramen
12 _____
13 _____
14 _____ (bone)

Figure 14.4 Label the bones and features of the floor of the cranial cavity as viewed from above.

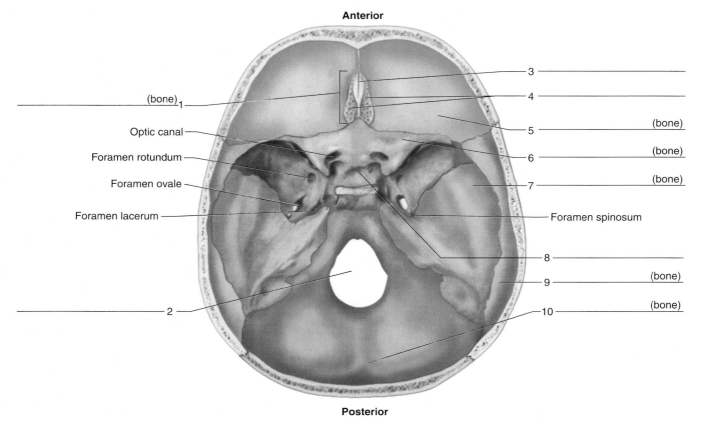

Anterior

(bone) 1
Optic canal
Foramen rotundum
Foramen ovale
Foramen lacerum
2

3 _____
4 _____
5 _____ (bone)
6 _____ (bone)
7 _____ (bone)
Foramen spinosum
8 _____
9 _____ (bone)
10 _____ (bone)

Posterior

Figure 14.5 Label the bones and features of the sagittal section of the skull.

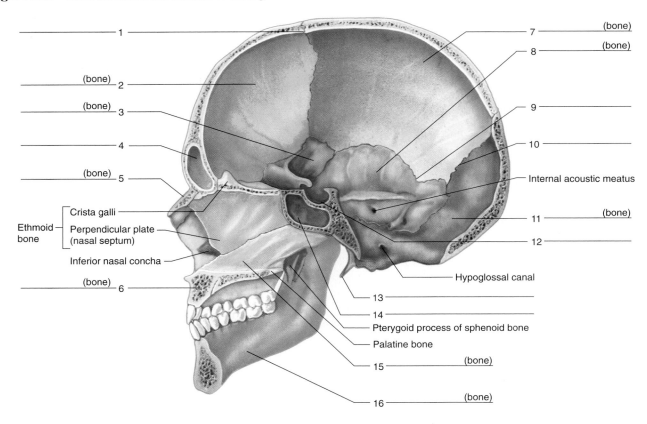

1 _____
(bone) 2 _____
(bone) 3 _____
4 _____
(bone) 5 _____

Ethmoid bone {
Crista galli
Perpendicular plate (nasal septum)
Inferior nasal concha
}

(bone) 6 _____

7 _____ (bone)
8 _____ (bone)
9 _____
10 _____
Internal acoustic meatus
11 _____ (bone)
12 _____
Hypoglossal canal
13 _____
14 _____
Pterygoid process of sphenoid bone
Palatine bone
15 _____ (bone)
16 _____ (bone)

5. Examine the **facial bones** of the articulated and sectioned skulls and the corresponding disarticulated bones. Locate the following:

maxilla (2)
   maxillary sinus
   palatine process
   alveolar process
   alveolar arch
palatine bone (2)
zygomatic bone (2)
   temporal process
   zygomatic arch
lacrimal bone (2)
nasal bone (2)
vomer bone (1)
inferior nasal concha (2)
mandible (1)
   ramus
   mandibular condyle
   coronoid process
   alveolar border
   mandibular foramen
   mental foramen

6. Complete Part C of the laboratory report.

LEARNING EXTENSION

Use colored pencils to differentiate the bones illustrated in figures 14.1 and 14.2. Select a different color for each bone in the series. This activity should help you locate various bones that are shown in different views in the figures. You can check your work by referring to the corresponding figures in the textbook, which are presented in full color.

7. Study table 7.8 of chapter 7 in the textbook. Locate the following features of the human skull:

carotid canal
foramen lacerum
foramen magnum
foramen ovale
foramen rotundum
foramen spinosum
greater palatine foramen
hypoglossal canal
incisive foramen
inferior orbital fissure

infraorbital foramen
internal acoustic meatus
jugular foramen
mandibular foramen
mental foramen
optic canal
stylomastoid foramen
superior orbital fissure
supraorbital foramen

8. Complete Parts D and E of the laboratory report.

DEMONSTRATION

Examine the fetal skull (fig. 14.6). Note that the skull is incompletely developed and that the cranial bones are separated by fibrous membranes. These membranous areas are called fontanels, or "soft spots." The fontanels close as the cranial bones grow together. The posterior fontanel usually closes within a few months after birth, whereas the anterior fontanel may not close until the middle or end of the second year. What other features characterize the fetal skull?

_____

_____

_____

_____

Critical Thinking Application

Examine the inside of the cranium on a sectioned skull. What area appears to be the weakest area? Explain your answer.

_____

_____

_____

_____

Web Quest

What are the functions of individual bones and features? Search these and review the anatomy of the skeleton at
www.mhhe.com/shier11
Click on Student Edition. Click on Martin Lab Manual, Web Quest.

Figure 14.6   Human fetal skeleton.

Fontanel (anterior)

NOTES

Name _____

Date _____

Section _____

SKULL

PART A

Match the bones in column A with the features in column B. Place the letter of your choice in the space provided. (Some answers are used more than once.)

Column A

a. Ethmoid bone
b. Frontal bone
c. Occipital bone
d. Parietal bone
e. Sphenoid bone
f. Temporal bone

Column B

_____ 1. Forms sagittal, coronal, squamous, and lambdoid sutures

_____ 2. Cribriform plate

_____ 3. Crista galli

_____ 4. External acoustic meatus

_____ 5. Foramen magnum

_____ 6. Mandibular fossa

_____ 7. Mastoid process

_____ 8. Middle nasal concha

_____ 9. Occipital condyle

_____ 10. Sella turcica

_____ 11. Styloid process

_____ 12. Supraorbital foramen

PART B

Complete the following statements:

1. The _____ suture joins the frontal bone to the parietal bones.

2. The parietal bones are firmly interlocked along the midline by the _____ suture.

3. The _____ suture joins the parietal bones to the occipital bone.

4. The temporal bones are joined to the parietal bones along the _____ sutures.

5. Name the three cranial bones that contain sinuses. _____

_____

6. Name a facial bone that contains a sinus. _____

PART C

Match the bones in column A with the characteristics in column B. Place the letter of your choice in the space provided.

Column A		Column B
a. Inferior nasal concha	_____ 1.	Forms bridge of nose
b. Lacrimal bone	_____ 2.	Only movable bone in the facial skeleton
c. Mandible	_____ 3.	Contains coronoid process
d. Maxilla	_____ 4.	Creates prominence of cheek inferior and lateral to the eye
e. Nasal bone		
f. Palatine bone	_____ 5.	Contains sockets of upper teeth
g. Vomer bone	_____ 6.	Forms inferior portion of nasal septum
h. Zygomatic bone	_____ 7.	Forms anterior portion of zygomatic arch
	_____ 8.	Scroll-shaped bone
	_____ 9.	Forms anterior roof of mouth
	_____ 10.	Contains mental foramen
	_____ 11.	Forms posterior roof of mouth
	_____ 12.	Scalelike part in medial wall of orbit

PART D

Match the passageways in column A with the structures transmitted through them in column B. Place the letter of your choice in the space provided.

Column A		Column B
a. Foramen magnum	_____ 1.	Maxillary division of trigeminal nerve
b. Foramen ovale	_____ 2.	Nerve fibers of spinal cord
c. Foramen rotundum	_____ 3.	Optic nerve
d. Incisive foramen	_____ 4.	Vagus and accessory nerves
e. Internal acoustic meatus		
f. Jugular foramen	_____ 5.	Nasopalatine nerves
g. Optic canal	_____ 6.	Mandibular division of trigeminal nerve
	_____ 7.	Vestibular and cochlear nerves

PART E

Identify the numbered bones and features of the skulls indicated in figures 14.7, 14.8, 14.9, 14.10, and 14.11.

Figure 14.7 Identify the bones and features indicated on this anterior view of the skull, using the terms provided.

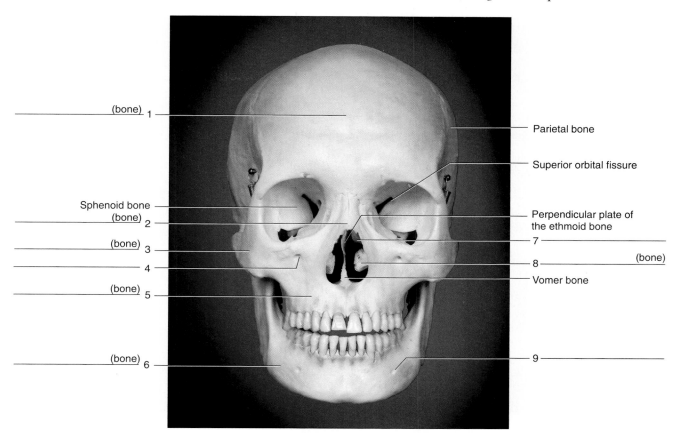

(bone) 1 _____

Parietal bone

Superior orbital fissure

Sphenoid bone _____
(bone) 2 _____

(bone) 3 _____

4 _____

(bone) 5 _____

(bone) 6 _____

Perpendicular plate of the ethmoid bone

7 _____

8 _____ (bone)

Vomer bone

9 _____

Terms:

Frontal bone
Inferior nasal concha
Infraorbital foramen
Mandible
Maxilla

Mental foramen
Middle nasal concha (of ethmoid bone)
Nasal bone
Zygomatic bone

Figure 14.8 Identify the bones and features indicated on this lateral view of the skull, using the terms provided.

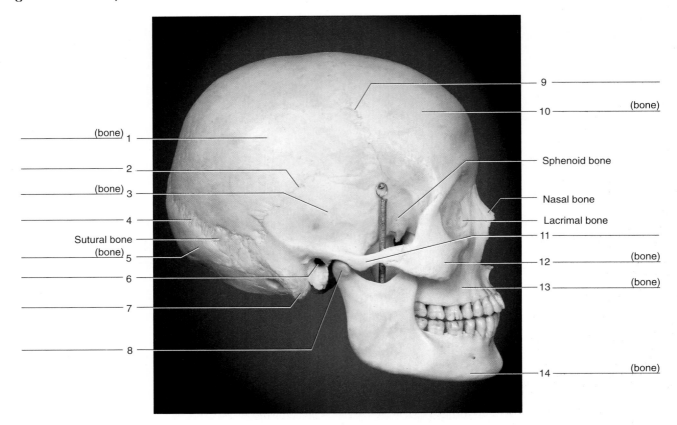

Terms:

Coronal suture	Mandible	Occipital bone	Temporal bone
External acoustic meatus	Mandibular condyle	Parietal bone	Zygomatic bone
Frontal bone	Mastoid process	Squamous suture	Zygomatic process
Lambdoid suture	Maxilla		(of temporal bone)

Figure 14.9 Identify the bones and features indicated on this inferior view of the skull, using the terms provided.

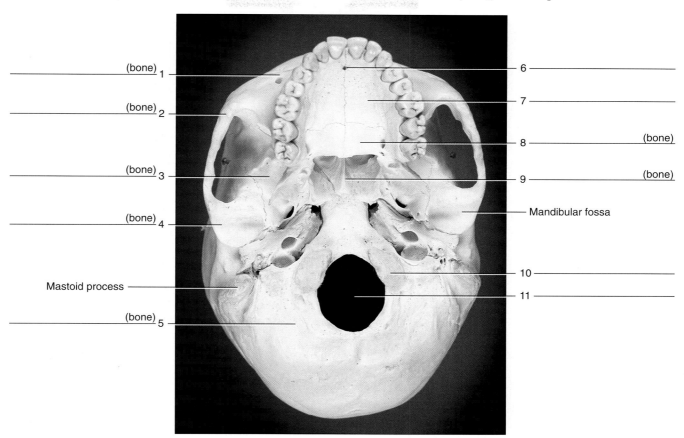

(bone) 1
(bone) 2
(bone) 3
(bone) 4
Mastoid process
(bone) 5

6
7
8 (bone)
9 (bone)
Mandibular fossa
10
11

Terms:

Foramen magnum	Occipital condyle	Temporal bone
Incisive foramen	Palatine bone	Vomer bone
Maxilla	Palatine process of maxilla	Zygomatic bone
Occipital bone	Sphenoid bone	

Figure 14.10 Identify the bones and features on this floor of the cranial cavity of a skull, using the terms provided.

_____ (bone) 1

Crista galli _____

Olfactory foramina _____

Cribriform plate _____

Optic canal _____

Foramen ovale _____

Foramen spinosum _____

_____ (bone) 2

_____ (bone) 3

_____ (bone) 4

5 _____ (bone)

6 _____ (bone)

7 _____

Foramen lacerum _____

Jugular foramen _____

8 _____

Terms:
Ethmoid bone
Foramen magnum
Frontal bone
Occipital bone
Parietal bone
Sella turcica
Sphenoid bone
Temporal bone

Figure 14.11 Identify the bones on this disarticulated skull, using the terms provided.

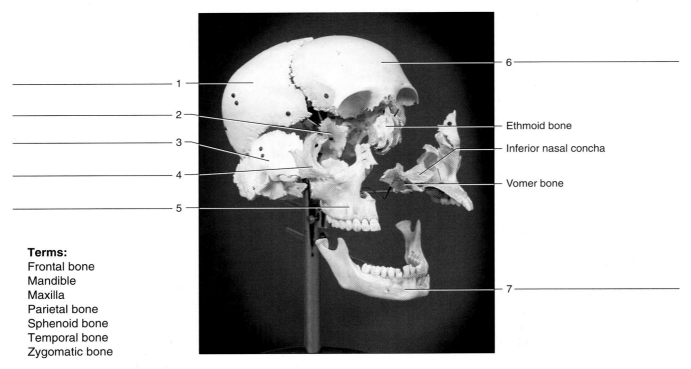

_____ 1

_____ 2

_____ 3

_____ 4

_____ 5

6 _____

Ethmoid bone _____

Inferior nasal concha _____

Vomer bone _____

7 _____

Terms:
Frontal bone
Mandible
Maxilla
Parietal bone
Sphenoid bone
Temporal bone
Zygomatic bone

114

VERTEBRAL COLUMN AND THORACIC CAGE

MATERIALS NEEDED

Textbook
Human skeleton, articulated
Samples of cervical, thoracic, and lumbar vertebrae
Human skeleton, disarticulated

The vertebral column, consisting of twenty-six bones, extends from the skull to the pelvis and forms the vertical axis of the human skeleton. The column is composed of many vertebrae, which are separated from one another by cartilaginous intervertebral discs and are held together by ligaments.

The thoracic cage surrounds the thoracic and upper abdominal cavities. It includes the ribs, the thoracic vertebrae, the sternum, and the costal cartilages.

PURPOSE OF THE EXERCISE

To examine the vertebral column and the thoracic cage of the human skeleton and to identify the bones and major features of these parts.

LEARNING OBJECTIVES

After completing this exercise, you should be able to

1. Identify the major features of the vertebral column.
2. Name the features of a typical vertebra.
3. Distinguish among a cervical, thoracic, and lumbar vertebra and locate the sacrum and coccyx.
4. Identify the structures of the thoracic cage.
5. Distinguish between true and false ribs.

PROCEDURE A—THE VERTEBRAL COLUMN

1. Review the section entitled "Vertebral Column" in chapter 7 of the textbook.
2. As a review activity, label figures 15.1, 15.2, 15.3, and 15.4.
3. Examine the vertebral column of the human skeleton and locate the following bones and features. At the same time, locate as many of the corresponding bones and features in your own skeleton as possible.

atlas (C1)	**(1)**
axis (C2)	**(1)**
vertebra prominens (C7)	**(1)**
cervical vertebrae (includes atlas, axis, and vertebra prominens)	**(7)**
thoracic vertebrae	**(12)**
lumbar vertebrae	**(5)**
intervertebral discs	
vertebral canal	
sacrum	**(1)**
coccyx	**(1)**
cervical curvature	
thoracic curvature	
lumbar curvature	
sacral curvature	
intervertebral foramina	

Critical Thinking Application

Note the four curvatures of the vertebral column. What functional advantages exist with curvatures for skeletal structure instead of a straight vertebral column?

_____

_____

_____

_____

4. Compare the available samples of cervical, thoracic, and lumbar vertebrae by noting differences in size and shape, and by locating the following features:

body
pedicles
vertebral foramen
laminae
spinous process
vertebral arch
transverse processes
superior articular processes

Figure 15.1 Label the bones and features of the vertebral column (right lateral view).

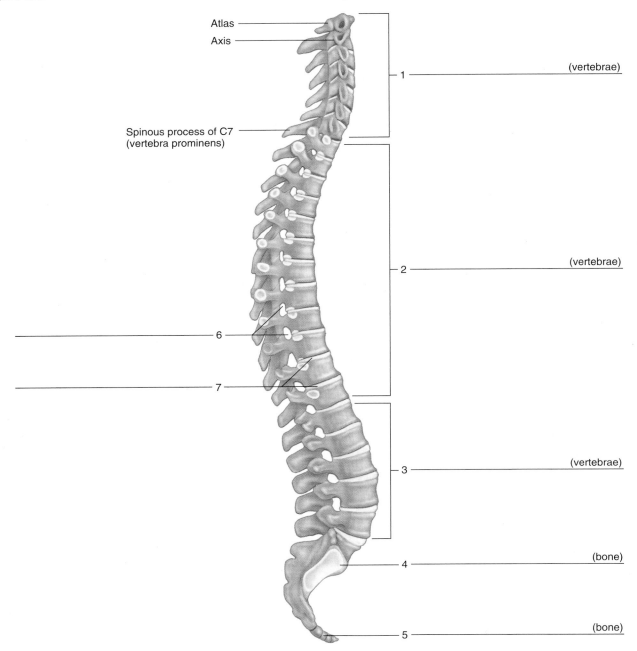

Atlas

Axis

Spinous process of C7
(vertebra prominens)

1 _____ (vertebrae)

2 _____ (vertebrae)

6 _____

7 _____

3 _____ (vertebrae)

4 _____ (bone)

5 _____ (bone)

inferior articular processes

transverse foramina

facets

dens of axis

5. Examine the sacrum and coccyx. Locate the following features:

sacrum

 superior articular process

 posterior sacral foramen

 anterior sacral foramen

 sacral promontory

 sacral canal

 tubercles

 sacral hiatus

coccyx

6. Complete Parts A and B of Laboratory Report 15.

PROCEDURE B—THE THORACIC CAGE

1. Review the section entitled "Thoracic Cage" in chapter 7 of the textbook.
2. As a review activity, label figure 15.5.

Figure 15.2 Label the superior features of (*a*) the atlas and the superior and right lateral features of (*b*) the axis by placing the correct numbers in the spaces provided. (The broken arrow indicates a transverse foramen.)

(a) Atlas (C1)

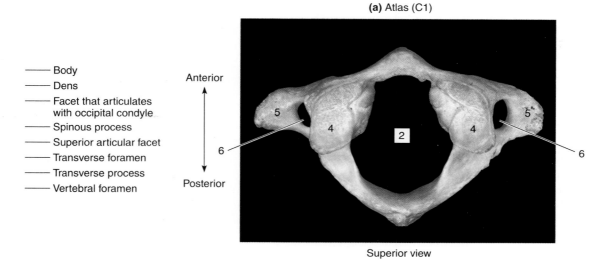

——— Body
——— Dens
——— Facet that articulates
　　 with occipital condyle
——— Spinous process
——— Superior articular facet
——— Transverse foramen
——— Transverse process
——— Vertebral foramen

Anterior

Posterior

Superior view

(b) Axis (C2)

Anterior

Posterior

Superior view

Right lateral view

Posterior ◄──────► Anterior

3. Examine the thoracic cage of the human skeleton and locate the following bones and features:

rib
　head
　tubercle
　neck
　shaft
　anterior (sternal) end
　facets
　true ribs (pairs 1–7)
　false ribs (pairs 8–12) (includes floating ribs)
　　floating ribs (pairs 11–12)
costal cartilages
sternum
　jugular (suprasternal) notch

　clavicular notch
　manubrium
　body
　xiphoid process
　sternal angle

4. Complete Parts C and D of the laboratory report.

Web Quest

What are the functions of individual bones and features? Search these and review the anatomy of the skeleton at
www.mhhe.com/shier11
Click on Student Edition. Click on Martin Lab Manual, Web Quest.

Figure 15.3 Label the superior and right lateral features of the (*a*) cervical, (*b*) thoracic, and (*c*) lumbar vertebrae by placing the correct numbers in the spaces provided. (The broken arrow indicates a transverse foramen.)

_____ Body
_____ Intervertebral (inferior) notch
_____ Lamina
_____ Pedicle
_____ Spinous process
_____ Superior articular process
_____ Transverse foramen
_____ Transverse process
_____ Vertebral foramen

Superior views   Right lateral views

(a) Cervical vertebra

Anterior

Posterior

(b) Thoracic vertebra

(c) Lumbar vertebra

Posterior ← → Anterior

Figure 15.4 Label the coccyx and the features of the sacrum: (*a*) anterior view; (*b*) posterior view.

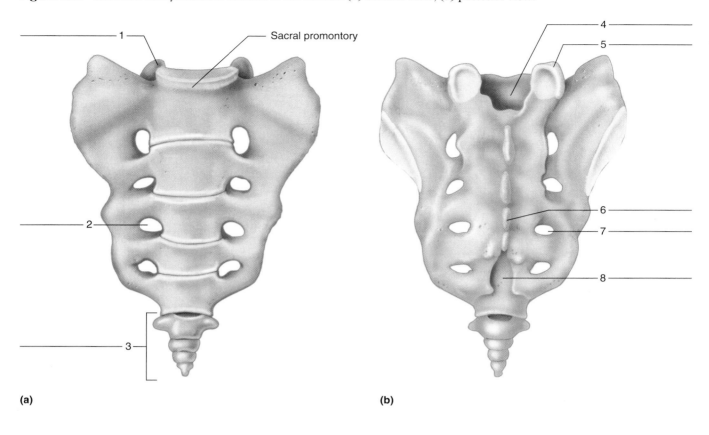

Sacral promontory

1

2

3

(a)

4

5

6

7

8

(b)

Figure 15.5 Label the bones and features of the thoracic cage.

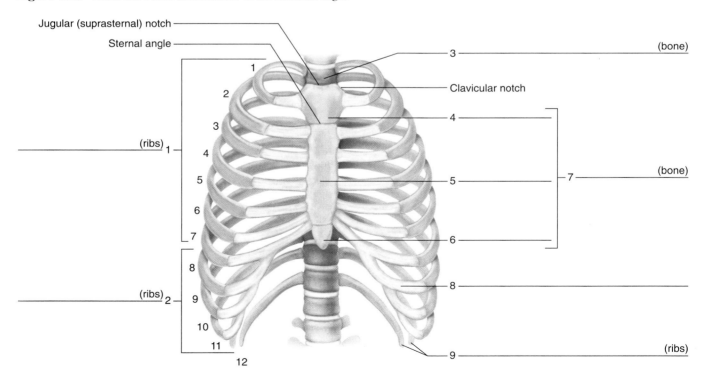

Jugular (suprasternal) notch

Sternal angle

1

2

3

(ribs) 1

4

5

6

7

(ribs) 2

8

9

10

11

12

3 (bone)

Clavicular notch

4

5

6

7 (bone)

8

9 (ribs)

NOTES

VERTEBRAL COLUMN AND THORACIC CAGE

PART A

Complete the following statements:

1. The vertebral column encloses and protects the _____.

2. The number of separate bones in the vertebral column of an adult is _____.

3. The _____ of the vertebrae support the weight of the head and trunk.

4. The _____ separate adjacent vertebrae, and they soften the forces created by walking.

5. The pedicles, laminae, and _____ of a vertebra form the vertebral arch.

6. The intervertebral foramina provide passageways for _____.

7. Transverse foramina of cervical vertebrae serve as passageways for _____ leading to the brain.

8. The first vertebra is also called the _____.

9. The second vertebra is also called the _____.

10. When the head is moved from side to side, the first vertebra pivots around the _____ of the second vertebra.

11. The _____ vertebrae have the largest and strongest bodies.

12. The number of vertebrae that fuse to form the sacrum is _____.

13. The joint between a coxa of the pelvis and the sacrum is called the _____ joint.

14. The upper, anterior margin of the sacrum that projects forward is called the _____.

15. An opening called the _____ exists at the tip of the sacral canal.

PART B

Based on your observations, compare typical cervical, thoracic, and lumbar vertebrae in relation to the characteristics indicated in the table. Consider characteristics such as size, shape, presence or absence, and unique features for your responses.

Vertebra	Number	Size	Body	Spinous Process	Transverse Foramina
Cervical					
Thoracic					
Lumbar					

PART C

Complete the following statements:

1. The adult skeleton of most men and women contains a total of _____ (number) bones.

2. The last two pairs of ribs that have no cartilaginous attachments to the sternum are sometimes called _____ ribs.

3. The tubercles of the ribs articulate with facets on the _____ processes of the thoracic vertebrae.

4. Costal cartilages are composed of _____ tissue.

5. The manubrium articulates with the _____ on its superior border.

6. List three general functions of the thoracic cage. _____

_____

PART D

Identify the bones and features indicated in the radiograph (X ray) of the neck in figure 15.6.

Figure 15.6 Identify the bones and features indicated in this radiograph (X ray) of the neck (lateral view), using the terms provided.

Terms:
Atlas
Axis
Body
Intervertebral disc
Spinous process
Transverse process

2 _____ (bone)

3 _____ (bone)

4 _____

5 _____

6 _____

Body of seventh cervical vertebra

1

Spinous process of C7 (vertebra prominens)

LABORATORY EXERCISE 16

PECTORAL GIRDLE AND UPPER LIMB

MATERIALS NEEDED

Textbook
Human skeleton, articulated
Human skeleton, disarticulated

For Learning Extension:

Colored pencils

The pectoral girdle consists of two clavicles and two scapulae. These parts support the upper limbs and serve as attachments for various muscles that move these limbs.

Each upper limb includes a humerus, a radius, an ulna, eight carpals, five metacarpals, and fourteen phalanges. These bones form the framework of the arm, forearm, and hand. They also function as parts of levers when the limbs are moved.

PURPOSE OF THE EXERCISE

To examine the bones of the pectoral girdle and upper limb and to identify the major features of these bones.

LEARNING OBJECTIVES

After completing this exercise, you should be able to

1. Locate and identify the bones of the pectoral girdle and their major features.
2. Locate and identify the bones of the upper limb and their major features.

PROCEDURE A—THE PECTORAL GIRDLE

1. Review the section entitled "Pectoral Girdle" in chapter 7 of the textbook.
2. As a review activity, label figures 16.1 and 16.2.
3. Examine the bones of the pectoral girdle and locate the following features. At the same time, locate as many of the corresponding surface bones and features of your own skeleton as possible.

clavicle
    medial (sternal) end
    lateral (acromial) end

scapula
    spine
    lateral (axillary) border
    medial (vertebral) border
    superior border
    acromion process
    coracoid process
    glenoid cavity (fossa)
    supraspinous fossa
    infraspinous fossa

 Critical Thinking Application

Why is the clavicle a bone that can easily fracture?

_____

_____

_____

_____

4. Complete Part A of Laboratory Report 16.

PROCEDURE B—THE UPPER LIMB

1. Review the section entitled "Upper Limb" in chapter 7 of the textbook.
2. As a review activity, label figures 16.3, 16.4, 16.5, and 16.6.
3. Examine the following bones and features of the upper limb:

humerus
    head
    greater tubercle
    lesser tubercle
    intertubercular groove
    anatomical neck

Figure 16.1 Label the bones and features of the right shoulder and upper limb (anterior view).

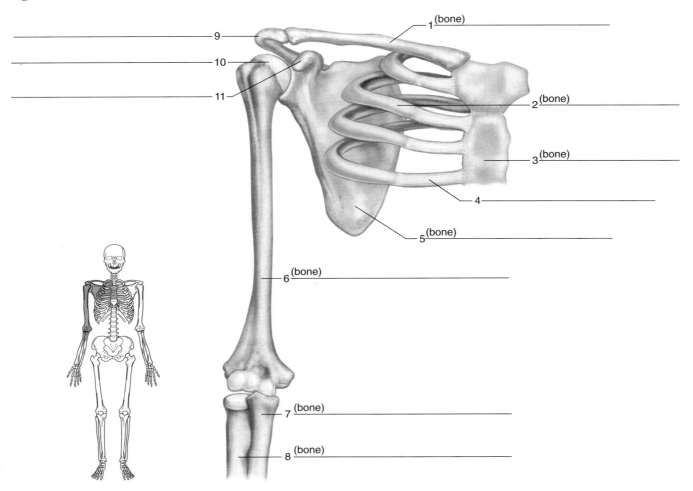

surgical neck

deltoid tuberosity

capitulum

trochlea

medial epicondyle

lateral epicondyle

coronoid fossa

olecranon fossa

radius

head

radial tuberosity

styloid process

ulnar notch

ulna

trochlear notch (semilunar notch)

radial notch

olecranon process

coronoid process

styloid process

head

carpal bones

proximal row (listed lateral to medial)

scaphoid

lunate

triquetrum

pisiform

distal row (listed medial to lateral)

hamate

capitate

trapezoid

trapezium

metacarpal bones

phalanges

proximal phalanx

middle phalanx

distal phalanx

Figure 16.2 Label (*a*) the posterior surface of the right scapula and (*b*) the lateral aspect of the right scapula.

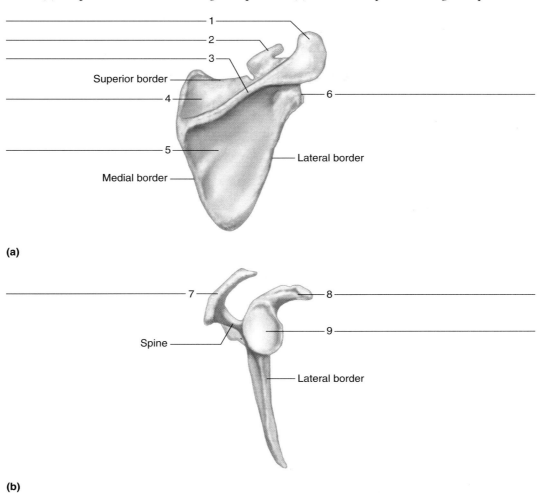

1

2

3

Superior border

4

5

Medial border

6

Lateral border

(a)

7

Spine

8

9

Lateral border

(b)

4. Complete Parts B, C, and D of the laboratory report.

The following mnemonic device will help you learn the eight carpals:

So Long Top Part
Here Comes The Thumb

The first letter of each word corresponds to the first letter of a carpal. Notice that this device arranges the carpals in order for the proximal, transverse row of four bones from lateral to medial, followed by the distal, transverse row from medial to lateral, which ends nearest the thumb. This arrangement assumes the hand is in the anatomical position.

LEARNING EXTENSION

Use different colored pencils to distinguish the individual bones in figure 16.6.

Web Quest

What are the functions of individual bones and features? Search these and review the anatomy of the skeleton at
www.mhhe.com/shier11
Click on Student Edition. Click on Martin Lab Manual, Web Quest.

Figure 16.3 Label the (*a*) anterior surface and (*b*) posterior surface of the right humerus.

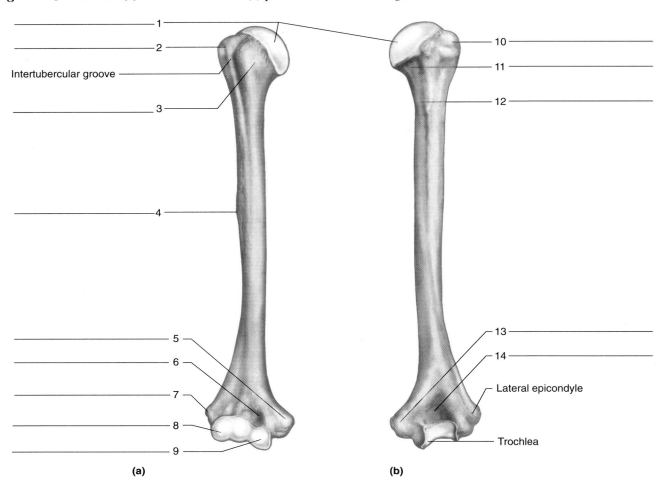

Intertubercular groove

Lateral epicondyle

Trochlea

(a)   (b)

Figure 16.4   Label the major anterior features of the right radius and ulna (anterior view).

Radius

Ulna

Styloid process

Figure 16.5   Label the bones and features of the right elbow, posterior view.

(bone)

(bone)

(bone)

Figure 16.6 Label the bones and groups of bones in this anterior view of the right hand.

Radius

Ulna

8

Hamate

9

Pisiform

Medial

Lateral

1
2
3
4
5

10

11

12

1
2
3
4
5
6
7

PECTORAL GIRDLE AND UPPER LIMB

PART A

Complete the following statements:

1. The pectoral girdle is an incomplete ring because it is open in the back between the _____ .

2. The medial ends of the clavicles articulate with the _____ of the sternum.

3. The lateral ends of the clavicles articulate with the _____ of the scapulae.

4. The _____ is a bone that serves as a brace between the sternum and the scapula.

5. The _____ divides the scapula into unequal portions.

6. The tip of the shoulder is the _____ of the scapula.

7. At the lateral end of the scapula, the _____ curves anteriorly and inferiorly from the clavicle.

8. The glenoid cavity of the scapula articulates with the _____ of the humerus.

PART B

Match the bones in column A with the bones and features in column B. Place the letter of your choice in the space provided.

Column A

a. Carpals
b. Humerus
c. Metacarpals
d. Phalanges
e. Radius
f. Ulna

Column B

_____ 1. Capitate

_____ 2. Coronoid fossa

_____ 3. Deltoid tuberosity

_____ 4. Greater tubercle

_____ 5. Five palmar bones

_____ 6. Fourteen bones in digits

_____ 7. Intertubercular groove

_____ 8. Lunate

_____ 9. Olecranon fossa

_____ 10. Radial tuberosity

_____ 11. Trapezium

_____ 12. Trochlear notch

PART C

Identify the bones and features indicated in the radiographs of figures 16.7, 16.8, and 16.9.

Figure 16.7 Identify the bones and features indicated on this radiograph of the elbow, using the terms provided.

Terms:
Head of radius
Humerus
Olecranon process
Radius
Ulna

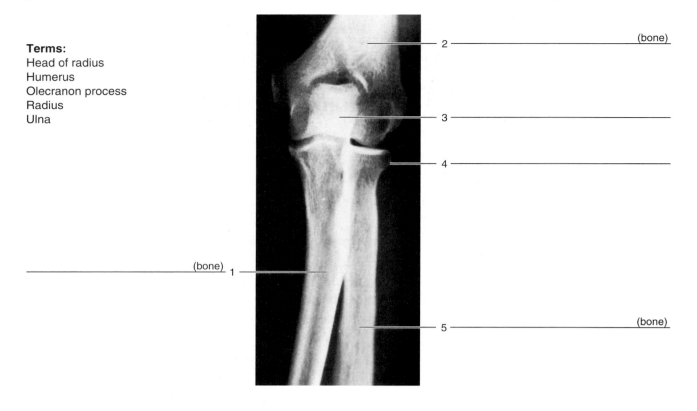

2 _____ (bone)

3 _____

4 _____

(bone) 1 _____

5 _____ (bone)

Figure 16.8 Identify the bones and features indicated on this radiograph of the shoulder, using the terms provided.

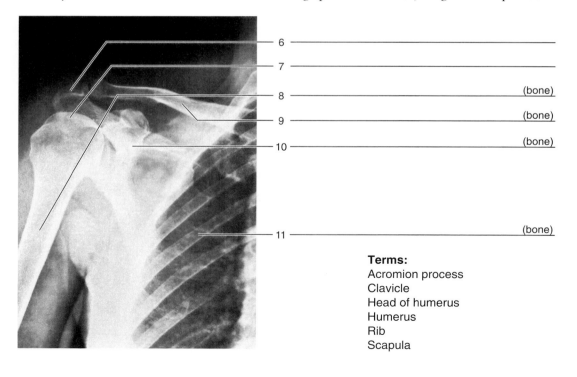

6 _____

7 _____

8 _____ (bone)

9 _____ (bone)

10 _____ (bone)

11 _____ (bone)

Terms:
Acromion process
Clavicle
Head of humerus
Humerus
Rib
Scapula

Figure 16.9 Identify the bones indicated on this radiograph of the left hand, using the terms provided.

Terms:
Carpals
Distal phalanx
Metacarpals
Phalanges
Proximal phalanx

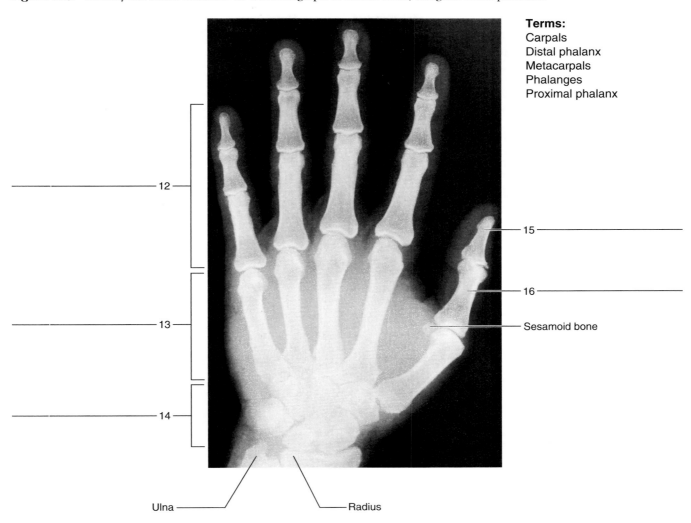

12

13

14

15

16

Sesamoid bone

Ulna

Radius

Figure 16.10 Identify the bones that are numbered on this anterior view of the right hand, using the terms provided.

Terms:
Capitate
Distal phalanges
Hamate
Lunate
Metacarpals
Middle phalanges
Pisiform
Proximal phalanges
Scaphoid
Trapezium
Trapezoid
Triquetrum

PART D

Identify the bones of the hand in figure 16.10.

1. _____
2. _____
3. _____
4. _____
5. _____
6. _____

7. _____
8. _____
9. _____
10. _____
11. _____
12. _____

PELVIC GIRDLE AND LOWER LIMB

MATERIALS NEEDED

Textbook
Human skeleton, articulated
Human skeleton, disarticulated
Male and female pelves

For Learning Extension:

Colored pencils

The pelvic girdle includes two coxae (hipbones) that articulate with each other anteriorly at the symphysis pubis and posteriorly with the sacrum. Together, the pelvic girdle, sacrum, and coccyx comprise the pelvis. The pelvis, in turn, provides support for the trunk of the body and provides attachments for the lower limbs.

The bones of the lower limb form the framework of the thigh, leg, and foot. Each limb includes a femur, a patella, a tibia, a fibula, seven tarsals, five metatarsals, and fourteen phalanges.

PURPOSE OF THE EXERCISE

To examine the bones of the pelvic girdle and lower limb and to identify the major features of these bones.

LEARNING OBJECTIVES

After completing this exercise, you should be able to

1. Locate and identify the bones of the pelvic girdle and their major features.
2. Locate and identify the bones of the lower limb and their major features.

PROCEDURE A—THE PELVIC GIRDLE

1. Review the section entitled "Pelvic Girdle" in chapter 7 of the textbook.
2. As a review activity, label figures 17.1 and 17.2.

Figure 17.1 Label the bones of the pelvis (posterior view).

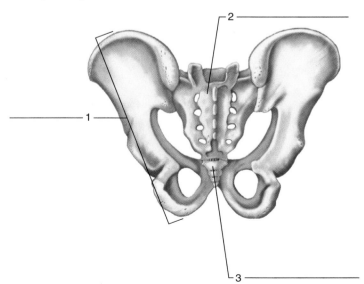

Figure 17.2 Label (*a*) the lateral and (*b*) the medial features of the right coxa.

(a)

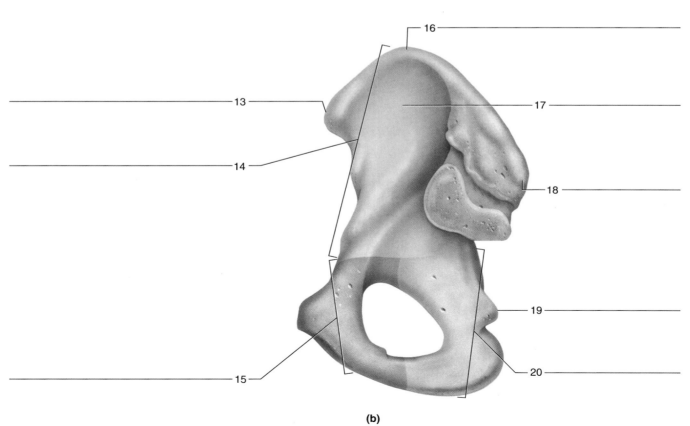

(b)

3. Examine the bones of the pelvic girdle and locate the following:

coxa (hipbone; pelvic bone; innominate)
>   acetabulum
>   ilium
>   iliac crest
>   iliac fossa
>   sacroiliac joint
>   anterior superior iliac spine
>   posterior superior iliac spine
>   greater sciatic notch
>   lesser sciatic notch
>   ischium
>   ischial tuberosity
>   ischial spine
>   pubis
>   symphysis pubis
>   pubic arch
>   obturator foramen

4. Complete Part A of Laboratory Report 17.

Critical Thinking Application

Examine the male and female pelves. Look for major differences between them. Note especially the flare of the iliac bones, the angle of the pubic arch, the distance between the ischial spines and ischial tuberosities, and the curve and width of the sacrum. In what ways are the differences you observed related to the function of the female pelvis as a birth canal?

_____
_____
_____
_____

PROCEDURE B—THE LOWER LIMB

1. Review the section entitled "Lower Limb" in chapter 7 of the textbook.

2. As a review activity, label figures 17.3, 17.4, 17.5, and 17.6.

3. Examine the bones of the lower limb and locate each of the following:

femur
>   head
>   fovea capitis
>   neck
>   greater trochanter
>   lesser trochanter
>   linea aspera
>   lateral condyle
>   medial condyle
>   lateral epicondyle
>   medial epicondyle

patella

tibia
>   medial condyle
>   lateral condyle
>   tibial tuberosity
>   anterior crest
>   medial malleolus

fibula
>   head
>   lateral malleolus

tarsal bones
>   talus
>   calcaneus
>   navicular
>   cuboid
>   lateral cuneiform
>   intermediate cuneiform
>   medial cuneiform

metatarsal bones

phalanges
>   proximal phalanx
>   middle phalanx
>   distal phalanx

4. Complete Parts B, C, and D of the laboratory report.

Figure 17.3 Label the features of (*a*) the anterior surface and (*b*) the posterior surface of the right femur.

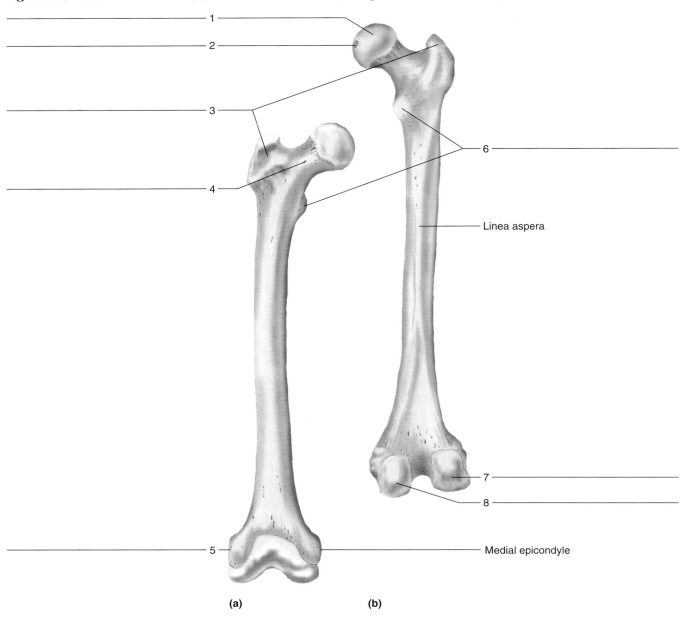

1 _____

2 _____

3 _____

4 _____

5 _____

6 _____

Linea aspera

7 _____

8 _____

Medial epicondyle

(a)   (b)

 LEARNING EXTENSION

Use different colored pencils to distinguish the individual bones in figure 17.6.

 Web Quest

What are the functions of individual bones and features? Search these and review the anatomy of the skeleton at

www.mhhe.com/shier11

Click on Student Edition. Click on Martin Lab Manual, Web Quest.

Figure 17.4 Label the bones and features of the right tibia and fibula in this anterior view.

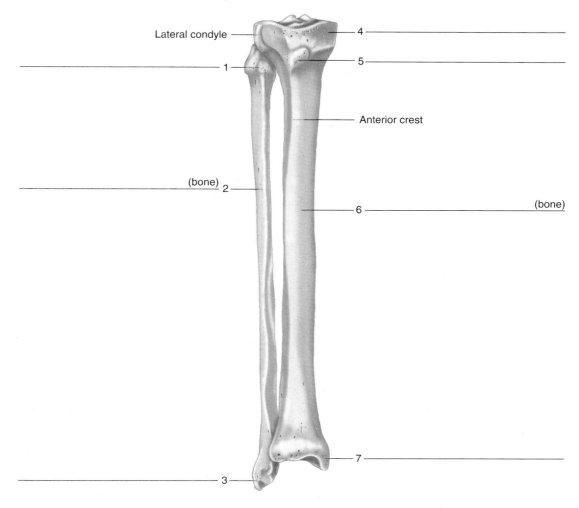

Lateral condyle — 4 —
— 1 — 5 —
Anterior crest
(bone) 2 —
6 — (bone)
— 3 — 7 —

Figure 17.5 Label the bones and features of the right knee, posterior view.

2 — (bone)
Lateral epicondyle
Lateral condyle
— 1 — 3 —
4 — (bone)
5 — (bone)

Figure 17.6 Label the bones of the superior surface of the right foot.

1

2

3

4

5

6

7

5

4

3

2

1

8

9

10

11

12

13

Name _____

Date _____

Section _____

PELVIC GIRDLE AND LOWER LIMB

PART A

Complete the following statements:

1. The pelvic girdle consists of two _____ .
2. The head of the femur articulates with the _____ of the coxa.
3. The _____ is the largest portion of the coxa.
4. The distance between the _____ represents the shortest diameter of the pelvic outlet.
5. The pubic bones come together anteriorly to form the joint called the _____ .
6. The _____ is the portion of the ilium that causes the prominence of the hip.
7. When a person sits, the _____ of the ischium supports the weight of the body.
8. The angle formed by the pubic bones below the symphysis pubis is called the _____ .
9. The _____ is the largest foramen in the skeleton.
10. The ilium joins the sacrum at the _____ joint.

PART B

Match the bones in column A with the features in column B. Place the letter of your choice in the space provided.

Column A		Column B
a. Femur	_____ 1.	Middle phalanx
b. Fibula	_____ 2.	Lesser trochanter
c. Metatarsals	_____ 3.	Medial malleolus
d. Patella	_____ 4.	Fovea capitis
e. Phalanges	_____ 5.	Calcaneus
f. Tarsals	_____ 6.	Lateral cuneiform
g. Tibia	_____ 7.	Tibial tuberosity
	_____ 8.	Talus
	_____ 9.	Linea aspera
	_____ 10.	Lateral malleolus
	_____ 11.	Sesamoid bone
	_____ 12.	Five bones that form the instep

PART C

Identify the bones and features indicated in the radiographs of figures 17.7, 17.8, and 17.9.

Figure 17.7 Identify the bones and features indicated on this radiograph of the pelvic region, using the terms provided.

Terms:
Head of femur
Ilium
Obturator foramen
Pubis
Sacrum
Symphysis pubis

3 _____

4 _____ (bone)

5 _____

6 _____

_____ 1

_____ 2

Figure 17.8 Identify the bones and features indicated on this radiograph of the knee, using the terms provided.

_____ (bone) 7

Terms:
Femur
Fibula
Head of fibula
Lateral condyle
Lateral epicondyle
Tibia

_____ (bone) 8

9 _____

10 _____

11 _____

12 _____ (bone)

Figure 17.9 Identify the bones indicated on this radiograph of the left foot, using the terms provided.

Navicular

Medial cuneiform

16

17

18

Sesamoid bone

13

14

15

Terms:
Calcaneus
Distal phalanx
Metatarsal
Proximal phalanx
Talus
Tibia

PART D

Identify the bones of the foot in figure 17.10.

Figure 17.10 Identify the bones indicated on this superior view of the right foot, using the terms provided.

Terms:
Calcaneus
Cuboid
Distal phalanges
Intermediate cuneiform
Lateral cuneiform
Medial cuneiform
Metatarsals
Middle phalanges
Navicular
Proximal phalanges
Talus

LABORATORY EXERCISE 18

JOINTS

 SAFETY

- Wear disposable gloves when handling the fresh animal joint.
- Wash your hands before leaving the laboratory.

Joints are junctions between bones. Although they vary considerably in structure, they can be classified according to the type of tissue that binds the bones together. Thus, the three groups of joints can be identified as (1) fibrous joints, (2) cartilaginous joints, and (3) synovial joints.

Movements occurring at freely movable synovial joints are due to the contractions of skeletal muscles. In each case, the type of movement depends on the kind of joint involved and the way in which the muscles are attached to the bones on either side of the joint.

PURPOSE OF THE EXERCISE

To examine examples of the three types of joints, to identify the major features of these joints, and to review the types of movements produced at synovial joints.

LEARNING OBJECTIVES

After completing this exercise, you should be able to

1. Distinguish among fibrous, cartilaginous, and synovial joints.

2. Identify examples of each type of joint.
3. Identify the major features of each type of joint.
4. Locate and identify examples of each of the six types of synovial joints.
5. Identify the types of movements that occur at synovial joints.
6. Describe the structure of the shoulder, elbow, hip, and knee joints.

PROCEDURE A—TYPES OF JOINTS

1. Review the section entitled "Classification of Joints" in chapter 8 of the textbook.
2. Examine the human skull and articulated skeleton to locate examples of the following types of joints:

   fibrous joints

   syndesmosis

   suture

   gomphosis

   cartilaginous joints

   synchondrosis

   symphysis

   synovial joints

3. Complete Part A of Laboratory Report 18.
4. Locate examples of the following types of synovial joints in the skeleton. At the same time, examine the corresponding joints in the models and in your own body. Experiment with each joint to experience its range of movements.

   ball-and-socket joint

   condyloid (ellipsoidal) joint

   gliding (plane) joint

   hinge joint

   pivot joint

   saddle joint

5. Complete Parts B and C of the laboratory report.

PROCEDURE B—JOINT MOVEMENTS

1. Review the section entitled "Types of Joint Movements" in chapter 8 of the textbook.
2. When the body is in anatomical position, most joints are extended and/or adducted. Skeletal muscle action involves the movable end (*insertion*) being pulled toward the stationary end (*origin*). In the limbs, the origin is usually proximal to the insertion; in the trunk, the origin is usually medial to the insertion. Use these concepts as reference points as you move joints. Move various parts of your own body to demonstrate the following joint movements:

> **flexion**
> **extension**
>> hyperextension
> **dorsiflexion**
> **plantar flexion**
> **abduction**
> **adduction**
> **rotation**
>> medial (internal)
>> lateral (external)
> **circumduction**
> **supination**
> **pronation**
> **eversion** (called pronation in some health professions)
> **inversion** (called supination in some health professions)
> **protraction**
> **retraction**
> **elevation**
> **depression**

3. Have your laboratory partner do some of the preceding movements and see if you can identify correctly the movements made.

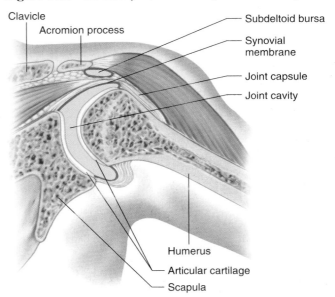

Figure 18.1 Shoulder joint structures (coronal section).

Clavicle
Acromion process
Subdeltoid bursa
Synovial membrane
Joint capsule
Joint cavity
Humerus
Articular cartilage
Scapula

 Critical Thinking Application

Describe a body position that can exist when all major body parts are flexed.

_____

_____

_____

4. Complete Part D of the laboratory report.

PROCEDURE C—EXAMPLES OF SYNOVIAL JOINTS

1. Study and compare the shoulder, elbow, hip, and knee joints in figures 18.1, 18.2, 18.3, 18.4, and 18.5.
2. Examine models of the shoulder, elbow, hip, and knee joints. Locate as many features as possible on the models that are illustrated in figures 18.1 through 18.5.
3. Complete Part E of the laboratory report.

 Web Quest

Why does the shoulder joint allow extensive movement? What is joint fluoroscopy? Search for these answers and review joints at
www.mhhe.com/shier11
Click on Student Edition. Click on Martin Lab Manual, Web Quest.

Figure 18.2 Elbow joint structures (sagittal section).

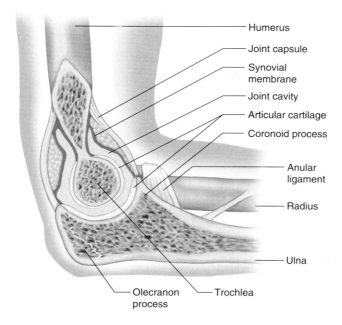

- Humerus
- Joint capsule
- Synovial membrane
- Joint cavity
- Articular cartilage
- Coronoid process
- Anular ligament
- Radius
- Ulna
- Olecranon process
- Trochlea

Figure 18.4 Knee joint structures (sagittal section).

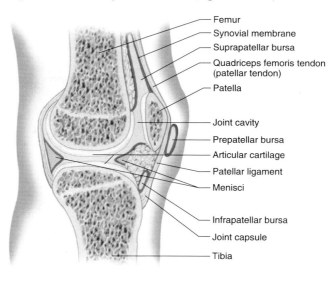

- Femur
- Synovial membrane
- Suprapatellar bursa
- Quadriceps femoris tendon (patellar tendon)
- Patella
- Joint cavity
- Prepatellar bursa
- Articular cartilage
- Patellar ligament
- Menisci
- Infrapatellar bursa
- Joint capsule
- Tibia

Figure 18.3 Hip joint structures (coronal section).

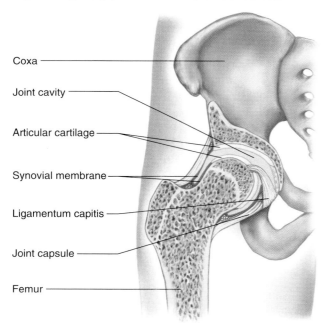

- Coxa
- Joint cavity
- Articular cartilage
- Synovial membrane
- Ligamentum capitis
- Joint capsule
- Femur

Figure 18.5 Anterior view of right knee (patella removed).

- Femur
- Lateral condyle
- Lateral meniscus
- Lateral condyle
- Fibular collateral ligament
- Fibula
- Tibia
- Posterior cruciate ligament
- Medial condyle
- Anterior cruciate ligament
- Medial meniscus
- Medial condyle
- Tibial collateral ligament
- Patellar ligament (cut)

NOTES

JOINTS

PART A

Match the terms in column A with the descriptions in column B. Place the letter of your choice in the space provided.

<table>
<tr><td colspan="2">Column A</td><td colspan="2">Column B</td></tr>
<tr><td>a.</td><td>Gomphosis</td><td>_____ 1.</td><td>Immovable joint between flat bones of the skull united by a thin layer of connective tissue</td></tr>
<tr><td>b.</td><td>Suture</td><td></td><td></td></tr>
<tr><td>c.</td><td>Symphysis</td><td>_____ 2.</td><td>Articular cartilages at joint attached by pad of fibrocartilage</td></tr>
<tr><td>d.</td><td>Synchondrosis</td><td>_____ 3.</td><td>Temporary joint in which bones are united by bands of hyaline cartilage</td></tr>
<tr><td>e.</td><td>Syndesmosis</td><td></td><td></td></tr>
<tr><td></td><td></td><td>_____ 4.</td><td>Slightly movable joint in which bones are united by interosseous ligament (anterior tibiofibular ligament)</td></tr>
<tr><td></td><td></td><td>_____ 5.</td><td>Joint formed by union of cone-shaped bony process in bony socket</td></tr>
</table>

PART B

Identify the types of joints that are numbered in figure 18.6.

1. _____

2. _____

3. _____

4. _____

5. _____

6. _____

7. _____

8. _____

9. _____

Figure 18.6 Identify the types of joints that are numbered in these illustrations.

PART C

Match the types of synovial joints in column A with the examples in column B. Place the letter of your choice in the space provided.

Column A	Column B
a. Ball-and-socket	_____ 1. Hip joint
b. Condyloid (ellipsoidal)	_____ 2. Metacarpal-phalanx
c. Gliding (plane)	_____ 3. Proximal radius-ulna
d. Hinge	_____ 4. Humerus-ulna of the elbow joint
e. Pivot	_____ 5. Phalanx-phalanx
f. Saddle	_____ 6. Shoulder joint
	_____ 7. Knee joint
	_____ 8. Carpal-metacarpal of the thumb
	_____ 9. Carpal-carpal
	_____ 10. Tarsal-tarsal

PART D

Identify the types of joint movements that are numbered in figure 18.7.

1. _____ (of head)
2. _____ (of shoulder)
3. _____ (of shoulder)
4. _____ (of hand)
5. _____ (of hand)
6. _____ (of arm at shoulder)
7. _____ (of arm at shoulder)
8. _____ (of hand at wrist)
9. _____ (of hand at wrist)
10. _____ (of thigh at hip)
11. _____ (of thigh at hip)
12. _____ (of lower limb at hip)
13. _____ (of chin/mandible)
14. _____ (of chin/mandible)

15. _____ (of vertebral column/trunk)
16. _____ (of vertebral column/trunk)
17. _____ (of head and neck)
18. _____ (of head and neck)
19. _____ (of arm at shoulder)
20. _____ (of arm at shoulder)
21. _____ (of forearm at elbow)
22. _____ (of forearm at elbow)
23. _____ (of thigh at hip)
24. _____ (of thigh at hip)
25. _____ (of leg at knee)
26. _____ (of leg at knee)
27. _____ (of foot at ankle)
28. _____ (of foot at ankle)

PART E

Complete the following table:

Name of Joint	Type of Joint	Bones Included	Types of Movement Possible
Shoulder joint			
Elbow joint			
Hip joint			
Knee joint			

Figure 18.7 Identify each of the types of movements that are numbered and illustrated: (*a*) anterior view; (*b*) lateral view of head; (*c*) lateral view. (Original illustration drawn by Ross Martin)

(a)

(b)

(c)

SKELETAL MUSCLE STRUCTURE

MATERIALS NEEDED

Textbook
Compound light microscope
Prepared microscope slide of skeletal muscle tissue
Human torso model with musculature
Model of skeletal muscle fiber

For Demonstration:

Fresh round beefsteak

 SAFETY

- Wear disposable gloves when handling the fresh beefsteak.
- Wash your hands before leaving the laboratory.

A skeletal muscle represents an organ of the muscular system and is composed of several kinds of tissues. These tissues include skeletal muscle tissue, nervous tissue, blood, and various connective tissues.

Each skeletal muscle is surrounded by connective tissue. The connective tissue often extends beyond the end of a muscle, providing an attachment to other muscles or to bones. Connective tissue also extends into the structure of a muscle and separates it into compartments.

PURPOSE OF THE EXERCISE

To review the structure of a skeletal muscle.

LEARNING OBJECTIVES

After completing this exercise, you should be able to

1. Describe how connective tissue is associated with muscle tissue within a skeletal muscle.

2. Name and locate the major structures of a skeletal muscle fiber on a model.
3. Distinguish between the origin and insertion of a muscle.
4. Describe the general actions of prime movers (agonists), synergists, and antagonists.

PROCEDURE

1. Review the section entitled "Skeletal Muscle Tissue" in chapter 5 of the textbook.
2. Reexamine the microscopic structure of skeletal muscle by observing a prepared microscope slide of this tissue. Use figure 19.1 of skeletal muscle tissue to locate the following features:

   skeletal muscle fiber (cell)
   nuclei
   striations (alternating light and dark)

3. Review the section entitled "Structure of a Skeletal Muscle" in chapter 9 of the textbook.
4. As a review activity, label figure 19.2 and study figure 19.3.
5. Examine the torso and locate examples of fascia, tendons, and aponeuroses. Locate examples of tendons in your own body.
6. Complete Part A of Laboratory Report 19.

DEMONSTRATION

Examine the fresh round beefsteak. It represents a cross section through the beef thigh muscles. Note the white lines of connective tissue that separate the individual skeletal muscles. Also note how the connective tissue extends into the structure of a muscle and separates it into small compartments of muscle tissue. Locate the epimysium and the perimysium of the deep fascia.

Figure 19.1   Structures found in skeletal muscle fibers (cells) (250× micrograph enlarged to 700×).

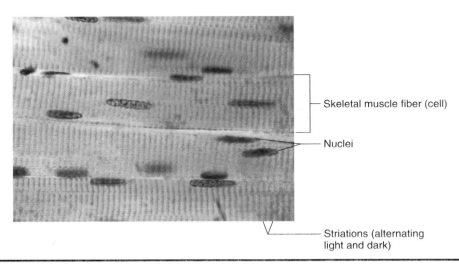

— Skeletal muscle fiber (cell)

— Nuclei

— Striations (alternating light and dark)

Figure 19.2   Label the structures of a skeletal muscle.

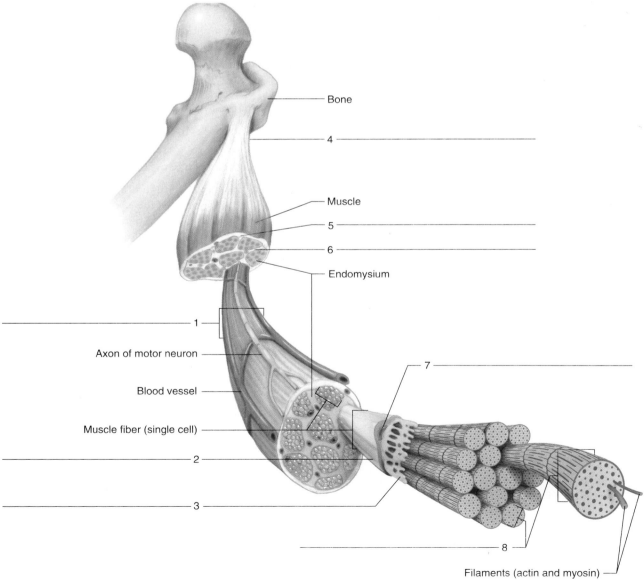

Bone

4

Muscle

5

6

Endomysium

1

Axon of motor neuron

7

Blood vessel

Muscle fiber (single cell)

2

3

8

Filaments (actin and myosin)

Figure 19.3 Structures of a skeletal muscle fiber.

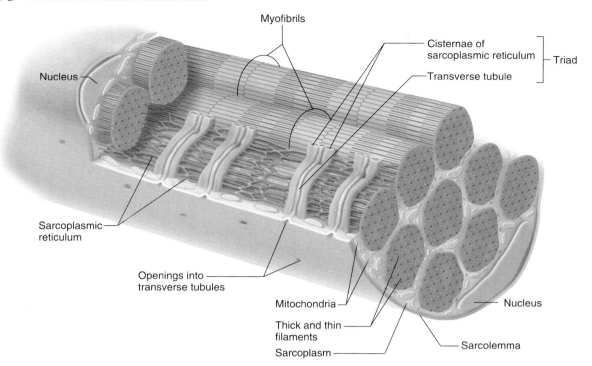

7. Examine the model of the skeletal muscle fiber and locate the following:

   sarcolemma
   sarcoplasm
   myofibril
   　thick (myosin) filament
   　thin (actin) filament
   sarcomere
   　A band (dark)
   　I band (light)
   　H zone
   　M line
   　Z line
   sarcoplasmic reticulum
   　cisternae
   transverse tubules

8. Complete Part B of the laboratory report.
9. Review the section entitled "Skeletal Muscle Actions" in chapter 9 of the textbook.
10. Provide labels for figure 19.4.
11. Locate the biceps brachii and its origins and insertions in the human torso model and in your own body.
12. Make various movements with your upper limb at the shoulder and elbow. For each movement, determine the location of the muscles functioning as prime movers (agonists) and as antagonists. **Remember, when a prime mover contracts (shortens) and a joint moves, its antagonist relaxes (lengthens).**
13. Complete Part C of the laboratory report.

Figure 19.4   Label the major features of the upper limb.

(bone) 4

5

(bone) 6

1

2

3

Name _____

Date _____

Section _____

SKELETAL MUSCLE STRUCTURE

PART A

Match the terms in column A with the definitions in column B. Place the letter of your choice in the space provided.

Column A	Column B
a. Endomysium	_____ 1. Membranous channel extending inward from muscle fiber membrane
b. Epimysium	
c. Fascia	_____ 2. Cytoplasm of a muscle fiber
d. Fascicle	_____ 3. Network of connective tissue that extends throughout the muscular system
e. Myosin	
f. Perimysium	_____ 4. Layer of connective tissue that separates a muscle into small bundles called fascicles
g. Sarcolemma	
h. Sarcomere	_____ 5. Cell membrane of a muscle fiber
i. Sarcoplasm	_____ 6. Layer of connective tissue that surrounds a skeletal muscle
j. Sarcoplasmic reticulum	
k. Tendon	_____ 7. Unit of alternating light and dark striations between Z lines
l. Transverse tubule	
	_____ 8. Layer of connective tissue that surrounds an individual muscle fiber
	_____ 9. Cellular organelle in muscle fiber corresponding to the endoplasmic reticulum
	_____ 10. Cordlike part that attaches a muscle to a bone
	_____ 11. Protein found within thick myofibril
	_____ 12. A small bundle of muscle fibers

PART B

Provide the labels for the electron micrograph in figure 19.5.

1. _____
2. _____
3. _____
4. _____

Figure 19.5 Identify the bands and lines of the striations in this transmission electron micrograph of relaxed sarcomeres (16,000×), using the terms provided.

Terms:
A band (dark)
I band (light)
Sarcomere
Z line

PART C

Complete the following statements:

1. The _____ of a muscle is usually attached to a fixed part.

2. The _____ of a muscle is usually attached to a movable part.

3. The name *biceps* means _____ .

4. The forearm is flexed at the elbow when the _____ muscle contracts.

5. A muscle responsible for most of a movement is called a(n) _____ .

6. Assisting muscles are called _____ .

7. Antagonists are muscles that resist the actions of _____ and cause movement in the opposite direction.

MUSCLES OF THE FACE, HEAD, AND NECK

MATERIALS NEEDED

Textbook
Human torso model with musculature
Human skull
Human skeleton, articulated

The skeletal muscles of the face and head include the muscles of facial expression, which lie just beneath the skin, the muscles of mastication, which are attached to the mandible, and the muscles that move the head, which are located in the neck.

PURPOSE OF THE EXERCISE

To review the locations, actions, origins, and insertions of the muscles of the face, head, and neck.

LEARNING OBJECTIVES

After completing this exercise, you should be able to

1. Locate and identify the muscles of facial expression, the muscles of mastication, and the muscles that move the head.
2. Describe and demonstrate the action of each of these muscles.
3. Locate the origin and insertion of each of these muscles in a human skeleton and the musculature of the human torso model.

PROCEDURE

1. Review the sections entitled "Muscles of Facial Expression," "Muscles of Mastication," and "Muscles That Move the Head and Vertebral Column" in chapter 9 of the textbook.

2. As a review activity, label figures 20.1, 20.2, and 20.3.
3. Locate the following muscles in the human torso model and in your own body whenever possible:

   epicranius (frontalis and occipitalis)
   orbicularis oculi
   orbicularis oris
   buccinator
   zygomaticus major
   zygomaticus minor
   platysma
   masseter
   temporalis
   medial pterygoid
   lateral pterygoid
   sternocleidomastoid
   splenius capitis
   semispinalis capitis
   longissimus capitis (of erector spinae group)

4. Demonstrate the action of these muscles in your own body.
5. Locate the origins and insertions of these muscles in the human skull and skeleton.
6. Complete Parts A, B, and C of Laboratory Report 20.

Web Quest

Determine the origin, insertion, action, nerve innervation, and blood supply of all the major muscles.

Identify muscles and detailed explanations from an interactive site.

Find information about these topics at www.mhhe.com/shier11

Click on Student Edition. Click on Martin Lab Manual, Web Quest.

Figure 20.1 Label the muscles of expression and mastication.

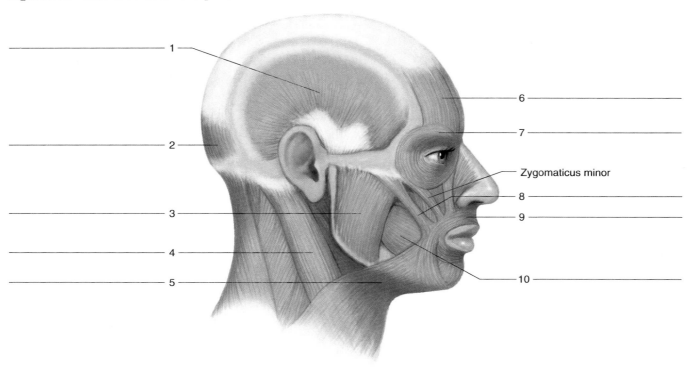

Zygomaticus minor

Figure 20.2 Label these muscles of mastication.

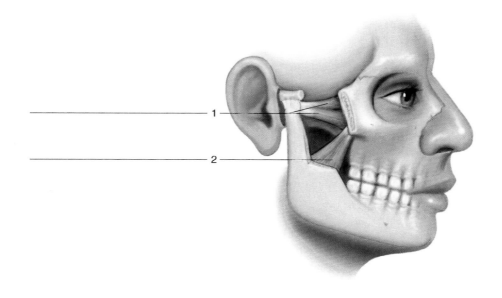

Figure 20.3 Label these deep muscles of the posterior neck (trapezius removed), using the terms provided.

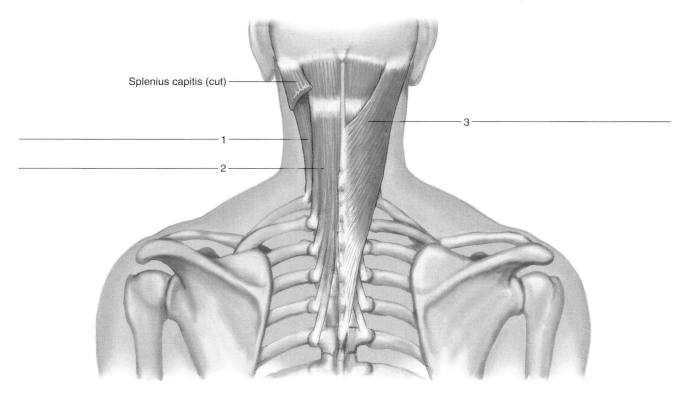

Splenius capitis (cut)

1

2

3

Terms:
Longissimus capitis (erector spinae)
Semispinalis capitis
Splenius capitis

NOTES

MUSCLES OF THE FACE, HEAD, AND NECK

PART A

Complete the following statements:

1. When the _____ contracts, the corner of the mouth is drawn upward.
2. The _____ acts to compress the wall of the cheeks when air is blown out of the mouth.
3. The _____ causes the lips to close and pucker.
4. The _____ and platysma help to lower the mandible.
5. The temporalis acts to _____ .
6. The _____ pterygoid can close the jaw and pull it sideways.
7. The _____ pterygoid can protrude the jaw, pull the jaw sideways, and open the mouth.
8. The _____ can close the eye, as in blinking.
9. The _____ can pull the head toward the chest.
10. The _____ can pull the head to one side, rotate it, or bring it into an upright position (extend head).
11. The muscle used for pouting and to express horror is the _____ .
12. The muscle used to smile and laugh is the _____ .

PART B

Name the muscle indicated by the following combinations of origin and insertion.

Origin	Insertion	Muscle
1. Occipital bone	Skin and muscle around eye	_____
2. Zygomatic bone	Orbicularis oris	_____
3. Zygomatic arch	Lateral surface of mandible	_____
4. Sphenoid bone	Anterior surface of mandibular condyle	_____
5. Anterior surface of sternum and upper clavicle	Mastoid process of temporal bone	_____
6. Outer surfaces of mandible and maxilla	Orbicularis oris	_____
7. Fascia in upper chest	Lower border of mandible and skin around corner of mouth	_____
8. Temporal bone	Coronoid process and anterior ramus of mandible	_____
9. Spinous processes of cervical and thoracic vertebrae	Mastoid process of temporal bone and occipital bone	_____
10. Processes of cervical and thoracic vertebrae	Occipital bone	_____

PART C

Critical Thinking Application

Identify the muscles of various facial expressions in the photographs of figure 20.4.

1. _____

2. _____

3. _____

4. _____

5. _____

Figure 20.4   Identify the muscles of expression being contracted in each of these photographs (*a–c*), using the terms provided.

(a)

(b)

Terms:
Epicranius/frontalis
Orbicularis oculi
Orbicularis oris
Platysma
Zygomaticus major

(c)

MUSCLES OF THE CHEST, SHOULDER, AND UPPER LIMB

MATERIALS NEEDED

Textbook
Human torso model
Human skeleton, articulated
Muscular models of the upper limb

The muscles of the chest and shoulder are responsible for moving the scapula and arm, whereas those within the arm and forearm move joints in the elbow and hand.

PURPOSE OF THE EXERCISE

To review the locations, actions, origins, and insertions of the muscles in the chest, shoulder, and upper limb.

LEARNING OBJECTIVES

After completing this exercise, you should be able to

1. Locate and identify the muscles of the chest, shoulder, and upper limb.
2. Describe and demonstrate the action of each of these muscles.
3. Locate the origin and insertion of each of these muscles.

PROCEDURE

1. Review the sections entitled "Muscles That Move the Pectoral Girdle," "Muscles That Move the Arm," "Muscles That Move the Forearm," and "Muscles That Move the Hand" in chapter 9 of the textbook.
2. As a review activity, label figures 21.1, 21.2, 21.3, and 21.4.
3. Locate the following muscles in the human torso model and models of the upper limb. Also locate in your own body as many of the muscles as you can.

muscles that move the pectoral girdle
  trapezius
  rhomboid major
  rhomboid minor
  levator scapulae
  serratus anterior
  pectoralis minor
muscles that move the arm
  coracobrachialis
  pectoralis major
  teres major
  latissimus dorsi
  supraspinatus
  deltoid
  subscapularis
  infraspinatus
  teres minor
muscles that move the forearm
  biceps brachii
  brachialis
  brachioradialis
  triceps brachii
  supinator
  pronator teres
  pronator quadratus
muscles that move the hand
  flexor carpi radialis
  flexor carpi ulnaris
  palmaris longus
  flexor digitorum profundus
  flexor digitorum superficialis
  extensor carpi radialis longus
  extensor carpi radialis brevis
  extensor carpi ulnaris
  extensor digitorum

Figure 21.1 Label the muscles of the posterior shoulder. Superficial muscles are illustrated on the left side and deep muscles on the right side.

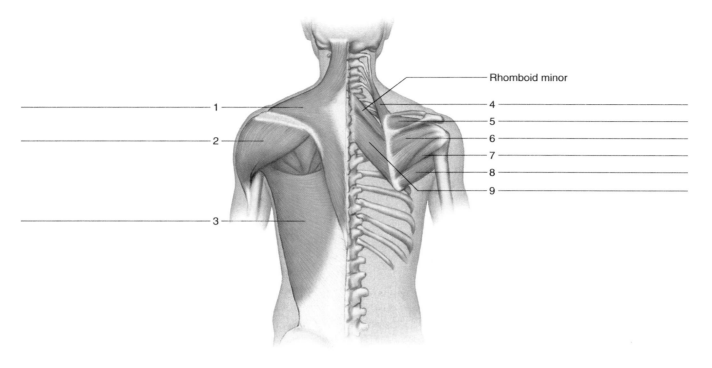

Rhomboid minor

1
2
3

4
5
6
7
8
9

Figure 21.2 Label the muscles of the anterior chest. Superficial muscles are illustrated on the left side and deep muscles on the right side.

Trapezius

1
2

External intercoastal

3
4

5

4. Demonstrate the action of these muscles in your own body.
5. Locate the origins and insertions of these muscles in the human skeleton.
6. Complete Parts A, B, and C of Laboratory Report 21.

Web Quest

Determine the origin, insertion, action, nerve innervation, and blood supply of all the major muscles.

   Identify muscles and detailed explanations from an interactive site.

   Find information about these topics at www.mhhe.com/shier11

Click on Student Edition. Click on Martin Lab Manual, Web Quest.

Figure 21.3 Label (*a*) the muscles of the posterior shoulder and arm and (*b*) the muscles of the anterior shoulder and arm, with the rib cage removed.

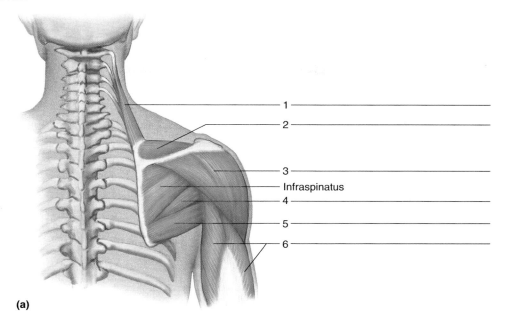

1 —————————————————
2 —————————————————
3 —————————————————
Infraspinatus
4 —————————————————
5 —————————————————
6 —————————————————

(a)

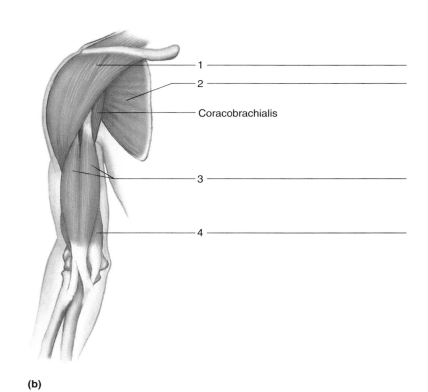

1 —————————————————
2 —————————————————
Coracobrachialis
3 —————————————————
4 —————————————————

(b)

Figure 21.4 Label (*a*) the muscles of the anterior forearm and (*b*) the muscles of the posterior forearm.

Biceps brachii

Brachialis

Supinator

_____ 1 _____

_____ 2 _____

Extensor carpi radialis longus

_____ 3 _____

_____ 4 _____

Flexor carpi ulnaris

Pronator quadratus

Retinaculum

(a)

Triceps brachii

Brachioradialis

3 _____

_____ 1 _____

_____ 2 _____

Extensor carpi radialis brevis

4 _____

Retinaculum

(b)

MUSCLES OF THE CHEST, SHOULDER, AND UPPER LIMB

PART A

Match the muscles in column A with the actions in column B. Place the letter of your choice in the space provided.

Column A	**Column B**
a. Brachialis	_____ 1. Abducts arm
b. Coracobrachialis	_____ 2. Pulls arm forward and across chest and rotates arm medially
c. Deltoid	
d. Extensor carpi ulnaris	_____ 3. Flexes and adducts hand at the wrist
e. Flexor carpi ulnaris	_____ 4. Raises and adducts scapula
f. Infraspinatus	_____ 5. Raises ribs in forceful inhalation or pulls scapula forward and downward
g. Pectoralis major	
h. Pectoralis minor	_____ 6. Used to thrust shoulder anteriorly, as when pushing something
i. Rhomboid major	
j. Serratus anterior	_____ 7. Flexes the forearm at the elbow
k. Teres major	_____ 8. Flexes and adducts arm at the shoulder along with pectoralis major
l. Triceps brachii	
	_____ 9. Extends the forearm at the elbow
	_____ 10. Extends, adducts, and rotates arm medially
	_____ 11. Extends and adducts hand at the wrist
	_____ 12. Rotates arm laterally

PART B

Name the muscle indicated by the following combinations of origin and insertion.

Origin	Insertion	Muscle
1. Spines of upper thoracic vertebrae	Medial border of scapula	_____
2. Outer surfaces of upper ribs	Ventral surface of scapula	_____
3. Sternal ends of upper ribs	Coracoid process of scapula	_____
4. Coracoid process of scapula	Shaft of humerus	_____
5. Lateral border of scapula	Intertubercular groove of humerus	_____
6. Anterior surface of scapula	Lesser tubercle of humerus	_____
7. Lateral border of scapula	Greater tubercle of humerus	_____
8. Anterior shaft of humerus	Coronoid process of ulna	_____
9. Medial epicondyle of humerus and coronoid process of ulna	Lateral surface of radius	_____
10. Distal lateral end of humerus	Lateral surface of radius above styloid process	_____
11. Medial epicondyle of humerus	Base of second and third metacarpals	_____
12. Medial epicondyle of humerus	Fascia of palm	_____

PART C

Critical Thinking Application

Identify the muscles indicated in figure 21.5.

1. _____
2. _____
3. _____
4. _____
5. _____
6. _____
7. _____
8. _____
9. _____
10. _____
11. _____

12. _____
13. _____
14. _____
15. _____
16. _____
17. _____
18. _____
19. _____
20. _____
21. _____

168

Figure 21.5 Identify the muscles that appear as body surface features in these photographs (*a*, *b*, and *c*), using the terms provided.

Terms:
Biceps brachii
Deltoid
External oblique
Pectoralis major
Rectus abdominis
Serratus anterior
Sternocleidomastoid
Trapezius

1
2
3
4
5
6
7
8

(a)

Terms:
Biceps brachii
Deltoid
Infraspinatus
Latissimus dorsi
Trapezius
Triceps brachii

9
10
11
12
13
14

(b)

Figure 21.5 *Continued.*

Terms:
Biceps brachii
Brachioradialis
Deltoid
Pectoralis major
Serratus anterior
Trapezius
Triceps brachii

(c)

MUSCLES OF THE DEEP BACK, ABDOMINAL WALL, AND PELVIC OUTLET

MATERIALS NEEDED

Textbook
Human torso model with musculature
Human skeleton, articulated
Muscular models of male and female pelves

The deep muscles of the back extend the vertebral column. Because the muscles have numerous origins, insertions, and subgroups, the muscles overlap each other. The deep back muscles can extend the spine when contracting as a group but also help to maintain posture and normal spine curvatures.

The anterior and lateral walls of the abdomen contain broad, flattened muscles arranged in layers. These muscles connect the rib cage and vertebral column to the pelvic girdle.

The muscles of the pelvic outlet are arranged in two muscular sheets: (1) a deeper pelvic diaphragm that forms the floor of the pelvic cavity and (2) a urogenital diaphragm that fills the space within the pubic arch.

PURPOSE OF THE EXERCISE

To review the actions, origins, and insertions of the muscles of the deep back, abdominal wall, and pelvic outlet.

LEARNING OBJECTIVES

After completing this exercise, you should be able to

1. Locate and identify the muscles of the deep back, abdominal wall, and pelvic outlet.
2. Describe the action of each of these muscles.
3. Locate the origin and insertion of each of these muscles.

PROCEDURE

1. Review the sections entitled "Muscles of the Abdominal Wall" and "Muscles of the Pelvic Outlet" in chapter 9 of the textbook.
2. As a review activity, label figures 22.1, 22.2, 22.3, and 22.4.
3. Locate the following muscles in the human torso model:

   erector spinae group
   iliocostalis (lateral group)
   longissimus (intermediate group)
   spinalis (medial group)
   external oblique
   internal oblique
   transversus abdominis
   rectus abdominis

4. Demonstrate the actions of these muscles in your own body.
5. Locate the origin and insertion of each of these muscles in the human skeleton.
6. Complete Part A of Laboratory Report 22.
7. Locate the following muscles in the models of the male and female pelves:

   levator ani
   coccygeus
   superficial transversus perinei
   bulbospongiosus
   ischiocavernosus

8. Locate the origin and insertion of each of these muscles in the human skeleton.
9. Complete Part B of the laboratory report.

Figure 22.1 Label the three deep back muscle groups of the erector spinae group, using the terms provided. (*Note:* The three erector spinae muscle groups are not illustrated on both sides of the body.)

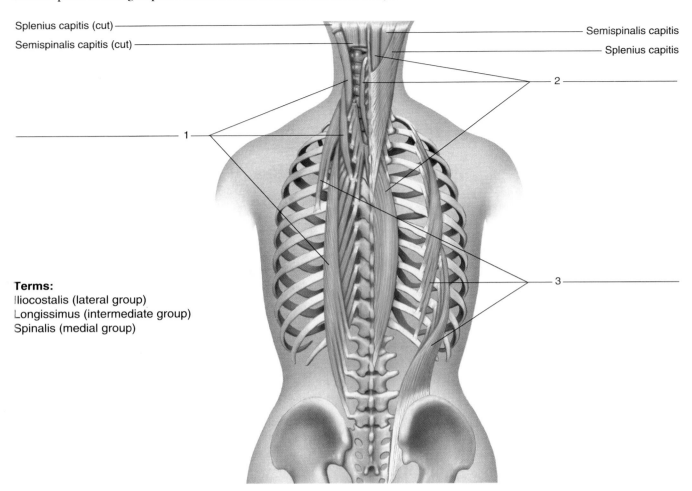

Splenius capitis (cut)

Semispinalis capitis (cut)

Semispinalis capitis

Splenius capitis

1

2

3

Terms:
Iliocostalis (lateral group)
Longissimus (intermediate group)
Spinalis (medial group)

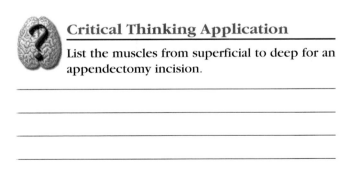

Critical Thinking Application

List the muscles from superficial to deep for an appendectomy incision.

_____

_____

_____

_____

Web Quest

Determine the origin, insertion, action, nerve innervation, and blood supply of all the major muscles.

Identify muscles and detailed explanations from an interactive site.

Find information about these topics at www.mhhe.com/shier11

Click on Student Edition. Click on Martin Lab Manual, Web Quest.

Figure 22.2 Label the muscles of the abdominal wall.

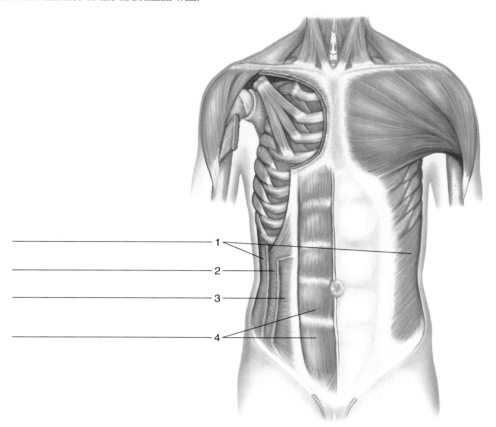

Figure 22.3   Label the muscles of the male pelvic outlet.

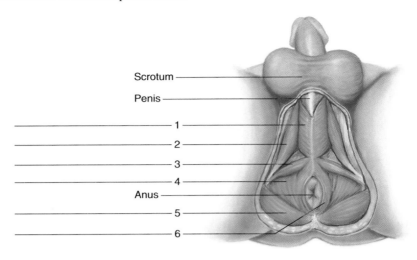

Scrotum

Penis

1

2

3

4

Anus

5

6

Figure 22.4   Label the muscles of the female pelvic outlet.

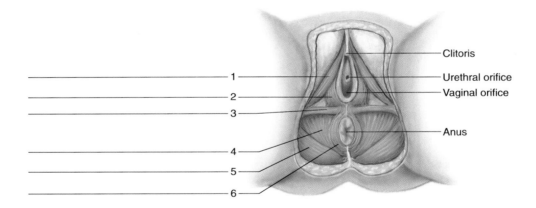

1

2

3

4

5

6

Clitoris

Urethral orifice

Vaginal orifice

Anus

Name _____

Date _____

Section _____

MUSCLES OF THE DEEP BACK, ABDOMINAL WALL, AND PELVIC OUTLET

PART A

Complete the following statements:

1. A band of tough connective tissue in the midline of the anterior abdominal wall called the _____ serves as a muscle attachment.

2. The _____ muscle spans from the ribs and sternum to the pubic bones.

3. The _____ forms the third layer (deepest layer) of the abdominal wall muscles.

4. The action of the external oblique muscle is to_____ .

5. The action of the rectus abdominis is to _____ .

6. The iliocostalis, longissimus, and spinalis muscles together form the _____ .

PART B

Complete the following statements:

1. The levator ani and coccygeus together form the _____ .

2. The levator ani provides a sphincterlike action in the _____ .

3. The action of the coccygeus is to _____
   _____ .

4. The _____ surrounds the base of the penis.

5. In females, the bulbospongiosus acts to _____ .

6. The ischiocavernosus extends from the margin of the pubic arch to the_____ .

7. In the female, the _____ muscles are separated by the vagina, urethra, and anal canal.

8. The action of the superficial transversus perinei is to _____ .

9. The coccygeus extends from the coccyx and sacrum to the _____ .

10. The _____ assists in closing the urethra.

NOTES

MUSCLES OF THE HIP AND LOWER LIMB

The muscles that move the thigh are attached to the femur and to some part of the pelvic girdle. Those attached anteriorly primarily act to flex the thigh at the hip, whereas those attached posteriorly act to extend, abduct, or rotate the thigh.

The muscles that move the leg connect the tibia or fibula to the femur or to the pelvic girdle. They function to flex or extend the leg at the knee. Other muscles, located in the leg, act to move the foot.

PURPOSE OF THE EXERCISE

To review the actions, origins, and insertions of the muscles that move the thigh, leg, and foot.

LEARNING OBJECTIVES

After completing this exercise, you should be able to

1. Locate and identify the muscles that move the thigh, leg, and foot.
2. Describe and demonstrate the actions of each of these muscles.
3. Locate the origin and insertion of each of these muscles.

PROCEDURE

1. Review the sections entitled "Muscles That Move the Thigh," "Muscles That Move the Leg," and "Muscles That Move the Foot" in chapter 9 of the textbook.

2. As a review activity, label figures 23.1, 23.2, 23.3, 23.4, 23.5, and 23.6.
3. Locate the following muscles in the human torso model and in the lower limb models. Also locate as many of them as possible in your own body.

muscles that move the thigh
   iliopsoas group
      psoas major
      iliacus
   psoas minor
   gluteus maximus
   gluteus medius
   gluteus minimus
   tensor fasciae latae
   pectineus
   adductor longus
   adductor magnus
   adductor brevis
   gracilis
muscles that move the leg
   hamstring group
      biceps femoris
      semitendinosus
      semimembranosus
   sartorius
   quadriceps femoris group
      rectus femoris
      vastus lateralis
      vastus medialis
      vastus intermedius
muscles that move the foot
   tibialis anterior
   fibularis (peroneus) tertius
   extensor digitorum longus
   gastrocnemius
   soleus

flexor digitorum longus

tibialis posterior

fibularis (peroneus) longus

fibularis (peroneus) brevis

4. Demonstrate the action of each of these muscles in your own body.
5. Locate the origin and insertion of each of these muscles in the human skeleton.
6. Complete Parts A, B, and C of Laboratory Report 23.

Web Quest

Determine the origin, insertion, action, nerve innervation, and blood supply of all the major muscles.

Identify muscles and detailed explanations from an interactive site.

Find information about these topics at www.mhhe.com/shier11

Click on Student Edition. Click on Martin Lab Manual, Web Quest.

Figure 23.1 Label the muscles of the anterior right hip and thigh.

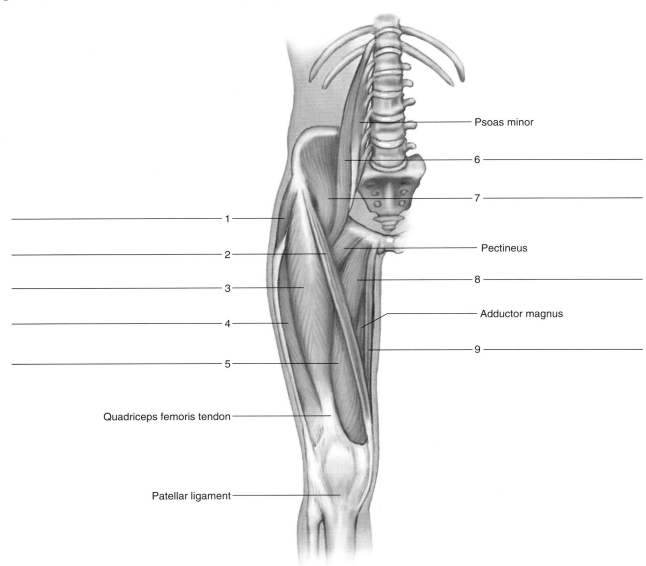

Figure 23.2 Label the muscles of the lateral right hip and thigh.

1

2

3

4

Sartorius

5

6

Iliotibial tract (band)

Figure 23.3 Label the muscles of the posterior right hip and thigh.

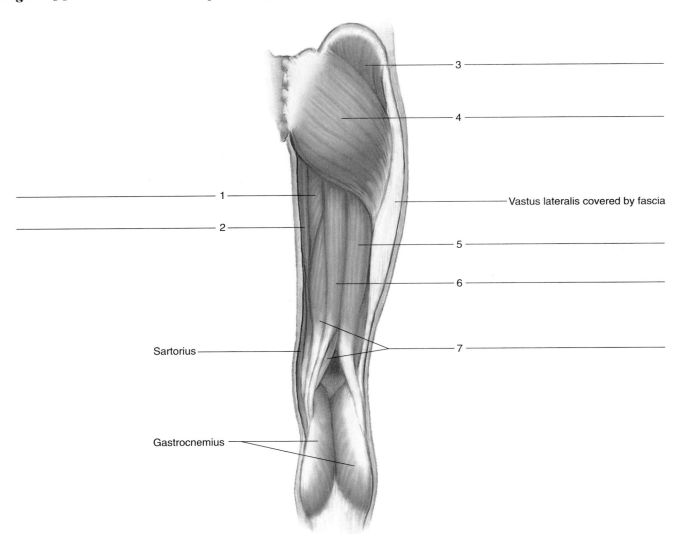

3

4

1

2

Vastus lateralis covered by fascia

5

6

Sartorius

7

Gastrocnemius

Figure 23.4 Label the muscles of the anterior right leg.

Patellar ligament

Gastrocnemius

1

2

3

Soleus

Fibularis (peroneus) brevis

Tibia

Extensor retinacula

Figure 23.5   Label the muscles of the lateral right leg.

Iliotibial tract (band)

1

2

3

4

5

6

Fibularis (peroneus) tertius

Retinaculum

Figure 23.6 Label the muscles of the posterior right leg.

1 — Fibularis (peroneus) longus

2 — Calcaneal tendon

Flexor digitorum longus

Retinaculum

NOTES

Name _____

Date _____

Section _____

MUSCLES OF THE HIP AND LOWER LIMB

PART A

Match the muscles in column A with the actions in column B. Place the letter of your choice in the space provided.

Column A		Column B
a.	Biceps femoris	_____ 1. Adducts thigh
b.	Fibularis (peroneus) longus	_____ 2. Plantar flexion and eversion of foot
c.	Fibularis (peroneus) tertius	
d.	Gluteus medius	_____ 3. Flexes thigh at the hip
e.	Gracilis	_____ 4. Abducts thigh and rotates it laterally
f.	Psoas major and iliacus	
g.	Quadriceps femoris group	_____ 5. Dorsiflexion and eversion of foot
h.	Sartorius	_____ 6. Abducts thigh and rotates it medially
i.	Tibialis anterior	
j.	Tibialis posterior	_____ 7. Plantar flexion and inversion of foot
		_____ 8. Flexes leg at the knee
		_____ 9. Extends leg at the knee
		_____ 10. Dorsiflexion and inversion of foot

PART B

Name the muscle indicated by the following combinations of origin and insertion.

Origin	Insertion	Muscle
1. Lateral surface of ilium	Greater trochanter of femur	_____
2. Ischial tuberosity	Posterior surface of femur	_____
3. Anterior superior iliac spine	Medial surface of tibia	_____
4. Lateral and medial condyles of femur	Posterior surface of calcaneus	_____
5. Anterior iliac crest	Fascia (iliotibial tract) of the thigh	_____
6. Greater trochanter and posterior surface of femur	Patella to tibial tuberosity	_____
7. Ischial tuberosity	Medial surface of tibia	_____
8. Medial surface of femur	Patella to tibial tuberosity	_____
9. Posterior surface of tibia	Distal phalanges of four lateral toes	_____
10. Lateral condyle and lateral surface of tibia	Cuneiform and first metatarsal	_____

PART C

Critical Thinking Application

Identify the muscles indicated in figure 23.7.

1. _____
2. _____
3. _____
4. _____
5. _____
6. _____
7. _____
8. _____

Figure 23.7 Identify the muscles that appear as lower limb surface features in these photographs (*a* and *b*), using the terms provided.

(a) Left thigh, anterior view

(b) Right lower limb, medial view

Terms:

Gastrocnemius
Rectus femoris
Sartorius
Soleus

Tibialis anterior
Vastus lateralis
Vastus medialis
Vastus medialis

CAT DISSECTION: MUSCULATURE

MATERIALS NEEDED

Textbook
Preserved cat (double injection)
Dissecting tray
Dissecting instruments
Large plastic bag
Identification tag
Disposable gloves
Bone shears
Human torso model
Human upper and lower limb models

For Demonstration:

Cat skeleton

⚠ SAFETY

- Wear disposable gloves when working on the cat dissection.
- Dispose of tissue remnants and gloves as instructed.
- Wash the dissecting tray and instruments as instructed.
- Wash your laboratory table.
- Wash your hands before leaving the laboratory.

Although the aim of this exercise is to become more familiar with the human musculature, human cadavers are not always available for dissection. Instead, preserved cats often are used for dissection because they are relatively small and can be purchased from biological suppliers. Also, as mammals, cats have many features in common with humans, including similar skeletal muscles (with similar names).

On the other hand, cats make use of four limbs for support, whereas humans use only two limbs. Because the musculature of each type of organism is adapted to provide for its special needs, comparisons of the muscles of cats and humans may not be precise.

As you continue your dissection of various systems of the cat, many anatomical similarities between cats and humans will be observed. These fundamental similarities are called homologous structures. Although homologous structures have a similar structure and embryological origin, the functions are sometimes different.

PURPOSE OF THE EXERCISE

To observe the musculature of the cat and to compare it with that of the human.

LEARNING OBJECTIVES

After completing this exercise, you should be able to

1. Name and locate the major skeletal muscles of the cat.
2. Name and locate the corresponding muscles of the human.
3. Name the origins, insertions, and actions of the muscles designated by the laboratory instructor.

MUSCLE DISSECTION TECHNIQUES

Dissect: to expose the entire length of the muscle from origin to insertion. Most of the procedures are accomplished with blunt probes used to separate various connective tissues that hold adjacent structures together. It does not mean to remove or to cut into the muscles or other organs.

Transect: to cut through the muscle near its midpoint. The cut is perpendicular to the muscle fibers.

Reflect: to lift a transected muscle aside to expose deeper muscles or other organs.

PROCEDURE A—SKIN REMOVAL

1. Cats usually are preserved with a solution that prevents microorganisms from causing the tissues to decompose. However, because fumes from this preserving fluid may be annoying and may irritate skin, be sure to work in a well-ventilated room and wear disposable gloves to protect your hands.
2. Obtain a preserved cat, a dissecting tray, a set of dissecting instruments, a large plastic bag, and an identification tag.
3. If the cat is in a storage bag, dispose of any excess preserving fluid in the bag, as directed by the laboratory instructor. However, you may want to

save some of the preserving fluid to keep the cat moist until you have completed your work later in the year.

4. If the cat is too wet with preserving fluid, blot the cat dry with paper towels.

5. Remove the skin from the cat. To do this, follow these steps:

   a. Place the cat in the dissecting tray with its ventral surface down.

   b. Use a sharp scalpel to make a short, shallow incision through the skin in the dorsal midline at the base of the cat's neck.

   c. Insert the pointed blade of a dissecting scissors through the opening in the skin and cut along the dorsal midline, following the tips of the vertebral spinous processes to the base of the tail (fig. 24.1).

   d. Use the scissors to make an incision encircling the region of the tail, anus, and genital organs. Do not remove the skin from this area.

   e. Use bone shears or a bone saw to sever the tail at its base and discard it (optional procedure).

   f. From the incision at the base of the tail, cut along the lateral surface of each hindlimb to the paw, and encircle the ankle. Also clip off the claws from each paw to prevent them from tearing the plastic storage bag and scratching your skin.

   g. Make an incision from the initial cut at the base of the neck to encircle the neck.

Figure 24.1 Incisions to be made for removing the skin of the cat.

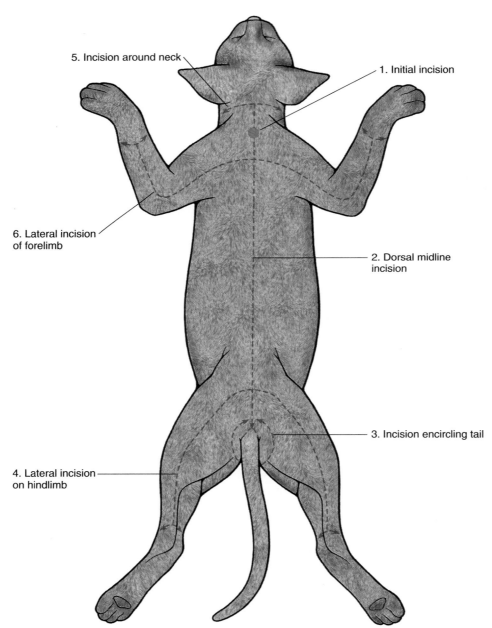

5. Incision around neck

1. Initial incision

6. Lateral incision of forelimb

2. Dorsal midline incision

3. Incision encircling tail

4. Lateral incision on hindlimb

h. From the incision around the neck, cut along the lateral surface of each forelimb to the paw and encircle the wrist (fig. 24.1).

i. Grasp the skin on either side of the dorsal midline incision, and carefully pull the skin laterally away from the body. At the same time, use your fingers or a blunt probe to help remove the skin from the underlying muscles by separating the loose connective tissue (superficial fascia). As you pull the skin away, you may note a thin sheet of muscle tissue attached to it. This muscle is called the *cutaneous maximus,* and it functions to move the cat's skin. Humans lack the cutaneous maximus, but a similar sheet of muscle (platysma) is present in the neck of a human.

j. As you remove the skin, work toward the ventral surface, then work toward the head, and finally work toward the tail. Pull the skin over each limb as if you were removing a glove.

k. If the cat is a female, note the mammary glands on the ventral surface of the thorax and abdomen (fig. 24.2). These glands will adhere to the skin and can be removed from it and discarded.

l. After the skin has been pulled away, carefully remove as much of the remaining connective tissue as possible to expose the underlying skeletal muscles. The muscles should appear light brown and fibrous.

6. After skinning the cat, follow these steps:

a. Discard the tissues you have removed as directed by the laboratory instructor.

Figure 24.2 Mammary glands on the ventral surface of the cat's thorax and abdomen.

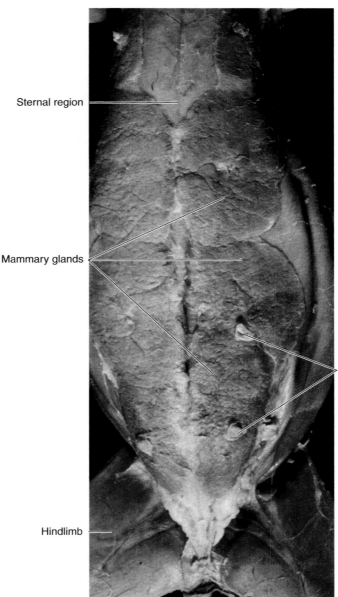

Sternal region

Mammary glands

Mammary papillae (teats or nipples)

Hindlimb

b. Wrap the skin around the cat to help keep its body moist, and place it in a plastic storage bag.

c. Write your name in pencil on an identification tag, and tie the tag to the storage bag so that you can identify your specimen.

7. Observe the recommended safety procedures for the conclusion of a laboratory session.

PROCEDURE B—SKELETAL MUSCLE DISSECTION

1. The purpose of a skeletal muscle dissection is to separate the individual muscles from any surrounding tissues and thus expose the muscles for observation. To do a muscle dissection, follow these steps:

   a. Use the appropriate figure as a guide and locate the muscle to be dissected in the specimen.

   b. Use a blunt probe or a finger to separate the muscle from the surrounding connective tissue along its natural borders. The muscle should separate smoothly. If the border appears ragged, you probably have torn the muscle fibers.

2. If it is necessary to cut through (transect) a superficial muscle to observe a deeper one, use scissors to transect the muscle about halfway between its origin and insertion. Then, lift aside (reflect) the cut ends, leaving their attachments intact.

3. The following procedures will instruct you to dissect some of the larger and more easily identified muscles of the cat. In each case, the procedure will include the names of the muscles to be dissected, figures illustrating their locations, and tables listing

the origins, insertions, and actions of the muscles. (More detailed dissection instructions can be obtained by consulting an additional guide or atlas for cat dissection.) As you dissect each muscle, study the figures and tables in chapter 9 of the textbook and identify any corresponding (homologous) muscles of the human body. Also locate these homologous muscles in the human torso model or models of the human upper and lower limbs.

DEMONSTRATION

Refer to the cat skeleton to help you to locate origins and insertions of the cat's muscles. Reference to the cat skeleton will also help you visualize the actions of these muscles, if you remember that a muscle's insertion is pulled toward its origin.

PROCEDURE C—MUSCLES OF THE HEAD AND NECK

1. Place the cat in the dissecting tray with its ventral surface up.

2. Remove the skin and underlying connective tissues from one side of the neck, forward to the chin, and up to the ear.

3. Study figures 24.3 and 24.4, and then locate and dissect the following muscles:

sternomastoid	**mylohyoid**
sternohyoid	**masseter**
digastric	

Figure 24.3 Muscles on the ventral surface of the cat's head and neck.

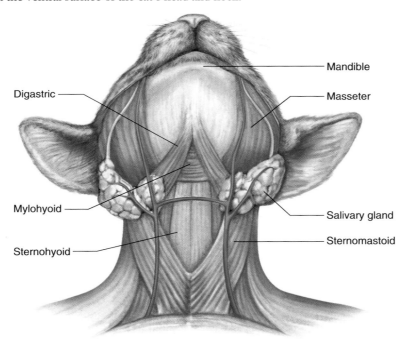

Figure 24.4 Deep muscles on the right ventral surface of the cat's neck.

Digastric
Masseter
Stylohyoid
Sternomastoid (cut)
Cleidomastoid
Sternomastoid (cut)

Mandible
Mylohyoid
Sternohyoid

Table 24.1 Muscles of the Head and Neck

Muscle	Origin	Insertion	Action
Sternomastoid	Manubrium of sternum	Mastoid process of temporal bone	Turns and depresses head
Sternohyoid	Costal cartilage	Hyoid bone	Depresses hyoid bone
Digastric	Mastoid process and occipital bone	Ventral border of mandible	Depresses mandible
Mylohyoid	Inner surface of mandible	Hyoid bone	Raises floor of mouth
Masseter	Zygomatic arch	Coronoid fossa of mandible	Elevates mandible
Hyoglossus	Hyoid bone	Tongue	Pulls tongue back
Styloglossus	Styloid process	Tip of tongue	Pulls tongue back
Geniohyoid	Inner surface of mandible	Hyoid bone	Pulls hyoid bone forward
Cleidomastoid	Clavicle	Mastoid process	Turns head to side
Thyrohyoid	Thyroid cartilage	Hyoid bone	Raises larynx
Sternothyroid	Sternum	Thyroid cartilage	Pulls larynx back

4. To find the deep muscles of the cat's neck and chin, carefully remove the sternomastoid, sternohyoid, and mylohyoid muscles from the right side.
5. Study figure 24.5, and locate the following muscles:

hyoglossus
cleidomastoid
styloglossus
thyrohyoid
geniohyoid
sternothyroid

6. See table 24.1 for the origins, insertions, and actions of these head and neck muscles.
7. Complete Part A of Laboratory Report 24.

PROCEDURE D—MUSCLES OF THE THORAX

1. Place the cat in the dissecting tray with its ventral surface up.
2. Remove any remaining fat and connective tissue to expose the muscles in the walls of the thorax and abdomen.

Figure 24.5 Deep muscles of the cat's neck and chin regions.

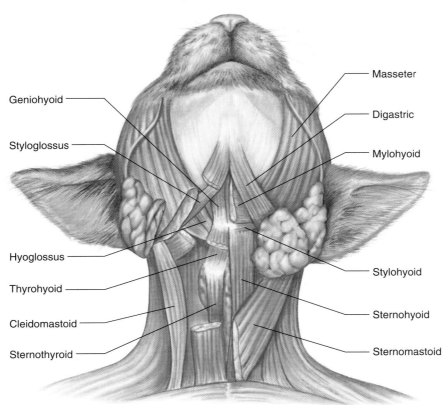

Geniohyoid

Styloglossus

Hyoglossus

Thyrohyoid

Cleidomastoid

Sternothyroid

Masseter

Digastric

Mylohyoid

Stylohyoid

Sternohyoid

Sternomastoid

3. Study figures 24.6 and 24.7. Transect the superficial pectoantebrachialis to expose the entire pectoralis major. Locate and dissect the following pectoral muscles:

pectoantebrachialis   **pectoralis minor**

pectoralis major   **xiphihumeralis**

4. To find the deep thoracic muscles, transect the pectoralis minor, pectoralis major, and pectoantebrachialis muscles, and reflect their cut edges to the sides. Remove the underlying fat and connective tissues to expose the following muscles, as shown in figure 24.8:

scalenus   **levator scapulae**

serratus ventralis   **transversus costarum**

5. See table 24.2 for the origins, insertions, and actions of these muscles.

PROCEDURE E—MUSCLES OF THE ABDOMINAL WALL

1. Study figures 24.6 and 24.9
2. Locate the *external oblique* muscle in the abdominal wall.

3. Make a shallow, longitudinal incision through the external oblique. Lift up the cut edge and expose the *internal oblique* muscle beneath (fig. 24.6). Note that the fibers of the internal oblique run at a right angle to those of the external oblique.
4. Make a longitudinal incision through the internal oblique. Lift up the cut edge and expose the *transversus abdominis* muscle.
5. Expose the *rectus abdominis* muscle on one side of the midventral line. This muscle lies beneath an aponeurosis.
6. See table 24.3 for the origins, insertions, and actions of these muscles.
7. Complete Part B of the laboratory report.

PROCEDURE F—MUSCLES OF THE SHOULDER AND BACK

1. Place the cat in the dissecting tray with its dorsal surface up.
2. Remove any remaining fat and connective tissue to expose the muscles of the shoulder and back.

Figure 24.6 Muscles of the cat's thorax and abdomen.

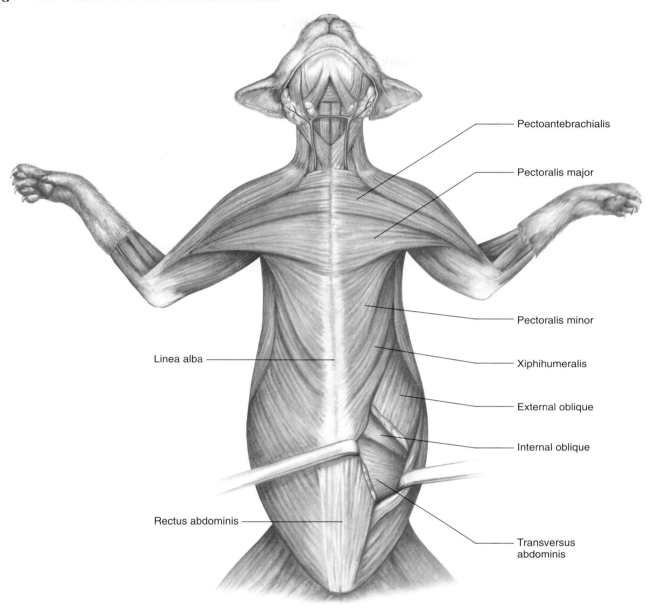

- Pectoantebrachialis
- Pectoralis major
- Pectoralis minor
- Xiphihumeralis
- External oblique
- Internal oblique
- Transversus abdominis

Linea alba

Rectus abdominis

Table 24.2 Muscles of the Thorax

Muscle	Origin	Insertion	Action
Pectoantebrachialis	Manubrium of sternum	Fascia of forelimb	Adducts forelimb
Pectoralis major	Manubrium of sternum and costal cartilages	Greater tubercle of humerus	Adducts and rotates forelimb
Pectoralis minor	Sternum	Proximal end of humerus	Adducts and rotates forelimb
Xiphihumeralis	Xiphoid process of sternum	Proximal end of humerus	Adducts forelimb
Scalenus	Ribs	Cervical vertebrae	Flexes neck
Serratus ventralis	Ribs	Scapula	Pulls scapula ventrally and posteriorly
Levator scapulae	Cervical vertebrae	Scapula	Pulls scapula ventrally and anteriorly
Transversus costarum	Sternum	First rib	Pulls sternum toward head

Figure 24.7 Superficial muscles of the cat's thorax.

- Pectoralis major
- Pectoantebrachialis
- Pectoralis major
- Latissimus dorsi
- Pectoralis minor
- Xiphihumeralis

Figure 24.8 Deep muscles of the cat's thorax.

- Levator scapulae
- Transverus costarum
- Scalenus
- Serratus ventralis
- Rectus abdominis
- Pectoralis major
- Pectoantebrachialis
- Pectoralis minor
- Xiphihumeralis

Table 24.3 Muscles of the Abdominal Wall

Muscle	Origin	Insertion	Action
External oblique	Ribs and fascia of back	Linea alba	Compresses abdominal wall
Internal oblique	Fascia of back	Linea alba	Compresses abdominal wall
Transversus abdominis	Lower ribs	Linea alba	Compresses abdominal wall
Rectus abdominis	Symphysis pubis	Sternum and costal cartilages	Compresses abdominal wall and flexes trunk

Figure 24.9 Superficial muscles of the cat's thorax and abdomen.

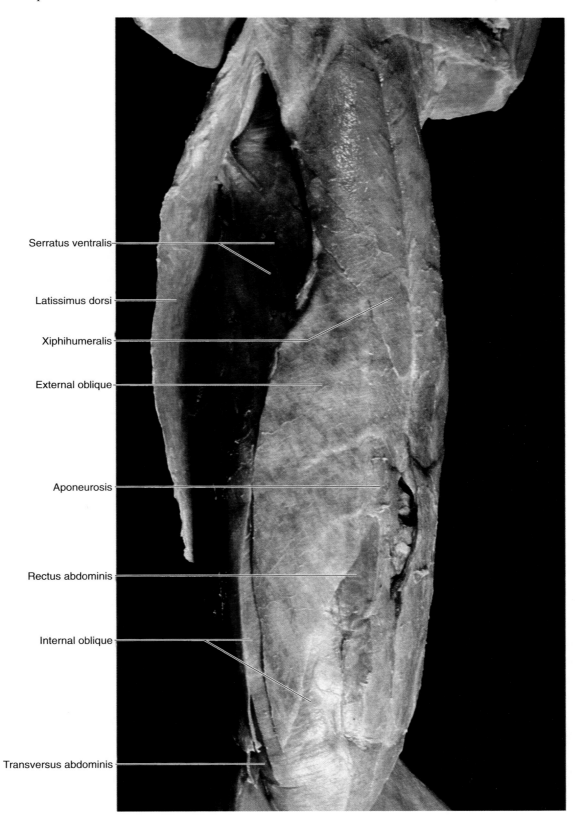

Serratus ventralis

Latissimus dorsi

Xiphihumeralis

External oblique

Aponeurosis

Rectus abdominis

Internal oblique

Transversus abdominis

Figure 24.10 Superficial muscles of the cat's shoulder and back (*right side*); deep muscles of the shoulder and back (*left side*).

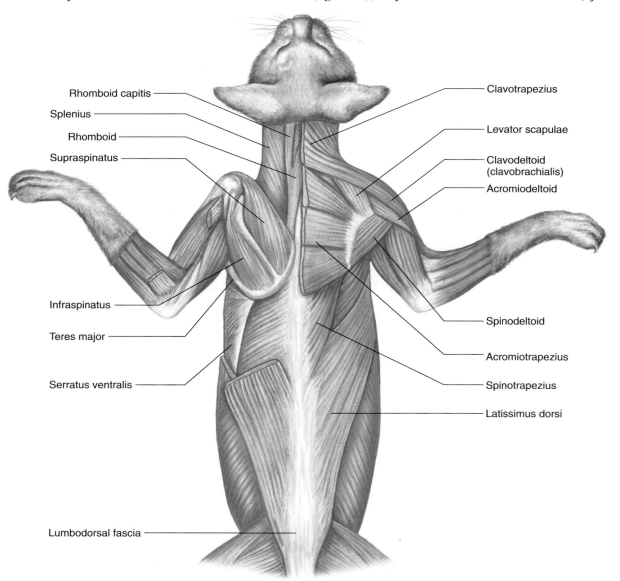

Rhomboid capitis

Splenius

Rhomboid

Supraspinatus

Infraspinatus

Teres major

Serratus ventralis

Lumbodorsal fascia

Clavotrapezius

Levator scapulae

Clavodeltoid (clavobrachialis)

Acromiodeltoid

Spinodeltoid

Acromiotrapezius

Spinotrapezius

Latissimus dorsi

3. Study figures 24.10 and 24.11, and then locate and dissect the following superficial muscles:

clavotrapezius	**acromiodeltoid**
acromiotrapezius	**spinodeltoid**
spinotrapezius	**latissimus dorsi**
clavodeltoid	

Note: The clavodeltoid (clavobrachialis) appears as a continuation of the clavotrapezius.

4. Using scissors, transect the latissimus dorsi and the group of trapezius muscles. Lift aside their cut edges and remove any underlying fat and connective tissue. Study figures 24.10 and 24.12, and then

locate and dissect the following deep muscles of the shoulder and back:

supraspinatus	**infraspinatus**
teres major	**rhomboid**
rhomboid capitis	**splenius**

5. See table 24.4 for the origins, insertions, and actions of these muscles in the shoulder and back.

6. Complete Part C of the laboratory report.

PROCEDURE G—MUSCLES OF THE FORELIMB

1. Place the cat in the dissecting tray with its ventral surface up.

2. Remove any remaining fat and connective tissue from a forelimb to expose the muscles.

Figure 24.11 Muscles of the cat's shoulder and back.

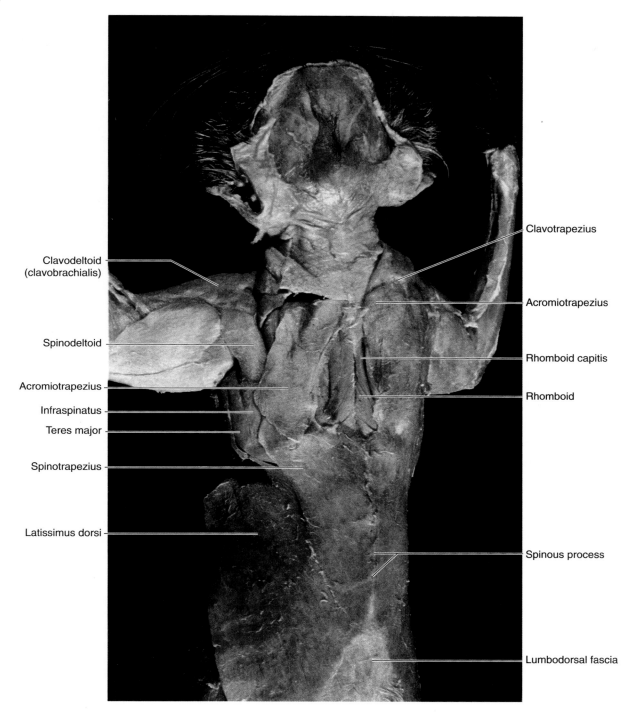

Clavodeltoid (clavobrachialis)

Spinodeltoid

Acromiotrapezius

Infraspinatus

Teres major

Spinotrapezius

Latissimus dorsi

Clavotrapezius

Acromiotrapezius

Rhomboid capitis

Rhomboid

Spinous process

Lumbodorsal fascia

3. Study figure 24.13*a*, and then locate and dissect the following muscles from the medial surface of the upper forelimb:

epitrochlearis

triceps brachii

4. Transect the pectoral muscles (pectoantebrachialis, pectoralis major, and pectoralis minor) and lift aside their cut edges.

5. Study figures 24.13*b* and 24.14, and then locate and dissect the following muscles:

coracobrachialis

biceps brachii

long head of the triceps brachii

medial head of the triceps brachii

6. Study figures 24.15*a* and 24.16, which show the lateral surface of the upper forelimb.

Figure 24.12 Deep muscles of the cat's back.

Clavotrapezius (reflected)
Supraspinatus
Rhomboid capitis
Serratus ventralis
Acromiotrapezius (reflected)
Rhomboid

Table 24.4 Muscles of the Shoulder and Back

Muscle	Origin	Insertion	Action
Clavotrapezius	Occipital bone of skull and spines of cervical vertebrae	Clavicle	Pulls clavicle upward
Acromiotrapezius	Spines of cervical and thoracic vertebrae	Spine and acromion process of scapula	Pulls scapula upward
Spinotrapezius	Spines of thoracic vertebrae	Spine of scapula	Pulls scapula upward and back
Clavodeltoid	Clavicle	Ulna near semilunar notch	Flexes forelimb
Acromiodeltoid	Acromion process of scapula	Proximal end of humerus	Flexes and rotates forelimb
Spinodeltoid	Spine of scapula	Proximal end of humerus	Flexes and rotates forelimb
Latissimus dorsi	Thoracic and lumbar vertebrae	Proximal end of humerus	Pulls forelimb upward and back
Supraspinatus	Fossa above spine of scapula	Greater tubercle of humerus	Extends forelimb
Infraspinatus	Fossa below spine of scapula	Greater tubercle of humerus	Rotates forelimb
Teres major	Posterior border of scapula	Proximal end of humerus	Rotates forelimb
Rhomboid	Spines of cervical and thoracic vertebrae	Medial border of scapula	Pulls scapula back
Rhomboid capitis	Occipital bone of skull	Medial border of scapula	Pulls scapula forward
Splenius	Fascia of neck	Occipital bone	Turns and raises head

7. Locate the lateral head of the triceps muscle, transect it, and lift aside its cut edges.
8. Study figure 24.15*b*. Locate and dissect the following deeper muscles:

   anconeus
   brachialis

9. Separate the muscles in the lower forelimb into an *extensor group* (fig. 24.15*a*) and a *flexor group* (fig. 24.13*a*). Generally, the extensors are located on the posterior surface of the lower forelimb, and the flexors are located on the anterior surface. A thick, tough layer of fascia

Figure 24.13 (*a*) Superficial muscles of the cat's medial forelimb. (*b*) Deep muscles of the medial forelimb.

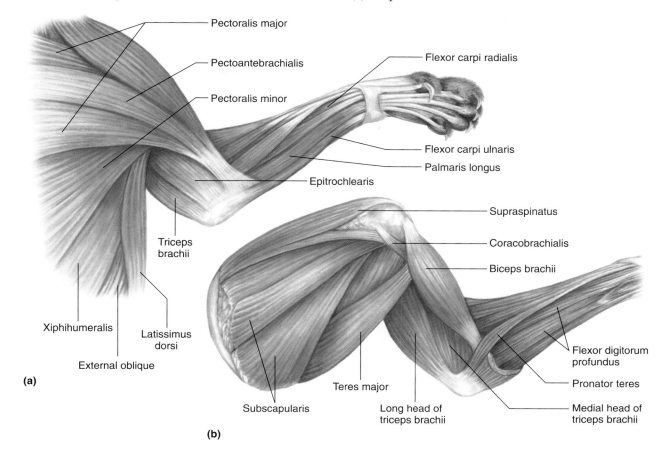

Pectoralis major

Pectoantebrachialis

Pectoralis minor

Flexor carpi radialis

Flexor carpi ulnaris

Palmaris longus

Epitrochlearis

Supraspinatus

Coracobrachialis

Biceps brachii

Triceps brachii

Xiphihumeralis

Latissimus dorsi

External oblique

(a)

Subscapularis

Teres major

Long head of triceps brachii

Flexor digitorum profundus

Pronator teres

Medial head of triceps brachii

(b)

Figure 24.14 Deep muscles of the cat's right medial forelimb.

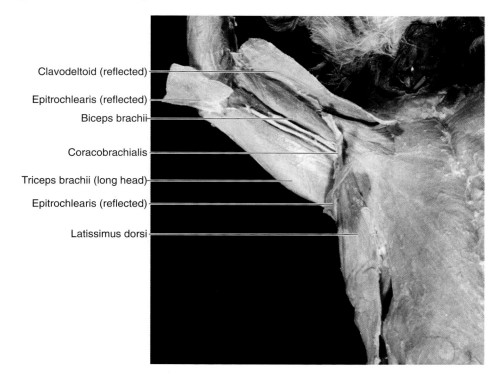

Clavodeltoid (reflected)

Epitrochlearis (reflected)

Biceps brachii

Coracobrachialis

Triceps brachii (long head)

Epitrochlearis (reflected)

Latissimus dorsi

Figure 24.15 (*a*) Superficial muscles of the cat's lateral forelimb. (*b*) Deep muscles of the lateral forelimb.

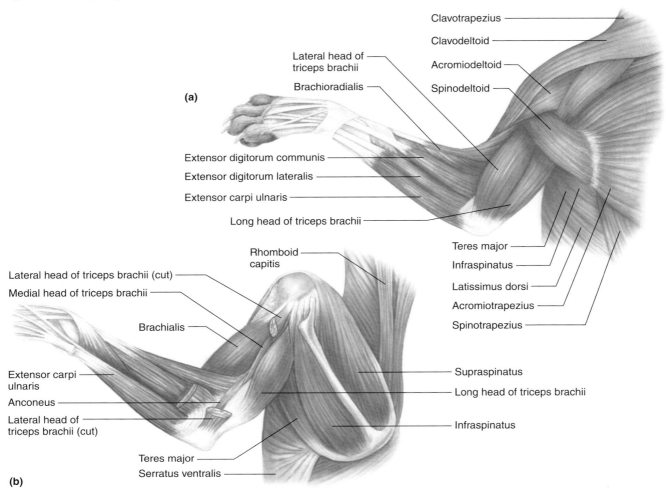

(a)

Clavotrapezius
Clavodeltoid
Acromiodeltoid
Spinodeltoid

Lateral head of triceps brachii
Brachioradialis

Extensor digitorum communis
Extensor digitorum lateralis
Extensor carpi ulnaris
Long head of triceps brachii

Teres major
Infraspinatus
Latissimus dorsi
Acromiotrapezius
Spinotrapezius

Rhomboid capitis

Lateral head of triceps brachii (cut)
Medial head of triceps brachii

Brachialis

Extensor carpi ulnaris
Anconeus
Lateral head of triceps brachii (cut)

Teres major
Serratus ventralis

Supraspinatus
Long head of triceps brachii

Infraspinatus

(b)

Table 24.5 Muscles of the Forelimb

Muscle	Origin	Insertion	Action
Coracobrachialis	Coracoid process of scapula	Proximal end of humerus	Adducts forelimb
Epitrochlearis	Fascia of latissimus dorsi	Olecranon process of ulna	Extends forelimb
Biceps brachii	Border of glenoid cavity of scapula	Radial tuberosity of radius	Flexes forelimb
Triceps brachii			
Lateral head	Deltoid tuberosity of humerus	Olecranon process of ulna	Extends forelimb
Long head	Border of glenoid cavity of scapula	Olecranon process of ulna	Extends forelimb
Medial head	Shaft of humerus	Olecranon process of ulna	Extends forelimb
Anconeus	Lateral epicondyle of humerus	Olecranon process of ulna	Extends forelimb
Brachialis	Lateral surface of humerus	Proximal end of ulna	Flexes forelimb
Brachioradialis	Shaft of humerus	Distal end of radius	Supinates lower forelimb
Extensor digitorum communis	Lateral surface of humerus	Digits two to five	Extends digits
Extensor digitorum lateralis	Lateral surface of humerus	Digits two to five	Extends digits
Extensor carpi ulnaris	Lateral epicondyle of humerus and ulna	Fifth metacarpal	Extends wrist
Flexor carpi ulnaris	Medial epicondyle of humerus	Carpals	Flexes wrist
Palmaris longus	Medial epicondyle of humerus	Digits	Flexes digits
Flexor carpi radialis	Medial epicondyle of humerus	Second and third metacarpals	Flexes metacarpals
Pronator teres	Medial epicondyle of humerus	Radius	Pronates lower forelimb
Flexor digitorum profundus	Radius, ulna, and medial epicondyle of humerus	Distal phalanges	Flexes digits

Figure 24.16 Superficial muscles of the cat's left lateral forelimb, dorsal view.

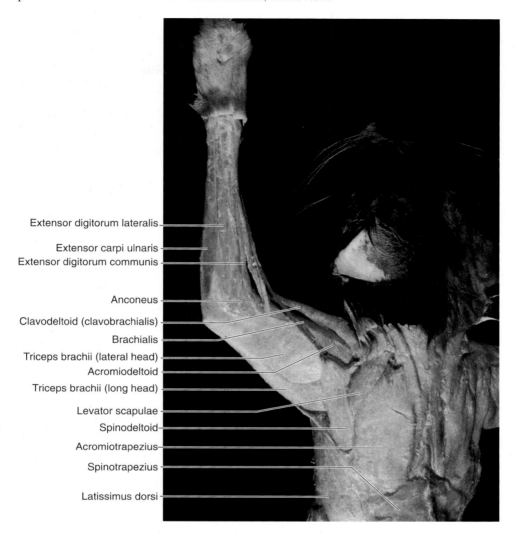

Extensor digitorum lateralis
Extensor carpi ulnaris
Extensor digitorum communis

Anconeus
Clavodeltoid (clavobrachialis)
Brachialis
Triceps brachii (lateral head)
Acromiodeltoid
Triceps brachii (long head)
Levator scapulae
Spinodeltoid
Acromiotrapezius
Spinotrapezius
Latissimus dorsi

(antebrachial fascia) surrounds the forelimb. Remove this fascia to expose and dissect the following muscles:

brachioradialis

extensor digitorum communis

extensor digitorum lateralis

extensor carpi ulnaris

flexor carpi ulnaris

palmaris longus

flexor carpi radialis

pronator teres

10. Transect the flexor carpi ulnaris, palmaris longus, and flexor carpi radialis to expose the flexor digitorum profundus.
11. See table 24.5 for the origins, insertions, and actions of these muscles of the forelimb.
12. Complete Part D of the laboratory report.

PROCEDURE H—MUSCLES OF THE HIP AND HINDLIMB

1. Place the cat in the dissecting tray with its ventral surface up.
2. Remove any remaining fat and connective tissue from the hip and hindlimb to expose the muscles.
3. Study figures 24.17a and 24.18, and then locate and dissect the following muscles from the medial surface of the thigh:

    sartorius

    gracilis

4. Using scissors, transect the sartorius and gracilis, and lift aside their cut edges to observe the deeper muscles of the thigh.

Figure 24.17 (*a*) Superficial muscles of the cat's medial hindlimb. (*b*) Deep muscles of the medial hindlimb.

Rectus abdominis

External oblique

Vastus medialis

Adductor longus

Sartorius

Adductor femoris

Gracilis

Semitendinosus

(a)

Tensor fasciae latae

Rectus femoris

Adductor longus

Vastus medialis

Adductor femoris

Semimembranosus

Semitendinosus

(b)

5. Study figures 24.17*b* and 24.19, and then locate and dissect the following muscles:

rectus femoris
vastus medialis
adductor longus
adductor femoris
semimembranosus
semitendinosus
tensor fasciae latae

6. Transect the tensor fasciae latae and rectus femoris muscles and turn their ends aside. Locate the *vastus intermedius* and *vastus lateralis* muscles beneath (fig. 24.20). (*Note:* In some specimens, the vastus intermedius, vastus lateralis, and vastus medialis muscles are closely united by connective tissue and are difficult to separate.)

7. Study figures 24.21*a* and 24.22, and then locate and dissect the following muscles from the lateral surface of the hip and thigh:

biceps femoris
caudofemoralis
gluteus maximus

8. Using scissors, transect the tensor fasciae latae and biceps femoris, and lift aside their cut edges to observe the deeper muscles of the thigh.

9. Locate and dissect the following muscles:

tenuissimus
gluteus medius

(*Note:* The tenuissimus muscle and the sciatic nerve may adhere tightly to the dorsal surface of the biceps femoris muscle. Take care to avoid cutting these structures.)

10. On the lateral surface of the lower hindlimb (figs. 24.21 and 24.23), locate and dissect the following muscles:

gastrocnemius
soleus
tibialis anterior
fibularis (peroneus) group

11. See table 24.6 for the origins, insertions, and actions of these muscles of the hip and hindlimb.

12. Complete Part E of the laboratory report.

Figure 24.18 Superficial muscles of the cat's hindlimb, medial view.

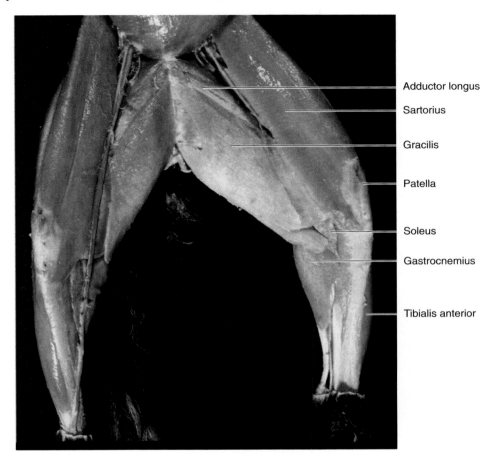

Adductor longus

Sartorius

Gracilis

Patella

Soleus

Gastrocnemius

Tibialis anterior

Figure 24.19 Deep muscles of the cat's hindlimb, medial view.

Sartorius (reflected)

Vastus lateralis

Rectus femoris

Adductor longus

Vastus medialis
Adductor femoris
Sartorius (reflected)
Semimembranosus
Gracilis (reflected)
Semitendinosus

Gracilis (reflected)

Figure 24.20 Other deep muscles of the cat's thigh, medial view.

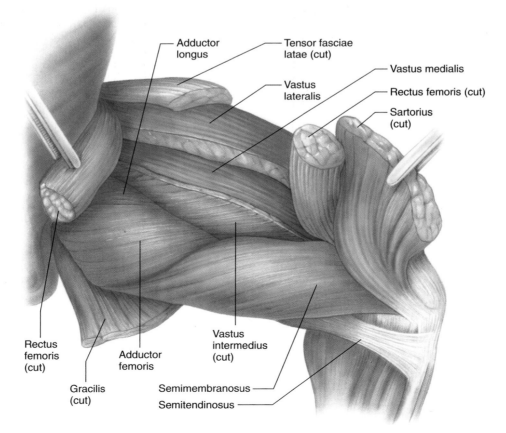

Adductor longus

Tensor fasciae latae (cut)

Vastus lateralis

Vastus medialis

Rectus femoris (cut)

Sartorius (cut)

Rectus femoris (cut)

Adductor femoris

Gracilis (cut)

Vastus intermedius (cut)

Semimembranosus

Semitendinosus

Figure 24.21 (*a*) Superficial muscles of the cat's lateral hindlimb. (*b*) Deep muscles of the lateral hindlimb.

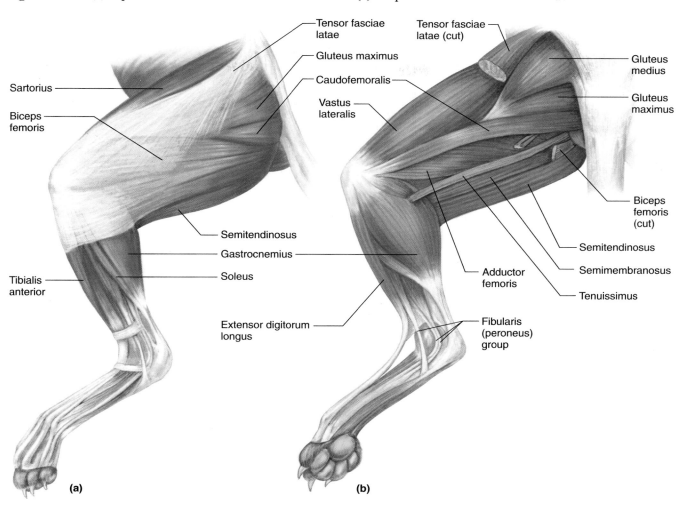

Figure 24.22 Muscles of the cat's hindlimb, lateral view.

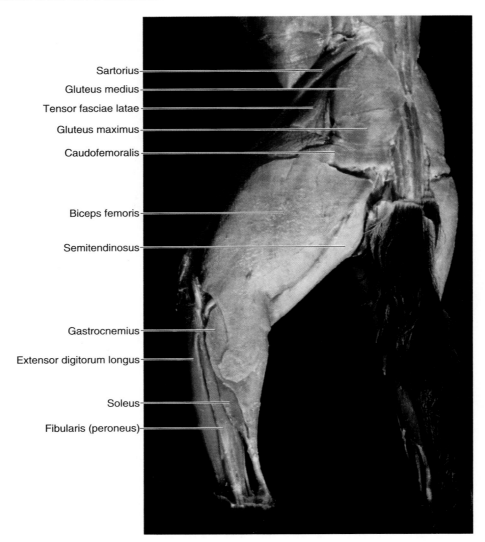

Sartorius

Gluteus medius

Tensor fasciae latae

Gluteus maximus

Caudofemoralis

Biceps femoris

Semitendinosus

Gastrocnemius

Extensor digitorum longus

Soleus

Fibularis (peroneus)

Figure 24.23 Deep muscles of the cat's hindlimb, lateral view.

Tensor fasciae latae
Sartorius

Sciatic nerve
Biceps femoris (reflected)
Semimembranosus
Tenuissimus

Semitendinosus

Gastrocnemius

Soleus
Fibularis (peroneus) tertius
Extensor digitorum longus

Table 24.6 Muscles of the Hip and Hindlimb

Muscle	Origin	Insertion	Action
Sartorius	Crest of ilium	Fascia of knee and proximal end of tibia	Rotates and extends hindlimb
Gracilis	Symphysis pubis and ischium	Proximal end of tibia	Adducts hindlimb
Quadriceps femoris			
Vastus lateralis	Shaft of femur and greater trochanter	Patella	Extends hindlimb
Vastus intermedius	Shaft of femur	Patella	Extends hindlimb
Rectus femoris	Ilium	Patella	Extends hindlimb
Vastus medialis	Shaft of femur	Patella	Extends hindlimb
Adductor longus	Pubis	Proximal end of femur	Adducts hindlimb
Adductor femoris	Pubis and ischium	Shaft of femur	Adducts hindlimb
Semimembranosus	Ischial tuberosity	Medial epicondyle of femur	Extends thigh
Tensor fasciae latae	Ilium	Fascia of thigh	Extends thigh
Biceps femoris	Ischial tuberosity	Patella and tibia	Abducts thigh and flexes lower hindlimb
Tenuissimus	Second caudal vertebra	Tibia and fascia of biceps femoris	Abducts thigh and flexes lower hindlimb
Semitendinosus	Ischial tuberosity	Crest of tibia	Flexes lower hindlimb
Caudofemoralis	Caudal vertebrae	Patella	Abducts thigh and extends lower hindlimb
Gluteus maximus	Sacral and caudal vertebrae	Greater trochanter of femur	Abducts thigh
Gluteus medius	Ilium, and sacral and caudal vertebrae	Greater trochanter of femur	Abducts thigh
Gastrocnemius	Lateral and medial epicondyles of femur	Calcaneus	Extends foot
Soleus	Proximal end of fibula	Calcaneus	Extends foot
Tibialis anterior	Proximal end of tibia and fibula	First metatarsal	Flexes foot
Fibularis (peroneus) group	Shaft of fibula	Metatarsals	Flexes foot

Notes

Name _____

Date _____

Section _____

CAT DISSECTION: MUSCULATURE

PART A

Complete the following statements:

1. The _____ muscle of the human is homologous to the sternomastoid muscle of the cat.
2. The _____ muscle elevates the mandible in the human and in the cat.
3. Two muscles of the cat that are inserted on the hyoid bone are the _____ and the

    _____ .

PART B

Complete the following:
Name two muscles that are found in the thoracic wall of the cat but are absent in the human.

1. _____
2. _____

Name two muscles that are found in the thoracic wall of the cat and the human.

3. _____
4. _____

Name four muscles that are found in the abdominal wall of the cat and the human.

5. _____
6. _____
7. _____
8. _____

PART C

Complete the following:
Name three muscles of the cat that together correspond to the trapezius muscle in the human.

1. _____
2. _____
3. _____

Name three muscles of the cat that together correspond to the deltoid muscle in the human.

4. _____
5. _____
6. _____

Name the muscle in the cat and in the human that occupies the fossa above the spine of the scapula.

7. _____

Name the muscle in the cat and in the human that occupies the fossa below the spine of the scapula.

8. _____

Name two muscles found in the cat and in the human that can rotate the forelimb.

9. _____

10. _____

PART D

Complete the following:
Name two muscles found in the cat and in the human that can flex the forelimb.

1. _____

2. _____

Name a muscle found in the cat but absent in the human that can extend the forelimb.

3. _____

Name a muscle that has three heads, can extend the forelimb, and is found in the cat and in the human.

4. _____

PART E

Each of the muscles in figure 24.24 is found both in the cat and in the human. Identify each of the numbered muscles in the figure by placing its name in the space next to its number.

_____

Figure 24.24 Identify the numbered muscles that occur in both the cat and the human.

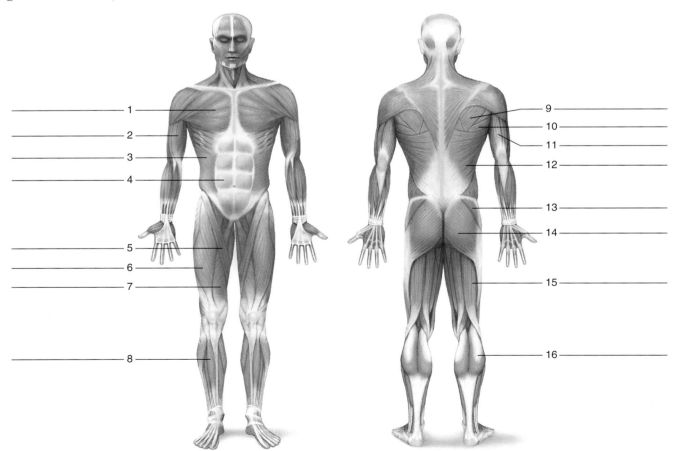

NERVOUS TISSUE AND NERVES

Nervous tissue, which occurs in the brain, spinal cord, and nerves, contains neurons and neuroglial cells. The neurons are the basic structural and functional units of the nervous system involved in decision-making processes, detecting stimuli, and conducting messages. The neuroglial cells perform various supportive and protective functions for neurons.

PURPOSE OF THE EXERCISE

To review the characteristics of nervous tissue and to observe neurons, neuroglial cells, and various features of the nerves.

LEARNING OBJECTIVES

After completing this exercise, you should be able to

1. Describe the general characteristics of nervous tissue.
2. Distinguish between neurons and neuroglial cells.
3. Identify the major structures of a neuron and a nerve.

PROCEDURE

1. Review the sections entitled "General Functions of the Nervous System" and "Classification of Neurons and Neuroglial Cells" in chapter 10 of the textbook.
2. As a review activity, label figures 25.1 and 25.2.

3. Complete Parts A and B of Laboratory Report 25.
4. Obtain a prepared microscope slide of a spinal cord smear. Using low-power magnification, search the slide and locate the relatively large, deeply stained cell bodies of motor neurons (multipolar neurons).
5. Observe a single motor neuron, using high-power magnification, and note the following features:

   cell body

   nucleus

   nucleolus

   chromatophilic substance (Nissl bodies)

   neurofibrils (threadlike structures extending into the nerve fibers)

   dendrites

   axon (nerve fiber)

   Compare the slide to the neuron model and to figure 25.3. You also may note small, darkly stained nuclei of neuroglial cells around the motor neuron.
6. Sketch and label a single motor (efferent) neuron in the space provided in Part C of the laboratory report.
7. Obtain a prepared microscope slide of a dorsal root ganglion. Search the slide and locate a cluster of sensory neuron cell bodies. You also may note bundles of nerve fibers passing among groups of neuron cell bodies (fig. 25.4).
8. Sketch and label a single sensory (afferent) neuron cell body in the space provided in Part C of the laboratory report.
9. Obtain a prepared microscope slide of neuroglial cells. Search the slide and locate some darkly stained astrocytes with numerous long, slender processes (fig. 25.5).
10. Sketch a single neuroglial cell in the space provided in Part C of the laboratory report.
11. Obtain a prepared microscope slide of a nerve. Locate the cross section of the nerve and note the many round nerve fibers inside. Also note the dense layer of connective tissue (perineurium) that encircles the nerve fibers and holds them together in a bundle. The individual nerve fibers are surrounded by a layer of more delicate connective tissue (endoneurium) (fig. 25.6).

Figure 25.1 Label this diagram of a motor neuron.

Chromatophilic substance
(Nissl bodies)

5

6

1

Neurofibrils

2

Axonal hillock

Impulse

7

3

Nucleus

4

Myelin (cut)

Figure 25.2 Label the features of the myelinated axon (nerve fiber).

1 _____

2 _____

3 _____

Neurofibril

4 _____

Figure 25.3 Micrograph of a multipolar neuron and neuroglial cells from a spinal cord smear (100× micrograph enlarged to 600×).

Neuroglial cells

Dendrites

Cell body

Nucleolus

Nucleus

Axon (nerve fiber)

Figure 25.4 Micrograph of a dorsal root ganglion (50× micrograph enlarged to 100×).

Sensory neuron cell bodies

Nerve fibers

Figure 25.6 Cross section of a bundle of neurons within a nerve (400×).

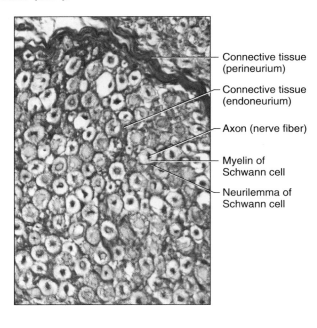

Connective tissue (perineurium)

Connective tissue (endoneurium)

Axon (nerve fiber)

Myelin of Schwann cell

Neurilemma of Schwann cell

Figure 25.5 Micrograph of astrocytes (250× micrograph enlarged to 1,000×).

Blood vessel

Astrocyte

Figure 25.7 Longitudinal section of a nerve (250× micrograph enlarged to 2,000×).

Node of Ranvier
Axon (nerve fiber)
Neurilemma of Schwann cell
Myelin of Schwann cell

12. Using high-power magnification, observe a single nerve fiber and note the following features:

    central axon

    myelin around the axon (actually, most of the myelin may have been dissolved and lost during the slide preparation)

    neurilemma

13. Sketch and label a single nerve fiber with Schwann cell (cross section) in the space provided in Part D of the laboratory report.

14. Locate the longitudinal section of the nerve on the slide (fig. 25.7). Note the following:

    central axons

    myelin of Schwann cells

    neurilemma of Schwann cells

    nodes of Ranvier

15. Sketch and label a single nerve fiber with Schwann cell (longitudinal section) in the space provided in Part D of the laboratory report.

LEARNING EXTENSION

O btain a prepared microscope slide of Purkinje cells. To locate these neurons, search the slide for large, flask-shaped cell bodies. Note that each cell body has one or two large, thick dendrites that give rise to branching networks of fibers. These cells are found in a particular region of the brain (cerebellar cortex).

NOTES

NERVOUS TISSUE AND NERVES

PART A

Match the terms in column A with the descriptions in column B. Place the letter of your choice in the space provided.

Column A

a. Astrocyte
b. Axon
c. Chromatophilic substance (Nissl bodies)
d. Collateral
e. Dendrite
f. Myelin
g. Neurilemma
h. Neurofibrils

Column B

_____ 1. Sheath of Schwann cell containing cytoplasm and nucleus that encloses myelin

_____ 2. Corresponds to rough endoplasmic reticulum in other cells

_____ 3. Network of fine threads within nerve fiber

_____ 4. Substance of Schwann cell composed of lipoprotein

_____ 5. Neuron process with many branches that conducts an impulse toward the cell body

_____ 6. Branch of an axon

_____ 7. Star-shaped neuroglial cell between neurons and blood vessels

_____ 8. Nerve fiber arising from a slight elevation of the cell body that conducts an impulse away from the cell body

PART B

Match the terms in column A with the descriptions in column B. Place the letter of your choice in the space provided.

Column A

a. Effector
b. Ependyma
c. Ganglion
d. Interneuron
e. Microglia
f. Motor (efferent) neuron
g. Oligodendrocyte
h. Sensory (afferent) neuron

Column B

_____ 1. Transmits impulse from sensory to motor neuron within central nervous system

_____ 2. Transmits impulse out of the brain or spinal cord to effectors

_____ 3. Transmits impulse into brain or spinal cord from receptors

_____ 4. Myelin-forming neuroglial cell in brain and spinal cord

_____ 5. Phagocytic neuroglial cell

_____ 6. Structure capable of responding to motor impulse

_____ 7. Specialized mass of neuron cell bodies outside the brain or spinal cord

_____ 8. Covers the inside spaces of the ventricles

PART C

1. Sketch a single motor neuron. Label the cell body, nucleus, nucleolus, and cell processes (dendrite and axon).

2. Sketch and label a single sensory neuron cell body.

3. Sketch a single neuroglial cell.

PART D

1. Sketch and label a single nerve fiber with Schwann cell (cross section).

2. Sketch and label a single nerve fiber with Schwann cell (longitudinal section).

MENINGES AND SPINAL CORD

MATERIALS NEEDED

Textbook
Compound light microscope
Prepared microscope slide of a spinal cord cross section
    with spinal nerve roots
Spinal cord model

For Demonstration:

Preserved spinal cord with meninges intact

The meninges consist of layers of membranes located between the bones of the skull and vertebral column and the soft tissues of the central nervous system. They include the dura mater, the arachnoid mater, and the pia mater.

The spinal cord is a column of nerve fibers that extends down through the vertebral canal. Together with the brain, it makes up the central nervous system.

Neurons within the spinal cord provide a two-way communication system between the brain and body parts outside the central nervous system. The cord also contains the processing centers for spinal reflexes.

PURPOSE OF THE EXERCISE

To review the characteristics of the meninges and the spinal cord and to observe the major features of these structures.

LEARNING OBJECTIVES

After completing this exercise, you should be able to

1. Name the layers of the meninges and describe the structure of each.
2. Identify the major features of the spinal cord.
3. Locate the ascending and descending tracts of the spinal cord.

PROCEDURE A—MENINGES

1. Review the section entitled "Meninges" in chapter 11 of the textbook.
2. Complete Part A of Laboratory Report 26.

DEMONSTRATION

Observe the preserved section of spinal cord. Note the heavy covering of dura mater, which is firmly attached to the cord on each side by a set of ligaments (denticulate ligaments) originating in the pia mater. The intermediate layer of meninges, the arachnoid mater, is devoid of blood vessels, but in a live human being, the space beneath this layer contains cerebrospinal fluid. The pia mater, which is closely attached to the surface of the spinal cord, contains many blood vessels. What are the functions of these layers?

_____

_____

_____

_____

PROCEDURE B—STRUCTURE OF THE SPINAL CORD

1. Review the section entitled "Spinal Cord" in chapter 11 of the textbook.
2. As a review activity, label figures 26.1 and 26.2. Study figure 26.3.
3. Complete Parts B and C of the laboratory report.
4. Obtain a prepared microscope slide of a spinal cord cross section. Use the low power of the microscope to locate the following features:

posterior median sulcus
anterior median fissure
central canal
gray matter
    gray commissure
    posterior horn
    lateral horn
    anterior horn
white matter
    posterior funiculus
    lateral funiculus
    anterior funiculus

Figure 26.1 Label the features of the spinal cord and the surrounding structures.

Posterior/Dorsal

Spinous process

(matter)

(matter)

1

2

6

7

Dorsal root ganglion

3

Spinal nerve

4

Arachnoid mater

Pia mater

5

Dura mater

Anterior/Ventral

Figure 26.2 Label this cross section of the spinal cord, including the features of the white and gray matter.

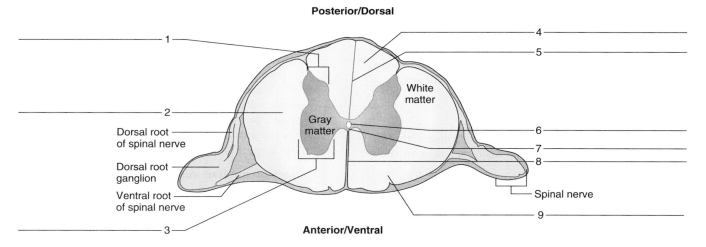

Posterior/Dorsal

1

4

5

2

White
matter

Gray
matter

Dorsal root
of spinal nerve

Dorsal root
ganglion

6

7

8

Ventral root
of spinal nerve

Spinal nerve

3

9

Anterior/Ventral

Figure 26.3 Major ascending and descending tracts within a cross section of the spinal cord. Ascending tracts are in orange, descending tracts in tan, and are shown only on one side. This pattern varies with the level of the spinal cord. This pattern is representative of the midcervical region. (*Note:* These tracts are not visible as individually stained structures on microscope slides.)

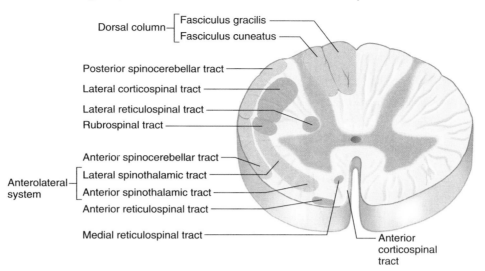

Dorsal column ⎡ Fasciculus gracilis
⎣ Fasciculus cuneatus

Posterior spinocerebellar tract

Lateral corticospinal tract

Lateral reticulospinal tract

Rubrospinal tract

Anterior spinocerebellar tract

Anterolateral system ⎡ Lateral spinothalamic tract
⎣ Anterior spinothalamic tract

Anterior reticulospinal tract

Medial reticulospinal tract

Anterior corticospinal tract

roots of spinal nerve
   dorsal roots
   dorsal root ganglia
   ventral roots

5. Observe the model of the spinal cord, and locate the features listed in step 4.
6. Complete Part D of the laboratory report.

Web Quest

Describe the development of the nervous system, and review the brain, cranial nerves, spinal cord, and CSF. Search these at
www.mhhe.com/shier11
Click on Student Edition. Click on Martin Lab Manual, Web Quest.

NOTES

MENINGES AND SPINAL CORD

PART A

Match the terms in column A with the descriptions in column B. Place the letter of your choice in the space provided.

Column A		Column B
a.	Arachnoid mater	_____ 1. Band of pia mater that attaches dura mater to cord
b.	Denticulate ligament	_____ 2. Channel through which venous blood flows
c.	Dural sinus	_____ 3. Outermost layer of meninges
d.	Dura mater	_____ 4. Follows irregular contours of spinal cord surface
e.	Epidural space	_____ 5. Contains cerebrospinal fluid
f.	Pia mater	_____ 6. Thin, weblike middle membrane
g.	Subarachnoid space	_____ 7. Separates dura mater from bone of vertebra

PART B

Complete the following statements:

1. Each of the thirty-one segments of the spinal cord gives rise to a pair of _____ .

2. The bulge in the spinal cord that gives off nerves to the upper limbs is called the _____ .

3. The bulge in the spinal cord that gives off nerves to the lower limbs is called the _____ .

4. The _____ is a groove that extends the length of the spinal cord posteriorly.

5. In a spinal cord cross section, the posterior _____ of the gray matter resemble the upper wings of a butterfly.

6. The cell bodies of motor neurons are found in the _____ horns of the spinal cord.

7. The _____ connects the gray matter on the left and right sides of the spinal cord.

8. The _____ in the gray commissure of the spinal cord contains cerebrospinal fluid and is continuous with the ventricles of the brain.

9. The white matter of the spinal cord is divided into anterior, lateral, and posterior _____ .

10. The longitudinal bundles of nerve fibers within the spinal cord comprise major nerve pathways called _____ .

11. Collectively, the dura mater, arachnoid mater, and pia mater are called the _____ .

PART C

Match the nerve tracts in column A with the descriptions in column B. Place the letter of your choice in the space provided.

Column A

a.   Corticospinal
b.   Fasciculus gracilis
c.   Lateral spinothalamic
d.   Posterior spinocerebellar
e.   Reticulospinal

Column B

_____   1.   Ascending tract to the brain to interpret touch, pressure, and body movements

_____   2.   Descending tract whose fibers conduct motor impulses to sweat glands and muscles to control tone

_____   3.   Descending tract whose fibers conduct motor impulses to skeletal muscles

_____   4.   Ascending tract to the cerebellum necessary for coordination of skeletal muscles

_____   5.   Ascending tract to the brain to give rise to sensations of temperature and pain

PART D

Identify the features indicated in the spinal cord cross section of figure 26.4.

1.   _____   5.   _____

2.   _____   6.   _____

3.   _____   7.   _____

4.   _____   8.   _____

Figure 26.4   Micrograph of a spinal cord cross section with spinal nerve roots (35×). Identify the features, using the terms provided.

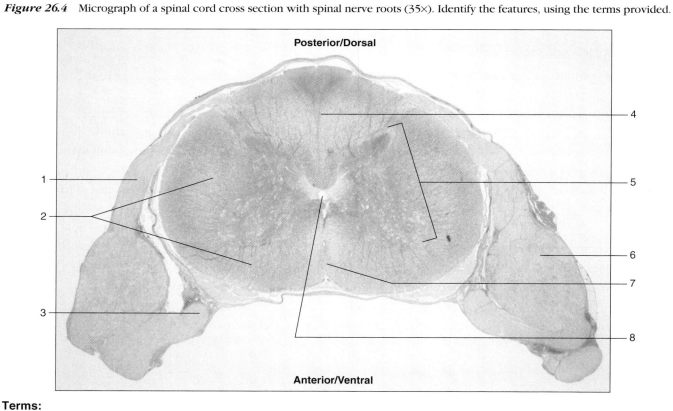

Terms:

Anterior median fissure	Dorsal root ganglion	Gray matter	Ventral root of spinal nerve
Central canal	Dorsal root of spinal nerve	Posterior median sulcus	White matter

224

REFLEX ARC AND REFLEXES

MATERIALS NEEDED

Textbook
Rubber percussion hammer

A reflex arc represents the simplest type of nerve pathway found in the nervous system. This pathway begins with a receptor at the dendrite end of a sensory (afferent) neuron. The sensory neuron leads into the central nervous system and may communicate with one or more interneurons. Some of these interneurons, in turn, communicate with motor (efferent) neurons, whose axons (nerve fibers) lead outward to effectors.

Thus, when a sensory receptor is stimulated by some kind of change occurring inside or outside the body, nerve impulses may pass through a reflex arc, and, as a result, effectors may respond. Such an automatic, subconscious response is called a reflex.

Most reflexes demonstrated in this lab are stretch reflexes. When a muscle is stretched by a tap over its tendon, stretch receptors (proprioceptors) called *muscle spindles* are stretched within the muscle, which initiates an impulse over a reflex arc. A sensory (afferent) neuron conducts an impulse from the muscle spindle into the gray matter of the spinal cord, where it synapses with a motor (efferent) neuron, which conducts the impulse to the effector muscle. The stretched muscle responds by contracting to resist or reverse further stretching. These stretch reflexes are important to maintain proper posture, balance, and movements. Observations of many of these reflexes in clinical tests on patients may indicate damage to a level of the spinal cord or peripheral nerves of the particular reflex arc.

PURPOSE OF THE EXERCISE

To review the characteristics of reflex arcs and reflex behavior and to demonstrate some of the reflexes that occur in the human body.

LEARNING OBJECTIVES

After completing this exercise, you should be able to

1. Describe a reflex arc.
2. Distinguish between a reflex arc and a reflex.
3. Identify and demonstrate several reflex actions that occur in humans.

PROCEDURE

1. Review the section entitled "Reflex Arcs" in chapter 11 of the textbook and "Proprioception" in chapter 12 of the textbook.
2. As a review activity, label figure 27.1.
3. Complete Part A of Laboratory Report 27.
4. Work with a laboratory partner to demonstrate each of the reflexes listed. (See fig. 27.2 also.) *It is important that muscles involved in the reflexes be totally relaxed in order to observe proper responses.* After each demonstration, record your observations in the table provided in Part B of the laboratory report.
   a. *Knee-jerk reflex (patellar reflex).* Have your laboratory partner sit on a table (or sturdy chair) with legs relaxed and hanging freely over the edge without touching the floor. Gently strike your partner's patellar ligament (just below the patella) with the blunt side of a rubber percussion hammer. The normal response is a moderate extension of the leg at the knee joint.
   b. *Ankle-jerk reflex.* Have your partner kneel on a chair with back toward you and with feet slightly dorsiflexed over the edge and relaxed. Gently strike the calcaneal tendon (just above its insertion on the calcaneus) with the blunt side of the rubber hammer. The normal response is plantar flexion of the foot.
   c. *Biceps-jerk reflex.* Have your partner place a bare arm bent about 90° at the elbow on the table. Press your thumb on the inside of the elbow over the tendon of the biceps brachii, and gently strike your thumb with the rubber hammer. Watch the biceps brachii for a response. The response might be a slight twitch of the muscle or flexion of the forearm at the elbow joint.
   d. *Triceps-jerk reflex.* Have your partner lie supine with an upper limb bent about 90° across the abdomen. Gently strike the tendon of the triceps brachii near its insertion just proximal to the olecranon process at the tip of the elbow. Watch the triceps brachii for a response. The response might be a slight twitch of the muscle or extension of the forearm at the elbow joint.

Figure 27.1 Label this diagram of a withdrawal (polysynaptic) reflex arc by placing the correct numbers in the spaces provided. Most reflexes demonstrated in this lab are stretch (monosynaptic) reflex arcs and lack the interneuron.

___ Effector

___ Interneuron

___ Motor (efferent) neuron

___ Receptor

___ Sensory (afferent) neuron

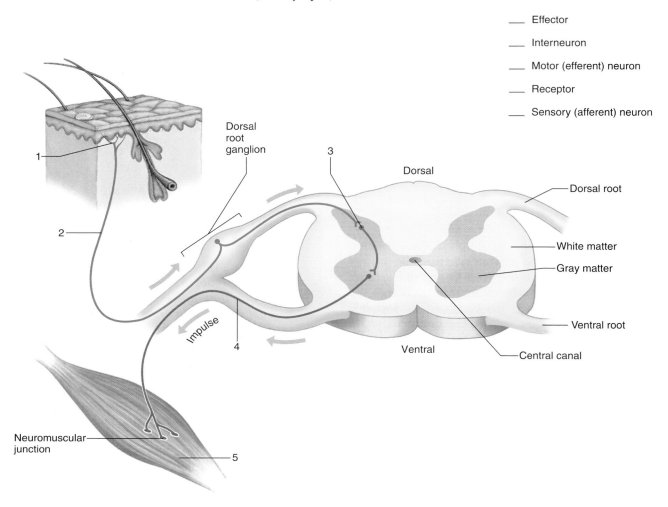

e. *Plantar reflex.* Have your partner remove a shoe and sock and lie supine with the lateral surface of the foot resting on the table. Draw the metal tip of the rubber hammer, applying firm pressure, over the sole from the heel to the base of the large toe. The normal response is flexion (curling) of the toes and plantar flexion of the foot. If the toes spread apart and dorsiflexion of the great toe occurs, the reflex is the abnormal *Babinski reflex* response (normal in infants until the nerve fibers have complete myelinization). If the Babinski reflex occurs later in life, it may indicate damage to the corticospinal tract of the CNS.

5. Complete Part B of the laboratory report.

Figure 27.2 Demonstrate each of the following reflexes: (*a*) knee-jerk reflex; (*b*) ankle-jerk reflex; (*c*) biceps-jerk reflex; (*d*) triceps-jerk reflex; and (*e*) plantar reflex.

(a) Knee-jerk reflex

(b) Ankle-jerk reflex

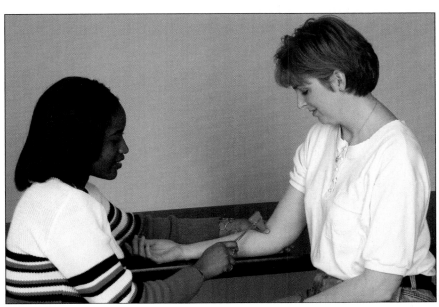

(c) Biceps-jerk reflex

Figure 27.2 Continued.

(d) Triceps-jerk reflex

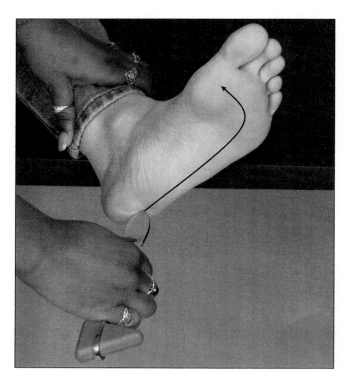

(e) Plantar reflex

Name _____

Date _____

Section _____

REFLEX ARC AND REFLEXES

PART A

Complete the following statements:

1. _____ are routes followed by nerve impulses as they pass through the nervous system.

2. Interneurons in a withdrawal reflex are located in the _____ .

3. _____ are automatic subconscious responses to external or internal stimuli.

4. Effectors of a reflex arc are glands and _____ .

5. A knee-jerk reflex employs only _____ and motor neurons.

6. The effector muscle of the knee-jerk reflex is the _____ .

7. The sensory stretch receptors of the knee-jerk reflex are located in the _____ muscle.

8. The knee-jerk reflex helps the body to maintain _____ .

9. The sensory receptors of a withdrawal reflex are located in the _____ .

10. _____ muscles in the limbs are the effectors of a withdrawal reflex.

11. The normal plantar reflex results in _____ of toes.

12. Stroking the sole of the foot in infants results in dorsiflexion and toes that spread apart, called the _____ reflex.

PART B

1. Complete the following table:

Reflex Tested	Response Observed	Effector Muscle Involved
Knee-jerk		
Ankle-jerk		
Biceps-jerk		
Triceps-jerk		
Plantar		

2. List the major events that occur in the knee-jerk reflex, from the striking of the patellar ligament to the resulting response. _____

_____

_____

_____

_____

Critical Thinking Application

What characteristics do the reflexes you demonstrated have in common?

_____

_____

_____

BRAIN AND CRANIAL NERVES

MATERIALS NEEDED

Textbook
Dissectible model of the human brain
Preserved human brain
Anatomical charts of the human brain

The brain, the largest and most complex part of the nervous system, contains nerve centers associated with sensory functions and is responsible for sensations and perceptions. It issues motor commands to skeletal muscles and carries on higher mental activities. It also functions to coordinate muscular movements, and it contains centers and nerve pathways necessary for the regulation of internal organs.

Twelve pairs of cranial nerves arise from the ventral surface of the brain and are designated by number and name. Although most of these nerves conduct both sensory and motor impulses, some contain only sensory fibers associated with special sense organs. Others are primarily composed of motor fibers and are involved with the activities of muscles and glands.

PURPOSE OF THE EXERCISE

To review the structural and functional characteristics of the human brain and cranial nerves.

LEARNING OBJECTIVES

After completing this exercise, you should be able to

1. Identify the major structures in the human brain.
2. Locate the major functional regions of the brain.
3. Identify each of the cranial nerves.
4. List the functions of each cranial nerve.

PROCEDURE A—HUMAN BRAIN

1. Review the section entitled "Brain" in chapter 11 of the textbook.
2. As a review activity, label figures 28.1, 28.2, and 28.3.
3. Complete Part A of Laboratory Report 28.

4. Observe the anatomical charts, dissectible model, and preserved specimen of the human brain. Locate each of the following features:

cerebrum
cerebral hemispheres
corpus callosum
convolutions (gyri)
sulci
    central sulcus
    lateral sulcus
fissures
    longitudinal fissure
    transverse fissure
lobes
    frontal lobe
    parietal lobe
    temporal lobe
    occipital lobe
    insula
cerebral cortex
basal nuclei (basal ganglia, a widely used clinical term)
    caudate nucleus
    putamen
    globus pallidus
ventricles
    lateral ventricles
    third ventricle
    fourth ventricle
    choroid plexuses
    cerebral aqueduct
diencephalon
    thalamus
    hypothalamus
    optic chiasma
    mammillary bodies
    pineal gland

Figure 28.1 Label this diagram by placing the correct numbers in the spaces provided.

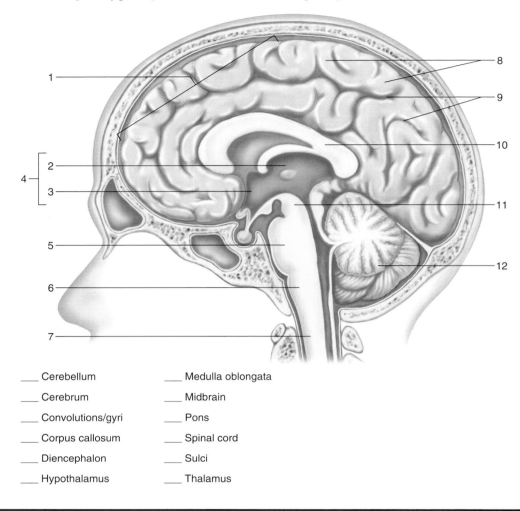

___ Cerebellum	___ Medulla oblongata
___ Cerebrum	___ Midbrain
___ Convolutions/gyri	___ Pons
___ Corpus callosum	___ Spinal cord
___ Diencephalon	___ Sulci
___ Hypothalamus	___ Thalamus

Figure 28.2 Label the lobes of the cerebrum, using the terms provided.

Terms:
Frontal lobe
Occipital lobe
Parietal lobe
Temporal lobe

Figure 28.3 Label the functional areas of the cerebrum, using the terms provided. (*Note:* These areas are not visible as distinct parts of the brain.)

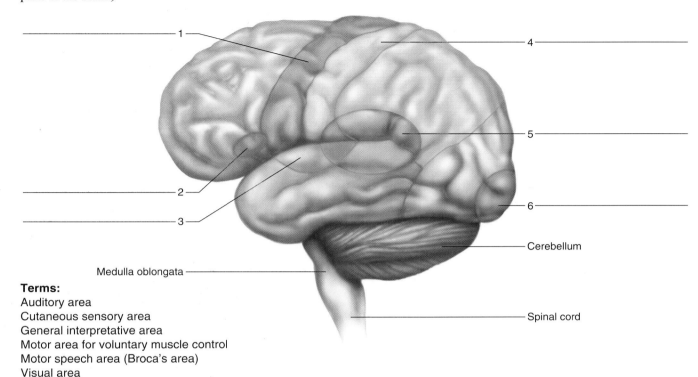

Medulla oblongata

Cerebellum

Spinal cord

Terms:
Auditory area
Cutaneous sensory area
General interpretative area
Motor area for voluntary muscle control
Motor speech area (Broca's area)
Visual area

cerebellum
>   lateral hemispheres
>   vermis
>   cerebellar cortex
>   arbor vitae
>   cerebellar peduncles

brainstem
>   midbrain
>>   cerebral aqueduct
>>   cerebral peduncles
>>   corpora quadrigemina
>   pons
>   medulla oblongata

5. Locate the labeled areas in figure 28.3 that represent the following functional regions of the cerebrum:

   motor area for voluntary muscle control

   motor speech area (Broca's area)

   cutaneous sensory area

   auditory area

   visual area

   general interpretative area

6. Complete Parts B and C of the laboratory report.

PROCEDURE B—CRANIAL NERVES

1. Review the section entitled "Cranial Nerves" in chapter 11 of the textbook.
2. As a review activity, label figure 28.4.
3. Observe the model and preserved specimen of the human brain, and locate as many of the following cranial nerves as possible:

   olfactory nerves (I)
   optic nerves (II)
   oculomotor nerves (III)
   trochlear nerves (IV)
   trigeminal nerves (V)
   abducens nerves (VI)
   facial nerves (VII)
   vestibulocochlear nerves (VIII)
   glossopharyngeal nerves (IX)
   vagus nerves (X)
   accessory nerves (XI)
   hypoglossal nerves (XII)

Figure 28.4 Provide the names of the cranial nerves in this ventral view.

(VII) Facial nerve — 7

1

2

3

4 — (IV) Trochlear nerve

5

6

8

9

10

11

12 — (XII) Hypoglossal nerve

The following mnemonic device will help you learn the twelve pairs of cranial nerves in the proper order:

Old **Op**ie **oc**casionally **tr**ies **trig**onometry, **a**nd **f**eels **very glo**omy, **vagu**e, **a**nd **hypo**active.[1]

4. Complete Part D of the laboratory report.

Web Quest

Describe the development of the nervous system, and review the brain, cranial nerves, spinal cord, and CSF. Search these at www.mhhe.com/shier11
Click on Student Edition. Click on Martin Lab Manual, Web Quest.

1. From *HAPS-EDucator*, Winter 2002. An official publication of the Human Anatomy & Physiology Society (HAPS).

Name _____

Date _____

Section _____

BRAIN AND CRANIAL NERVES

PART A

Match the terms in column A with the descriptions in column B. Place the letter of your choice in the space provided.

Column A

a.   Central sulcus
b.   Cerebral cortex
c.   Convolution (gyrus)
d.   Corpus callosum
e.   Falx cerebelli
f.   Hypothalamus
g.   Insula
h.   Medulla oblongata
i.   Midbrain
j.   Optic chiasma
k.   Pineal gland
l.   Pons

Column B

_____ 1.   Structure formed by the crossing-over of the optic nerves

_____ 2.   Part of diencephalon that forms lower walls and floor of third ventricle

_____ 3.   Cone-shaped structure attached to upper posterior portion of diencephalon

_____ 4.   Connects cerebral hemispheres

_____ 5.   Ridge on surface of cerebrum

_____ 6.   Separates frontal and parietal lobes

_____ 7.   Part of brainstem between diencephalon and pons

_____ 8.   Rounded bulge on underside of brainstem

_____ 9.   Part of brainstem continuous with the spinal cord

_____ 10.   A layer of dura mater that separates cerebellar hemispheres

_____ 11.   Cerebral lobe located deep within lateral sulcus

_____ 12.   Thin layer of gray matter on surface of cerebrum

PART B

Complete the following table:

Structure	Location	Major Functions
Broca's area		
Cardiac center		
Cerebellar peduncles		
Cerebral peduncles		
Corpora quadrigemina		
Frontal eye fields		
Hypothalamus		
Limbic system		
Respiratory center		
Reticular formation		
Thalamus		
Vasomotor center		

PART C

Identify the features indicated in the midsagittal section of the right half of the human brain in figure 28.5.

1. _____

2. _____

3. _____

4. _____

5. _____

6. _____

7. _____

8. _____

9. _____

10. _____

Figure 28.5 Identify the features on this midsagittal section of the right half of the human brain, using the terms provided.

Terms:

Brainstem	Hypothalamus
Cerebellum	Medulla oblongata
Cerebrum	Midbrain
Corpus callosum	Pons
Diencephalon	Thalamus

PART D

Indicate by name and number which cranial nerve(s) is (are) most closely associated with each of the following functions:

1. Sense of hearing _____
2. Sense of taste _____
3. Sense of sight _____
4. Sense of smell _____
5. Sense of equilibrium _____
6. Conducting sensory impulses from upper teeth _____
7. Conducting sensory impulses from lower teeth _____
8. Raising eyelids _____
9. Focusing lenses of eyes _____
10. Adjusting amount of light entering eye _____
11. Moving eyes _____
12. Stimulating salivary secretions _____
13. Movement of trapezius and sternocleidomastoid muscles _____
14. Muscular movements associated with speech _____
15. Muscular movements associated with swallowing _____

DISSECTION OF THE SHEEP BRAIN

MATERIALS NEEDED

Dissectible model of human brain
Preserved sheep brain
Dissecting tray
Dissection instruments
Long knife

For Demonstration:

Coronal sections of sheep brains

 SAFETY

- Wear disposable gloves when handling the sheep brains.
- Save or dispose of the brains as instructed.
- Wash your hands before leaving the laboratory.

Mammalian brains have many features in common. Because human brains may not be available, sheep brains often are dissected as an aid to understanding mammalian brain structure. However, as in the cat, the adaptations of the sheep differ from the adaptations of the human, so comparisons of their structural features may not be precise.

PURPOSE OF THE EXERCISE

To observe the major features of the sheep brain and to compare these features with those of the human brain.

LEARNING OBJECTIVES

After completing this exercise, you should be able to

1. Identify the major structures of the sheep brain.
2. Locate the larger cranial nerves of the sheep brain.
3. List several differences and similarities between the sheep brain and the human brain.

PROCEDURE

1. Obtain a preserved sheep brain and rinse it thoroughly in water to remove as much of the preserving fluid as possible.

2. Examine the surface of the brain for the presence of meninges. (The outermost layers of these membranes may have been lost during removal of the brain from the cranial cavity.) If meninges are present, locate the following:

   dura mater—the thick, opaque outer layer
   arachnoid mater—the delicate, transparent middle layer that is attached to the undersurface of the dura mater
   pia mater—the thin, vascular layer that adheres to the surface of the brain (should be present)

3. Remove any remaining dura mater by pulling it gently from the surface of the brain.
4. Position the brain with its ventral surface down in the dissecting tray. Study figure 29.1, and locate the following structures on the specimen:

   cerebral hemispheres
   convolutions (gyri)
   sulci
   longitudinal fissure
   frontal lobe
   parietal lobe
   temporal lobe
   occipital lobe
   cerebellum
   medulla oblongata

5. Gently separate the cerebral hemispheres along the longitudinal fissure and expose the transverse band of white fibers within the fissure that connects the hemispheres. This band is the *corpus callosum.*
6. Bend the cerebellum and medulla oblongata slightly downward and away from the cerebrum (fig. 29.2). This will expose the *pineal gland* in the upper midline and the *corpora quadrigemina,* which consists of four rounded structures associated with the midbrain.
7. Position the brain with its ventral surface upward. Study figures 29.3 and 29.4, and locate the following structures on the specimen:

   longitudinal fissure
   olfactory bulbs

Figure 29.1 Dorsal surface of the sheep brain.

Sulcus
Convolution (gyrus)
Cerebral hemisphere
Cerebellum
Medulla oblongata

Frontal lobe
Parietal lobe
Temporal lobe
Longitudinal fissure
Occipital lobe

Figure 29.2 Gently bend the cerebellum and medulla oblongata away from the cerebrum to expose the pineal gland and the corpora quadrigemina.

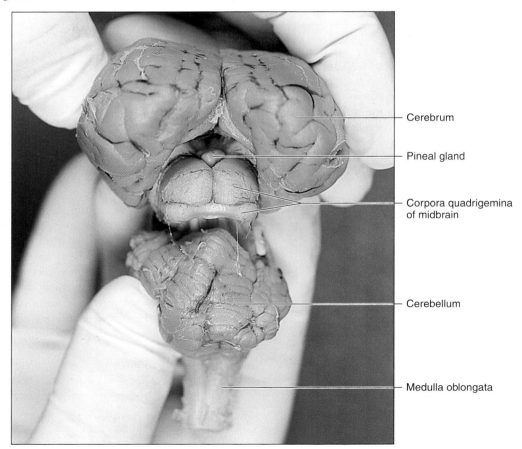

Cerebrum
Pineal gland
Corpora quadrigemina of midbrain
Cerebellum
Medulla oblongata

Figure 29.3 Lateral surface of the sheep brain.

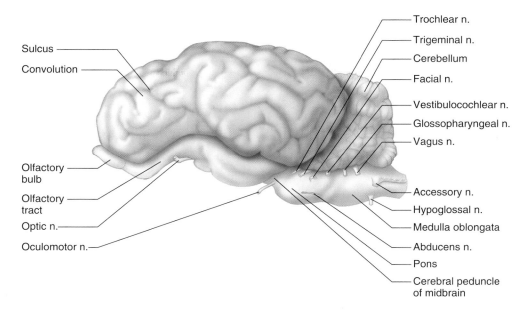

Sulcus
Convolution
Olfactory bulb
Olfactory tract
Optic n.
Oculomotor n.

Trochlear n.
Trigeminal n.
Cerebellum
Facial n.
Vestibulocochlear n.
Glossopharyngeal n.
Vagus n.
Accessory n.
Hypoglossal n.
Medulla oblongata
Abducens n.
Pons
Cerebral peduncle of midbrain

Figure 29.4 Ventral surface of the sheep brain.

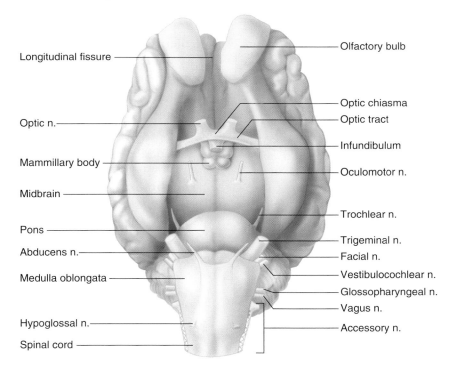

Longitudinal fissure
Optic n.
Mammillary body
Midbrain
Pons
Abducens n.
Medulla oblongata
Hypoglossal n.
Spinal cord

Olfactory bulb
Optic chiasma
Optic tract
Infundibulum
Oculomotor n.
Trochlear n.
Trigeminal n.
Facial n.
Vestibulocochlear n.
Glossopharyngeal n.
Vagus n.
Accessory n.

optic nerves
optic chiasma
optic tract
mammillary bodies
infundibulum (pituitary stalk)
midbrain
pons

8. Although some of the cranial nerves may be missing or are quite small and difficult to find, locate as many of the following as possible, using figures 29.3 and 29.4 as references:

oculomotor nerves
trochlear nerves
trigeminal nerves

241

Figure 29.5 Midsagittal section of the right half of the sheep brain dissection.

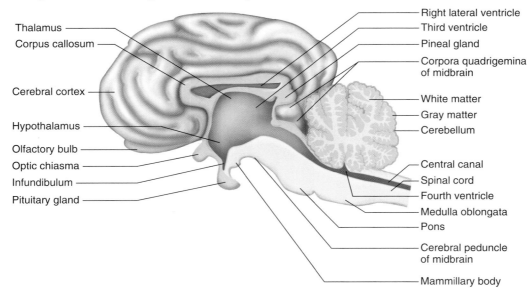

Thalamus
Corpus callosum
Cerebral cortex
Hypothalamus
Olfactory bulb
Optic chiasma
Infundibulum
Pituitary gland

Right lateral ventricle
Third ventricle
Pineal gland
Corpora quadrigemina of midbrain
White matter
Gray matter
Cerebellum
Central canal
Spinal cord
Fourth ventricle
Medulla oblongata
Pons
Cerebral peduncle of midbrain
Mammillary body

abducens nerves
facial nerves
vestibulocochlear nerves
glossopharyngeal nerves
vagus nerves
accessory nerves
hypoglossal nerves

9. Using a long, sharp knife, cut the sheep brain along the midline to produce a midsagittal section. Study figures 29.5 and 29.6, and locate the following structures on the specimen:

cerebrum
    cerebral hemisphere
    cerebral cortex
    white matter
    gray matter
olfactory bulb
corpus callosum
cerebellum
    white matter
    gray matter
lateral ventricle
third ventricle

fourth ventricle
diencephalon
    optic chiasma
    infundibulum
    pituitary gland (this structure may be missing)
    mammillary bodies
    thalamus
    hypothalamus
    pineal gland
midbrain
    corpora quadrigemina
    cerebral peduncles
pons
medulla oblongata

DEMONSTRATION

Observe a sheep brain from a coronal section. Note the longitudinal fissure, gray matter, white matter, corpus callosum, lateral ventricles, third ventricle, and thalamus.

10. Dispose of the sheep brain as directed by the laboratory instructor.
11. Complete Parts A and B of Laboratory Report 29.

Figure 29.6 Midsagittal section of the right half of the sheep brain dissection.

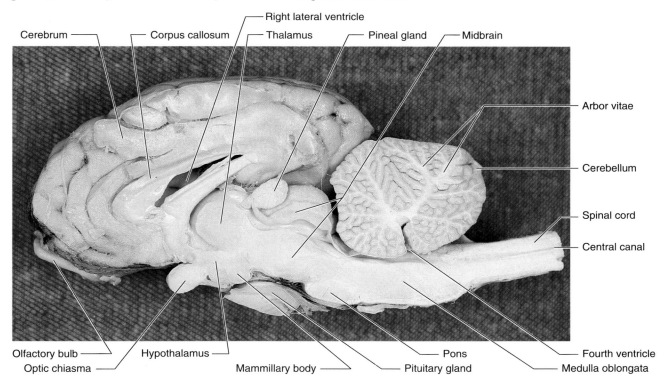

Cerebrum

Corpus callosum

Right lateral ventricle

Thalamus

Pineal gland

Midbrain

Arbor vitae

Cerebellum

Spinal cord

Central canal

Olfactory bulb

Optic chiasma

Hypothalamus

Mammillary body

Pituitary gland

Pons

Fourth ventricle

Medulla oblongata

NOTES

Name _____

Date _____

Section _____

DISSECTION OF THE SHEEP BRAIN

PART A

Answer the following questions:

1. How do the relative sizes of the sheep and human cerebral hemispheres differ? _____
   _____
   _____

2. How do the convolutions and sulci of the sheep cerebrum compare with the human cerebrum in numbers? _____
   _____
   _____

3. What is the significance of the differences you noted in your answers for questions 1 and 2? _____
   _____
   _____

4. What difference did you note in the structures of the sheep cerebellum and the human cerebellum?_____
   _____
   _____

5. How do the sizes of the olfactory bulbs of the sheep brain compare with those of the human brain?_____
   _____
   _____

6. Based on their relative sizes, which of the cranial nerves seems to be most highly developed in the sheep brain?
   _____
   _____

7. What is the significance of the observations you noted in your answers for questions 5 and 6? _____
   _____
   _____

PART B

Critical Thinking Application

Prepare a list of at least six features to illustrate ways in which the brains of sheep and humans are similar.

1. _____

2. _____

3. _____

4. _____

5. _____

6. _____

Interpret the significance of these similarities. _____

_____

_____

_____

RECEPTORS AND GENERAL SENSES

MATERIALS NEEDED

Textbook
Marking pen (washable)
Millimeter ruler
Bristle or sharp pencil
Forceps (fine points) or measuring calipers
Blunt metal probes
Three beakers (250 mL)
Warm tap water or 45°C (113°F) water bath
Cold water (ice water)
Thermometer

For Demonstration:

Prepared microscope slides of tactile (Meissner's) and
   lamellated (Pacinian) corpuscles
Compound light microscope

Sensory receptors are sensitive to changes that occur within the body and its surroundings. Each type of receptor is particularly sensitive to a distinct kind of environmental change and is much less sensitive to other forms of stimulation. When receptors are stimulated, they initiate nerve impulses that travel into the central nervous system. The raw form in which these receptors send information to the brain is called *sensation.* The way our brains interpret this information is called *perception.*

The sensory receptors found widely distributed throughout skin, muscles, joints, and visceral organs are associated with **general senses.** These senses include touch, pressure, temperature, pain, and the senses of muscle movement and body position.

Sensory receptors that are more specialized and confined to the head are associated with **special senses.** Laboratory Exercises 31 through 35 describe the special senses.

PURPOSE OF THE EXERCISE

To review the characteristics of sensory receptors and general senses and to investigate some of the general senses associated with the skin.

LEARNING OBJECTIVES

After completing this exercise, you should be able to

1. Name four general types of receptors associated with the body surface.
2. Explain how a sensation results.
3. List the general senses.
4. Determine the distribution of touch, warm, and cold receptors in a region of skin.
5. Determine the two-point threshold of a region of skin.

PROCEDURE A—RECEPTORS

1. Review the sections entitled "Receptors, Sensations, and Perception" and "General Senses" in chapter 12 of the textbook.
2. Complete Part A of Laboratory Report 30.

DEMONSTRATION

Observe the tactile (Meissner's) corpuscle with the microscope set up by the laboratory instructor. This type of receptor is abundant in the superficial dermis in outer regions of the body, such as in the fingertips, soles, lips, and external genital organs. It is responsible for the sensation of light touch. (See fig. 30.1 and chapter 6 of the textbook.)

Observe the lamellated (Pacinian) corpuscle in the second demonstration microscope. This corpuscle is composed of many layers of connective tissue cells and has a nerve fiber in its central core. Lamellated corpuscles are numerous in the hands, feet, joints, and external genital organs. They are responsible for the sense of deep pressure (fig. 30.2). How are tactile and lamellated corpuscles similar?

_____

_____

How are they different?

_____

_____

Figure 30.1 Tactile (Meissner's) corpuscles, such as this one, are responsible for the sensation of light touch (250×).

- Epidermis
- Tactile corpuscle in dermal papilla
- Dermis

Figure 30.2 Lamellated (Pacinian) corpuscles, such as this one, are responsible for the sensation of deep pressure (25× micrograph enlarged to 100×).

- Dermis
- Lamellated corpuscle
- Nerve fiber

PROCEDURE B—SENSE OF TOUCH

1. Investigate the distribution of touch receptors in your laboratory partner's skin. To do this, follow these steps:
   a. Use a marking pen and a millimeter ruler to prepare a square with 2.5 cm on each side on the skin of your partner's inner wrist, near the palm.
   b. Divide the square into smaller squares with 0.5 cm on a side, producing a small grid.
   c. Ask your partner to rest the marked wrist on the tabletop and to keep his or her eyes closed throughout the remainder of the experiment.
   d. Press the end of a bristle on the skin in some part of the grid, using just enough pressure to cause the bristle to bend. A sharp pencil could be used as an alternate device.
   e. Ask your partner to report whenever the touch of the bristle is felt. Record the results in Part B of the laboratory report.
   f. Continue this procedure until you have tested twenty-five different locations on the grid. Move randomly through the grid to help prevent anticipation of the next stimulation site.
2. Test two other areas of exposed skin in the same manner, and record the results in Part B of the laboratory report.
3. Answer the questions in Part B of the laboratory report.

PROCEDURE C—TWO-POINT THRESHOLD

1. Test your partner's ability to recognize the difference between one and two points of skin being stimulated simultaneously. To do this, follow these steps:
   a. Have your partner place a hand with the palm up on the table and close his or her eyes.
   b. Hold the tips of a forceps tightly together and gently touch the skin of your partner's index finger.
   c. Ask your partner to report if it feels like one or two points are touching the finger.
   d. Allow the tips of the forceps or the points of the measuring calipers to spread so they are 1 mm apart, press both points against the skin simultaneously, and ask your partner to report as before.
   e. Repeat this procedure, allowing the tips of the forceps to spread more each time until your partner can feel both tips being pressed against the skin. The minimum distance between the tips of the forceps when both can be felt is called the *two-point threshold.* As soon as you are able to distinguish two points, two separate receptors are being stimulated instead of only one receptor.
   f. Record the two-point threshold for the skin of the index finger in Part C of the laboratory report.
2. Repeat this procedure to determine the two-point threshold of the palm, the back of the hand, the back of the neck, the leg, and the sole. Record the results in Part C of the laboratory report.
3. Answer the questions in Part C of the laboratory report.

PROCEDURE D—SENSE OF TEMPERATURE

1. Investigate the distribution of *warm receptors* in your partner's skin. To do this, follow these steps:
    a. Mark a square with 2.5 cm sides on your partner's palm.
    b. Prepare a grid by dividing the square into smaller squares, 0.5 cm on a side.
    c. Have your partner rest the marked palm on the table and close his or her eyes.
    d. Heat a blunt metal probe by placing it in a beaker of warm (hot) water (about 40–45°C/ 104–113°F) for a minute or so. *(Be sure the probe does not get so hot that it burns the skin.)* Use a thermometer to monitor the appropriate warm water from the tap or the water bath.
    e. Wipe the probe dry and touch it to the skin on some part of the grid.
    f. Ask your partner to report if the probe feels warm. Then record the results in Part D of the laboratory report.
    g. Keep the probe warm, and repeat the procedure until you have randomly tested twenty-five different locations on the grid.

2. Investigate the distribution of *cold receptors* by repeating the procedure. Use a blunt metal probe that has been cooled by placing it in ice water for a minute or so. Record the results in Part D of the laboratory report.

3. Answer the questions in Part D of the laboratory report.

 LEARNING EXTENSION

Prepare three beakers of water of different temperatures. One beaker should contain warm water (about 40°C/ 104°F), one should be room temperature (about 22°C/ 72°F), and one should contain cold water (about 10°C/ 50°F). Place the index finger of one hand in the warm water and, at the same time, place the index finger of the other hand in the cold water for about 2 minutes. Then, simultaneously move both index fingers into the water at room temperature. What temperature do you sense with each finger? How do you explain the resulting perceptions?

_____

_____

_____

_____

NOTES

Name _____

Date _____

Section _____

RECEPTORS AND GENERAL SENSES

PART A—RECEPTORS

Complete the following statements:

1. _____ are receptors that are sensitive to changes in the concentrations of chemicals.

2. Whenever tissues are damaged, _____ receptors are likely to be stimulated.

3. Receptors that are sensitive to temperature changes are called _____ .

4. _____ are sensitive to changes in the intensity of light energy.

5. A sensation may seem to fade away when receptors are continuously stimulated as a result of _____ .

6. Tactile (Meissner's) corpuscles are responsible for the sense of light _____ .

7. Lamellated (Pacinian) corpuscles are responsible for the sense of deep _____ .

8. Warm receptors are most sensitive to temperatures between _____ .

9. Cold receptors are most sensitive to temperatures between _____ .

10. Pain receptors are widely distributed but are lacking in the nervous tissue of the _____ .

11. When visceral pain is felt in some region other than the part being stimulated, the phenomenon is called

_____ .

PART B—SENSE OF TOUCH

1. Record a + to indicate where the bristle was felt and a *0* to indicate where it was not felt.

Skin of wrist

2. Show distribution of touch receptors in two other regions of skin.

Region tested _____   Region tested _____

3. Answer the following questions:

   a. How do you describe the pattern of distribution for touch receptors in the regions of the skin you tested?

   _____

   _____

   b. How does the concentration of touch receptors seem to vary from region to region? _____

   _____

PART C—TWO-POINT THRESHOLD

1. Record the two-point threshold in millimeters for skin in each of the following regions:

   Index finger _____

   Palm _____

   Back of hand _____

   Back of neck _____

   Leg _____

   Sole _____

2. Answer the following questions:

   a. What region of the skin tested has the greatest ability to discriminate two points? _____

   b. What region of the skin has the least sensitivity to this test? _____

   c. What is the significance of these observations in questions *a* and *b*? _____

   _____

   _____

PART D—SENSE OF TEMPERATURE

1. Record a + to indicate where warm was felt and a *0* to indicate where it was not felt.

   Skin of palm

2. Record a + to indicate where cold was felt and a *0* to indicate where it was not felt.

   Skin of palm

3. Answer the following questions:

   a. How do temperature receptors appear to be distributed in the skin of the palm? _____

   _____

   b. Compare the distribution and concentration of warm and cold receptors in the skin of the palm. _____

   _____

   _____

LABORATORY EXERCISE 31

SMELL AND TASTE

MATERIALS NEEDED

For Procedure A—Sense of Smell (Olfaction)

Textbook
Set of substances in stoppered bottles:
    cinnamon, sage, vanilla, garlic powder, oil of clove,
    oil of wintergreen, and perfume

For Procedure B—Sense of Taste (Gustation)

Textbook
Paper cups (small)
Cotton swabs (sterile; disposable)
5% sucrose solution
5% NaCl solution
1% acetic acid or unsweetened lemon juice
0.5% quinine sulfate solution or 0.1% Epsom salt solution

For Demonstrations:

Compound light microscope
Prepared microscope slides of olfactory epithelium and
    of taste buds

For Learning Extension:

Pieces of apple, potato, carrot, and onion

 SAFETY

- Prepare fresh solutions for use in Procedure B.
- Wash your hands before starting the taste experiment.
- Use a clean cotton swab for each test. Do not dip a
  used swab into a test solution.
- Dispose of used cotton swabs and paper towels as
  directed.
- Wash your hands before leaving the laboratory.

The senses of smell (olfaction) and taste (gustation) are dependent upon chemoreceptors that are stimulated by various chemicals dissolved in liquids. The receptors of smell are found in the olfactory organs, which are located in the upper parts of the nasal cavity and in a portion of the nasal septum. The receptors of taste occur in the taste buds, which are sensory organs primarily found on the surface of the tongue. Chemicals are considered odorless and tasteless if receptor sites for them are absent.

These senses function closely together, because substances that are tasted often are smelled at the same moment, and they play important roles in the selection of foods.

PURPOSE OF THE EXERCISE

To review the structures of the organs of smell and taste and to investigate the abilities of smell and taste receptors to discriminate various chemical substances.

LEARNING OBJECTIVES

After completing this exercise, you should be able to

1. Describe the general characteristics of the smell (olfactory) receptors.
2. Describe the general characteristics of the taste (gustatory) receptors.
3. Explain how the senses of smell and taste function together.
4. Determine the time needed for olfactory sensory adaptation to occur.
5. Determine the distribution of taste receptors on the surface of the tongue and mouth cavity.

PROCEDURE A—SENSE OF SMELL (OLFACTION)

1. Review the section entitled "Sense of Smell" in chapter 12 of the textbook.
2. As a review activity, label figure 31.1.
3. Complete Part A of Laboratory Report 31.

DEMONSTRATION

Observe the olfactory epithelium in the microscope set up by the laboratory instructor. The olfactory receptor cells are spindle-shaped, bipolar neurons with spherical nuclei. They also have six to eight cilia at their distal ends. The supporting cells are pseudostratified columnar epithelial cells. However, in this region the tissue lacks goblet cells. (See fig. 31.2 and chapter 5 of the textbook.)

Figure 31.1 Label this diagram of the olfactory organ by placing the correct numbers in the spaces provided.

___ Cilia

___ Columnar epithelial cells

___ Cribriform plate of ethmoid bone

___ Nasal cavity

___ Nerve fibers within olfactory bulb

___ Olfactory nerves

___ Olfactory receptor cells

(a)

(b)

Figure 31.2 Olfactory receptors have cilia at their distal ends (250×).

4. Test your laboratory partner's ability to recognize the odors of the bottled substances available in the laboratory. To do this, follow these steps:
   a. Have your partner keep his or her eyes closed.
   b. Remove the stopper from one of the bottles, and hold it about 4 cm under your partner's nostrils for about 2 seconds.
   c. Ask your partner to identify the odor, and then replace the stopper.
   d. Record your partner's response in Part B of the laboratory report.
   e. Repeat steps *b–d* for each of the bottled substances.

5. Repeat the preceding procedure, using the same set of bottled substances, but present them to your partner in a different sequence. Record the results in Part B of the laboratory report.

6. Wait 10 minutes and then determine the time it takes for your partner to experience olfactory sensory adaptation. To do this, follow these steps:
   a. Ask your partner to breathe in through the nostrils and exhale through the mouth.
   b. Remove the stopper from one of the bottles, and hold it about 4 cm under your partner's nostrils.
   c. Keep track of the time that passes until your partner is no longer able to detect the odor of the substance.
   d. Record the result in Part B of the laboratory report.
   e. Wait 5 minutes and repeat this procedure, using a different bottled substance.
   f. Test a third substance in the same manner.
   g. Record the results as before.

7. Complete Part B of the laboratory report.

PROCEDURE B—SENSE OF TASTE (GUSTATION)

1. Review the section entitled "Sense of Taste" in chapter 12 of the textbook.
2. As a review activity, label figure 31.3.
3. Complete Part C of the laboratory report.

DEMONSTRATION

Observe the oval-shaped taste bud in the microscope set up by the laboratory instructor. Note the surrounding epithelial cells. The taste pore, an opening into the taste bud, may be filled with taste hairs (microvilli). Within the taste bud there are supporting cells and thinner taste-receptor cells, which often have lightly stained nuclei (fig. 31.4).

4. Map the distribution of the receptors for the primary taste sensations on your partner's tongue. To do this, follow these steps:
   a. Ask your partner to rinse his or her mouth with water and then partially dry the surface of the tongue with a paper towel.
   b. Moisten a clean cotton swab with 5% sucrose solution, and touch several regions of your partner's tongue with the swab.
   c. Each time you touch the tongue, ask your partner to report if a sweet sensation is experienced.
   d. Test the tip, sides, and back of the tongue in this manner.
   e. Test some other representative areas inside the mouth cavity such as the cheek, gums, and roof of the mouth (hard and soft palate) for a sweet sensation.

Figure 31.3   Label this diagram by placing the correct numbers in the spaces provided.

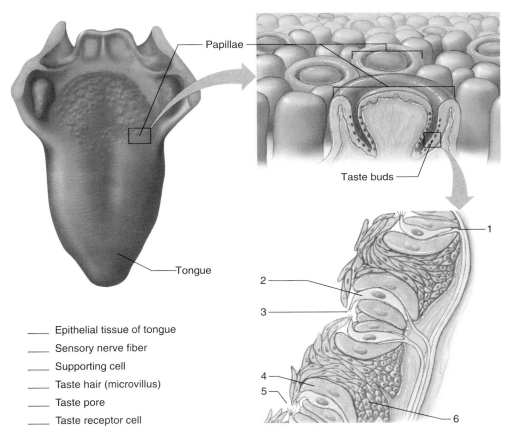

_____ Epithelial tissue of tongue

_____ Sensory nerve fiber

_____ Supporting cell

_____ Taste hair (microvillus)

_____ Taste pore

_____ Taste receptor cell

Figure 31.4 Taste receptors are found in taste buds such as this one (250× micrograph enlarged to 1,500×).

Taste pore
Taste hairs
Taste bud
Taste cell
Supporting cell

f. Record your partner's responses in Part D of the laboratory report.

g. Have your partner rinse his or her mouth and dry the tongue again, and repeat the preceding procedure, using each of the other three test solutions—NaCl, acetic acid, and quinine or Epsom salt solution. Be sure to use a fresh swab for each test substance and dispose of used swabs and paper towels as directed.

5. Complete Part D of the laboratory report.

 LEARNING EXTENSION

Test your laboratory partner's ability to recognize the tastes of apple, potato, carrot, and onion. To do this, follow these steps:

1. Have your partner close his or her eyes and hold the nostrils shut.
2. Place a small piece of one of the test substances on your partner's tongue.
3. Ask your partner to identify the substance without chewing or swallowing it.
4. Repeat the procedure for each of the other substances.

How do you explain the results of this experiment?

_____

_____

_____

SMELL AND TASTE

PART A

Complete the following statements:

1. Olfactory, or smell, receptors are _____ neurons surrounded by columnar epithelial cells.

2. The distal ends of the olfactory neurons are covered with hairlike _____.

3. Before gaseous substances can stimulate the olfactory receptors, they must be dissolved in _____ that surrounds the cilia.

4. The axons of olfactory receptors pass through small openings in the _____ of the ethmoid bone.

5. Olfactory bulbs lie on either side of the _____ of the ethmoid bone.

6. The sensory impulses pass from the olfactory bulbs through the _____ to the interpreting centers of the brain.

7. The olfactory interpreting centers are located deep within the temporal lobes and at the base of the _____ lobes of the cerebrum.

8. Olfactory sensations usually fade rapidly as a result of _____.

9. Olfactory receptor neurons are the only parts of the nervous system that come in contact with the _____ directly.

10. A chemical would be considered _____ if a person lacks a particular receptor site on the cilia of the olfactory neurons.

PART B—SENSE OF SMELL

1. Record the results (as +, if recognized; as *0*, if unrecognized) from the tests of odor recognition in the following table:

| Substance Tested | Odor Reported | |
	First Trial	Second Trial

2. Record the results of the olfactory sensory adaptation time in the following table:

Substance Tested	Adaptation Time in Seconds

3. Complete the following:

   a. How do you describe your partner's ability to recognize the odors of the substances you tested? _____
   _____
   _____

   b. Compare your experimental results with others in the class. Did you find any evidence to indicate that individuals may vary in their abilities to recognize odors? Explain your answer. _____
   _____
   _____
   _____
   _____

Critical Thinking Application

Does the time it takes for sensory adaptation to occur seem to vary with the substances tested? Explain your answer.

_____
_____
_____
_____

PART C

Complete the following statements:

1. Taste receptor cells are modified _____ cells.
2. The opening to a taste bud is called a _____ .
3. The _____ of a taste cell are its sensitive part.
4. Before the taste of a substance can be detected, the substance must be dissolved in _____ .
5. Substances that stimulate taste cells seem to bind with _____ sites on the surfaces of taste hairs.
6. Sour receptors are mainly stimulated by _____ .
7. Salt receptors are mainly stimulated by ionized inorganic _____ .
8. Alkaloids usually have a _____ taste.

PART D—SENSE OF TASTE

1. *Taste receptor distribution.* Record a + to indicate where a taste sensation seemed to originate and a *0* if no sensation occurred when the spot was stimulated.

Sucrose (sweet sensation)

NaCl (salt sensation)

Acetic acid (sour sensation)

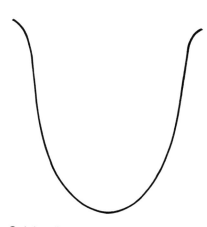

Quinine (bitter sensation)

2. Complete the following:

a. Describe how each type of taste receptor is distributed on the surface of your partner's tongue. _____

_____

_____

_____

_____

_____

b. Describe other locations inside the mouth where any sensations of sweet, salt, sour, or bitter were located.

_____

_____

_____

_____

c. How do your experimental results compare with the distribution of taste receptors described in chapter 12 of the textbook? _____

_____

_____

_____

d. How does your taste distribution map on the tongue compare to those of other students in the class? _____

_____

_____

EAR AND HEARING

MATERIALS NEEDED

Textbook
Dissectible ear model
Watch that ticks
Tuning fork (128 or 256 cps)
Rubber hammer
Cotton
Meterstick

For Demonstrations:

Compound light microscope
Prepared microscope slide of cochlea (section)
Audiometer

The ear is composed of outer (external), middle, and inner (internal) parts. The outer structures gather sound waves and direct them inward to the tympanic membrane. The parts of the middle ear, in turn, transmit vibrations from the tympanic membrane (eardrum) to the inner ear, where the hearing receptors are located. As they are stimulated, these receptors initiate nerve impulses to pass over the vestibulocochlear nerve into the auditory cortex of the brain, where the impulses are interpreted and the sensations of hearing are created.

PURPOSE OF THE EXERCISE

To review the structural and functional characteristics of the ear and to conduct some simple hearing tests.

LEARNING OBJECTIVES

After completing this exercise, you should be able to

1. Identify the major structures of the ear.
2. Describe the functions of the structures of the ear.
3. Trace the pathway of sound vibrations from the tympanic membrane to the hearing receptors.
4. Conduct several simple hearing tests.

PROCEDURE A—STRUCTURE AND FUNCTION OF THE EAR

1. Review the section entitled "Sense of Hearing" in chapter 12 of the textbook.
2. As a review activity, label figures 32.1, 32.2, and 32.3.

3. Examine the dissectible model of the ear and locate the following features:

   outer (external) ear
      auricle
      external acoustic meatus
      tympanic membrane (eardrum)
   middle ear
      tympanic cavity
      auditory ossicles (fig. 32.4)
         malleus
         incus
         stapes
      oval window
      tensor tympani
      stapedius
   auditory tube (eustachian tube; pharyngotympanic tube)
   inner (internal) ear
      osseous labyrinth
      membranous labyrinth
      cochlea
      round window
      semicircular canals
      vestibule
   vestibulocochlear nerve
      vestibular nerve (balance branch)
      cochlear nerve (hearing branch)

DEMONSTRATION

Observe the section of the cochlea in the microscope set up by the laboratory instructor. Locate one of the turns of the cochlea, and using figures 32.3 and 32.5 as a guide, identify the *scala vestibuli, cochlear duct (scala media), scala tympani, vestibular membrane, basilar membrane,* and the *organ of Corti.*

4. Complete Parts A and B of Laboratory Report 32.

Figure 32.1 Label the major structures of the ear.

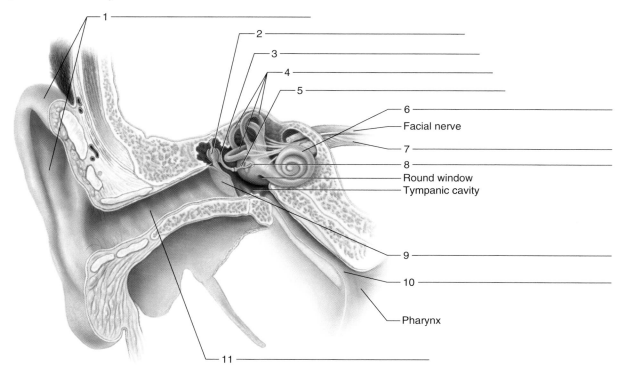

1 _____

2 _____

3 _____

4 _____

5 _____

6 _____

Facial nerve

7 _____

8 _____

Round window

Tympanic cavity

9 _____

10 _____

Pharynx

11 _____

PROCEDURE B—HEARING TESTS

Perform the following tests in a quiet room, using your laboratory partner as the test subject.

1. *Auditory acuity test.* To conduct this test, follow these steps:
   a. Have the test subject sit with eyes closed.
   b. Pack one of the subject's ears with cotton.
   c. Hold a ticking watch close to the open ear, and slowly move it straight out and away from the ear.
   d. Have the subject indicate when the sound of the ticking can no longer be heard.
   e. Use a meterstick to measure the distance in centimeters from the ear to the position of the watch.
   f. Repeat this procedure to test the acuity of the other ear.
   g. Record the test results in Part C of the laboratory report.
2. *Sound localization test.* To conduct this test, follow these steps:
   a. Have the subject sit with eyes closed.
   b. Hold the ticking watch somewhere within the audible range of the subject's ears, and ask the subject to point to the watch.
   c. Move the watch to another position and repeat the request. In this manner, determine how accurately the subject can locate the watch when it is in each of the following positions: in front of the head, behind the head, above the head, on the right side of the head, and on the left side of the head.
   d. Record the test results in Part C of the laboratory report.
3. *Rinne test.* This test is done to assess possible conduction deafness by comparing bone and air conduction. To conduct this test, follow these steps:
   a. Obtain a tuning fork and strike it with a rubber hammer, or on the heel of your hand, causing it to vibrate.
   b. Place the end of the fork's handle against the subject's mastoid process behind one ear. Have the prongs of the fork pointed downward and away from the ear, and be sure nothing is touching them (fig. 32.6*a*). The sound sensation is that of bone conduction. If no sound is experienced, nerve deafness exists.
   c. Ask the subject to indicate when the sound is no longer heard.
   d. Then quickly remove the fork from the mastoid process and position it in the air close to the opening of the nearby external acoustic meatus (fig. 32.6*b*).
      If hearing is normal, the sound (from air conduction) will be heard again; if there is conductive impairment, the sound will not be heard. Conductive impairment involves outer or

Figure 32.2 Label the structures of the inner ear by placing the correct numbers in the spaces provided.

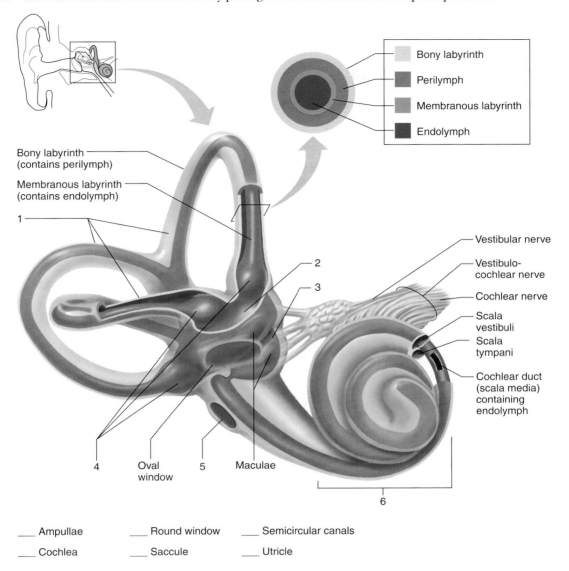

Bony labyrinth

Perilymph

Membranous labyrinth

Endolymph

Bony labyrinth (contains perilymph)

Membranous labyrinth (contains endolymph)

1

2

3

4

Oval window

5

Maculae

6

Vestibular nerve

Vestibulo-cochlear nerve

Cochlear nerve

Scala vestibuli

Scala tympani

Cochlear duct (scala media) containing endolymph

___ Ampullae   ___ Round window   ___ Semicircular canals

___ Cochlea   ___ Saccule   ___ Utricle

middle ear defects. Hearing aids can improve hearing for conductive deafness because bone conduction transmits the sound into the inner ear. Surgery could possibly correct this type of defect.

e. Record the test results in Part C of the laboratory report.

4. *Weber test.* This test is used to distinguish possible conduction or sensory deafness. To conduct this test, follow these steps:

a. Strike the tuning fork with the rubber hammer.

b. Place the handle of the fork against the subject's forehead in the midline (fig. 32.7).

c. Ask the subject to indicate if the sound is louder in one ear than in the other or if it is equally loud in both ears.

If hearing is normal, the sound will be equally loud in both ears. If there is conductive impairment, the sound will appear louder in the affected ear. If some degree of sensory (nerve) deafness exists, the sound will be louder in the normal ear. The impairment involves the organ of Corti or the cochlear nerve. Hearing aids will not improve sensory deafness.

d. Have the subject experience the effects of conductive impairment by packing one ear with cotton and repeating the Weber test. Usually the sound appears louder in the plugged (or impaired) ear because extraneous sounds from the room are blocked out.

e. Record the test results in Part C of the laboratory report.

5. Complete Part C of the laboratory report.

Figure 32.3 Label the structures associated with the organ of Corti of a cochlea.

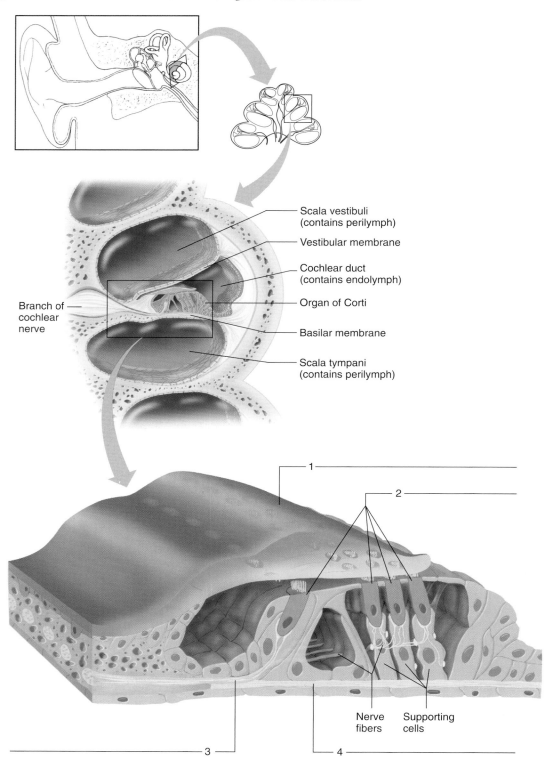

Scala vestibuli
(contains perilymph)

Vestibular membrane

Cochlear duct
(contains endolymph)

Organ of Corti

Basilar membrane

Scala tympani
(contains perilymph)

Branch of
cochlear
nerve

1

2

Nerve
fibers

Supporting
cells

3

4

Figure 32.4 Middle ear bones (auditory ossicles) superimposed on a penny to show their relative size. The arrangement of the malleus, incus, and stapes in the enlarged photograph resembles the articulations in the middle ear.

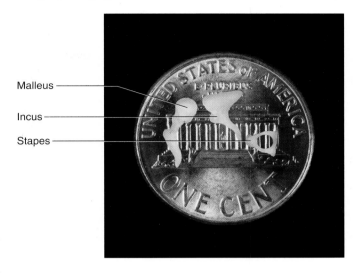

Malleus

Incus

Stapes

Figure 32.5 A section through the cochlea (22×).

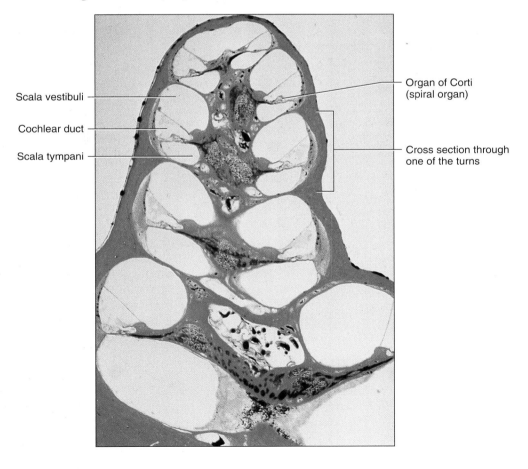

Scala vestibuli

Cochlear duct

Scala tympani

Organ of Corti
(spiral organ)

Cross section through
one of the turns

Figure 32.6 Rinne test: (*a*) first placement of vibrating tuning fork until sound is no longer heard; (*b*) second placement of tuning fork to assess air conduction.

(a)

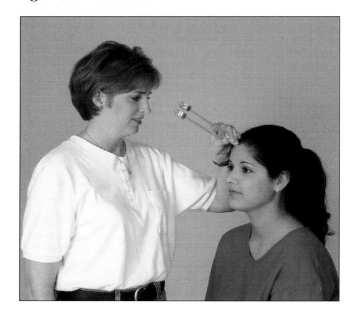

(b)

Figure 32.7 Weber test.

DEMONSTRATION

Ask the laboratory instructor to demonstrate the use of the audiometer. This instrument produces sound vibrations of known frequencies that are transmitted to one or both ears of a test subject through earphones. The audiometer can be used to determine the threshold of hearing for different sound frequencies, and, in the case of hearing impairment, it can be used to determine the percentage of hearing loss for each frequency.

Web Quest

What are the causes of hearing impairment? Search this site and review the anatomy and physiology of the ear at

www.mhhe.com/shier11

Click on Student Edition. Click on Martin Lab Manual, Web Quest.

Critical Thinking Application

Ear structures from the outer ear into the inner ear are progressively smaller. Using results obtained from the hearing tests, explain this advantage.

_____

_____

_____

_____

EAR AND HEARING

PART A

Match the terms in column A with the descriptions in column B. Place the letter of your choice in the space provided.

Column A	Column B
a. Auditory tube	_____ 1. Auditory ossicle attached to tympanic membrane
b. Ceruminous gland	_____ 2. Air-filled space containing auditory ossicles
c. External acoustic meatus	_____ 3. Contacts hairs of hearing receptors
d. Malleus	_____ 4. Leads from oval window to apex of cochlea
e. Membranous labyrinth	_____ 5. S-shaped tube leading to tympanic membrane
f. Osseous labyrinth	_____ 6. Wax-secreting structure
g. Scala tympani	_____ 7. Cone-shaped, semitransparent membrane attached to malleus
h. Scala vestibuli	
i. Stapes	_____ 8. Auditory ossicle attached to oval window
j. Tectorial membrane	_____ 9. Contains endolymph
k. Tympanic cavity	_____ 10. Bony canal of inner ear in temporal bone
l. Tympanic membrane (eardrum)	_____ 11. Connects middle ear and pharynx
	_____ 12. Extends from apex of cochlea to round window

PART B

Label the structures indicated in the micrograph of the organ of Corti (spiral organ) in figure 32.8.

Figure 32.8 Label the structures associated with this organ of Corti (spiral organ) region of a cochlea, using the terms provided (75× micrograph enlarged to 300×).

Terms:
Basilar membrane
Cochlear duct
Hair cells
Scala tympani
Tectorial membrane

PART C

1. Results of auditory acuity test:

Ear Tested	Audible Distance (cm)
Right	
Left	

2. Results of sound localization test:

Actual Location	Reported Location
Front of the head	
Behind the head	
Above the head	
Right side of the head	
Left side of the head	

3. Results of experiments using tuning forks:

Test	Left Ear (normal or impaired)	Right Ear (normal or impaired)
Rinne		
Weber		

4. Summarize the results of the hearing tests you conducted on your laboratory partner.

_____
_____
_____
_____
_____
_____
_____
_____

NOTES

LABORATORY EXERCISE 33

EQUILIBRIUM

 SAFETY

- Do not pick subjects who have frequent motion sickness.
- Have four people surround the subject in the swivel chair in case the person falls from vertigo or loss of balance.
- Stop your experiment if the subject becomes nauseated.

The sense of equilibrium involves two sets of sensory organs. One set helps to maintain the stability of the head and body when they are motionless and produces a sense of static (gravitational) equilibrium. The other set is concerned with balancing the head and body when they are moved suddenly and produces a sense of dynamic (rotational) equilibrium.

The organs associated with the sense of static equilibrium are located within the vestibules of the inner ears, whereas those associated with the sense of dynamic equilibrium are found within the ampullae of the semicircular canals of the inner ear.

PURPOSE OF THE EXERCISE

To review the structure and function of the organs of equilibrium and to conduct some simple tests of equilibrium.

LEARNING OBJECTIVES

After completing this exercise, you should be able to

1. Distinguish between static and dynamic equilibrium.

2. Identify the organs of equilibrium and describe their functions.
3. Explain the role of vision in the maintenance of equilibrium.
4. Conduct the Romberg and Bárány tests of equilibrium.

PROCEDURE A—STRUCTURE AND FUNCTION OF ORGANS OF EQUILIBRIUM

1. Review the section entitled "Sense of Equilibrium" in chapter 12 of the textbook.
2. Complete Part A of Laboratory Report 33.

DEMONSTRATION

Observe the cross section of the semicircular canal through the ampulla in the microscope set up by the laboratory instructor. Note the crista ampullaris (figs. 33.1 and 33.2) projecting into the lumen of the membranous labyrinth, which in a living person is filled with endolymph. The space between the membranous and osseous labyrinths is filled with perilymph.

PROCEDURE B—TESTS OF EQUILIBRIUM

Perform the following tests, using a person as a test subject who is not easily disturbed by dizziness or rotational movement. Also have some other students standing close by to help prevent the test subject from falling during the tests. *The tests should be stopped immediately if the test subject begins to feel uncomfortable or nauseated.*

1. *Vision and equilibrium.* To demonstrate the importance of vision in the maintenance of equilibrium, follow these steps:
   a. Have the test subject stand erect on one foot for 1 minute with his or her eyes open.
   b. Observe the subject's degree of unsteadiness.
   c. Repeat the procedure with the subject's eyes closed. *Be prepared to prevent the subject from falling.*
2. *Romberg test.* To conduct this test, follow these steps:
   a. Position the test subject close to a chalkboard with the back toward the board.

Figure 33.1 The crista ampullaris is located within the ampulla of each semicircular canal.

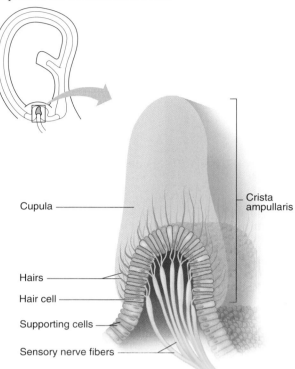

Cupula

Crista ampullaris

Hairs

Hair cell

Supporting cells

Sensory nerve fibers

Figure 33.2 A micrograph of a crista ampullaris (1,400×).

Cupula

Hair

Hair cell

Region of sensory nerve fibers

b. Place a bright light in front of the subject so that a shadow of the body is cast on the board.

c. Have the subject stand erect with feet close together and eyes staring straight ahead for a period of 3 minutes.

d. During the test, make marks on the chalkboard along the edge of the shadow of the subject's shoulders to indicate the range of side-to-side swaying.

e. Measure the maximum sway in centimeters and record the results in Part B of the laboratory report.

f. Repeat the procedure with the subject's eyes closed.

g. Position the subject so one side is toward the chalkboard.

h. Repeat the procedure with the eyes open.

i. Repeat the procedure with the eyes closed.

The Romberg test is used to evaluate a person's ability to integrate sensory information from proprioceptors and receptors within the organs of equilibrium and to relay appropriate motor impulses to postural muscles. A person who shows little unsteadiness when standing with feet together and eyes open, but who becomes unsteady when the eyes are closed, has a positive Romberg test.

3. *Bárány test.* To conduct this test, follow these steps:

a. Have the test subject sit on a swivel chair with his or her eyes closed, the head tilted forward about 30°, and the hands gripped firmly to the seat. Position four people around the chair for safety. *Be prepared to prevent the subject and the chair from tipping over.*

b. Rotate the chair ten rotations within 20 seconds.

c. Abruptly stop the movement of the chair. The subject will still have the sensation of continuous movement and might experience some dizziness (vertigo).

d. Have the subject open the eyes, and note the nature of the eye movements and their direction. (Such reflex eye movements are called *nystagmus.*) Also note the time it takes for the nystagmus to cease. Nystagmus will continue until the cupula is returned to an original position.

e. Record your observations in Part B of the laboratory report.

f. Allow the subject several minutes of rest, then repeat the procedure with the subject's head tilted nearly 90° onto one shoulder.

g. After another rest period, repeat the procedure with the subject's head bent forward so that the chin is resting on the chest.

In this test, when the head is tilted about 30°, the lateral semicircular canals receive maximal stimulation, and the nystagmus is normally from side to side. When the head is tilted at 90°, the superior canals are stimulated, and the nystagmus is up and down. When the head is bent forward with the chin on the chest, the posterior canals are stimulated, and the nystagmus is rotary.

4. Complete Part B of the laboratory report.

Laboratory Report **33**

Name _____

Date _____

Section _____

EQUILIBRIUM

PART A

Complete the following statements:

1. The organs of static equilibrium are located within two expanded chambers of the membranous labyrinth called the _____ and the saccule.

2. All of the balance organs are located within the _____ bone of the skull.

3. The receptor cells of these organs are found in the wall of the membranous labyrinth in a structure called the _____ .

4. Otoliths are small grains composed of _____ .

5. Sensory impulses travel from the organs of equilibrium to the brain on the _____ nerve.

6. The sensory organ of a semicircular canal lies within a swelling of the canal called the _____ .

7. The sensory organ within a semicircular canal is called a _____ .

8. The _____ of this sensory organ consists of a dome-shaped gelatinous mass.

9. When the head is moved, the fluid inside the membranous portion of a semicircular canal tends to remain stationary because of the _____ of the fluid.

10. Parts of the _____ of the brain interpret impulses from the semicircular canals.

PART B—TESTS OF EQUILIBRIUM

1. Vision and equilibrium test results:

   a. When the eyes are open, what sensory organs provide information needed to maintain equilibrium? _____
   _____
   _____

   b. When the eyes are closed, what sensory organs provide such information? _____
   _____
   _____

2. Romberg test results:

a. Record the test results in the following table.

Conditions	Maximal Movement (cm)
Back toward board, eyes open	
Back toward board, eyes closed	
Side toward board, eyes open	
Side toward board, eyes closed	

b. Did the test subject's unsteadiness increase when the eyes were closed? _____ What is the significance of this observation? _____
_____
_____

c. Why would you expect a person with impairment of the organs of equilibrium to become more unsteady when the eyes are closed? _____
_____
_____

3. Bárány test results:

a. Record the test results in the following table.

Position of Head	Description of Eye Movements	Time for Movement to Cease
Tilted 30° forward		
Tilted 90° onto shoulder		
Tilted forward, chin on chest		

b. Summarize the results of this test. _____
_____
_____

Critical Thinking Application

What additional sensory information would you expect a person with impairment of organs of equilibrium to use to supplement their relative lack of some sensory information?

_____
_____
_____

LABORATORY EXERCISE 34

EYE STRUCTURE

MATERIALS NEEDED

Textbook
Dissectible eye model
Compound light microscope
Prepared microscope slide of a mammalian eye (sagittal section)
Sheep or beef eye (fresh or preserved)
Dissecting tray
Dissecting instruments—forceps, sharp scissors, and dissecting needle

For Learning Extension:

Ophthalmoscope

 SAFETY

- Wear disposable gloves when working on the eye dissection.
- Dispose of tissue remnants and gloves as instructed.
- Wash the dissecting tray and instruments as instructed.
- Wash your laboratory table.
- Wash your hands before leaving the laboratory.

The eye contains photoreceptors, which are modified neurons located on its inner wall. Other parts of the eye provide protective functions or make it possible to move the eyeball. Still other structures serve to focus light entering the eye so that a sharp image is projected onto the receptor cells. Nerve impulses generated when the receptors are stimulated travel along the optic nerves to the brain, which interprets the impulses and creates the sensation of sight.

PURPOSE OF THE EXERCISE

To review the structure and function of the eye and to dissect a mammalian eye.

LEARNING OBJECTIVES

After completing this exercise, you should be able to

1. Identify the major structures of an eye.
2. Describe the functions of the structures of an eye.
3. List the structures through which light passes as it travels from the cornea to the retina.
4. Dissect a mammalian eye and identify its major features.

PROCEDURE A—STRUCTURE AND FUNCTION OF THE EYE

1. Review the sections entitled "Visual Accessory Organs," "Structure of the Eye," and "Visual Receptors" in chapter 12 of the textbook.
2. As a review activity, label figures 34.1, 34.2, and 34.3.
3. Complete Part A of Laboratory Report 34.
4. Examine the dissectible model of the eye and locate the following features:

eyelid
conjunctiva
orbicularis oculi
levator palpebrae superioris
lacrimal apparatus
    lacrimal gland
    canaliculi
    lacrimal sac
    nasolacrimal duct
extrinsic muscles
    superior rectus
    inferior rectus
    medial rectus
    lateral rectus
    superior oblique
    inferior oblique
trochlea (pulley)
outer (fibrous) tunic
    sclera
    cornea
middle (vascular) tunic
    choroid coat
    ciliary body
        ciliary processes
        ciliary muscles
        suspensory ligaments

Figure 34.1 Label the structures of the lacrimal apparatus.

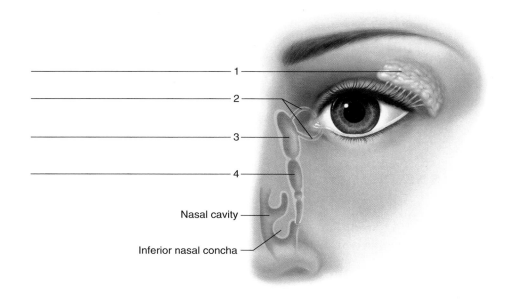

1 _____

2 _____

3 _____

4 _____

Nasal cavity

Inferior nasal concha

Figure 34.2 Label the extrinsic muscles of the right eye (lateral view).

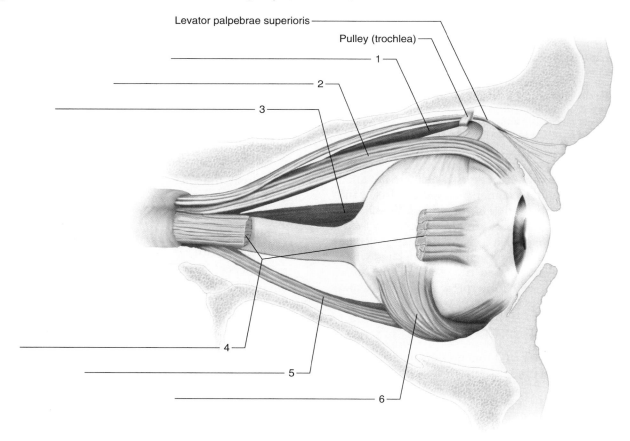

Levator palpebrae superioris

Pulley (trochlea)

1

2

3

4

5

6

Figure 34.3 Label the structures indicated in this transverse section of the right eye (superior view).

1

2

3

4

5

Medial rectus

6

7

(contents)

Anterior chamber

Posterior chamber

8

(cavity)

9

10

11

12

(contents)

Lateral rectus

14

15

16

(cavity)

13

iris

pupil (opening in center of iris)

inner (nervous) tunic

retina

macula lutea

fovea centralis

optic disc

optic nerve

lens

anterior cavity

anterior chamber

posterior chamber

aqueous humor

posterior cavity

vitreous humor

5. Obtain a microscope slide of a mammalian eye section, and locate as many of the features in step 4 as possible.

6. Using high-power magnification, observe the posterior portion of the eye wall, and locate the sclera, choroid coat, and retina.

7. Using high-power magnification, examine the retina, and note its layered structure (fig. 34.4). Locate the following:

nerve fibers leading to the optic nerve (innermost layer of the retina)

layer of ganglion cells

layer of bipolar neurons

nuclei of rods and cones

receptor ends of rods and cones

pigmented epithelium (outermost layer of the retina)

LEARNING EXTENSION

Use an ophthalmoscope to examine the interior of your laboratory partner's eye. This instrument consists of a set of lenses held in a rotating disc, a light source, and some mirrors that reflect the light into the test subject's eye.

The examination should be conducted in a dimly lighted room. Have your partner seated and staring straight ahead at eye level. Move the rotating disc of the ophthalmoscope so that the *O* appears in the lens selection window. Hold the instrument in your right hand with the end of your index finger on the rotating disc (fig. 34.5). Direct the light at a slight angle from a distance of about 15 cm into the subject's right eye. The light beam should pass along the inner edge of the pupil. Look through the instrument, and you should see a reddish, circular area—the interior of the eye. Rotate the disc of lenses to higher values until sharp focus is achieved.

Move the ophthalmoscope to within about 5 cm of the eye being examined *being very careful that the instrument does not touch the eye,* and again rotate the lenses to sharpen the focus (fig. 34.6). Locate the optic disc and the blood vessels that pass through it. Also locate the yellowish macula lutea by having your partner stare directly into the light of the instrument (fig. 34.7).

Examine the subject's iris by viewing it from the side and by using a lens with a +15 or +20 value.

PROCEDURE B—EYE DISSECTION

1. Obtain a mammalian eye, place it in a dissecting tray, and dissect it as follows:

   a. Trim away the fat and other connective tissues but leave the stubs of the *extrinsic muscles* and of the *optic nerve.* This nerve projects outward from the posterior region of the eyeball.

   b. Note the *conjunctiva,* which lines the inside of the eyelid and is reflected over the anterior

Figure 34.4 The cells of the retina are arranged in distinct layers (75×).

Direction of light

Inside of eye

Retina

Vitreous humor
Nerve fibers
Ganglion cells
Bipolar neurons
Nuclei of rods and cones
Receptor ends of rods and cones
Pigmented epithelium
Choroid coat
Sclera

Outside of eye

Figure 34.5 The ophthalmoscope is used to examine the interior of the eye.

Eyepiece

Rotating disc

Lens selection window

Handle of ophthalmoscope

Figure 34.6 (*a*) Rotate the disc of lenses until sharp focus is achieved. (*b*) Move the ophthalmoscope to within 5 cm of the eye to examine the optic disc.

(a)　　　　　　　　　　　　　　　　　　　　　　　　　　(b)

Figure 34.7 The interior of the eye as seen using an ophthalmoscope: (*a*) photograph with an arrow indicating the optic disc; (*b*) diagram.

(a)

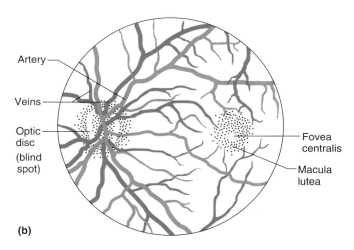

Artery

Veins

Optic disc (blind spot)

Fovea centralis

Macula lutea

(b)

surface of the eye, except for the cornea. Lift some of this thin membrane away from the eye with forceps and examine it.

c. Locate and observe the *cornea, sclera,* and *iris.* Also note the *pupil* and its shape. The cornea from a fresh eye will be transparent; when preserved, it becomes opaque.

d. Use sharp scissors to make a coronal section of the eye. To do this, cut through the wall about 1 cm from the margin of the cornea and continue all the way around the eyeball. Try not to damage the internal structures of the eye (fig. 34.8).

e. Gently separate the eyeball into anterior and posterior portions. Usually the jellylike vitreous humor will remain in the posterior portion, and the lens may adhere to it. Place the parts in the dissecting tray with their contents facing upward.

f. Examine the anterior portion of the eye, and locate the *ciliary body,* which appears as a dark, circular structure. Also note the *iris* and the *lens* if it remained in the anterior portion. The lens is normally attached to the ciliary body by many *suspensory ligaments,* which appear as delicate, transparent threads.

g. Use a dissecting needle to gently remove the lens, and examine it. If the lens is still transparent, hold it up and look through it at something in the distance and note that the lens inverts the image. The lens of a preserved eye is usually too opaque for this experience.

h. Examine the posterior portion of the eye. Note the *vitreous humor.* This jellylike mass helps to hold the lens in place anteriorly and

279

Figure 34.8 Prepare a coronal section of the eye.

— Margin of cornea

helps to hold the *retina* against the choroid coat.

i. Carefully remove the vitreous humor and examine the retina. This layer will appear as a thin, nearly colorless to cream-colored membrane that detaches easily from the choroid coat. Compare the structures identified to figure 34.9.

j. Locate the *optic disc*—the point where the retina is attached to the posterior wall of the eyeball and where the optic nerve originates.

Because there are no receptor cells in the optic disc, this region is also called the "blind spot."

k. Note the iridescent area of the choroid coat beneath the retina. This colored surface in ungulates (mammals having hoofs) is called the *tapetum fibrosum.* It serves to reflect light back through the retina, an action that is thought to aid the night vision of some animals. The tapetum fibrosum is lacking in the human eye.

l. Discard the tissues of the eye as directed by the laboratory instructor.

2. Complete Parts B and C of the laboratory report.

 Critical Thinking Application

A strong blow to the head might cause the retina to detach. From observations made during the eye dissection, explain why this could happen.

_____

_____

_____

_____

Web Quest

How do we see? Search this and review the anatomy and physiology of the eye at www.mhhe.com/shier11

Click on Student Edition. Click on Martin Lab Manual, Web Quest.

Figure 34.9 Internal structures of the beef eye dissection.

Choroid coat (reflected)

Sclera

Retina (partly detached)

Tapetum fibrosum (iridescent)

Cornea (posterior surface)

Pupil (opening in center of iris)

Iris

Ciliary body

Posterior portion

Anterior portion

Vitreous humor (transparent)

Lens

EYE STRUCTURE

PART A

Match the terms in column A with the descriptions in column B. Place the letter of your choice in the space provided.

Column A	Column B
a. Aqueous humor	_____ 1. Posterior five-sixths of middle (vascular) tunic
b. Choroid coat	_____ 2. White part of outer (fibrous) tunic
c. Ciliary muscles	_____ 3. Transparent anterior portion of outer tunic
d. Conjunctiva	_____ 4. Inner lining of eyelid
e. Cornea	_____ 5. Secretes tears
f. Iris	_____ 6. Fills posterior cavity of eye
g. Lacrimal gland	_____ 7. Area where optic nerve exits the eye
h. Optic disc	_____ 8. Smooth muscle that controls light entering the eye
i. Retina	_____ 9. Fills anterior and posterior chambers of the anterior cavity of the eye
j. Sclera	_____ 10. Contains visual receptors called rods and cones
k. Suspensory ligament	_____ 11. Connects lens to ciliary body
l. Vitreous humor	_____ 12. Cause lens to change shape

Complete the following:

13. List the structures and fluids through which light passes as it travels from the cornea to the retina. _____

_____

_____

_____

14. List three ways in which rods and cones differ in structure or function. _____

_____

_____

_____

_____

PART B

Complete the following:

1. Which tunic/layer of the eye was the most difficult to cut? _____

2. What kind of tissue do you think is responsible for this quality of toughness? _____

3. How do you compare the shape of the pupil in the dissected eye with your own pupil? _____
   _____
   _____

4. Where do you find aqueous humor in the dissected eye? _____
   _____
   _____

5. What is the function of the dark pigment in the choroid coat? _____
   _____
   _____

6. Describe the lens of the dissected eye. _____
   _____
   _____
   _____

7. Describe the vitreous humor of the dissected eye. _____
   _____
   _____
   _____

PART C

Identify the features of the eye indicated in figure 34.10.

a. Anterior portion of eye:

1. _____
2. _____
3. _____
4. _____
5. _____

b. Posterior portion of eye:

6. _____
7. _____
8. _____
9. _____
10. _____
11. _____

Figure 34.10 Sections of the eye: (*a*) anterior portion (10×); (*b*) posterior portion (53×). Identify the numbered features, using the terms provided.

(a)

(b)

Terms:
Aqueous humor
Choroid coat/middle tunic
Conjunctiva
Cornea
Iris
Lens
Optic disc
Optic nerve
Retina/inner tunic
Sclera/outer tunic
Vitreous humor

NOTES

VISUAL TESTS AND DEMONSTRATIONS

MATERIALS NEEDED

Snellen eye chart
3″ × 5″ card (plain)
3″ × 5″ card with word typed in center
Astigmatism chart
Meterstick
Metric ruler
Pen flashlight
Ichikawa's or Ishihara's color plates for colorblindness test

Normal vision (emmetropia) results when light rays from objects in the external environment are refracted by the cornea and lens of the eye and focused onto the photoreceptors of the retina. Irregular curvatures in the surface of the cornea or lens, inability to change the shape of the lens, or defects in the shape of the eyeball can result in defective vision.

PURPOSE OF THE EXERCISE

To conduct tests for visual acuity, astigmatism, accommodation, color vision, the blind spot, and certain reflexes of the eye.

LEARNING OBJECTIVES

After completing this exercise, you should be able to

1. Describe four conditions that can lead to defective vision.
2. Conduct the tests used to evaluate visual acuity, astigmatism, the ability to accommodate for close vision, and color vision.
3. Demonstrate the blind spot, photopupillary reflex, accommodation pupillary reflex, and convergence reflex.

PROCEDURE A—VISUAL TESTS

Perform the following visual tests, using your laboratory partner as a test subject. If your partner usually wears glasses, test each eye with and without the glasses.

1. *Visual acuity test.* Visual acuity (sharpness of vision) can be measured by using a Snellen eye chart (fig. 35.1). This chart consists of several sets of letters in different sizes printed on a white card.

The letters near the top of the chart are relatively large, and those in each lower set become smaller. At one end of each set of letters is an acuity value in the form of a fraction. One of the sets near the bottom of the chart, for example, is marked 20/20. The normal eye can clearly see these letters from the standard distance of 20 feet and thus is said to have 20/20 vision. The letter at the top of the chart is marked 20/200. The normal eye can read letters of this size from a distance of 200 feet. Thus, an eye that is able to read only the top letter of the chart from a distance of 20 feet is said to have 20/200 vision. This person has less than normal vision. A line of letters near the bottom of the chart is marked 20/15. The normal eye can read letters of this size from a distance of 15 feet, but a person might be able to read it from 20 feet. This person has better than normal vision.

To conduct the visual acuity test, follow these steps:
a. Hang the Snellen eye chart on a well-illuminated wall at eye level.
b. Have your partner stand 20 feet in front of the chart, gently cover the left eye with a 3″ × 5″ card, and read the smallest set of letters possible.
c. Record the visual acuity value for that set of letters in Part A of Laboratory Report 35.
d. Repeat the procedure, using the left eye.

2. *Astigmatism test.* Astigmatism is a condition that results from a defect in the curvature of the cornea or lens. As a consequence, some portions of the image projected on the retina are sharply focused, and other portions are blurred. Astigmatism can be evaluated by using an astigmatism chart (fig. 35.2). This chart consists of sets of black lines radiating from a central spot like the spokes of a wheel. To a normal eye, these lines appear sharply focused and equally dark; however, if the eye has an astigmatism, some sets of lines appear sharply focused and dark, while others are blurred and less dark.

To conduct the astigmatism test, follow these steps:
a. Hang the astigmatism chart on a well-illuminated wall at eye level.

Figure 35.1 The Snellen eye chart looks similar to this but is somewhat larger.

Figure 35.2 Astigmatism is evaluated using a chart such as this one.

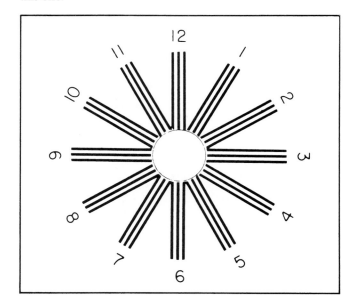

To evaluate the ability to accommodate, follow these steps:
  a. Hold the end of a meterstick against your partner's chin so that the stick extends outward at a right angle to the plane of the face (fig. 35.3).
  b. Have your partner close the left eye.
  c. Hold a 3″ × 5″ card with a word typed in the center at the distal end of the meterstick.
  d. Slide the card along the stick toward your partner's open eye, and locate the *point closest to the eye* where your partner can still see the letters of the word sharply focused. This distance is called the *near point of accommodation,* and it tends to increase with age (table 35.1).
  e. Repeat the procedure with the right eye closed.
  f. Record the results in Part A of the laboratory report.
4. *Color vision test.* Some people exhibit defective color vision because they lack certain cones, usually those sensitive to the reds or greens. Because this trait is an X-linked (sex-linked) inheritance, the condition is more prevalent in males (7%) than in females (0.4%). People who lack or possess decreased sensitivity to the red-sensitive cones possess protanopia colorblindness; those who lack or possess decreased sensitivity to green-sensitive cones possess deuteranopia colorblindness. The colorblindness condition is often more of a deficiency or a weakness than one of blindness. Laboratory Exercise 61 describes the genetics for colorblindness.

  b. Have your partner stand 20 feet in front of the chart, gently cover the left eye with a 3″ × 5″ card, focus on the spot in the center of the radiating lines, and report which lines, if any, appear more sharply focused and darker.
  c. Repeat the procedure, using the left eye.
  d. Record the results in Part A of the laboratory report.
3. *Accommodation test.* Accommodation is the changing of the shape of the lens that occurs when the normal eye is focused for close vision. It involves a reflex in which muscles of the ciliary body are stimulated to contract, releasing tension on the suspensory ligaments that are fastened to the lens capsule. This allows the capsule to rebound elastically, causing the surface of the lens to become more convex. The ability to accommodate is likely to decrease with age because the tissues involved tend to lose their elasticity.

Figure 35.3 To determine the near point of accommodation, slide the 3″ × 5″ card along the meterstick toward your partner's open eye until it reaches the closest location where your partner can still see the word sharply focused.

Table 35.1 Near Point of Accommodation

Age (years)	Average Near Point (cm)
10	7
20	10
30	13
40	20
50	45
60	90

To conduct the color vision test, follow these steps:

a. Examine the color test plates in Ichikawa's or Ishihara's book to test for any red-green color vision deficiency. Also examine figure 35.4.

b. Hold the test plates approximately 30 inches from the subject in bright light. All responses should occur within 3 seconds.

c. Compare your responses with the correct answers in Ichikawa's or Ishihara's book. Determine the percentage of males and females in your class who exhibit any color-deficient vision. If an individual exhibits color-deficient vision, determine if the condition is protanopia or deuteranopia.

d. Record the class results in Part A of the laboratory report.

5. Complete Part A of the laboratory report.

PROCEDURE B—VISUAL DEMONSTRATIONS

Perform the following demonstrations with the help of your laboratory partner.

1. *Blind-spot demonstration.* There are no photoreceptors in the optic disc, which is located where the nerve fibers of the retina leave the eye and enter the optic nerve. Consequently, this region of the retina is commonly called the *blind spot.*

To demonstrate the blind spot, follow these steps:

a. Close your left eye, hold figure 35.5 about 34 cm away from your face, and stare at the + sign in the figure with your right eye.

b. Move the figure closer to your face as you continue to stare at the + until the dot on the figure suddenly disappears. This happens when the image of the dot is focused on the optic disc. Measure the distance using a metric ruler or a meterstick.

c. Repeat the procedures with your right eye closed. This time stare at the dot, and the + will disappear when the image falls on the optic disc. Measure the distance.

d. Record the results in Part B of the laboratory report.

Critical Thinking Application

Under normal visual circumstances, explain why small objects are not lost from our vision.

_____

_____

_____

_____

_____

Figure 35.4 Samples of Ishihara's color plates. These plates are reproduced from *Ishihara's Tests for Colour Blindness* published by Kanehara & Co., Ltd., Tokyo, Japan, but tests for colorblindness cannot be conducted with this material. For accurate testing, the original plates should be used.

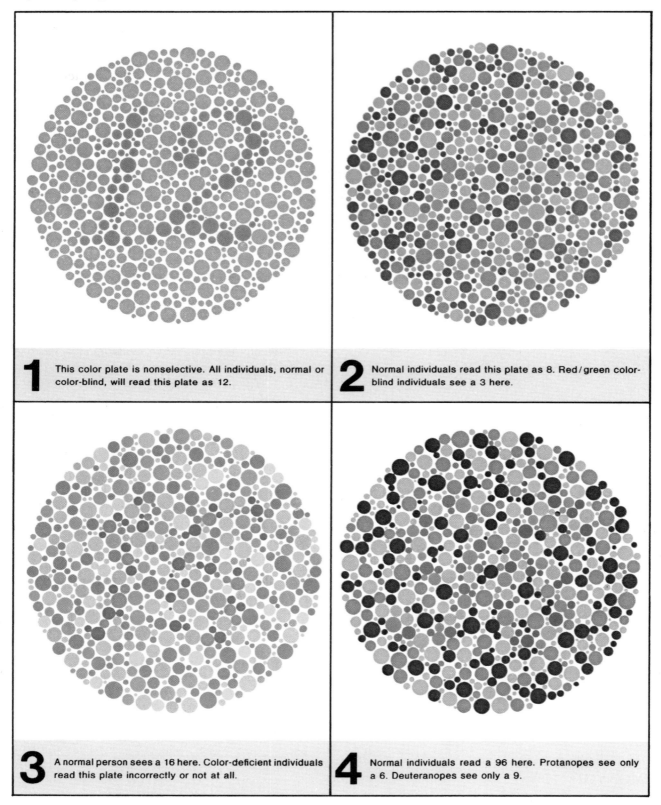

1 This color plate is nonselective. All individuals, normal or color-blind, will read this plate as 12.

2 Normal individuals read this plate as 8. Red/green color-blind individuals see a 3 here.

3 A normal person sees a 16 here. Color-deficient individuals read this plate incorrectly or not at all.

4 Normal individuals read a 96 here. Protanopes see only a 6. Deuteranopes see only a 9.

Figure 35.5 Blind-spot demonstration.

2. *Photopupillary reflex.* The smooth muscles of the iris control the size of the pupil. For example, when the intensity of light entering the eye increases, a photopupillary reflex is triggered, and the circular muscles of the iris are stimulated to contract. As a result, the size of the pupil decreases, and less light enters the eye.

   To demonstrate this reflex, follow these steps:
   a. Ask your partner to sit with his or her hands thoroughly covering his or her eyes for 2 minutes.
   b. Position a pen flashlight close to one eye with the light shining on the hand that covers the eye.
   c. Ask your partner to remove the hand quickly.
   d. Observe the pupil and note any change in its size.
   e. Have your partner remove the other hand, but keep that uncovered eye shielded from extra light.
   f. Observe both pupils and note any difference in their sizes.

3. *Accommodation pupillary reflex.* The pupil constricts as a normal accommodation reflex to focusing on close objects. To demonstrate the accommodation reflex, follow these steps:
   a. Have your partner stare for several seconds at some dimly illuminated object in the room that is more than 20 feet away.
   b. Observe the size of the pupil of one eye. Then hold a pencil about 25 cm in front of your partner's face, and have your partner stare at it.
   c. Note any change in the size of the pupil.

4. *Convergence reflex.* The eyes converge as a normal convergence reflex to focusing on close objects. To demonstrate the convergence reflex, follow these steps:
   a. Repeat the procedure outlined for the accommodation pupillary reflex.
   b. Note any change in the position of the eyeballs as your partner changes focus from the distant object to the pencil.

5. Complete Part B of the laboratory report.

NOTES

VISUAL TESTS AND DEMONSTRATIONS

PART A

1. Visual acuity test results:

Eye Tested	Acuity Values
Right eye	
Right eye with glasses (if applicable)	
Left eye	
Left eye with glasses (if applicable)	

2. Astigmatism test results:

Eye Tested	Darker Lines
Right eye	
Right eye with glasses (if applicable)	
Left eye	
Left eye with glasses (if applicable)	

3. Accommodation test results:

Eye Tested	Near Point (cm)
Right eye	
Right eye with glasses (if applicable)	
Left eye	
Left eye with glasses (if applicable)	

4. Color vision test results:

Condition	Males			Females		
	Class Number	**Class Percentage**	**Expected Percentage**	**Class Number**	**Class Percentage**	**Expected Percentage**
Normal color vision			93			99.6
Deficient red-green color vision			7			0.4
Protanopia (lack red-sensitive cones)			less-frequent type			less-frequent type
Deuteranopia (lack green-sensitive cones)			more-frequent type			more-frequent type

5. Complete the following:

a. What is meant by 20/70 vision? _____

_____

b. What is meant by 20/10 vision? _____

_____

c. What visual problem is created by astigmatism? _____

_____

d. Why does the near point of accommodation often increase with age? _____

_____

e. Describe the eye defect that causes color-deficient vision. _____

_____

PART B

1. Blind-spot results:
   a. Right eye distance _____
   b. Left eye distance _____

Complete the following:

2. Explain why an eye has a blind spot. _____

_____

3. Describe the photopupillary reflex. _____

_____

4. What difference did you note in the size of the pupils when one eye was exposed to bright light and the other eye was shielded from the light? _____

_____

5. Describe the accommodation pupillary reflex. _____

_____

6. Describe the convergence reflex. _____

_____

ENDOCRINE HISTOLOGY AND DIABETIC PHYSIOLOGY

MATERIALS NEEDED

For Procedure A—Endocrine Histology:

Textbook
Human torso model
Compound light microscope
Prepared microscope slides of the following:
    Pituitary gland
    Thyroid gland
    Parathyroid gland
    Adrenal gland
    Pancreas

For Procedure B—Insulin Shock:

500 mL beaker
Live small fish (1″ to 1.5″ goldfish, guppy, rosy red
    feeder, or other)
Small fish net
Insulin (regular U-100) (HumulinR in 10 mL vials has
    100 units/mL; store in refrigerator—do not freeze)
Syringes for U-100 insulin
10% glucose solution
Clock or timer

For Learning Extension:

Compound light microscope
Prepared microscope slides of the following:
    Normal human pancreas (stained for alpha and
      beta cells)
    Human pancreas of diabetic

SAFETY

- Review all the safety guidelines inside the front cover.
- Wear disposable gloves when handling the fish and syringes.
- Dispose of the used syringe and needle in the puncture-resistant container.
- Wash your hands before leaving the laboratory.

The endocrine system consists of ductless glands that act together with parts of the nervous system to help control body activities. The endocrine glands secrete hormones that are transported in body fluids and affect cells possessing appropriate receptor molecules. In this way, hormones influence the rate of metabolic reactions, the transport of substances through cell membranes, and the regulation of water and electrolyte balances. By controlling cellular activities, endocrine glands play important roles in the maintenance of homeostasis.

The primary "fuel" for the mitochondria of cells is sugar (glucose). Insulin produced by the beta cells of the pancreatic islets has a primary regulation role in the transport of blood sugar across the cell membranes. Some individuals do not produce enough of their own insulin; others might not have adequate transport of glucose into the body cells when cells lose insulin receptors. This rather common disease is called *diabetes mellitus*. Diabetes mellitus is a functional disease that might have its onset either during childhood or later in life.

The protein hormone insulin has several functions: it stimulates the liver and skeletal muscles to form glycogen from glucose; it inhibits the conversion of noncarbohydrates into glycogen; it promotes the facilitated diffusion of glucose across cell membranes of cells possessing insulin receptors (adipose tissue, cardiac muscle, and resting skeletal muscle); it decreases blood sugar (glucose); it increases protein synthesis; and it promotes fat storage in adipose cells. In a normal person, as blood sugar increases during nutrient absorption after a meal, a negative feedback mechanism creates an increase in insulin production by beta cells. This increase in insulin prevents blood sugar from sudden surges (hyperglycemia) by promoting glycogen production in the liver and an increase in the entry of glucose into muscle and adipose cells.

Between meals and during sleep, blood glucose levels decrease and insulin also decreases. When insulin concentration decreases, more glucose is available to enter cells that lack insulin receptors. Neurons, liver cells, kidney cells, and red blood cells lack insulin receptors and obtain their glucose by facilitated diffusion. These neurons depend upon blood glucose concentrations to enable cellular respiration and ATP production. When insulin is given as a medication for diabetes mellitus, blood glucose levels may drop drastically (hypoglycemia) if the individual does not eat some food. This can have significant effects on the nervous system, resulting in insulin shock.

Type 1 diabetes mellitus usually has a rapid onset relatively early in life, but it can occur in adults. It occurs when insulin is no longer produced; hence it is referred to as *insulin-dependent diabetes mellitus (IDDM)*. This autoimmune disorder occurs when the immune system destroys beta cells, resulting in a decrease in insulin production. This disorder affects about 10 to 15% of diabetics. The treatment for type 1 diabetes mellitus is to administer insulin, usually by injection.

Type 2 diabetes mellitus has a gradual onset, usually in those over age 40. It is also called *non-insulin-dependent diabetes mellitus (NIDDM)*. This disease results as body cells become less sensitive to insulin or lose insulin receptors and cannot respond to insulin even though insulin levels may remain normal. Risk factors for the onset of type 2 diabetes mellitus, which afflicts about 85 to 90% of diabetics, include heredity, obesity, and lack of exercise. Obesity is a major indicator for predicting type 2 diabetes; a weight loss of a mere 10 pounds will increase the body's sensitivity to insulin as a means of prevention. The treatments for type 2 diabetes mellitus include a diet that avoids foods that stimulate insulin production, weight control, exercise, and medications. (The causes and treatments for type 2 diabetes closely resemble those for coronary artery disease!)

PURPOSE OF THE EXERCISE

To examine microscopically the tissues of endocrine glands and to observe behavior changes that occur during insulin shock.

LEARNING OBJECTIVES

After completing this exercise, you should be able to

1. Name and locate the major endocrine glands.
2. Recognize tissue sections from the pituitary gland, thyroid gland, parathyroid glands, adrenal glands, and pancreas.
3. Compare the causes, symptoms, and treatments for type 1 and type 2 diabetes mellitus.
4. Observe the behavioral changes caused by insulin shock.
5. Observe the recovery from insulin shock when sugar is provided to cells.

PROCEDURE A—ENDOCRINE HISTOLOGY

1. Review the sections entitled "Pituitary Gland," "Thyroid Gland," "Parathyroid Glands," "Adrenal Glands," "Pancreas," and "Other Endocrine Glands" in chapter 13 of the textbook.
2. As a review activity, label figure 36.1.

Figure 36.1 Label the major endocrine glands.

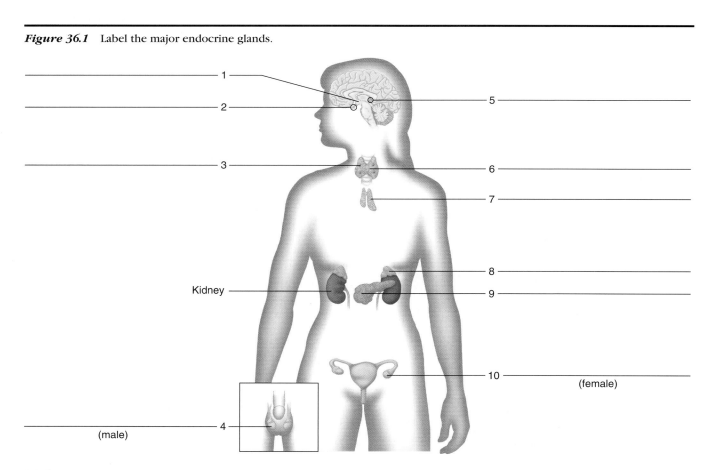

Kidney

(male)

(female)

3. Examine the human torso model and locate the following:

hypothalamus
pituitary stalk (infundibulum)
pituitary gland (hypophysis)
    anterior lobe (adenohypophysis)
    posterior lobe (neurohypophysis)
thyroid gland
parathyroid glands
adrenal glands (suprarenal glands)
    adrenal medulla
    adrenal cortex
pancreas
pineal gland
thymus gland
ovaries
testes

4. Examine the microscopic tissue sections of the following glands, and identify the features described:

Pituitary gland. To examine the pituitary tissue, follow these steps:
   a. Observe the tissues using low-power magnification (fig. 36.2).
   b. Locate the *pituitary stalk (infundibulum)*, the *anterior lobe* (the largest part of the gland), and the *posterior lobe.*
   c. Observe an area of the anterior lobe with high-power magnification. Locate a cluster of relatively large cells and identify some *acidophil cells,* which contain pink-stained granules, and some *basophil cells,* which contain blue-stained granules. These acidophil and basophil cells are hormone-secreting cells.
   d. Observe an area of the posterior lobe with high-power magnification. Note the numerous unmyelinated nerve fibers present in this lobe. Also locate some *pituicytes,* a type of neuroglial cell, scattered among the nerve fibers.
   e. Prepare labeled sketches of representative portions of the anterior and posterior lobes of the pituitary gland in Part A of Laboratory Report 36.

Thyroid gland. To examine the thyroid tissue, follow these steps:
   a. Use low-power magnification to observe the tissue (fig. 36.3). Note the numerous *follicles,* each of which consists of a layer of cells surrounding a colloid-filled cavity.
   b. Observe the tissue using high-power magnification. Note that the cells forming the wall of a follicle are simple cuboidal epithelial cells.
   c. Prepare a labeled sketch of a representative portion of the thyroid gland in Part A of the laboratory report.

Parathyroid gland. To examine the parathyroid tissue, follow these steps:
   a. Use low-power magnification to observe the tissue (fig. 36.4). Note that the gland consists of numerous tightly packed secretory cells.
   b. Switch to high-power magnification and locate two types of cells—a smaller form (chief cells) that are arranged in cordlike patterns and a

Figure 36.2   Micrograph of the pituitary gland (6×).

Hypothalamus

Pituitary stalk

Posterior lobe

Anterior lobe

Figure 36.3 Micrograph of the thyroid gland (100× micrograph enlarged to 300×).

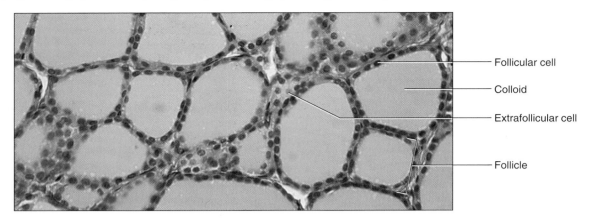

- Follicular cell
- Colloid
- Extrafollicular cell
- Follicle

Figure 36.4 Micrograph of the parathyroid gland (65×).

- Blood vessel
- Oxyphil cells
- Chief cells
- Adipose cell

Figure 36.5 Micrograph of the adrenal cortex and the adrenal medulla (75×).

- Capsule
- Zona glomerulosa
- Zona fasciculata
- Cortex
- Zona reticularis
- Medulla
- Chromaffin cells

larger form (oxyphil cells) that have distinct cell boundaries and are present in clusters. *Chief cells* secrete parathyroid hormone, whereas the function of *oxyphil cells* is not clearly understood.

c. Prepare a labeled sketch of a representative portion of the parathyroid gland in Part A of the laboratory report.

Adrenal gland. To examine the adrenal tissue, follow these steps:

a. Use low-power magnification to observe the tissue (fig. 36.5). Note the thin capsule of connective tissue that covers the gland. Just beneath the capsule, there is a relatively thick *adrenal cortex.* The central portion of the gland is the *adrenal medulla.* The cells of the cortex

are in three poorly defined layers. Those of the outer layer (zona glomerulosa) are arranged irregularly; those of the middle layer (zona fasciculata) are in long cords; and those of the inner layer (zona reticularis) are arranged in an interconnected network of cords. The cells of the medulla are relatively large and irregularly shaped, and they often occur in clusters.

b. Using high-power magnification, observe each of the layers of the cortex and the cells of the medulla.

c. Prepare labeled sketches of representative portions of the adrenal cortex and medulla in Part A of the laboratory report.

Figure 36.6 Micrograph of the pancreas (100×).

Pancreatic islet
(islet of Langerhans)

Endocrine cell

Exocrine (acinar) cells

Pancreas. To examine the pancreas tissue, follow these steps:

a. Use low-power magnification to observe the tissue (fig. 36.6). Note that the gland largely consists of deeply stained exocrine cells arranged in clusters around secretory ducts. These exocrine cells (acinar cells) secrete pancreatic juice rich in digestive enzymes. There are circular masses of lightly stained cells scattered throughout the gland. These clumps of cells constitute the *pancreatic islets (islets of Langerhans)*, and they represent the endocrine portion of the pancreas.

b. Examine an islet, using high-power magnification.

c. Prepare a labeled sketch of a representative portion of the pancreas in Part A of the laboratory report.

PROCEDURE B—INSULIN SHOCK

1. Review the sections entitled "Pancreas" and "Diabetes Mellitus—Clinical Application" in chapter 13 of the textbook, and the introduction to this lab.

2. Complete the table in Part B of the laboratory report.

3. A fish can be used to observe normal behavior, induced insulin shock, and recovery from insulin shock. The pancreatic islets are located in the pyloric ceca or other scattered regions in fish. The behavioral changes of fish when they experience insulin shock and recovery mimics those of humans. Observe a fish in 200 mL of aquarium water in a 500 mL beaker. Make your observations of swimming, gill cover (operculum), and mouth movements for 5 minutes. Record your observations in Part C of the laboratory report.

4. Add 200 units of room-temperature insulin slowly, using the syringe, into the water with the fish to induce insulin shock. Record the time or start the timer when the insulin is added. Watch for changes of the swimming, gill cover, and mouth movements as insulin diffuses into the blood at the gills. Signs of insulin shock might include rapid and irregular movements. As hypoglycemia occurs from the increased insulin absorption, the brain cells obtain less of the much-needed glucose, and epinephrine is secreted. Consequently, a rapid heart rate, anxiety, sweating, mental disorientation, impaired vision, dizziness, convulsions, and possible unconsciousness are complications during insulin shock. Record your observations of any behavioral changes and the time of the onset in Part C of the laboratory report.

5. After definite behavioral changes are observed, use the small fish net to move the fish into another 500 mL beaker containing 200 mL of a 10% room-temperature glucose solution. Record the time when the fish is transferred into this container. Make observations of any recovery of normal behaviors, including the amount of time involved. Record your observations in Part C of the laboratory report.

6. When the fish appears to be fully recovered, return the fish to its normal container. Dispose of the syringe according to directions from your laboratory instructor.

7. Complete Part C of the laboratory report.

LEARNING EXTENSION

Examine the normal pancreas under high-power magnification (fig. 36.6). Locate the clumps of cells that constitute the *pancreatic islets (islets of Langerhans)* that represent the endocrine portions of the organ. A pancreatic islet contains four distinct cells that secrete different hormones: *alpha cells,* which secrete glucagon, *beta cells,* which secrete insulin, *delta cells,* which secrete somatostatin, and *F cells,* which secrete pancreatic polypeptide. Some of the specially stained pancreatic islets allow for distinguishing the different types of cells. The normal pancreatic islet has about 80% beta cells, about 15% alpha cells, about 5% delta cells, and a small number of F cells. There are complex interactions among the four hormones affecting blood sugar, but in general, glucagon will increase blood sugar while insulin will lower blood sugar. Somatostatin acts as a paracrine secretion to inhibit alpha and beta cell secretions, and pancreatic polypeptide inhibits secretions from delta cells and digestive enzyme secretions from the pancreatic acini.

Examine the pancreas of a diabetic under high-power magnification (fig. 36.7). Locate a pancreatic islet and note the number of beta cells as compared to a normal number of beta cells in the normal pancreatic islet.

Describe the differences that you observed between a normal pancreatic islet and a pancreatic islet of a person with diabetes mellitus.

_____

_____

_____

_____

_____

_____

_____

Figure 36.7 Micrograph of pancreas showing indications of changes from diabetes mellitus (100×).

Exocrine (acinar) cells

Pancreatic islet

Areas of fibrosis and amyloid replacement of islet cells

Web Quest

Examine conditions, treatments, and preventions of diabetes mellitus. Search these at www.mhhe.com/shier11
Click on Student Edition. Click on Martin Lab Manual, Web Quest.

Name _____

Date _____

Section _____

ENDOCRINE HISTOLOGY AND DIABETIC PHYSIOLOGY

PART A

Sketch and label representative portions of the following endocrine glands:

Pituitary gland (____×) (anterior and posterior lobes)	Thyroid gland (____×)
Parathyroid gland (____×)	Adrenal gland (____x) (cortex and medulla)
Pancreas (____×)	

PART B

Complete the missing parts of the table of diabetes mellitus:

Characteristic	Type 1 Diabetes	Type 2 Diabetes
Onset age	Early age or adult	
Onset of symptoms		Slow
Percentage of diabetics		85–90%
Natural insulin levels	Below normal	
Beta cells of pancreatic islets		Not destroyed
Pancreatic islet cell antibodies	Present	
Risk factors of having the disease	Heredity	
Typical treatments	Insulin administration	
Untreated blood sugar levels		Hyperglycemia

PART C

1. Record your observations of normal behavior of the fish.

   a. Swimming movements: _____

   _____

   b. Gill cover movements: _____

   _____

   c. Mouth movements: _____

   _____

2. Record your observations of the fish after insulin was added to the water.

   a. Recorded time that insulin was added: _____

   b. Swimming movements: _____

   _____

   c. Gill cover movements: _____

   _____

   d. Mouth movements: _____

   _____

   e. Elapsed time until the insulin shock symptoms occurred: _____

3. Record your observations after the fish was transferred into a glucose solution.

   a. Recorded time that fish was transferred into the glucose solution:_____

   b. Describe any changes in the behavior of the fish that indicates a recovery from insulin shock. _____

   _____

   _____

   _____

   c. Elapsed time until indications of a recovery from insulin shock occurred: _____

   ### Critical Thinking Application

   Describe the importance for a type 1 diabetic of regulating insulin administration, meals, and exercise.

   _____

   _____

   _____

   _____

   _____

   _____

   _____

   _____

NOTES

BLOOD CELLS

MATERIALS NEEDED

Textbook
Compound light microscope
Prepared microscope slides of human blood
    (Wright's stain)
Colored pencils

For Demonstration:

Mammal blood other than human or contaminant-free
    human blood is suggested as a substitute for
    collected blood
Microscope slides (precleaned)
Sterile disposable blood lancets
Sterile absorbent cotton
70% alcohol
Slide staining rack and tray
Wright's stain
Distilled water

For Learning Extension:

Prepared slides of pathological blood, such as eosinophilia,
    leukocytosis, leukopenia, and lymphocytosis

 SAFETY

- It is important that students learn and practice correct procedures for handling body fluids. Consider using either mammal blood other than human or contaminant-free blood that has been tested and is available from various laboratory supply houses. Some of the procedures might be accomplished as demonstrations only. If student blood is used, it is important that students handle only their own blood.
- Use an appropriate disinfectant to wash the laboratory tables before and after the procedures.
- Wear disposable gloves when handling blood samples.
- Clean end of a finger with 70% alcohol before the puncture is performed.
- The sterile blood lancet should be used only once.
- Dispose of used lancets and blood-contaminated items in an appropriate container (never use the wastebasket).
- Wash your hands before leaving the laboratory.

Blood is a type of connective tissue whose cells are suspended in a liquid extracellular matrix. These cells are mainly formed in red bone marrow, and they include *red blood cells, white blood cells,* and some cellular fragments called *platelets.*

Red blood cells transport gases between the body cells and the lungs, white blood cells defend the body against infections, and platelets play an important role in stoppage of bleeding (hemostasis).

PURPOSE OF THE EXERCISE

To review the characteristics of blood cells, to examine them microscopically, and to perform a differential white blood cell count.

LEARNING OBJECTIVES

After completing this exercise, you should be able to

1. Describe the structure and function of red blood cells, white blood cells, and platelets.
2. Identify red blood cells, five types of white blood cells, and platelets on a stained blood slide.
3. Perform a differential white blood cell count.

WARNING

Because of the possibility of blood infections being transmitted from one student to another if blood slides are prepared in the classroom, it is suggested that commercially prepared blood slides be used in this exercise. The instructor, however, may wish to demonstrate the procedure for preparing such a slide. Observe all safety procedures for this lab.

DEMONSTRATION—BLOOD SLIDE PREPARATION

To prepare a stained blood slide, follow these steps:

1. Obtain two precleaned microscope slides. Avoid touching their flat surfaces.

Figure 37.1 To prepare a blood smear: (*a*) place a drop of blood about 2 cm from the end of a clean slide; (*b*) hold a second slide at about a 45° angle to the first one, allowing the blood to spread along its edge; (*c*) push the second slide over the surface of the first so that it pulls the blood with it; (*d*) observe the completed blood smear. The ideal smear should be 1½ inches in length, be evenly distributed, and contain a smooth, feathered edge.

2. Thoroughly wash hands with soap and water and dry them with paper towels.
3. Cleanse the end of the middle finger with some sterile cotton moistened with 70% alcohol and let the finger dry in the air.
4. Remove a sterile disposable blood lancet from its package without touching the sharp end.
5. Puncture the skin on the side near the tip of the middle finger with the lancet and properly discard the lancet.
6. Wipe away the first drop of blood with the cotton ball. Place a drop of blood about 2 cm from the end of a clean microscope slide.
7. Use a second slide to spread the blood across the first slide, as illustrated in figure 37.1. Discard the slide used for spreading the blood in the appropriate container.
8. Place the blood slide on a slide staining rack and let it dry in the air.
9. Put enough Wright's stain on the slide to cover the smear but not overflow the slide. Count the number of drops of stain that are used.
10. After 2–3 minutes, add an equal volume of distilled water to the stain and let the slide stand for 4 minutes. From time to time, gently blow on the liquid to mix the water and stain.
11. Flood the slide with distilled water until the blood smear appears light blue.
12. Tilt the slide to pour off the water, and let the slide dry in the air.

Figure 37.2 Blood cells illustrating some of the numerous variations of each type. Appearance characteristics for each cell pertains to a thin blood film using Wright's stain.

Neutrophils
- Fine light-purple granules
- Nucleus single to five lobes (highly variable)

Eosinophils
- Coarse reddish granules
- Nucleus usually bilobed

Basophils
- Coarse deep blue to almost black granules
- Nucleus usually S or U shaped
- Nucleus often almost hidden by granules

Lymphocytes
- Slightly larger than RBCs
- Thin rim of nearly clear cytoplasm
- Nearly round nucleus appears to fill most of cell in smaller lymphocytes
- Larger lymphocytes hard to distinguish from some monocytes

Monocytes
- Largest WBC; 2–3x larger than RBCs
- Cytoplasm nearly clear
- Nucleus round, kidney-shaped, oval, or lobed

Platelets
- Cell fragments
- Single to small clusters

Erythrocytes
- Lack nucleus (mature cell)
- Biconcave discs
- Thin centers appear almost hollow

13. Examine the blood smear with low-power magnification, and locate an area where the blood cells are well distributed. Observe these cells, using high-power magnification and then an oil immersion objective if one is available.

PROCEDURE A—TYPES OF BLOOD CELLS

1. Review the sections entitled "Characteristics of Red Blood Cells," "Types of White Blood Cells," and "Blood Platelets" in chapter 14 of the textbook.
2. Complete Part A of Laboratory Report 37.
3. Refer to figures 14.9–14.13 in the textbook and figure 37.2 as an aid in identifying the various types of blood cells. Study the functions of the blood cells listed in table 37.1. Use the prepared slide of blood and locate each of the following:

   red blood cell (erythrocyte)

   white blood cell (leukocyte)

      granulocytes

         neutrophil

         eosinophil

         basophil

      agranulocytes

         lymphocyte

         monocyte

   platelet (thrombocyte)

4. In Part B of the laboratory report, prepare sketches of single blood cells to illustrate each type. Pay particular attention to relative size, nuclear shape, and color of granules in the cytoplasm (if present).

Table 37.1   Cellular Components of Blood

Component	Function
Red blood cell (erythrocyte)	Transports oxygen and carbon dioxide
White blood cell (leukocyte)	Destroys pathogenic microorganisms and parasites and removes worn cells
Granulocytes	
1. Neutrophil	Phagocytizes small particles
2. Eosinophil	Kills parasites and helps control inflammation and allergic reactions
3. Basophil	Releases heparin and histamine
Agranulocytes	
1. Monocyte	Phagocytizes large particles
2. Lymphocyte	Provides immunity
Platelet (thrombocyte)	Helps control blood loss from broken vessels

Figure 37.3   Move the blood slide back and forth to avoid passing the same cells twice.

PROCEDURE B—DIFFERENTIAL WHITE BLOOD CELL COUNT

A differential white blood cell count is performed to determine the percentage of each of the various types of white blood cells present in a blood sample. The test is useful because the relative proportions of white blood cells may change in particular diseases. Neutrophils, for example, usually increase during bacterial infections, whereas eosinophils may increase during certain parasitic infections and allergic reactions.

1. To make a differential white blood cell count, follow these steps:
   a. Using high-power magnification or an oil immersion objective, focus on the cells at one end of a prepared blood slide where the cells are well distributed.
   b. Slowly move the blood slide back and forth, following a path that avoids passing over the same cells twice (fig. 37.3).
   c. Each time you encounter a white blood cell, identify its type and record it in Part C of the laboratory report.
   d. Continue searching for and identifying white blood cells until you have recorded 100 cells in the data table. Because *percent* means "parts of 100," for each type of white blood cell, the total number observed is equal to its percentage in the blood sample.
2. Complete Part C of the laboratory report.

✏️ LEARNING EXTENSION

Obtain a prepared slide of pathological blood that has been stained with Wright's stain. Perform a differential white blood cell count using this slide, and compare the results with the values for normal blood listed in table 37.2.

What differences do you note? _____

_____

_____

Table 37.2 Differential White Blood Cell Count

Cell Type	Normal Value (percent)	Elevated Levels May Indicate
Neutrophil	54–62	Bacterial infections, stress
Lymphocyte	25–33	Mononucleosis, whooping cough, viral infections
Monocyte	3–9	Malaria, tuberculosis, fungal infections
Eosinophil	1–3	Allergic reactions, autoimmune diseases, parasitic worms
Basophil	<1	Cancers, chicken pox, hypothyroidism

Web Quest

What are the functions of the various blood components? What do abnormal amounts indicate? Search these and review blood cell identification at

www.mhhe.com/shier11

Click on Student Edition. Click on Martin Lab Manual, Web Quest.

Notes

Laboratory Report **37**

Name _____

Date _____

Section _____

BLOOD CELLS

PART A

Complete the following statements:

1. Mature red blood cells are also called _____ .
2. The shape of a red blood cell can be described as a _____ disc.
3. The functions of red blood cells are _____ .
4. _____ is the oxygen-carrying substance in a red blood cell.
5. Red blood cells with high oxygen concentrations are bright red because of the presence of

    _____ .
6. Red blood cells cannot reproduce because they lack _____ when they are mature.
7. White blood cells are also called _____ .
8. White blood cells with granular cytoplasm are called _____ .
9. White blood cells lacking granular cytoplasm are called _____ .
10. Polymorphonuclear leukocyte is another name for a _____ with a segmented nucleus.
11. Normally, the most numerous white blood cells are _____ .
12. White blood cells whose cytoplasmic granules stain red in acid stain are called _____ .
13. _____ are normally the least abundant of the white blood cells.
14. _____ are the largest of the white blood cells.
15. _____ are small agranulocytes that have relatively large, round nuclei with thin rims of cytoplasm.
16. Upon an injury, platelets adhere to _____ found in connective tissue.
17. In the presence of damaged blood vessels, platelets release a substance called _____, which causes smooth muscle contraction.
18. In red bone marrow, blood cells develop from cells called _____ .

PART B

Sketch a single blood cell of each type in the following spaces. Use colored pencils to represent the stained colors of the cells. Label any features that can be identified.

Red blood cell (_____×)

Neutrophil (_____×)

Lymphocyte (_____×)

Monocyte (_____×)

Eosinophil (_____×)

Basophil (_____×)

Platelet (_____×)

PART C

1. *Differential White Blood Cell Count Data Table.* As you identify white blood cells, record them on the table by using a tally system, such as Ɨʜ̅ Il. Place tally marks in the "Number Observed" column, and total each of the five WBCs when the differential count is completed. Obtain a total of all five WBCs counted to determine the percent of each WBC type.

Type of WBC	Number Observed	Total	Percent
Neutrophil			
Lymphocyte			
Monocyte			
Eosinophil			
Basophil			
		Total of column	

2. How do the results of your differential white blood cell count compare with the normal values listed in table 37.2? _____

_____

_____

_____

_____

Critical Thinking Application

What is the difference between a differential white blood cell count and a total white blood cell count?

_____

_____

_____

_____

_____

NOTES

LABORATORY EXERCISE 38

BLOOD TESTING— A DEMONSTRATION

MATERIALS NEEDED

Mammal blood other than human or contaminant-free human blood is suggested as a substitute for collected blood
Textbook
Sterile disposable blood lancets
Sterile absorbent cotton
70% alcohol

For Demonstration A:

Heparinized microhematocrit capillary tube
Sealing clay (or Critocaps)
Microhematocrit centrifuge
Microhematocrit reader

For Demonstration B:

Hemoglobinometer
Lens paper
Hemolysis applicator

For Demonstration C:

Hemocytometer
Unopette system (a Becton Dickinson product) for counting red blood cells (see Instructor's Manual for a supplier)
Compound light microscope
Hand counter (tally)

For Demonstration D:

Hemocytometer
Unopette system (a Becton Dickinson product) for counting white blood cells (see Instructor's Manual for a supplier)
Compound light microscope
Hand counter (tally)

For Alternative Hemoglobin Content:

Tallquist test kit

 SAFETY

- It is important that students learn and practice correct procedures for handling body fluids. Consider using either mammal blood other than human or contaminant-free blood that has been tested and is available from various laboratory supply houses. Some of the procedures might be accomplished as demonstrations only. If student blood is used, it is important that students handle only their own blood.

- Use an appropriate disinfectant to wash the laboratory tables before and after the procedures.
- Wear disposable gloves when handling blood samples.
- Clean the end of a finger with 70% alcohol before the puncture is performed.
- The sterile blood lancet should be used only once.
- Dispose of used lancets and blood-contaminated items in an appropriate container (never use the wastebasket).
- Wash your hands before leaving the laboratory.

As an aid in identifying various disease conditions, tests are often performed on blood to determine how its composition compares with normal values. These tests commonly include hematocrit (red blood cell percentage), hemoglobin content, red blood cell count, and total white blood cell count. Common tests performed on the blood can be found in Appendix B of the textbook. Use the clinical significance in Appendix B for the tests in this lab to determine what factors can influence the normal values.

PURPOSE OF THE EXERCISE

To observe the blood tests used to determine hematocrit, hemoglobin content, red blood cell count, and total white blood cell count.

LEARNING OBJECTIVES

After completing this exercise, you should be able to

1. Determine the hematocrit in a blood sample.
2. Determine the hemoglobin content of a blood sample.
3. Describe how a red blood cell count is performed.
4. Describe how a total white blood cell count is performed.

WARNING

Because of the possibility of blood infections being transmitted from one student to another during blood-testing procedures, it is suggested that the following demonstrations be performed by the instructor. Observe all safety procedures listed for this lab.

DEMONSTRATION A—HEMATOCRIT

To determine the hematocrit (percentage of red blood cells) in a whole blood sample, the cells must be separated from the liquid plasma. This separation can be rapidly accomplished by placing a tube of blood in a centrifuge. The force created by the spinning motion of the centrifuge causes the cells to be packed into the lower end of the tube. Then the quantities of cells and plasma can be measured, and the percentage of cells (hematocrit or packed cell volume) can be calculated.

1. To determine the hematocrit in a blood sample, follow these steps:
   a. Lance the end of a finger to obtain a drop of blood. *See the demonstration in Laboratory Exercise 37 for directions.*
   b. Touch the drop of blood with the colored end of a heparinized capillary tube. Hold the tube tilted slightly upward so that the blood will easily move into it by capillary action (fig. 38.1). To prevent an air bubble, keep the tip in the blood until filled.
   c. Allow the blood to fill about two-thirds of the length of the tube.
   d. Hold a finger over the tip of the dry end so that blood will not drain out while you seal the blood end. Plug the blood end of the tube by pushing it with a rotating motion into sealing clay or by adding a plastic Critocap.
   e. Place the sealed tube into one of the numbered grooves of a microhematocrit centrifuge. The tube's sealed end should point outward from the center and should touch the rubber lining on the rim of the centrifuge (fig. 38.1).
   f. The centrifuge should be balanced by placing specimen tubes on opposite sides of the moving head, the inside cover should be tightened with the lock wrench, and the outside cover should be securely fastened.
   g. Run the centrifuge for 3–5 minutes.
   h. After the centrifuge has stopped, remove the specimen tube and note that the red blood cells have been packed into the bottom of the tube. The clear liquid on top of the cells is plasma.
   i. Use a microhematocrit reader to determine the percentage of red blood cells in the tube. If a microhematocrit reader is not available, measure the total length of the blood column in millimeters (red cells plus plasma) and the length of the red blood cell column alone in millimeters. Divide the red blood cell length by the total blood column length and multiply the answer by 100 to calculate the percentage of red blood cells.
   j. Record the test result in Part A of Laboratory Report 38.
2. Complete Part B of the laboratory report.

Figure 38.1 Steps in the hematocrit (red blood cell percentage) procedure: (*a*) load a heparinized capillary tube with blood; (*b*) plug the blood end of the tube with sealing clay; (*c*) place the tube in a microhematocrit centrifuge.

(a)

(b)

(c)

DEMONSTRATION B—HEMOGLOBIN CONTENT

Although the hemoglobin content of a blood sample can be measured in several ways, a common method uses a hemoglobinometer. This instrument is designed to compare the color of light passing through a hemolyzed blood sample with a standard color. The results of the test are expressed in grams of hemoglobin per 100 mL of blood or in percentage of normal values.

1. To measure the hemoglobin content of a blood sample, follow these steps:
   a. Obtain a hemoglobinometer and remove the blood chamber from the slot in its side.
   b. Separate the pieces of glass from the metal clip and clean them with 70% alcohol and lens paper. Note that one of the pieces of glass has two broad, U-shaped areas surrounded by depressions. The other piece is flat on both sides.
   c. Obtain a large drop of blood from a finger, as before.
   d. Place the drop of blood on one of the U-shaped areas of the blood chamber glass.
   e. Stir the blood with the tip of a hemolysis applicator until the blood appears clear rather than cloudy. This usually takes about 45 seconds.
   f. Place the flat piece of glass on top of the blood plate and slide both into the metal clip of the blood chamber.
   g. Push the blood chamber into the slot on the side of the hemoglobinometer, making sure that it is in all the way (fig. 38.2).
   h. Hold the hemoglobinometer in the left hand with the thumb on the light switch on the underside.
   i. Look into the eyepiece and note the green area that is split in half.
   j. Slowly move the slide on the side of the instrument back and forth with the right hand until the two halves of the green area look the same.
   k. Note the value in the upper scale (grams of hemoglobin per 100 mL of blood), indicated by the mark in the center of the movable slide.
   l. Record the test result in Part A of the laboratory report.
2. Complete Part C of the laboratory report.

ALTERNATIVE PROCEDURE

The *Tallquist method* can also be used to determine reasonably accurate hemoglobin content. The Tallquist test kit contains a special test paper, color scale, and directions.

Figure 38.2 Steps in the hemoglobin content procedure: (*a*) load the blood chamber with blood; (*b*) stir the blood with a hemolysis applicator; (*c*) place the blood chamber in the slot of the hemoglobinometer; (*d*) match the colors in the green area by moving the slide on the side of the instrument.

(a)

(b)

(c)

(d)

Figure 38.3 Location of the counting areas of a hemocytometer.

Depression

Ridge

Coverslip

Counting areas

Hemocytometer

Figure 38.4 The pattern of lines in a counting area of a hemocytometer. The squares marked with *R* are used to count red blood cells, whereas the squares marked with *W* are used to count white blood cells.

DEMONSTRATION C—RED BLOOD CELL COUNT

Although modern clinical laboratories commonly use electronic instruments to obtain blood cell counts, a hemocytometer provides a convenient and inexpensive way to count both red and white blood cells. This instrument is a special microscope slide on which there are two counting areas (fig. 38.3). Each counting area contains a grid of tiny lines forming nine large squares that are further subdivided into smaller squares (fig. 38.4).

The squares on the counting area have known dimensions. When a coverslip is placed over the area, it is held a known distance above the grid by glass ridges of the hemocytometer. Thus, when a liquid is placed under the coverslip, the volume of liquid covering each part of the grid can be calculated. Also, if the number of blood cells in a tiny volume of blood can be counted, it is possible to calculate the number that must be present in any larger volume.

When red blood cells are counted using a hemocytometer, a small sample of blood is drawn into a special pipette, and the blood is diluted to reduce the number of cells that must be counted. Some of the diluted blood is spread over the counting area, and with the aid of a microscope, all of the cells in the grid areas marked *R* are counted (fig. 38.4). The total count is multiplied by 10,000 to correct for the dilution and for the fact that only a small volume of blood was observed. The final result provides the number of red blood cells per cubic millimeter in the original blood sample.

1. To perform a red blood cell count, follow these steps:
   a. Examine a hemocytometer, and use a microscope to locate the grid of a counting area. Focus on the large central square of the grid with low-power and then with high-power

Figure 38.5 The Unopette system consists of a reservoir containing blood cell diluting fluid (*left*) and a plastic capillary tube within a plastic shield (*right*).

   magnification. Adjust the light intensity so that the lines are clear and sharp.
   b. Wash the hemocytometer with soap and water, and dry it. Place the coverslip over the counting areas and set the instrument aside.
   c. Examine the Unopette system for counting red blood cells, which consists of a reservoir containing blood cell diluting fluid and a plastic capillary tube assembly within a plastic shield (fig. 38.5).
   d. Place the Unopette reservoir on the table and gently force the pointed tip of the capillary tube

Figure 38.6 The Unopette capillary tube fills with blood by capillary action.

Figure 38.7 The Unopette dropper system being used to fill a hemocytometer with blood. When you squeeze the reservoir, a drop of diluted blood enters the counting areas under the coverslip by capillary action.

shield through the thin diaphragm at the top of the reservoir.

e. Lance the tip of a finger, as before, to obtain a drop of blood.

f. Remove the Unopette capillary tube from its shield and, holding the tube horizontally, touch the tip of the tube to the drop of blood. Allow the tube to fill completely with blood by capillary action (fig. 38.6).

g. Gently squeeze the reservoir, taking care not to expel any of its fluid content, and while maintaining pressure on the sides of the reservoir, insert the capillary tube through the punctured diaphragm of the reservoir. Release the pressure on the sides of the reservoir and allow the blood to be drawn into its chamber.

h. Hold the capillary tube assembly in the reservoir and gently squeeze the sides of the reservoir several times to mix the blood with the diluting fluid inside. Also, invert the reservoir a few times to aid this mixing process.

i. Remove the capillary tube assembly from the reservoir and insert the opposite end of the assembly into the top of the reservoir, thus converting the parts into a dropper system (fig. 38.7).

j. Gently squeeze the sides of the reservoir to expel some of the diluted blood from the capillary tube. Discard the first four drops of this mixture, and place the next drop of diluted blood at the edge of the coverslip near a counting area of the hemocytometer (fig. 38.7). If the hemocytometer is properly charged with diluted blood, the space between the counting area and the coverslip will be filled and will lack air bubbles, but no fluid will spill over into the depression on either side.

k. Place the hemocytometer on the microscope stage and focus on the large, central square of the counting area with the low-power objective

and then the high-power objective. Adjust the light so that the grid lines and blood cells are clearly visible.

l. Count all the cells in the five areas corresponding to those marked with *R* in figure 38.4. To obtain an accurate count, include cells that are touching the lines at the tops and left sides of the squares, but do not count those touching the bottoms and right sides of the squares. The use of a hand counter facilitates the counting task.

m. Multiply the total count by 10,000, and record the result (cells per cubic millimeter of blood) in Part A of the laboratory report.

n. Discard or clean the materials as directed by the laboratory instructor.

2. Complete Part D of the laboratory report.

DEMONSTRATION D—TOTAL WHITE BLOOD CELL COUNT

A hemocytometer is used to make a total white blood cell count in much the same way that it was used to count red blood cells. However, in the case of white cell counting, a diluting fluid is used that destroys red blood cells. Also, in making the white cell count, all of the cells in the four large squares marked *W* in figure 38.4 are included. The total count is multiplied by 50 to calculate the total number of white blood cells in a cubic millimeter of the blood sample.

1. To perform a total white blood cell count, follow these steps:

a. Clean the hemocytometer as before.

b. Lance the tip of a finger, as before, to obtain a drop of blood.

317

c. Repeat steps 1*c*–1*g* of the procedure for counting red blood cells, but use a Unopette system for counting white blood cells.

d. After mixing the blood with the diluting fluid in the reservoir, discard the first four drops of the mixture and charge the hemocytometer with diluted blood as before.

e. Use low-power magnification to locate the areas of the grid corresponding to those marked with *W* in figure 38.4.

f. Count all of the cells in the four large squares (remember that the red blood cells were destroyed by the white blood cell diluting fluid), following the same counting rules as before.

g. Multiply the total by 50, and record the result in Part A of the laboratory report.

h. Discard or clean the materials as directed by the laboratory instructor.

2. Complete Part E of the laboratory report.

ALTERNATIVE PROCEDURE

Laboratories in modern hospitals and clinics use updated hematology analyzers (fig. 38.8) for evaluations of the blood factors that are described in laboratory exercise 38. The more traditional procedures performed in these laboratory activities will help you to better understand each blood characteristic.

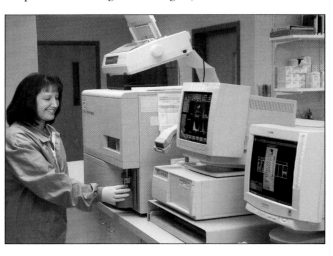

Figure 38.8 Modern hematology analyzer being used in the laboratory of a clinic. (*Note:* A tour of a laboratory in a modern hospital or clinic might be arranged.)

Laboratory Report 38

Name _____
Date _____
Section _____

BLOOD TESTING— A DEMONSTRATION

PART A

Blood test data:

Blood Test	Test Results	Normal Values
Hematocrit (mL per 100 mL blood)		Men: 40–54% Women: 37–47%
Hemoglobin content (g per 100 mL blood)		Men: 14–18 g/100mL Women: 12–16 g/100mL
Red blood cell count (cells per mm^3 blood)		Men: 4,600,000–6,200,000/mm^3 Women: 4,200,000–5,400,000/mm^3
White blood cell count (cells per mm^3 blood)		5,000–10,000/mm^3

PART B

Complete the following:

1. How does the hematocrit from the demonstration blood test compare with the normal value?

_____
_____

2. What conditions might produce a decreased red blood cell percentage? _____

_____
_____

3. What conditions might produce an increased red blood cell percentage? _____

_____
_____

PART C

Complete the following:

1. How does the hemoglobin content from the demonstration blood test compare with the normal value? _____

_____
_____

319

2. What conditions might produce a decreased hemoglobin content? _____

_____

_____

3. What conditions might produce an increased hemoglobin content? _____

_____

_____

_____

PART D

Complete the following:

1. How does the red blood cell count from the demonstration blood test compare with the normal value? _____

_____

_____

2. What conditions might produce a decreased red blood cell count? _____

_____

_____

_____

3. What conditions might produce an increased red blood cell count? _____

_____

_____

_____

PART E

Complete the following:

1. How does the white blood cell count from the demonstration blood test compare with the normal value? _____

_____

_____

2. What conditions might produce a decreased white blood cell count? _____

_____

_____

_____

3. What conditions might produce an increased white blood cell count? _____

_____

_____

_____

Critical Thinking Application

Which blood tests performed in this lab could be used to determine possible anemia?

_____

_____

_____

_____

BLOOD TYPING

MATERIALS NEEDED

Textbook
ABO blood-typing kit
Simulated blood-typing kits are suggested as a substitute
    for collected blood

For Demonstration:

Microscope slide
70% alcohol
Sterile absorbent cotton
Sterile blood lancet
Toothpicks
Anti-D serum
Slide warming box (Rh blood-typing box or Rh view box)

⚠ SAFETY

- It is important that students learn and practice correct procedures for handling body fluids. Consider using simulated blood-typing kits or contaminant-free blood that has been tested and is available from various laboratory supply houses. Some of the procedures might be accomplished as demonstrations only. If student blood is used, it is important that students handle only their own blood.
- Use an appropriate disinfectant to wash the laboratory tables before and after the procedures.
- Wear disposable gloves when handling blood samples.
- Clean the end of a finger with 70% alcohol before the puncture is performed.
- The sterile blood lancet should be used only once.
- Dispose of used lancets and blood-contaminated items in an appropriate container (never use the wastebasket).
- Wash your hands before leaving the laboratory.

---

lood typing involves identifying protein substances called *antigens* that are present in red blood cell membranes. Although there are many different antigens associated with human red blood cells, only a few of them are of clinical importance. These include the antigens of the ABO group and those of the Rh group.

To determine which antigens are present, a blood sample is mixed with blood-typing sera that contain known types of antibodies. If a particular antibody contacts a corresponding antigen, a reaction occurs, and the red blood cells clump together (agglutination). Thus, if blood cells are mixed with serum containing antibodies that react with antigen A and the cells clump together, antigen A must be present in those cells.

PURPOSE OF THE EXERCISE

To determine the ABO blood type of a blood sample and to observe an Rh blood-typing test.

LEARNING OBJECTIVES

After completing this exercise, you should be able to

1. Explain the basis of ABO blood typing.
2. Determine the ABO type of a blood sample.
3. Explain the basis of Rh blood typing.
4. Describe how the Rh type of a blood sample is determined.

WARNING

Because of the possibility of blood infections being transmitted from one student to another if blood testing is performed in the classroom, it is suggested that commercially prepared blood-typing kits containing virus-free human blood be used for ABO blood typing. The instructor may wish to demonstrate Rh blood typing. Observe all of the safety procedures listed for this lab.

ABO BLOOD TYPING

1. Review the section entitled "ABO Blood Group" in chapter 14 of the textbook.
2. Compete Part A of Laboratory Report 39.
3. Perform the ABO blood type test using the blood-typing kit. To do this, follow these steps:
   a. Obtain a clean microscope slide and mark across its center with a wax pencil to divide it into right and left halves. Also write "Anti-A" near the edge of the left half and "Anti-B" near the edge of the right half (fig. 39.1).

Figure 39.1 Slide prepared for ABO blood typing.

Table 39.1 Possible Reactions of ABO Blood-Typing Sera

Reactions		Blood Type	U.S. Frequency
Anti-A Serum	**Anti-B Serum**		
Clumping (agglutination)	No clumping	Type A	41%
No clumping	Clumping	Type B	9%
Clumping	Clumping	Type AB	3%
No clumping	No clumping	Type O	47%

Note: The inheritance of the ABO blood groups is described in Laboratory Exercise 61.

b. Place a small drop of blood on each half of the microscope slide. Work quickly so that the blood will not have time to clot.

c. Add a drop of anti-A serum to the blood on the left half and a drop of anti-B serum to the blood on the right half. Note the color coding of the anti-A and anti-B typing sera. To avoid contaminating the serum, avoid touching the blood with the serum while it is in the dropper; instead allow the serum to fall from the dropper onto the blood.

d. Use separate toothpicks to stir each sample of serum and blood together, and spread each over an area about as large as a quarter. Dispose of toothpicks in an appropriate container.

e. Examine the samples for clumping of blood cells (agglutination) after 2 minutes.

f. See table 39.1 and figure 39.2 for aid in interpreting the test results.

g. Discard contaminated materials as directed by the laboratory instructor.

4. Complete Part B of the laboratory report.

Critical Thinking Application

Judging from the observations of the blood-typing results, predict the components in the anti-A and anti-B sera that caused clumping.

_____

_____

_____

_____

DEMONSTRATION—RH BLOOD TYPING

1. Review the section entitled "Rh Blood Group" in chapter 14 of the textbook.

2. Complete Part C of the laboratory report.

3. To determine the Rh blood type of a blood sample, follow these steps:

a. Lance the tip of a finger. (See the demonstration procedures in Laboratory Exercise 37 for directions.) Place a small drop of blood in the center of a clean microscope slide.

Figure 39.2 Four possible results of the ABO test.

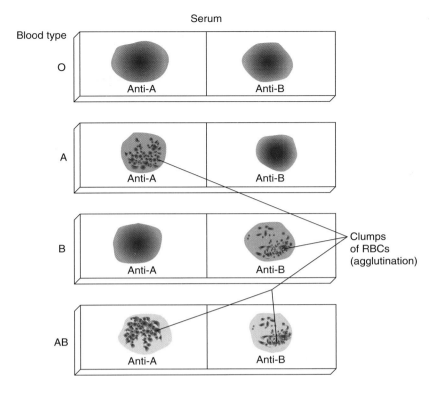

Serum

Blood type

O — Anti-A / Anti-B

A — Anti-A / Anti-B

B — Anti-A / Anti-B

AB — Anti-A / Anti-B

Clumps of RBCs (agglutination)

Figure 39.3 Slide warming box used for Rh blood typing.

Mixture of blood and anti-D serum

Plate heated to 45°C (113°F)

Rh TYPING BOX

ON / OFF

b. Add a drop of anti-D serum to the blood and mix them together with a clean toothpick.

c. Place the slide on the plate of a warming box (Rh blood-typing box or Rh view box) that has been prewarmed to 45°C (113°F) (fig. 39.3).

d. Slowly rock the box back and forth to keep the mixture moving, and watch for clumping (agglutination) of the blood cells. When clumping occurs in anti-D serum, the clumps usually are smaller than those that appear in anti-A or anti-B sera, so they may be less obvious. However, if clumping occurs, the blood is called Rh positive; if no clumping occurs *within 2 minutes,* the blood is called Rh negative.

e. Discard all contaminated materials in appropriate containers.

4. Complete Part D of the laboratory report.

NOTES

Name _____

Date _____

Section _____

BLOOD TYPING

PART A

Complete the following statements:

1. The antigens of the ABO blood group are located in the _____ .
2. The blood of every person contains one of (how many possible?) _____ combinations of antigens.
3. Type A blood contains antigen _____ .
4. Type B blood contains antigen _____ .
5. Type A blood contains antibody _____ in the plasma.
6. Type B blood contains antibody _____ in the plasma.
7. Persons with ABO blood type _____ are often called universal recipients.
8. Persons with ABO blood type _____ are often called universal donors.
9. Although antigens are present at the time of birth, antibodies usually do not appear in the blood until the age of _____ .

PART B

Complete the following:

1. What was the ABO type of the blood tested? _____
2. What ABO antigens are present in the red blood cells of this type of blood? _____
3. What ABO antibodies are present in the plasma of this type of blood? _____
4. If a person with this blood type needed a blood transfusion, what ABO type(s) of blood could be received safely? _____
5. If a person with this blood type was serving as a blood donor, what ABO blood type(s) could receive the blood safely? _____

PART C

Complete the following statements:

1. The Rh blood group was named after the _____ .
2. Of the antigens in the Rh group, the most important is _____ .
3. If red blood cells lack Rh antigens, the blood is called _____ .
4. Rh antibodies form only in persons with _____ type blood in response to special stimulation.
5. If an Rh-negative person who is sensitive to Rh-positive blood receives a transfusion of Rh-positive blood, the donor's cells are likely to _____ .
6. An Rh-negative woman who might be carrying an _____ fetus is given an injection of RhoGAM to prevent erythroblastosis fetalis (hemolytic disease of the newborn).

PART D

Complete the following:

1. What was the Rh type of the blood tested in the demonstration? _____
2. What Rh antigen is present in the red blood cells of this type of blood? _____
3. What Rh antibody is normally present in the plasma of this type of blood? _____
4. If a person with this blood type needed a blood transfusion, what type of blood could be received safely?

   _____
5. If a person with this blood type was serving as a blood donor, a person with what type of blood could receive the blood safely? _____

LABORATORY EXERCISE 40

HEART STRUCTURE

MATERIALS NEEDED

Textbook
Dissectible human heart model
Preserved sheep or other mammalian heart
Dissecting tray
Dissecting instruments

For Learning Extension:

Colored pencils

⚠ SAFETY

- Wear disposable gloves when working on the heart dissection.
- Save or dispose of the dissected heart as instructed.
- Wash the dissecting tray and instruments as instructed.
- Wash your laboratory table.
- Wash your hands before leaving the laboratory.

The heart is a muscular pump located within the mediastinum and resting upon the diaphragm. It is enclosed by the lungs, thoracic vertebrae, and sternum, and attached at its top (the base) are several large blood vessels. Its distal end extends downward to the left and terminates as a bluntly pointed apex.

The heart and the proximal ends of the attached blood vessels are enclosed by a double-layered pericardium. The innermost layer of this membrane (visceral pericardium) consists of a thin covering that is closely applied to the surface of the heart, whereas the outer layer (parietal pericardium with fibrous pericardium) forms a tough, protective sac surrounding the heart. Between the parietal and visceral layers of the pericardium is a space, the pericardial cavity, that contains a small volume of serous (pericardial) fluid.

PURPOSE OF THE EXERCISE

To review the structural characteristics of the human heart and to examine the major features of a mammalian heart.

LEARNING OBJECTIVES

After completing this exercise, you should be able to

1. Identify the major structural features of the human heart.
2. Compare the features of the human heart with those of another mammal.

PROCEDURE A—THE HUMAN HEART

1. Review the section entitled "Structure of the Heart" in chapter 15 of the textbook.
2. As a review activity, label figures 40.1, 40.2, and 40.3.
3. Complete Part A of Laboratory Report 40.
4. Examine the human heart model, and locate the following features:

heart
  base
  apex
pericardium (pericardial sac)
  fibrous pericardium (outer layer)
  parietal pericardium (inner lining of fibrous pericardium)
  visceral pericardium (epicardium)
pericardial cavity (between parietal and visceral pericardial membranes)
myocardium
endocardium
atria
  right atrium
  left atrium
  auricles
ventricles
  right ventricle
  left ventricle
atrioventricular orifices
atrioventricular valves (A-V valves)
  tricuspid valve (right atrioventricular valve)
  mitral valve (bicuspid valve; left atrioventricular valve)

Figure 40.1 Label this anterior view of the human heart.

Brachiocephalic veins

Right pulmonary
artery

Right pulmonary
veins

(chamber)

(chamber)

Marginal artery

1

2

3

(chamber)

4

5

6

Brachiocephalic artery

Left common carotid artery

Left subclavian artery

Ligamentum arteriosum

Left pulmonary artery

7

Left pulmonary veins

8

(chamber)

9

Circumflex artery

10

11

(chamber)

Anterior interventricular
(descending) artery

Adipose tissue

Apex of the heart

Figure 40.2 Label this posterior view of the human heart.

1

2

3

Left auricle

Circumflex artery

Cardiac vein

4

(chamber)

(chamber)

5

6

7

Right pulmonary
arteries

Right pulmonary
veins

8

(chamber)

9

Coronary sinus

Middle cardiac vein

Posterior interventricular
artery

10

(chamber)

Figure 40.3 Label this coronal section of the human heart. The arrows indicate the direction of blood flow.

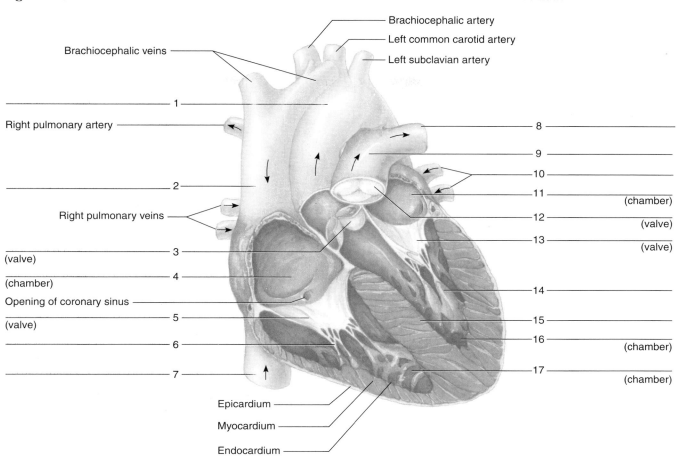

Brachiocephalic veins

Brachiocephalic artery

Left common carotid artery

Left subclavian artery

1

Right pulmonary artery

8

9

10

11
(chamber)

2

12
(valve)

Right pulmonary veins

13
(valve)

3
(valve)

4
(chamber)

Opening of coronary sinus

14

5
(valve)

15

6

16
(chamber)

7

17
(chamber)

Epicardium

Myocardium

Endocardium

chordae tendineae

papillary muscles

atrioventricular sulcus

interventricular sulci

    anterior sulcus

    posterior sulcus

superior vena cava

inferior vena cava

pulmonary trunk

pulmonary arteries

pulmonary veins

aorta

semilunar valves

    pulmonary valve

    aortic valve

left coronary artery

    circumflex artery

    anterior interventricular (descending) artery

right coronary artery

    posterior interventricular artery

    marginal artery

cardiac veins

    great cardiac vein

    middle cardiac vein

    small cardiac vein

coronary sinus

5. Complete Part B of the laboratory report.

 LEARNING EXTENSION

Use red and blue colored pencils to color the blood vessels in figure 40.3. Use red to illustrate a blood vessel high in oxygen, and use blue to illustrate a blood vessel low in oxygen. You can check your work by referring to the corresponding figures in the textbook, which are presented in full color.

PROCEDURE B—DISSECTION OF A SHEEP HEART

1. Obtain a preserved sheep heart. Rinse it in water thoroughly to remove as much of the preservative as possible. Also run water into the large blood vessels to force any blood clots out of the heart chambers.

Figure 40.4 Ventral surface of sheep heart.

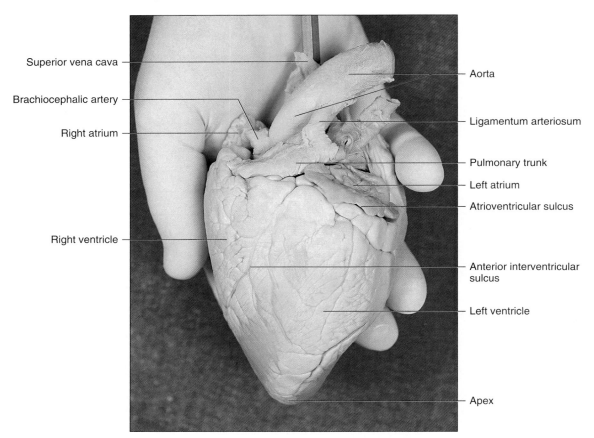

Superior vena cava

Brachiocephalic artery

Right atrium

Right ventricle

Aorta

Ligamentum arteriosum

Pulmonary trunk

Left atrium

Atrioventricular sulcus

Anterior interventricular sulcus

Left ventricle

Apex

2. Place the heart in a dissecting tray with its ventral surface up (fig. 40.4), and proceed as follows:
   a. Although the relatively thick *pericardial sac* probably is missing, look for traces of this membrane around the origins of the large blood vessels.
   b. Locate the *visceral pericardium,* which appears as a thin, transparent layer on the surface of the heart. Use a scalpel to remove a portion of this layer and expose the *myocardium* beneath. Also note the abundance of fat along the paths of various blood vessels. This adipose tissue occurs in the loose connective tissue that underlies the visceral pericardium.
   c. Identify the following:

   right atrium
   right ventricle
   left atrium
   left ventricle
   atrioventricular sulcus
   anterior interventricular sulcus

   d. Carefully remove the fat from the anterior interventricular sulcus, and expose the blood vessels that pass along this groove. They include

a branch of the *left coronary artery* (anterior interventricular artery) and a *cardiac vein.*

3. Examine the dorsal surface of the heart (fig. 40.5), and proceed as follows:
   a. Identify the *atrioventricular sulcus* and the *posterior interventricular sulcus.*
   b. Locate the stumps of two relatively thin-walled veins that enter the right atrium. Demonstrate this connection by passing a slender probe through them. The upper vessel is the *superior vena cava,* and the lower one is the *inferior vena cava.*

4. Open the right atrium. To do this, follow these steps:
   a. Insert a blade of the scissors into the superior vena cava and cut downward through the atrial wall (fig. 40.5).
   b. Open the chamber, locate the *tricuspid valve (right atrioventricular valve),* and examine its cusps.
   c. Also locate the opening to the *coronary sinus* between the valve and the inferior vena cava.
   d. Run some water through the tricuspid valve to fill the chamber of the right ventricle.
   e. Gently squeeze the ventricles, and watch the cusps of the valve as the water moves up against them.

Figure 40.5 Dorsal surface of sheep heart. To open the right atrium, insert a blade of the scissors into the superior (anterior in sheep) vena cava and cut downward.

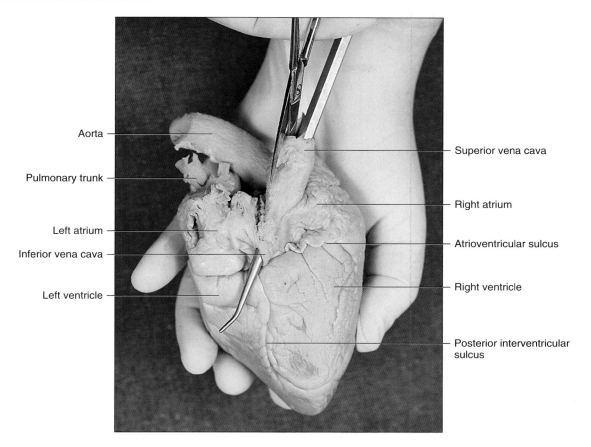

Aorta

Pulmonary trunk

Left atrium

Inferior vena cava

Left ventricle

Superior vena cava

Right atrium

Atrioventricular sulcus

Right ventricle

Posterior interventricular sulcus

5. Open the right ventricle as follows:
   a. Continue cutting downward through the tricuspid valve and the right ventricular wall until you reach the apex of the heart.
   b. Locate the *chordae tendineae* and the *papillary muscles.*
   c. Find the opening to the *pulmonary trunk,* and use the scissors to cut upward through the wall of the right ventricle. Follow the pulmonary trunk until you have exposed the *pulmonary valve.*
   d. Examine the valve and its cusps.
6. Open the left side of the heart. To do this, follow these steps:
   a. Insert the blade of the scissors through the wall of the left atrium and cut downward to the apex of the heart.
   b. Open the left atrium, and locate the four openings of the *pulmonary veins.* Pass a slender probe through each opening, and locate the stump of its vessel.
   c. Examine the *bicuspid valve (left atrioventricular valve)* and its cusps.
   d. Also examine the left ventricle, and compare the thickness of its wall with that of the right ventricle.

7. Locate the aorta, which leads away from the left ventricle, and proceed as follows:
   a. Compare the thickness of the aortic wall with that of a pulmonary artery.
   b. Use scissors to cut along the length of the aorta to expose the *aortic valve* at its base.
   c. Examine the cusps of the valve, and locate the openings of the *coronary arteries* just distal to them.
8. As a review, locate and identify the stumps of each of the major blood vessels associated with the heart.
9. Discard or save the specimen as directed by the laboratory instructor.
10. Complete Part C of the laboratory report.

Web Quest

Trace blood flow through an animated heart at various rates. Identify heart structures and take an animated tour of the heart. Search these at www.mhhe.com/shier11

Click on Student Edition. Click on Martin Lab Manual, Web Quest.

NOTES

Name _____

Date _____

Section _____

HEART STRUCTURE

PART A

Match the terms in column A with the descriptions in column B. Place the letter of your choice in the space provided.

Column A	Column B

Column A

a. Aorta
b. Cardiac vein
c. Coronary artery
d. Coronary sinus
e. Endocardium
f. Mitral (bicuspid) valve
g. Myocardium
h. Papillary muscle
i. Pericardial cavity
j. Pericardial sac
k. Pulmonary trunk
l. Tricuspid valve

Column B

_____ 1. Structure from which chordae tendineae originate

_____ 2. Prevents blood movement from right ventricle to right atrium

_____ 3. Membranes around heart

_____ 4. Prevents blood movement from left ventricle to left atrium

_____ 5. Gives rise to left and right pulmonary arteries

_____ 6. Drains blood from myocardium into right atrium

_____ 7. Inner lining of heart chamber

_____ 8. Layer largely composed of cardiac muscle tissue

_____ 9. Space containing serous fluid to reduce friction during heartbeats

_____ 10. Drains blood from myocardial capillaries

_____ 11. Supplies blood to heart muscle

_____ 12. Distributes blood to body organs (systemic circuit) except lungs

PART B

Locate the labeled features and identify the numbered features in figure 40.6 of a dissectible human heart model (coronal section).

Figure 40.6 Identify the features indicated on this anterior view of a coronal section of a human heart model, using the terms provided. (*Note:* The pulmonary valve is not shown on the portion of the model photographed.)

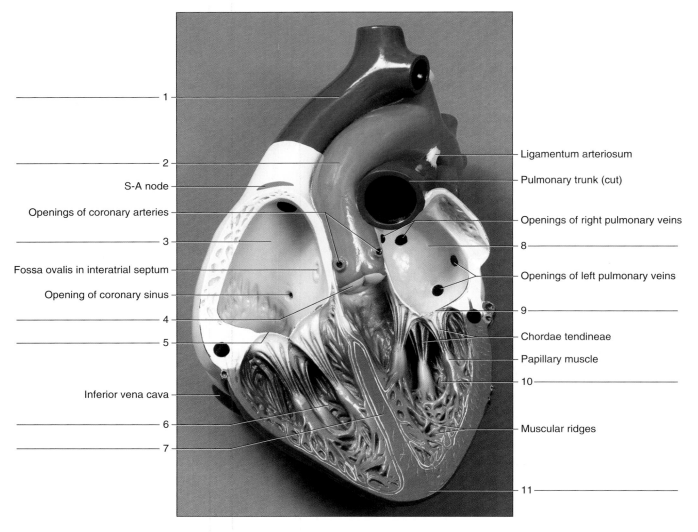

1

2

S-A node

Openings of coronary arteries

3

Fossa ovalis in interatrial septum

Opening of coronary sinus

4

5

Inferior vena cava

6

7

Ligamentum arteriosum

Pulmonary trunk (cut)

Openings of right pulmonary veins

8

Openings of left pulmonary veins

9

Chordae tendineae

Papillary muscle

10

Muscular ridges

11

Terms:

Aorta	Mitral (bicuspid) valve
Aortic valve	Right atrium
Apex	Right ventricle
Interventricular septum	Superior vena cava
Left atrium	Tricuspid valve
Left ventricle	

PART C

Complete the following:

1. Compare the structure of the tricuspid valve with that of the pulmonary valve._____
_____
_____
_____
_____

2. Describe the action of the tricuspid valve when you squeezed the water-filled right ventricle. _____
_____
_____
_____
_____

3. Describe the function of the chordae tendineae and the papillary muscles. _____
_____
_____
_____
_____

4. What is the significance of the difference in thickness between the wall of the aorta and the wall of the
   pulmonary trunk? _____
_____
_____
_____
_____

5. List in order the major blood vessels, chambers, and valves through which blood must pass in traveling from a
   vena cava to the aorta. _____
_____
_____
_____
_____
_____

Critical Thinking Application

What is the significance of the difference in thickness of the ventricular walls?

_____
_____
_____
_____

NOTES

CARDIAC CYCLE

MATERIALS NEEDED

Textbook

For Procedure A—Heart Sounds:

Stethoscope
70% alcohol
Absorbent cotton

For Procedure B—Electrocardiogram:

Electrocardiograph (or other instrument for recording
    an ECG)
Cot or table
70% alcohol
Absorbent cotton
Electrode cream (paste)
Plate electrodes and cables
Lead selector switch

A set of atrial contractions while the ventricular walls relax, followed by ventricular contractions while the atrial walls relax, constitutes a cardiac cycle. Such a cycle is accompanied by blood pressure changes within the heart chambers, movement of blood in and out of the chambers, and opening and closing of heart valves. These valves closing produce vibrations in the tissues and thus create the sounds associated with the heartbeat.

A number of electrical changes also occur in the myocardium as it contracts and relaxes. These changes can be detected by using metal electrodes and an instrument called an *electrocardiograph.* The recording produced by the instrument is an *electrocardiogram,* or *ECG (EKG).*

PURPOSE OF THE EXERCISE

To review the events of a cardiac cycle, to become acquainted with normal heart sounds, and to record an electrocardiogram.

LEARNING OBJECTIVES

After completing this exercise, you should be able to

1. Describe the major events of a cardiac cycle.
2. Identify the sounds produced during a cardiac cycle.
3. Record an electrocardiogram.

4. Identify the components of a normal ECG pattern.
5. Describe the phases of a cardiac cycle represented by each part of a normal ECG pattern.

PROCEDURE A—HEART SOUNDS

1. Review the sections entitled "Cardiac Cycle" and "Heart Sounds" in chapter 15 of the textbook.
2. Complete Part A of Laboratory Report 41.
3. Listen to your own heart sounds. To do this, follow these steps:
    a. Obtain a stethoscope, and clean its earpieces and the diaphragm by using cotton moistened with alcohol.
    b. Fit the earpieces into your ear canals so that the angles are positioned in the forward direction.
    c. Firmly place the diaphragm (or bell) of the stethoscope on the chest over the fifth intercostal space near the apex of the heart (fig. 41.1) and listen to the sounds. This is a good location to hear the first sound (*lubb*) of a cardiac cycle when the A-V valves are closing, which occurs during ventricular systole (contraction).
    d. Move the diaphragm to the second intercostal space, just to the left of the sternum, and listen to the sounds from this region. You should be able to hear the second sound (*dupp*) of the cardiac cycle clearly when the semilunar valves are closing, which occurs during ventricular diastole (relaxation).
    e. It is possible to hear sounds associated with the aortic and pulmonary valves by listening from the second intercostal space on either side of the sternum. The aortic valve sound comes from the right, and the pulmonary valve sound from the left. The sound associated with the mitral valve can be heard from the fifth intercostal space at the nipple line on the left. The sound of the tricuspid valve can be heard at the fifth intercostal space just to the right of the sternum (fig. 41.1).
4. Inhale slowly and deeply, and exhale slowly while you listen to the heart sounds from each of the locations as before. Note any changes that have occurred in the sounds.

Figure 41.1 The first sound (lubb) of a cardiac cycle can be heard by placing the diaphragm of a stethoscope over the fifth intercostal space near the apex of the heart. The second sound (dupp) can be heard over the second intercostal space, just left of the sternum. The thoracic regions circled indicate where the sounds of each heart valve are most easily heard.

Clavicle

Manubrium of sternum

Aortic area

Body of sternum

Tricuspid area

Xiphoid process of sternum

Jugular (suprasternal) notch

Sternal angle

Secondary intercostal space

Pulmonary area

Fifth intercostal space

Mitral area

5. Exercise moderately outside the laboratory for a few minutes so that other students listening to heart sounds will not be disturbed. After the exercise period, listen to the heart sounds and note any changes that have occurred in them. *This exercise should be avoided by anyone with health risks.*

6. Complete Part B of the laboratory report.

PROCEDURE B—ELECTROCARDIOGRAM

1. Review sections entitled "Cardiac Conduction System," "Electrocardiogram," and "Arrhythmias— Clinical Application" in chapter 15 of the textbook.

2. Complete Part C of the laboratory report.

3. The laboratory instructor will demonstrate the proper adjustment and use of the instrument available to record an electrocardiogram.

4. Record your laboratory partner's ECG. To do this, follow these steps:

   a. Have your partner lie on a cot or table close to the electrocardiograph, remaining as relaxed and still as possible.

   b. Scrub the electrode placement locations with cotton moistened with alcohol (fig. 41.2). Apply a small quantity of electrode cream to the skin

Figure 41.2 To record an ECG, attach electrodes to the wrists and ankles.

on the insides of the wrists and ankles. (Any jewelry on the wrists or ankles should be removed.)

c. Spread some electrode cream over the inner surfaces of four plate electrodes and attach one to each of the prepared skin areas (fig. 41.2). Make sure there is good contact between the skin and the metal of the electrodes. The electrode plate on the right ankle is the grounding system.

d. Attach the plate electrodes to the corresponding cables of a lead selector switch. When an ECG recording is made, only two electrodes are used at a time, and the selector switch allows various combinations of electrodes (leads) to be activated. Three standard limb leads placed on the two wrists and the left ankle are used for an ECG. This arrangement has become known as *Einthoven's triangle,*[1] which enables the recording of the potential difference between any two of the electrodes.

The standard Leads I, II, and III are called bipolar leads because they are the potential difference between two electrodes (a positive and a negative). Lead I measures the potential difference between the right wrist (negative) and the left wrist (positive). Lead II measures the potential difference between the right wrist and the left ankle, and Lead III measures the potential difference between the left wrist and the left ankle. The right ankle is always the ground.

e. Turn on the recording instrument and adjust it as previously demonstrated by the laboratory instructor. The paper speed should be set at 2.5 cm/second. This is the standard speed for ECG recordings.

f. Set the lead selector switch to Lead I (right wrist, left wrist electrodes), and record the ECG for 1 minute.

g. Set the lead selector switch to Lead II (right wrist, left ankle electrodes), and record the ECG for 1 minute.

h. Set the lead selector switch to Lead III (left wrist, left ankle electrodes), and record the ECG for 1 minute.

Figure 41.3 Components of a normal ECG pattern with a time scale.

i. Remove the electrodes and clean the cream from the metal and skin.

j. Use figure 41.3 to label the ECG components of the results from Leads I, II, and III. The P-Q interval is often called the P-R interval because the Q wave is often small or absent. The normal P-Q interval is 0.12–0.20 seconds. The normal QRS complex duration is less than 0.10 seconds.

5. Complete Part D of the laboratory report.

Web Quest

Identify normal heart sounds and a murmur.
    What is the purpose of stress electrocardiography? Compare normal and abnormal ECGs.
    Search these at
www.mhhe.com/shier11
Click on Student Edition. Click on Martin Lab Manual, Web Quest.

---

[1]Willem Einthoven (1860–1927), a Dutch physiologist, received the Nobel prize for physiology or medicine for his work with electrocardiograms.

NOTES

Name _____

Date _____

Section _____

CARDIAC CYCLE

PART A

Complete the following statements:

1. About _____ % of the blood from the atria passes into the ventricles before the atrial walls contract.
2. The period during which a heart chamber is contracting is called _____ .
3. The period during which a heart chamber is relaxing is called _____ .
4. During ventricular contraction, the A-V valves (tricuspid and mitral valves) are _____ .
5. During ventricular relaxation, the A-V valves are _____ .
6. The pulmonary and aortic valves open when the pressure in the _____ exceeds the pressure in the pulmonary trunk and aorta.
7. Heart sounds are due to _____ in heart tissues created by changes in blood flow.
8. The first sound of a cardiac cycle occurs when the _____ are closing.
9. The second sound of a cardiac cycle occurs when the _____ are closing.
10. The sound created when blood leaks back through an incompletely closed valve is called a

    _____ .

PART B

Complete the following:

1. What changes did you note in the heart sounds when you inhaled deeply?

    _____

    _____

2. What changes did you note in the heart sounds following the exercise period?

    _____

    _____

PART C

Complete the following statements:

1. The fibers of the cardiac conduction system are specialized _____ tissue.
2. Normally, the _____ node serves as the pacemaker of the heart.
3. The _____ node is located in the inferior portion of the interatrial septum.
4. The large fibers on the distal side of the A-V node make up the _____ .
5. The fibers that carry cardiac impulses from the interventricular septum into the myocardium are called _____ .

6. An _____ is a recording of electrical changes occurring in the myocardium during the cardiac cycle.

7. Between cardiac cycles, cardiac muscle fibers remain _____ with no detectable electrical changes.

8. The P wave corresponds to depolarization of the muscle fibers of the _____ .

9. The QRS complex corresponds to depolarization of the muscle fibers of the _____ .

10. The T wave corresponds to repolarization of the muscle fibers of the _____ .

11. Why is atrial repolarization not observed in the ECG? _____

_____

12. A rapid heartbeat is called _____ ; a slow heartbeat is called _____ .

PART D

1. Attach a short segment of the ECG recording from each of the three leads you used, and label the waves of each.

Lead I

Lead II

Lead III

2. What differences do you find in the ECG patterns of these leads?_____
_____
_____
_____
_____
_____

3. How much time passed from the beginning of the P wave to the beginning of the QRS complex (P-Q interval, or P-R interval) in the ECG from Lead I? _____

4. What is the significance of this P-Q (P-R) interval? _____
_____
_____
_____
_____

5. How can you determine the heart rate from an electrocardiogram?_____
_____
_____
_____

6. What was your heart rate as determined from the ECG? _____

Critical Thinking Application

If a person's heart rate is 72 beats per minute, determine the number of QRS complexes that would have appeared on an ECG during the first 30 seconds.

_____
_____
_____

NOTES

BLOOD VESSELS

MATERIALS NEEDED

Textbook
Compound light microscope
Prepared microscope slides:
    artery cross section
    vein cross section
Live frog or goldfish
Frog Ringer's solution
Paper towel
Rubber bands
Frog board or heavy cardboard (with a 1-inch hole cut
    in one corner)
Dissecting pins
Thread
Masking tape

For Learning Extension:

Ice
Hot plate
Thermometer

SAFETY

- Wear disposable gloves when handling the live frogs.
- Return the frogs to the location indicated after the
  experiment.
- Wash your hands before leaving the laboratory.

The blood vessels form a closed system of tubes that carry blood to and from the heart, lungs, and body cells. These tubes include arteries and arterioles that conduct blood away from the heart; capillaries in which exchanges of substances occur between the blood and surrounding tissues; and venules and veins that return blood to the heart.

PURPOSE OF THE EXERCISE

To review the structure and functions of blood vessels and to observe examples of blood vessels microscopically.

LEARNING OBJECTIVES

After completing this exercise, you should be able to

1. Describe the structure and functions of arteries, capillaries, and veins.

2. Distinguish cross sections of arteries and veins microscopically.
3. Identify the three major layers in the wall of an artery or vein.
4. Identify the types of blood vessels in the web of a frog's foot.

PROCEDURE

1. Review the section entitled "Blood Vessels" in chapter 15 of the textbook.
2. As a review activity, label figures 42.1 and 42.2.
3. Complete Part A of Laboratory Report 42.
4. Obtain a microscope slide of an artery cross section and examine it using low-power and high-power magnification. Identify the three distinct layers (tunics) of the arterial wall. The inner layer (*tunica interna*) is composed of an endothelium (simple squamous epithelium) and appears as a wavy line due to an abundance of elastic fibers that have recoiled just beneath it. The middle layer (*tunica media*) consists of numerous concentrically arranged smooth muscle cells with elastic fibers scattered among them. The outer layer (*tunica externa*) contains connective tissue that is rich in collagenous fibers (fig. 42.3).
5. Prepare a labeled sketch of the arterial wall in Part B of the laboratory report.
6. Obtain a slide of a vein cross section and examine it as you did the artery cross section. Note the thinner wall and larger lumen relative to an artery of comparable size. Identify the three layers of the wall, and prepare a labeled sketch in Part B of the laboratory report.
7. Complete Part B of the laboratory report.
8. Observe the blood vessels in the webbing of a frog's foot. (As a substitute for a frog, a live goldfish could be used to observe circulation in the tail.) To do this, follow these steps:
   a. Obtain a live frog. Wrap its body in a moist paper towel, leaving one foot extending outward. Secure the towel with rubber bands, but be careful not to wrap the animal so tightly that it could be injured. Try to keep the nostrils exposed.

Figure 42.1 Label the tunics of the wall of this artery and vein.

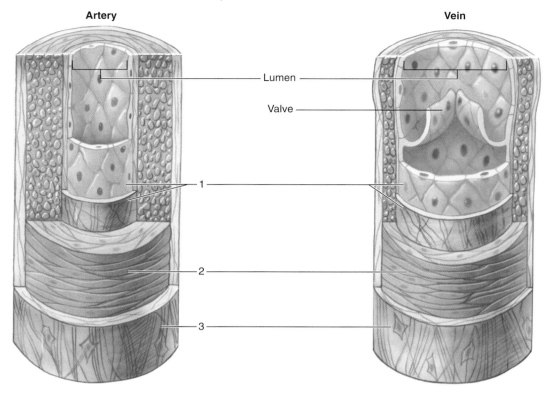

Artery   Vein

Lumen

Valve

1

2

3

Figure 42.2 Label this arteriole by placing the correct numbers in the spaces provided.

1

2

3

4

___ Arteriole

___ Capillary

___ Endothelium

___ Smooth muscle cell

b. Place the frog on a frog board or on a piece of heavy cardboard with the foot near the hole in one corner.

c. Fasten the wrapped body to the board with masking tape.

d. Carefully spread the web of the foot over the hole and secure it to the board with dissecting pins and thread (fig. 42.4). Keep the web moist with frog Ringer's solution.

e. Secure the board on the stage of a microscope with heavy rubber bands and position it so that the web is beneath the objective lens.

f. Focus on the web, using low-power magnification, and locate some blood vessels. Note the movement of the blood cells and the direction of the blood flow. You might notice that red blood cells of frogs are nucleated. Identify an arteriole, a capillary, and a venule.

g. Examine each of these vessels with high-power magnification.

LEARNING EXTENSION

Investigate the effect of temperature change on the blood vessels of the frog's foot by flooding the web with a small quantity of ice water. Observe the blood vessels with low-power magnification and note any changes in their diameters or the rate of blood flow. Remove the ice water and replace it with water heated to about 35°C (95°F). Repeat your observations. What do you conclude from this experiment?

_____

_____

_____

_____

h. When finished, return the frog to the location indicated by your instructor. The microscope lenses and stage will likely need cleaning after the experiment.

9. Complete Part C of the laboratory report.

Figure 42.3 Cross section of an artery and a vein (5×).

Artery

Vein

Outer layer (tunica externa)
Middle layer (tunica media)
Inner layer (tunica interna)
Lumen with blood cells

Lumen with blood cells

Tunica interna
Tunica media
Tunica externa

Figure 42.4 Spread the web of the foot over the hole and secure it to the board with pins and thread.

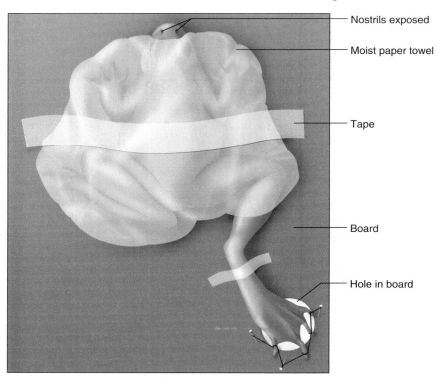

Nostrils exposed

Moist paper towel

Tape

Board

Hole in board

Name _____

Date _____

Section _____

BLOOD VESSELS

PART A

Complete the following statements:

1. Simple squamous epithelial tissue called _____ forms the inner linings of the tunica interna of blood vessels.

2. The _____ of an artery wall contains many smooth muscle cells.

3. The _____ of an artery wall is largely composed of connective tissue.

4. When contraction of the smooth muscle in a blood vessel wall occurs, the vessel is referred to as being in a condition of _____ .

5. Relaxation of the smooth muscle in a blood vessel wall results in the vessel being in a condition of _____ .

6. The smallest blood vessels are called _____ .

7. The protective tight arrangement between the capillaries and tissues of the brain is called the blood-brain _____ .

8. Tissues with high rates of metabolism tend to have _____ densities of capillaries.

9. _____ are composed of smooth muscles that encircle the entrances to capillaries and thus can control the distribution of blood within tissues.

10. The process called _____ provides the most important means of transfer of biochemicals through capillary walls.

11. Oxygen and carbon dioxide move easily through most areas of cell membranes because they are soluble in _____ .

12. Water moves through capillary walls by passing through _____ in the cell membranes and through slitlike openings between the endothelial cells.

13. Filtration results when substances are forced through capillary walls by _____ pressure.

14. The presence of plasma proteins in blood increases its _____ pressure as compared to tissue fluids.

15. _____ in certain veins close if blood begins to back up in the vein.

16. _____ are vessels with large lumens that serve as blood reservoirs.

PART B

1. Sketch and label a section of an arterial wall.

2. Sketch and label a section of a venous wall.

3. Describe the differences you noted in the structures of the arterial and venous walls. Mention each of the three layers of the wall. _____

_____

_____

_____

_____

Critical Thinking Application

Explain the functional significance of the differences you noted in the structures of the arterial and venous walls.

_____

_____

_____

_____

PART C

Complete the following:

1. How did you distinguish between arterioles and venules when you observed the vessels in the web of the frog's foot? _____

   _____

   _____

   _____

   _____

   _____

2. How did you recognize capillaries in the web? _____

   _____

   _____

   _____

   _____

3. What differences did you note in the rate of blood flow through the arterioles, capillaries, and venules? _____

   _____

   _____

   _____

   _____

4. Did you observe any evidence of precapillary sphincter activity? Explain your answer. _____

   _____

   _____

   _____

   _____

NOTES

PULSE RATE AND BLOOD PRESSURE

MATERIALS NEEDED

Textbook
Clock with second hand
Sphygmomanometer
Stethoscope
70% alcohol
Absorbent cotton

For Demonstration:

Pulse pickup transducer or plethysmogram
Physiological recording apparatus

The surge of blood that enters the arteries each time the ventricles of the heart contract causes the elastic walls of these vessels to swell. Then, as the ventricles relax, the walls recoil. This alternate expanding and recoiling of an arterial wall can be felt as a pulse in vessels that run close to the surface of the body.

The force exerted by the blood pressing against the inner walls of arteries also creates blood pressure. This pressure reaches a maximum during ventricular contraction and then drops to its lowest level while the ventricles are relaxed.

PURPOSE OF THE EXERCISE

To examine the pulse, determine the pulse rate, measure blood pressure, and investigate the effects of body position and exercise on pulse rate and blood pressure.

LEARNING OBJECTIVES

After completing this exercise, you should be able to

1. Determine pulse rate.
2. Test the effects of various factors on pulse rate.
3. Measure blood pressure using a sphygmomanometer.
4. Test the effects of various factors on blood pressure.

PROCEDURE A—PULSE RATE

1. Review the sections entitled "Arterial Blood Pressure" and "Measurement of Arterial Blood Pressure— Clinical Application" in chapter 15 of the textbook.
2. Complete Part A of Laboratory Report 43.
3. Examine your laboratory partner's radial pulse. To do this, follow these steps:
   a. Have your partner sit quietly, remaining as relaxed as possible.
   b. Locate the pulse by placing your index and middle fingers over the radial artery on the anterior surface of the wrist. Do not use your thumb for sensing the pulse because you may feel a pulse coming from an artery in the thumb itself.
   c. Note the characteristics of the pulse. That is, could it be described as regular or irregular, strong or weak, hard or soft?
   d. To determine the pulse rate, count the number of pulses that occur in 1 minute. This can be accomplished by counting pulses in 30 seconds and multiplying that number by 2.
4. Repeat the procedure and determine the pulse rate in each of the following conditions:
   a. immediately after lying down;
   b. 3-5 minutes after lying down;
   c. immediately after standing;
   d. 3-5 minutes after standing quietly;
   e. immediately after 3 minutes of moderate exercise *(omit if the person has health problems);*
   f. 3-5 minutes after exercise has ended.
5. Complete Part B of the laboratory report.

DEMONSTRATION

If the equipment is available, the laboratory instructor will demonstrate how a photoelectric pulse pickup transducer or plethysmogram can be used together with a physiological recording apparatus to record the pulse. Such a recording allows an investigator to analyze certain characteristics of the pulse more precisely than is possible using a finger to examine the pulse. For example, the pulse rate can be determined very accurately from a recording, and the heights of the pulse waves provide information about the blood pressure.

PROCEDURE B—BLOOD PRESSURE

1. Measure your laboratory partner's arterial blood pressure. To do this, follow these steps:
   a. Obtain a sphygmomanometer and a stethoscope.
   b. Clean the earpieces and the diaphragm of the stethoscope with cotton moistened with 70% alcohol.
   c. Have your partner sit quietly with bare upper limb resting on a table at heart level. Have the person remain as relaxed as possible.
   d. Locate the brachial artery at the antecubital space. Wrap the cuff of the sphygmomanometer around the arm so that its lower border is about 2.5 cm above the bend of the elbow. Center the bladder of the cuff in line with the *brachial pulse* (fig. 43.1).
   e. Palpate the *radial pulse.* Close the valve on the neck of the rubber bulb connected to the cuff, and pump air from the bulb into the cuff. Inflate the cuff while watching the sphygmomanometer, and note the pressure when the pulse disappears. (This is a rough estimate of the systolic pressure.) Immediately deflate the cuff.
   f. Position the stethoscope over the brachial artery. Reinflate the cuff to a level 30 mm Hg higher than the point where the pulse disappeared during palpation.
   g. Slowly open the valve of the bulb until the pressure in the cuff drops at a rate of about 2 or 3 mm Hg per second.
   h. Listen for sounds (Korotkoff sounds) from the brachial artery. When the first loud tapping sound is heard, record the reading as the systolic pressure. This indicates the pressure exerted against the arterial wall during systole.
   i. Continue to listen to the sounds as the pressure drops, and note the level when the last sound is heard. Record this reading as the diastolic pressure, which measures the constant arterial resistance.
   j. Release all of the pressure from the cuff.
   k. Repeat the procedure until you have two blood pressure measurements from each arm, allowing 2–3 minutes of rest between readings.
   l. Average your readings and enter them in the table in Part C of the laboratory report.
2. Measure your partner's blood pressure in each of the following conditions:
   a. 3–5 minutes after lying down;
   b. 3–5 minutes after standing quietly;
   c. immediately after 3 minutes of moderate exercise *(omit if the person has health problems);*
   d. 3–5 minutes after exercise has ended.
3. Complete Part C of the laboratory report.

Figure 43.1 Blood pressure is commonly measured by using a sphygmomanometer (blood pressure cuff). The use of a column of mercury is the most accurate measurement, but due to environmental concerns, it has been replaced by alternative gauges and digital readouts.

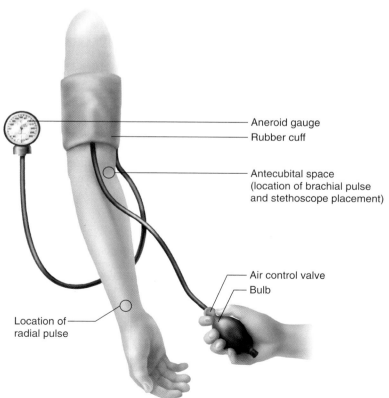

Aneroid gauge
Rubber cuff

Antecubital space
(location of brachial pulse
and stethoscope placement)

Air control valve
Bulb

Location of
radial pulse

PULSE RATE AND BLOOD PRESSURE

PART A

Complete the following statements:

1. The term *blood pressure* most commonly is used to refer to systemic _____ pressure.
2. The maximum pressure achieved during ventricular contraction is called _____ pressure.
3. The lowest pressure that remains in the arterial system during ventricular relaxation is called _____ pressure.
4. The pulse rate is equal to the _____ rate.
5. A pulse that feels full and is not easily compressed is produced by an elevated _____ .
6. The instrument commonly used to measure systemic arterial blood pressure is called a (an) _____ .
7. Blood pressure is expressed in units of _____ .
8. The upper number of the fraction used to record blood pressure indicates the _____ pressure.
9. The difference between the systolic and diastolic pressure is called the _____ .
10. The _____ artery in the arm is the standard systemic artery in which blood pressure is measured.

PART B

1. Enter your observations of pulse characteristics and pulse rates in the table.

Test Subject	Pulse Characteristics	Pulse Rate
Sitting		
Lying down		
3–5 minutes later		
Standing		
3–5 minutes later		
After exercise		
3–5 minutes later		

2. Summarize the effects of body position and exercise on the characteristics and rates of the pulse. _____

_____

_____

_____

PART C

1. Enter the initial measurements of blood pressure in the table.

Reading	Blood Pressure in Right Arm	Blood Pressure in Left Arm
First		
Second		
Average		

2. Enter your test results in the table.

Test Subject	Blood Pressure
3–5 minutes after lying down	
3–5 minutes after standing	
After 3 minutes of moderate exercise	
3–5 minutes later	

3. Summarize the effects of body position and exercise on blood pressure. _____
_____
_____
_____
_____

4. Summarize any correlations between pulse rate and blood pressure from any of the experimental conditions.
_____
_____
_____
_____

Critical Thinking Application

When a pulse is palpated and counted, which blood pressure (systolic or diastolic) would be characteristic at that moment? Explain your answer.

_____
_____
_____

ARTERIES AND VEINS

The blood vessels of the cardiovascular system can be divided into two major pathways—the pulmonary circuit and the systemic circuit. Within each circuit, arteries transport blood away from the heart. After exchanges of gases, nutrients, and wastes have occurred between the blood and the surrounding tissues, veins return the blood to the heart.

PURPOSE OF THE EXERCISE

To review the major circulatory pathways and to locate the major arteries and veins on anatomical charts and in the human torso model.

LEARNING OBJECTIVES

After completing this exercise, you should be able to

1. Distinguish and trace the pulmonary and systemic circuits.
2. Locate the major arteries in these circuits on a chart or model.
3. Locate the major veins in these circuits on a chart or model.

PROCEDURE A—PATHS OF CIRCULATION

1. Review the sections entitled "Pulmonary Circuit" and "Systemic Circuit" in chapter 15 of the textbook.
2. As a review activity, label figure 44.1.
3. Locate the following blood vessels on the available anatomical charts and the human torso model:

pulmonary trunk	1
pulmonary arteries	2
pulmonary veins	4
aorta	1
superior vena cava	1
inferior vena cava	1

Critical Thinking Application

Why is the left ventricle wall thicker than the right ventricle wall?

_____

_____

_____

_____

PROCEDURE B—THE ARTERIAL SYSTEM

1. Review the section entitled "Arterial System" in chapter 15 of the textbook.
2. As a review activity, label figures 44.2, 44.3, 44.4, and 44.5.
3. Locate the following arteries of the systemic circuit on the charts and human torso model:

aorta
    ascending aorta
    aortic arch (arch of aorta)
    thoracic aorta
    abdominal aorta
branches of the aorta
    coronary arteries
    brachiocephalic artery
    left common carotid artery
    left subclavian artery
    celiac artery
        gastric artery
        splenic artery
        hepatic artery
    superior mesenteric artery
    suprarenal arteries
    renal arteries
    gonadal arteries
        ovarian arteries
        testicular arteries
    inferior mesenteric artery

Figure 44.1 Label the major blood vessels associated with the pulmonary and systemic circuits, using the terms provided.

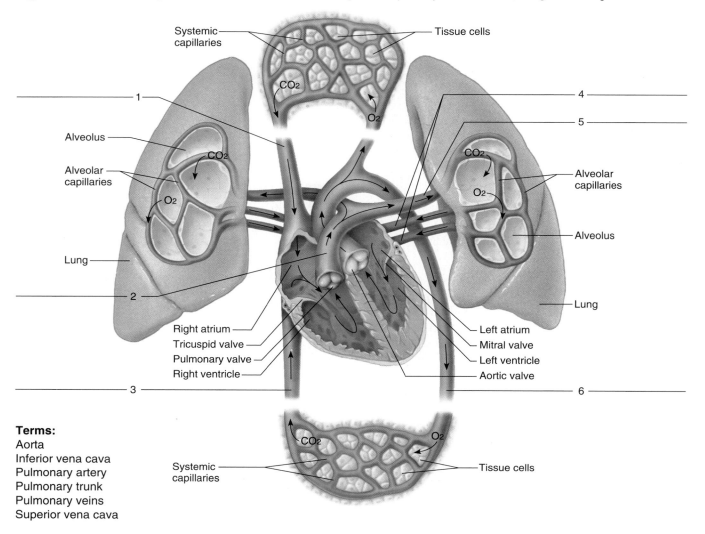

Systemic capillaries

Tissue cells

CO_2

1

Alveolus

CO_2

Alveolar capillaries

O_2

Lung

2

Right atrium
Tricuspid valve
Pulmonary valve
Right ventricle

3

4

5

CO_2

O_2

Alveolar capillaries

Alveolus

Lung

Left atrium
Mitral valve
Left ventricle
Aortic valve

6

CO_2

O_2

Systemic capillaries

Tissue cells

Terms:
Aorta
Inferior vena cava
Pulmonary artery
Pulmonary trunk
Pulmonary veins
Superior vena cava

middle sacral artery
common iliac arteries
arteries to neck, head, and brain
  vertebral arteries
  thyrocervical arteries
  common carotid arteries
  external carotid arteries
    superior thyroid artery
    facial artery
    superficial temporal artery
  internal carotid arteries
arteries to shoulder and upper limb
  axillary artery
  brachial artery
  deep brachial artery
  ulnar artery
  radial artery

arteries to the thoracic and abdominal walls
  internal thoracic artery
  anterior intercostal artery
  posterior intercostal artery
arteries to pelvis and lower limb
  common iliac artery
  internal iliac artery
  external iliac artery
  femoral artery
  deep femoral artery
  popliteal artery
  anterior tibial artery
  dorsalis pedis artery (dorsal pedis artery)
  posterior tibial artery

4. Complete Parts A and B of Laboratory Report 44.

Figure 44.2 Label the arteries supplying the right side of the neck and head. (Note that the clavicle has been removed.)

Occipital artery —

Thyrocervical artery —

1
2
3
4
5
6
7
8

PROCEDURE C—THE VENOUS SYSTEM

1. Review the section entitled "Venous System" in chapter 15 of the textbook.
2. As a review activity, label figures 44.6, 44.7, 44.8, 44.9, and 44.10.
3. Locate the following veins of the systemic circuit on the charts and the human torso model:

veins from brain, head, and neck
- external jugular veins
- internal jugular veins
- subclavian veins
- brachiocephalic veins
- superior vena cava

veins from upper limb and shoulder
- radial vein
- ulnar vein
- brachial vein
- basilic vein
- axillary vein
- cephalic vein
- median cubital vein (antecubital vein)
- subclavian vein

veins of the abdominal and thoracic walls
- internal thoracic veins
- intercostal veins
- azygos vein
- posterior intercostal veins
- superior hemiazygos vein
- inferior hemiazygos vein

veins of the abdominal viscera
- hepatic portal vein
- gastric vein
- superior mesenteric vein
- splenic vein
- inferior mesenteric vein
- hepatic vein
- gonadal vein
- renal vein
- suprarenal vein

veins from lower limb and pelvis
- anterior tibial vein
- posterior tibial vein
- popliteal vein
- femoral vein

Figure 44.3 Label the major arteries of the shoulder and upper limb.

great saphenous vein
small saphenous vein
external iliac vein
internal iliac vein
common iliac vein
inferior vena cava

4. Complete Parts C, D, and E of the laboratory report.

Web Quest

Identify the major arteries and veins, and describe their functions. Observe an animation of the exchanges in a capillary. Search these at www.mhhe.com/shier11
Click on Student Edition. Click on Martin Lab Manual, Web Quest.

Figure 44.4 Label the arteries associated with the abdominal aorta.

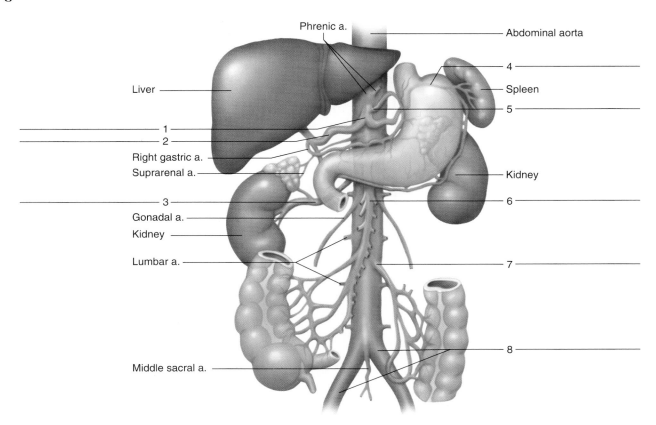

Phrenic a.

Abdominal aorta

Liver

4

Spleen

1

5

2

Right gastric a.

Suprarenal a.

Kidney

3

6

Gonadal a.

Kidney

Lumbar a.

7

Middle sacral a.

8

Figure 44.5 Label the major arteries supplying the pelvis and lower limb, using the terms provided.

1 _____

2 _____

3 _____

(on posterior side)

4 _____

5 _____

6 _____

Inguinal ligament

7 _____

8 _____

9 _____

Anterior view

Terms:
Abdominal aorta
Anterior tibial artery
Common iliac artery
Deep femoral artery
Dorsalis pedis artery
External iliac artery
Femoral artery
Internal iliac artery
Popliteal artery

Figure 44.6 Label the major veins associated with the head and neck. (Note that the clavicle has been removed.)

1

2

3

4

5

Figure 44.7 Label the veins associated with the thoracic wall, using the terms provided.

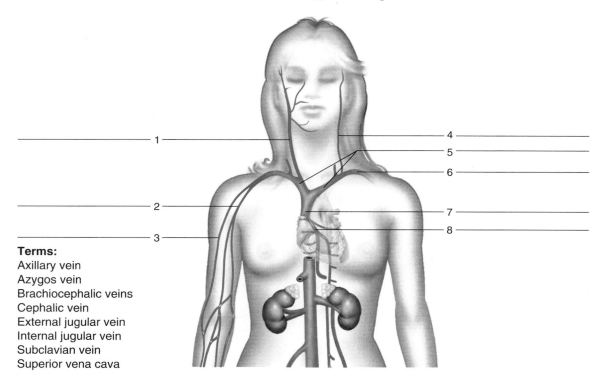

Terms:
Axillary vein
Azygos vein
Brachiocephalic veins
Cephalic vein
External jugular vein
Internal jugular vein
Subclavian vein
Superior vena cava

Figure 44.8 Label the veins of the upper limb and shoulder.

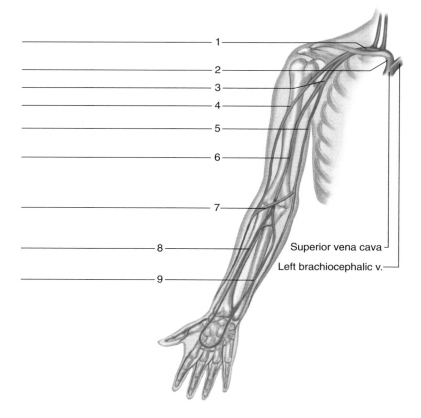

Superior vena cava

Left brachiocephalic v.

Figure 44.9 Label the veins that drain the abdominal viscera (hepatic portal system).

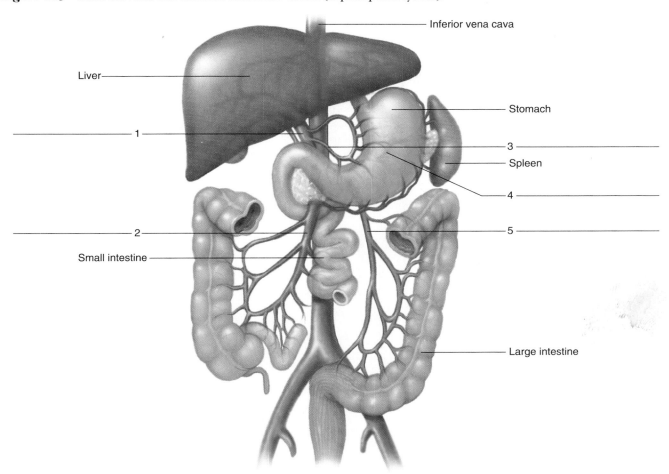

Inferior vena cava

Liver

Stomach

1

3

Spleen

4

2

5

Small intestine

Large intestine

Figure 44.10 Label the veins of the pelvis and lower limb, using the terms provided.

1
2
3
4
Inguinal ligament
5
6
7
(on posterior side)
8

Terms:
Anterior tibial vein
Common iliac vein
External iliac vein
Femoral vein
Great saphenous vein
Inferior vena cava
Internal iliac vein
Popliteal vein

Anterior view

Name _____

Date _____

Section _____

ARTERIES AND VEINS

PART A

Match the arteries in column A with the regions supplied in column B. Place the letter of your choice in the space provided.

Column A	Column B
a. Anterior tibial	_____ 1. Jaw, teeth, and face
b. Celiac	_____ 2. Kidney
c. Deep brachial	_____ 3. Upper digestive tract, spleen, and liver
d. External carotid	_____ 4. Foot and toes
e. Inferior mesenteric	_____ 5. Gluteal muscles
f. Internal carotid	_____ 6. Triceps muscle
g. Internal iliac	_____ 7. Adrenal gland
h. Phrenic	_____ 8. Diaphragm
i. Popliteal	_____ 9. Lower colon
j. Renal	_____ 10. Brain
k. Suprarenal	_____ 11. Forearm muscles
l. Ulnar	_____ 12. Knee joint

PART B

Provide the name of the missing artery in each of the following sequences:

1. Brachiocephalic artery, _____, right axillary artery

2. Ascending aorta, _____, thoracic aorta

3. Abdominal aorta, _____, ascending colon

4. Abdominal aorta, _____, descending colon

5. Brachiocephalic artery, _____, right external carotid artery

6. Subclavian artery, _____, basilar artery

7. External carotid artery, _____, lips

8. Axillary artery, _____, radial artery

9. Common iliac artery, _____, femoral artery

10. Pulmonary trunk, _____, lungs

PART C

Match each vein in column A with the vein it drains into from column B. Place the letter of your choice in the space provided.

Column A

a. Anterior tibial
b. Basilic
c. Brachiocephalic
d. Common iliac
e. External jugular
f. Femoral
g. Popliteal
h. Radial

Column B

_____ 1. Popliteal

_____ 2. Axillary

_____ 3. Inferior vena cava

_____ 4. Subclavian

_____ 5. Brachial

_____ 6. Superior vena cava

_____ 7. Femoral

_____ 8. External iliac

PART D

Provide the name of the missing vein or veins in each of the following sequences:

1. Right subclavian vein, _____, superior vena cava

2. Posterior tibial vein, _____, femoral vein

3. Internal iliac vein, _____, inferior vena cava

4. Median cubital vein, _____, axillary vein

5. Dorsalis pedis vein, _____, popliteal vein

6. Great saphenous vein, _____, external iliac vein

7. Liver, _____, inferior vena cava

8. Lungs, _____, left atrium

9. Kidney, _____, inferior vena cava

PART E

Label the major arteries and veins indicated in figure 44.11.

Figure 44.11 Label the major arteries and veins of the systemic and pulmonary circuits, using the terms provided.

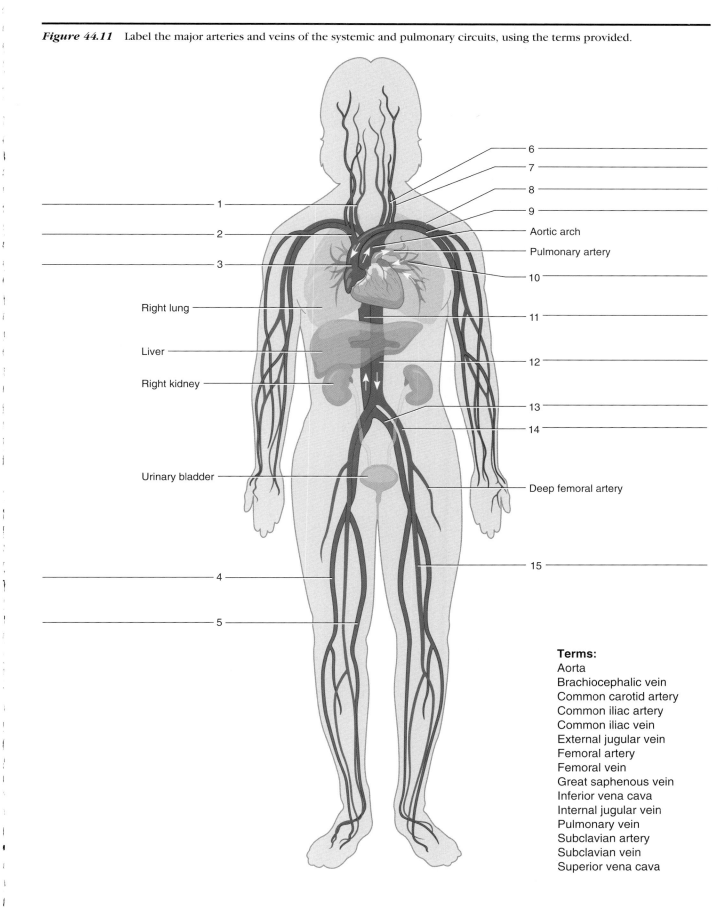

6
7
8
9
Aortic arch
Pulmonary artery
10
11
12
13
14

Deep femoral artery

15

1
2
3

Right lung

Liver

Right kidney

Urinary bladder

4

5

Terms:
Aorta
Brachiocephalic vein
Common carotid artery
Common iliac artery
Common iliac vein
External jugular vein
Femoral artery
Femoral vein
Great saphenous vein
Inferior vena cava
Internal jugular vein
Pulmonary vein
Subclavian artery
Subclavian vein
Superior vena cava

NOTES

LABORATORY EXERCISE 45

CAT DISSECTION: CARDIOVASCULAR SYSTEM

MATERIALS NEEDED

Preserved cat
Dissecting tray
Dissecting instruments
Disposable gloves
Human torso model

 SAFETY

- Wear disposable gloves when working on the cat dissection.
- Dispose of tissue remnants and gloves as instructed.
- Wash the dissecting tray and instruments as instructed.
- Wash your laboratory table.
- Wash your hands before leaving the laboratory.

In this laboratory exercise, you will dissect the major organs of the cardiovascular system of the cat. As before, while you are examining the organs of the cat, compare them with the corresponding organs of the human torso model.

If the cardiovascular system of the cat has been injected, the arteries will be filled with red latex, and the veins will be filled with blue latex. This will make it easier for you to trace the vessels as you dissect them.

PURPOSE OF THE EXERCISE

To examine the major organs of the cardiovascular system of the cat and to compare them with the corresponding organs of the human torso model.

LEARNING OBJECTIVES

After completing this exercise, you should be able to

1. Locate and identify the major organs of the cardiovascular system of the cat.
2. Identify the corresponding organs in the human torso model.
3. Compare the features of the cardiovascular system of the cat with those of the human.

PROCEDURE A—THE ARTERIAL SYSTEM

1. Place the preserved cat in the dissecting tray with its ventral surface up.
2. Open the thoracic cavity, and expose its contents. To do this, follow these steps:
   a. Make a longitudinal incision passing anteriorly from the diaphragm along one side of the sternum. Continue the incision through the neck muscles to the mandible. Try to avoid damaging the internal organs as you cut.
   b. Make a lateral cut on each side along the anterior surface of the diaphragm, and cut the diaphragm loose from the thoracic wall.
   c. Spread the sides of the thoracic wall outward, and use a scalpel to make a longitudinal cut along each side of the inner wall of the rib cage to weaken the ribs. Continue to spread the thoracic wall laterally to break the ribs so that the flaps of the wall will remain open (figs. 45.1 and 45.2).
3. Note the location of the heart and the large blood vessels associated with it. Slit the outer *parietal pericardium* that surrounds the heart by cutting with scissors along the midventral line. Note how this membrane is connected to the *visceral pericardium* that is attached to the surface of the heart. Locate the *pericardial cavity,* the space between the two layers of the pericardium.
4. Examine the heart (see figs. 40.1, 40.2, and 40.3, as well as figs. 45.2 and 45.3). It should be noted that the arrangement of blood vessels coming off the aortic arch is different in the cat. Locate the following:

   right atrium
   left atrium
   right ventricle
   left ventricle
   pulmonary trunk
   aorta
   coronary arteries

371

Figure 45.1 Arteries of the cat's thorax, neck, and forelimb.

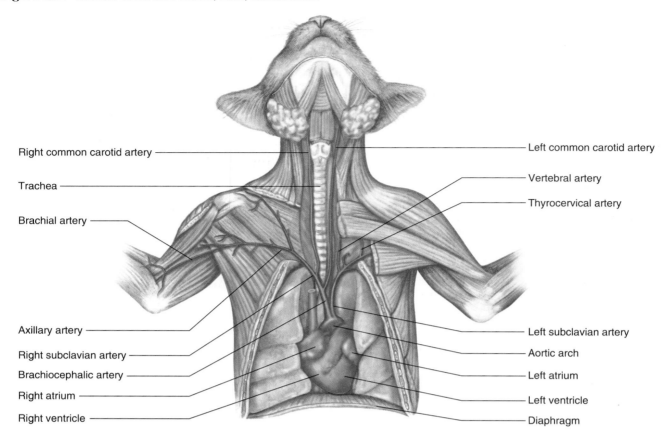

Right common carotid artery

Trachea

Brachial artery

Axillary artery

Right subclavian artery

Brachiocephalic artery

Right atrium

Right ventricle

Left common carotid artery

Vertebral artery

Thyrocervical artery

Left subclavian artery

Aortic arch

Left atrium

Left ventricle

Diaphragm

5. Use a scalpel to open the heart chambers by making a cut along the frontal plane from its apex to its base. Remove any remaining latex from the chambers. Examine the valves between the chambers, and note the relative thicknesses of the chamber walls (fig. 45.4). Do not remove the heart as it is needed for future examination of the relationship between major blood vessels.

6. Using figures 45.1, 45.3, and 45.4 as guides, locate and dissect the following arteries of the thorax and neck:

aortic arch
brachiocephalic artery (on right only)
right subclavian artery
left subclavian artery
right common carotid artery
left common carotid artery

7. Trace the right subclavian artery into the forelimb, and locate the following arteries:

vertebral artery
thyrocervical artery

subscapular artery
axillary artery
brachial artery
radial artery
ulnar artery

8. Open the abdominal cavity. To do this, follow these steps:
   a. Use scissors to make an incision through the body wall along the midline from the symphysis pubis to the diaphragm.
   b. Make a lateral incision through the body wall along either side of the inferior border of the diaphragm and along the bases of the thighs.
   c. Reflect the flaps created in the body wall as you would open a book, and expose the contents of the abdominal cavity.
   d. Note the *parietal peritoneum* that forms the inner lining of the abdominal wall. Also note the *greater omentum,* a structure composed of a double layer of peritoneum that hangs from the

Figure 45.2 Features of the cat's neck and thoracic cavity.

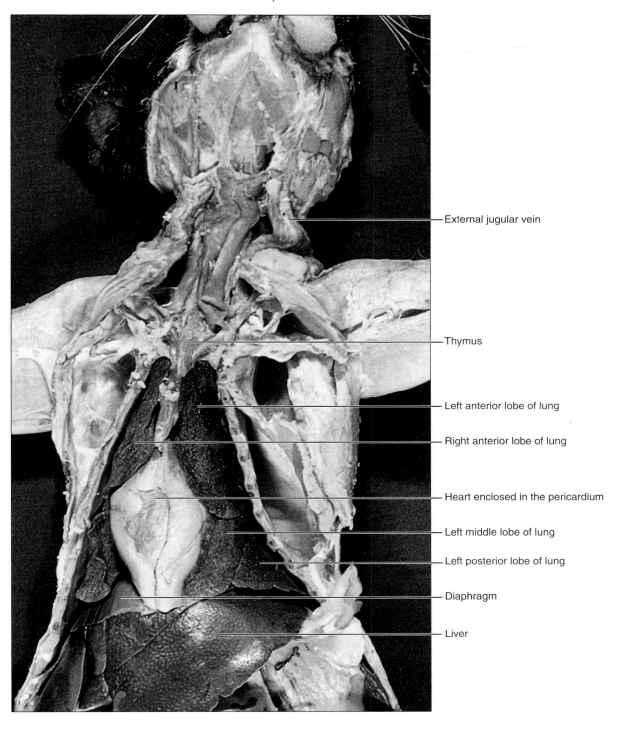

External jugular vein

Thymus

Left anterior lobe of lung

Right anterior lobe of lung

Heart enclosed in the pericardium

Left middle lobe of lung

Left posterior lobe of lung

Diaphragm

Liver

Figure 45.3 Blood vessels of the cat's upper forelimb and neck.

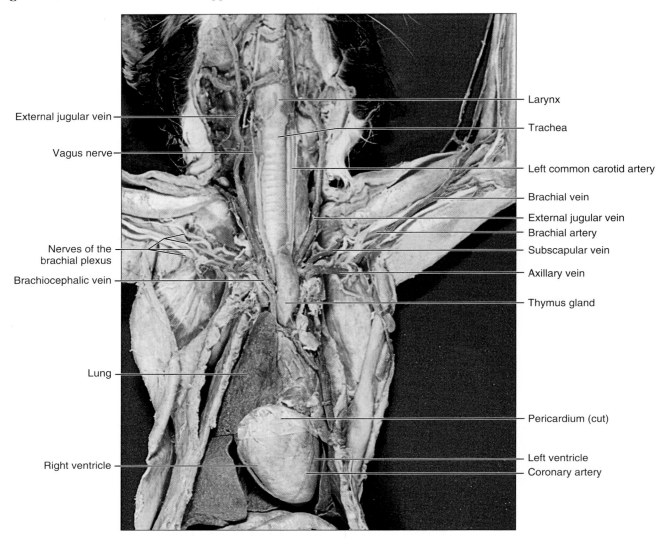

External jugular vein

Vagus nerve

Nerves of the brachial plexus

Brachiocephalic vein

Lung

Right ventricle

Larynx

Trachea

Left common carotid artery

Brachial vein

External jugular vein

Brachial artery

Subscapular vein

Axillary vein

Thymus gland

Pericardium (cut)

Left ventricle

Coronary artery

border of the stomach and covers the lower abdominal organs like a fatty apron (fig. 45.5).

9. As you expose and dissect blood vessels, try not to destroy other visceral organs needed for future studies.

Using figures 45.6, 45.7, and 45.8 as guides, locate and dissect the following arteries of the abdomen:

abdominal aorta (unpaired)

celiac artery (unpaired)

hepatic artery (unpaired)

gastric artery (unpaired)

splenic artery (unpaired)

anterior mesenteric artery (corresponds to superior mesenteric artery)

renal arteries (paired)

adrenolumbar arteries (paired)

gonadal arteries (paired)

posterior mesenteric artery (corresponds to inferior mesenteric artery)

iliolumbar arteries (paired)

external iliac arteries (paired)

internal iliac arteries (paired)

caudal artery (unpaired)

Figure 45.4 Blood vessels of the cat's neck and thorax.

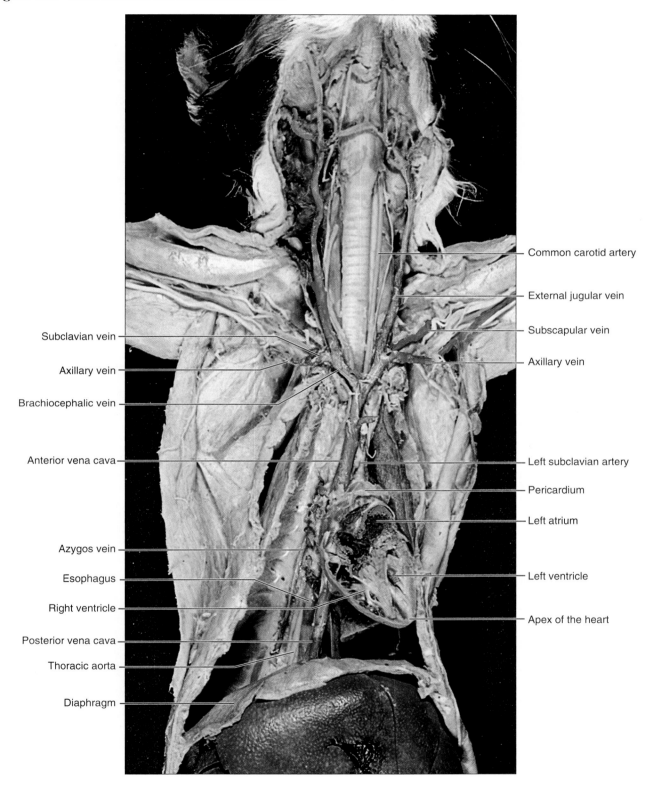

Common carotid artery

External jugular vein

Subscapular vein

Axillary vein

Subclavian vein

Axillary vein

Brachiocephalic vein

Anterior vena cava

Left subclavian artery

Pericardium

Left atrium

Azygos vein

Esophagus

Right ventricle

Left ventricle

Posterior vena cava

Apex of the heart

Thoracic aorta

Diaphragm

Figure 45.5 Organs of the cat's thoracic and abdominal cavities.

Heart
(within
pericardium)

Diaphragm

Gallbladder

Greater omentum

Small intestine

Abdominal wall
(lined with parietal
peritoneum)

Urinary bladder

Lung

Liver

Stomach

Spleen

Kidney

Descending
colon

Figure 45.6 Arteries of the cat's abdomen and hindlimb.

Right adrenolumbar artery

Abdominal aorta

External iliac artery

Femoral artery

Diaphragm

Celiac artery

Anterior mesenteric artery

Renal artery

Gonadal artery

Posterior mesenteric artery

Iliolumbar artery

Internal iliac artery

Caudal artery

Deep femoral artery

10. Trace the external iliac artery into the right hindlimb (fig. 45.9), and locate the following:

femoral artery
deep femoral artery

11. Complete Part A of Laboratory Report 45.

PROCEDURE B—THE VENOUS SYSTEM

1. Examine the heart again, and locate the following veins:

anterior vena cava (corresponds to superior vena cava)

posterior vena cava (corresponds to inferior vena cava)
pulmonary veins

2. Using figures 45.3, 45.4, and 45.10 as guides, locate and dissect the following veins in the thorax and neck:

right brachiocephalic vein
left brachiocephalic vein
right subclavian vein
left subclavian vein
internal jugular vein
external jugular vein

Figure 45.7 Arteries of the cat's abdomen, left lateral view.

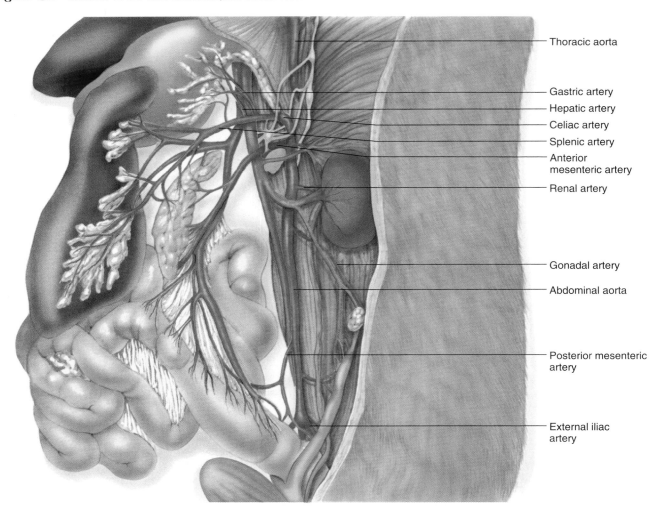

- Thoracic aorta
- Gastric artery
- Hepatic artery
- Celiac artery
- Splenic artery
- Anterior mesenteric artery
- Renal artery
- Gonadal artery
- Abdominal aorta
- Posterior mesenteric artery
- External iliac artery

3. Trace the right subclavian vein into the forelimb, and locate the following veins:

   axillary vein
   subscapular vein
   brachial vein
   long thoracic vein

4. Using figures 45.8, 45.11, and 45.12 as guides, locate and dissect the following veins in the abdomen:

   posterior vena cava
   adrenolumbar vein
   anterior mesenteric vein (corresponds to superior mesenteric vein)
   posterior mesenteric vein (corresponds to inferior mesenteric vein)

   hepatic portal vein
   splenic vein
   renal vein
   gonadal vein
   iliolumbar vein
   common iliac vein
   internal iliac vein
   external iliac vein

5. Trace the external iliac vein into the hindlimb (fig. 45.9), and locate the following veins:

   femoral vein
   deep femoral vein

6. Complete Part B of the laboratory report.

Figure 45.8 Blood vessels of the cat's abdominal cavity, with the digestive organs removed.

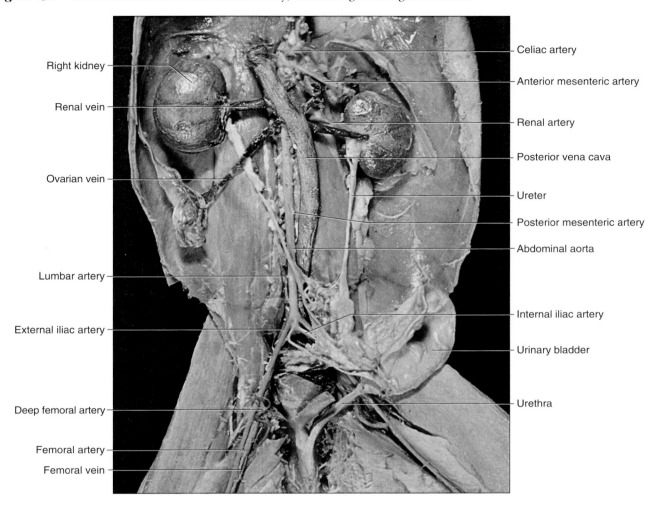

Right kidney

Renal vein

Ovarian vein

Lumbar artery

External iliac artery

Deep femoral artery

Femoral artery

Femoral vein

Celiac artery

Anterior mesenteric artery

Renal artery

Posterior vena cava

Ureter

Posterior mesenteric artery

Abdominal aorta

Internal iliac artery

Urinary bladder

Urethra

Figure 45.9   Blood vessels of the cat's upper hindlimb.

External iliac vein

Femoral vein

External iliac artery

Deep femoral artery

Femoral artery

Figure 45.10   Veins of the cat's thorax, neck, and forelimb.

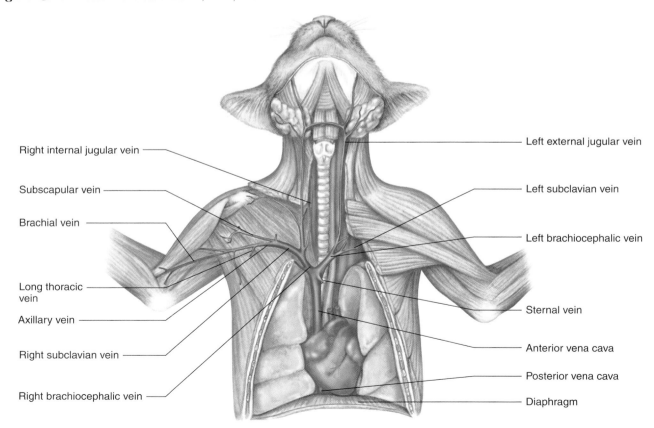

Right internal jugular vein

Subscapular vein

Brachial vein

Long thoracic vein

Axillary vein

Right subclavian vein

Right brachiocephalic vein

Left external jugular vein

Left subclavian vein

Left brachiocephalic vein

Sternal vein

Anterior vena cava

Posterior vena cava

Diaphragm

Figure 45.11 Veins of the cat's abdomen and hindlimb.

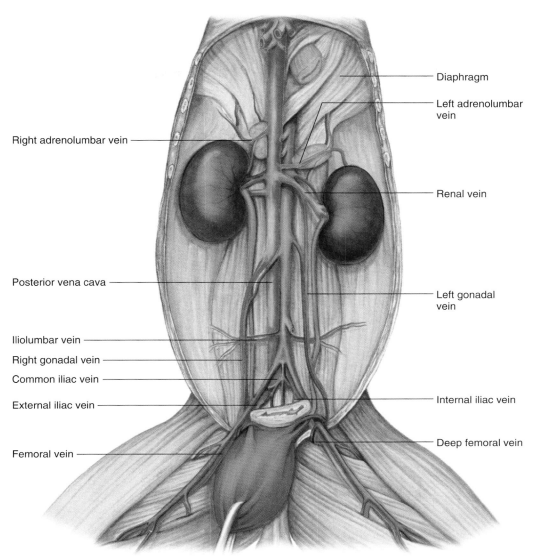

Right adrenolumbar vein

Posterior vena cava

Iliolumbar vein

Right gonadal vein

Common iliac vein

External iliac vein

Femoral vein

Diaphragm

Left adrenolumbar vein

Renal vein

Left gonadal vein

Internal iliac vein

Deep femoral vein

Figure 45.12 Veins of the cat's abdomen, left lateral view.

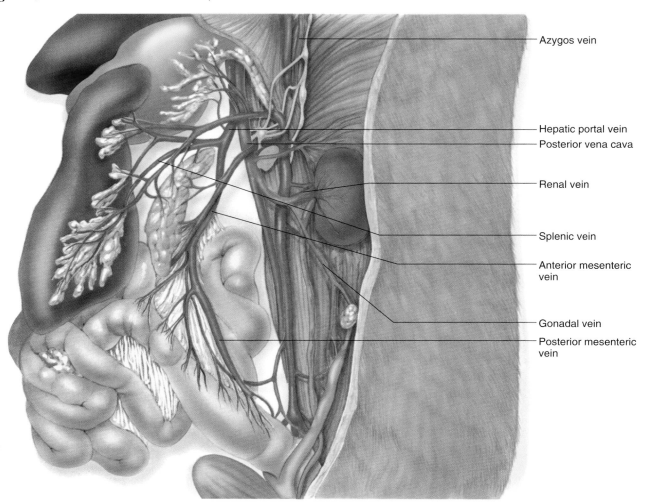

Azygos vein

Hepatic portal vein
Posterior vena cava

Renal vein

Splenic vein

Anterior mesenteric
vein

Gonadal vein

Posterior mesenteric
vein

Name _____

Date _____

Section _____

Cat Dissection: Cardiovascular System

PART A

Complete the following:

1. Describe the position and attachments of the parietal pericardium of the heart of the cat. _____
   _____
   _____
   _____

2. Describe the relative thicknesses of the walls of the heart chambers of the cat. _____
   _____
   _____
   _____

3. Explain how the wall thicknesses are related to the functions of the chambers. _____
   _____
   _____
   _____
   _____
   _____

4. Compare the origins of the common carotid arteries of the cat with those of the human. _____
   _____
   _____
   _____
   _____

5. Compare the origins of the iliac arteries of the cat with those of the human. _____
   _____
   _____
   _____

PART B

Complete the following:

1. Compare the origins of the brachiocephalic veins of the cat with those of the human. _____

    _____

    _____

    _____

2. Compare the relative sizes of the external and internal jugular veins of the cat with those of the human. _____

    _____

    _____

    _____

    _____

    _____

3. List twelve veins that cats and humans have in common.

    _____

    _____

    _____

    _____

    _____

    _____

LABORATORY EXERCISE 46

LYMPHATIC SYSTEM

 SAFETY

- Wear disposable gloves when working on the cat demonstration.
- Wash your hands before leaving the laboratory.

The lymphatic system is a vast collection of cells and biochemicals that travel in lymphatic capillaries and vessels, and the organs and glands that produce them. The system is closely associated with the cardiovascular system and includes a network of vessels that assist in the circulation of body fluids. These vessels provide pathways through which excess fluid can be transported away from interstitial spaces within most tissues and returned to the bloodstream. Without the lymphatic system, this fluid would accumulate in tissue spaces, producing edema.

The organs of the lymphatic system also help defend the tissues against infections by filtering particles from lymph and by supporting the activities of lymphocytes that furnish immunity against specific disease-causing agents or pathogens.

PURPOSE OF THE EXERCISE

To review the structure of the lymphatic system and to observe the microscopic structure of a lymph node, thymus, and spleen.

LEARNING OBJECTIVES

After completing this exercise, you should be able to

1. Locate and identify the major lymphatic pathways in an anatomical chart or model.
2. Locate and identify the major chains of lymph nodes (lymph glands) in an anatomical chart or model.
3. Describe the structure of a lymph node.
4. Identify the major microscopic structures of a lymph node, thymus, and spleen.

PROCEDURE A— LYMPHATIC PATHWAYS

1. Review the section entitled "Lymphatic Pathways" in chapter 16 of the textbook.
2. As a review activity, label figure 46.1.
3. Complete Part A of Laboratory Report 46.
4. Observe the human torso model and the anatomical chart of the lymphatic system, and locate the following features:

lymphatic vessels
lymph nodes
lymphatic trunks
    lumbar trunk
    intestinal trunk
    intercostal trunk
    bronchomediastinal trunk
    subclavian trunk
    jugular trunk
collecting ducts
    thoracic (left lymphatic) duct
    right lymphatic duct
internal jugular veins
subclavian veins

Figure 46.1 Label the diagram by placing the correct numbers in the spaces provided.

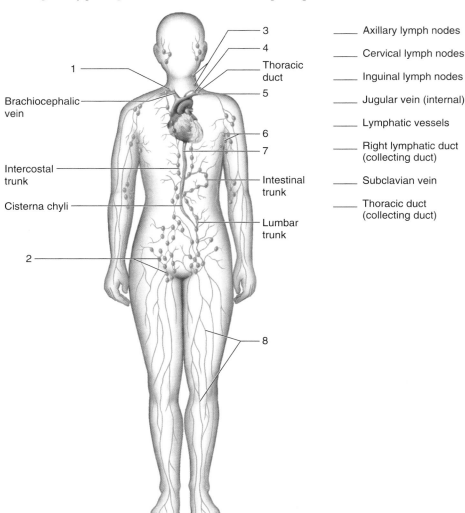

_____ Axillary lymph nodes

_____ Cervical lymph nodes

_____ Inguinal lymph nodes

_____ Jugular vein (internal)

_____ Lymphatic vessels

_____ Right lymphatic duct (collecting duct)

_____ Subclavian vein

_____ Thoracic duct (collecting duct)

Labels on diagram: 3, 4, Thoracic duct, 5, 6, 7, 1, Brachiocephalic vein, Intercostal trunk, Cisterna chyli, 2, Intestinal trunk, Lumbar trunk, 8

DEMONSTRATION

Examine the collecting ducts in the thorax of the preserved cat. The *thoracic duct* joins the venous system near the junction of the left subclavian vein and the left external jugular vein (see fig. 45.10). Trace this duct posteriorly, and note its beaded appearance, which is due to the presence of valves in the vessel. These valves prevent the backflow of lymph.

Look for the short *right lymphatic duct,* which joins the venous system near the junction of the right subclavian vein and the right external jugular vein. How do the collecting ducts compare in size?

_____

_____

What is the significance of this observation?

_____

_____

_____

PROCEDURE B—LYMPH NODES

1. Review the section entitled "Lymph Nodes" in chapter 16 of the textbook.
2. As a review activity, label figure 46.2.
3. Complete Part B of the laboratory report.
4. Observe the anatomical chart of the lymphatic system and the human torso model, and locate the clusters of lymph nodes in the following regions:

   cervical region
   axillary region
   inguinal region
   pelvic cavity
   abdominal cavity
   thoracic cavity

Figure 46.2 Label this diagram of a lymph node by placing the correct numbers in the spaces provided.

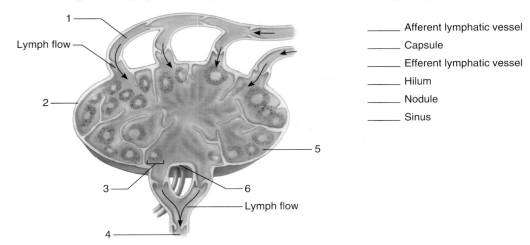

_____ Afferent lymphatic vessel
_____ Capsule
_____ Efferent lymphatic vessel
_____ Hilum
_____ Nodule
_____ Sinus

Figure 46.3 Micrograph of a lymph node (5×).

5. Palpate the lymph nodes in your cervical region. They are located along the lower border of the mandible and between the ramus of the mandible and the sternocleidomastoid muscle. They feel like small, firm lumps.

6. Obtain a prepared microscope slide of a lymph node and observe it, using low-power magnification (fig. 46.3). Identify the *capsule* that surrounds the node and is mainly composed of collagenous fibers, the *lymph nodules* that appear as dense masses near the surface of the node, and the *lymph sinus* that appears as narrow space between the nodules and the capsule.

7. Using high-power magnification, examine a nodule within the lymph node. Note that the nodule contains densely packed *lymphocytes.*

8. Prepare a labeled sketch of a representative section of a lymph node in Part D of the laboratory report.

PROCEDURE C—THYMUS AND SPLEEN

1. Review the section entitled "Thymus and Spleen" in chapter 16 of the textbook.

2. Locate the thymus and spleen in the anatomical chart of the lymphatic system and on the human torso model.

3. Complete Part C of the laboratory report.

4. Obtain a prepared microscope slide of human thymus and observe it, using low-power magnification (fig. 46.4). Note how the thymus is subdivided into *lobules* by *septa* of connective tissue that contain blood vessels. Identify the *capsule* of loose connective tissue that surrounds the thymus, the outer *cortex* of a lobule that is composed of densely packed cells and is deeply stained, and the inner *medulla* of a lobule that is composed of loosely packed lymphocytes and epithelial cells and is lightly stained.

5. Examine the cortex tissue of a lobule using high-power magnification. The cells of the cortex are composed of densely packed *lymphocytes* among some epithelial cells and *macrophages*. Some of these cortical cells may be undergoing mitosis, so their chromosomes may be visible.

6. Prepare a labeled sketch of a representative section of the thymus in Part D of the laboratory report.

Figure 46.4 A section of the thymus gland (10× micrograph enlarged to 20×).

Lobule

Septum of connective tissue

Medulla

Cortex

Figure 46.5 Micrograph of a section of the spleen (15×).

Red pulp   White pulp

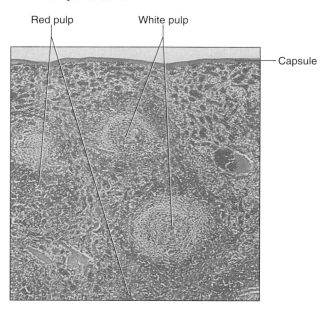

Capsule

7. Obtain a prepared slide of the human spleen and observe it, using low-power magnification (fig. 46.5). Identify the *capsule* of dense connective tissue that surrounds the spleen. Note that the tissues of the spleen include circular *nodules of white* (in unstained tissue) *pulp* that are enclosed in a matrix of *red pulp.*

8. Using high-power magnification, examine a nodule of white pulp and red pulp. The cells of the white pulp are mainly *lymphocytes.* Also, there may be an arteriole centrally located in the nodule. The cells of the red pulp are mostly red blood cells with many lymphocytes and macrophages.

9. Prepare a labeled sketch of a representative section of the spleen in Part D of the laboratory report.

Web Quest

Locate the six major areas of lymph nodes, and identify the components of the lymphatic system. Search these at

www.mhhe.com/shier11

Click on Student Edition. Click on Martin Lab Manual, Web Quest.

Name _____

Date _____

Section _____

LYMPHATIC SYSTEM

PART A

Complete the following statements:

1. Lymphatic pathways begin as _____ that merge to form lymphatic vessels.
2. The wall of a lymphatic capillary consists of a single layer of _____ cells.
3. Once tissue (interstitial) fluid is inside a lymph capillary, the fluid is called _____ .
4. Lymphatic vessels have walls that are similar to those of _____ but thinner.
5. Lymphatic vessels contain _____ that help prevent the backflow of lymph.
6. Lymphatic vessels usually lead to _____ that filter the fluid being transported.
7. The lymphatic trunk that drains the abdominal viscera is called the _____ trunk.
8. The lymphatic trunk that drains the head and neck is called the _____ trunk.
9. The _____ is the larger and longer of the two lymphatic collecting ducts.

PART B

Complete the following statements:

1. Lymph nodes contain large numbers of white blood cells called _____ and macrophages that fight invading microorganisms.
2. The indented region where blood vessels and nerves join a lymph node is called the _____ .
3. _____ that contain germinal centers are the structural units of a lymph node.
4. The spaces within a lymph node are called _____ through which lymph circulates.
5. Lymph enters a node through a(an) _____ lymphatic vessel.
6. The partially encapsulated lymph nodes in the pharynx are called _____ .
7. The aggregations of lymph nodules found within the mucosal lining of the small intestine are called

_____ .

8. The lymph nodes in the cervical region are associated with the lymphatic vessels that drain the

_____ .

9. The lymph nodes associated with the lymphatic vessels that drain the lower limbs are located in the _____ region.

PART C

Complete the following statements:

1. The thymus is located in the _____ , anterior to the aortic arch.
2. The thymus reaches its greatest size during infancy and early childhood and tends to decrease in size following _____ .
3. As a person ages, the thymus tissue is often replaced by _____ .
4. The lymphocytes of the thymus develop from precursor cells that originated in the _____ .
5. The hormones secreted by the thymus are called _____ .
6. The _____ is the largest of the lymphatic organs.
7. Blood vessels enter the spleen through the region called the _____ .
8. The sinuses within the spleen contain _____ .
9. The tiny islands (nodules) of tissue within the spleen that contain many lymphocytes comprise the _____ .
10. The _____ of the spleen contains large numbers of red blood cells, lymphocytes, and macrophages.
11. _____ within the spleen engulf and destroy foreign particles and cellular debris.

PART D

Lymph node sketch (_____×)	Thymus sketch (_____×)
Spleen sketch (_____×)	

390

LABORATORY EXERCISE 47

DIGESTIVE ORGANS

MATERIALS NEEDED

Textbook
Human torso model
Head model, sagittal section
Skull with teeth
Teeth, sectioned
Tooth model, sectioned
Paper cup
Compound light microscope
Prepared microscope slides of the following:
    Parotid gland (salivary gland)
    Esophagus
    Stomach (fundus)
    Pancreas (exocrine portion)
    Small intestine (jejunum)
    Large intestine

The digestive system includes the organs associated with the alimentary canal and several accessory structures. The alimentary canal, which is a muscular tube, passes through the body from the opening of the mouth to the anus. It includes the mouth, pharynx, esophagus, stomach, small intestine, and large intestine. The function of the canal is to move substances throughout its length. It is specialized in various regions to store, digest, and absorb food materials and to eliminate the residues. The accessory organs, which include the salivary glands, liver, gallbladder, and pancreas, secrete products into the alimentary canal that aid digestive functions.

PURPOSE OF THE EXERCISE

To review the structure and function of the digestive organs and to examine the tissues of these organs microscopically.

LEARNING OBJECTIVES

After completing this exercise, you should be able to

1. Locate the major digestive organs.
2. Describe the functions of these organs.
3. Recognize tissue sections of these organs.
4. Identify the major features of each tissue section.

PROCEDURE A—MOUTH AND SALIVARY GLANDS

1. Review the sections entitled "Mouth" and "Salivary Glands" in chapter 17 of the textbook.
2. As a review activity, label figures 47.1, 47.2, and 47.3.
3. Examine the head model (sagittal section) and a skull. Locate the following structures:

oral cavity
vestibule
tongue
    lingual frenulum
    papillae
lingual tonsils
palate
    hard palate
    soft palate
    uvula
palatine tonsils
pharyngeal tonsils (adenoids)
gums (gingivae)
teeth
    incisors
    cuspids (canines)
    bicuspids (premolars)
    molars

4. Examine a sectioned tooth and a tooth model. Locate the following features:

crown
    enamel
    dentin
neck
root
    pulp cavity
    cementum
    root canal

Figure 47.1   Label the major features of the mouth.

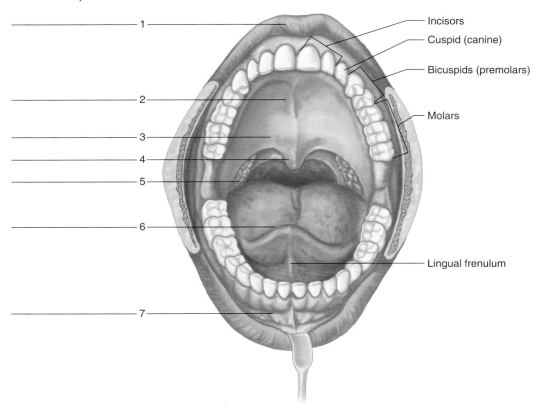

Incisors
Cuspid (canine)
Bicuspids (premolars)
Molars
Lingual frenulum

Figure 47.2   Label the features associated with the major salivary glands.

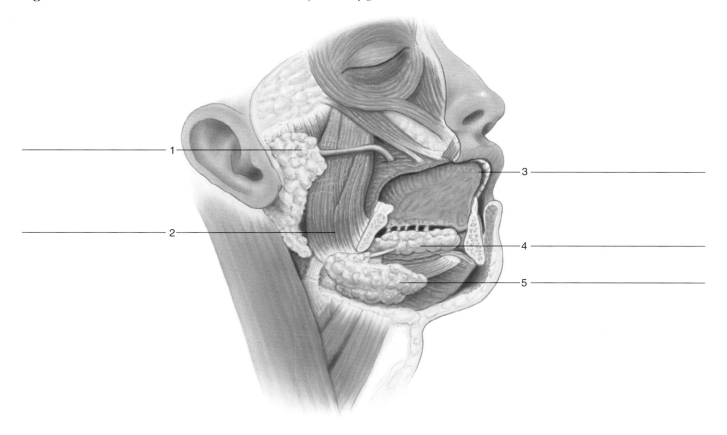

Figure 47.3 Label the features of this cuspid (canine) tooth.

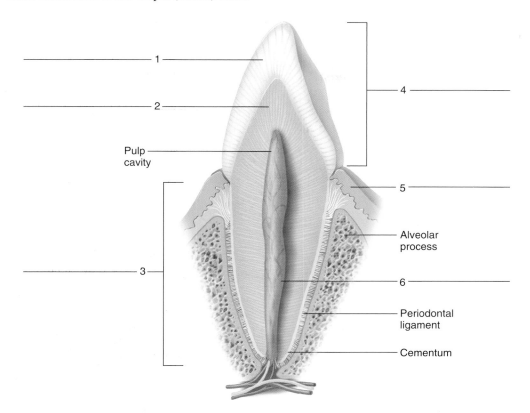

Pulp cavity

Alveolar process

Periodontal ligament

Cementum

5. Observe the head of the human torso model, and locate the following:

parotid salivary gland
parotid duct (Stensen's duct)
submandibular salivary gland
submandibular duct (Wharton's duct)
sublingual salivary gland

6. Examine a microscopic section of a parotid gland, using low- and high-power magnification. Note the numerous glandular cells arranged in clusters around small ducts. Also note a larger secretory duct surrounded by lightly stained cuboidal epithelial cells (fig. 47.4).
7. Complete Part A of Laboratory Report 47.

PROCEDURE B—PHARYNX AND ESOPHAGUS

1. Review the section entitled "Pharynx and Esophagus" in chapter 17 of the textbook.
2. As a review activity, label figure 47.5.
3. Observe the human torso model, and locate the following features:

pharynx
    nasopharynx
        opening to auditory tube (eustachian tube)
    oropharynx
    laryngopharynx
    constrictor muscles
epiglottis
esophagus
    esophageal hiatus
lower esophageal sphincter (cardiac sphincter)

4. Have your partner take a swallow from a cup of water. Carefully watch the movements in the anterior region of the neck. What steps in the swallowing process did you observe?

_____
_____
_____
_____

5. Examine a microscopic section of esophagus wall, using low-power magnification (fig. 47.6). Note that the inner lining is composed of stratified squamous epithelium and that there are layers of muscle tissue in the wall. Locate some mucous glands in the submucosa. They appear as clusters of lightly stained cells.
6. Complete Part B of the laboratory report.

Figure 47.4 Micrograph of the parotid salivary gland (300×).

Glandular cell

Secretory duct

Figure 47.5 Label the features associated with the pharynx.

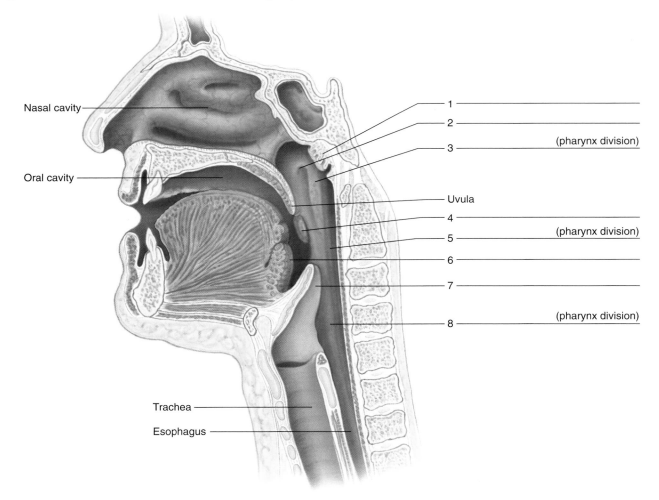

Nasal cavity

Oral cavity

1

2

(pharynx division)

3

Uvula

4

(pharynx division)

5

6

7

(pharynx division)

8

Trachea

Esophagus

Figure 47.6 Micrograph of a cross section of the esophagus (10 ×).

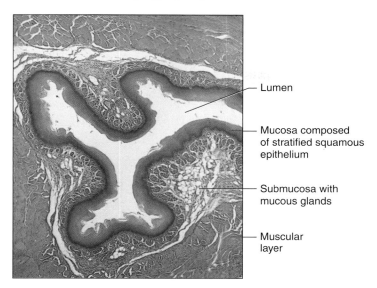

Lumen

Mucosa composed of stratified squamous epithelium

Submucosa with mucous glands

Muscular layer

PROCEDURE C—THE STOMACH

1. Review the section entitled "Stomach" in chapter 17 of the textbook.
2. As a review activity, label figures 47.7 and 47.8.
3. Observe the human torso model, and locate the following features of the stomach:

rugae	**pyloric canal**
cardiac region	**pyloric sphincter (valve)**
fundic region	**lesser curvature**
body region	**greater curvature**
pyloric region	

4. Examine a microscopic section of stomach wall, using low-power magnification. Note how the inner lining of simple columnar epithelium dips inward to form gastric pits. The gastric glands are tubular structures that open into the gastric pits. Near the deep ends of these glands, you should be able to locate some intensely stained (bluish) chief cells and some lightly stained (pinkish) parietal cells (fig. 47.9). What are the functions of these cells?

_____

_____

_____

_____

_____

5. Complete Part C of the laboratory report.

PROCEDURE D—PANCREAS AND LIVER

1. Review the sections entitled "Pancreas," "Liver," and "Small Intestine" in chapter 17 of the textbook.
2. As a review activity, label figure 47.10.
3. Observe the human torso model, and locate the following structures:

pancreas
pancreatic duct
liver
    right lobe
    quadrate lobe
    caudate lobe
    left lobe
round ligament (ligamentum teres)
falciform ligament
coronary ligament
gallbladder
hepatic ducts
common hepatic duct
cystic duct
common bile duct
hepatopancreatic sphincter (sphincter of Oddi)

Figure 47.7 Label the major regions of the stomach and associated structures.

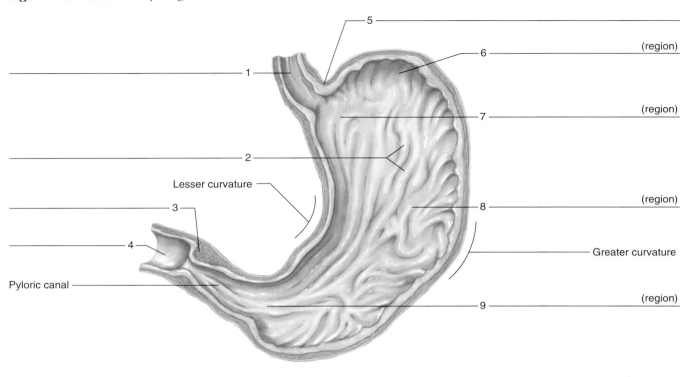

5 _____

6 _____ (region)

1 _____

7 _____ (region)

2 _____

Lesser curvature

3 _____

8 _____ (region)

4 _____

Greater curvature

Pyloric canal _____

9 _____ (region)

Figure 47.8 Label the lining of the stomach by placing the correct numbers in the spaces provided.

_____ Chief cell

_____ Gastric gland

_____ Gastric pits

_____ Mucosa

_____ Mucous cell

_____ Parietal cell

_____ Submucosa

Figure 47.9 Micrograph of the mucosa of the stomach wall (50× micrograph enlarged to 100×).

Simple columnar epithelium

Mucous cell

Gastric pit

Parietal cell

Gastric gland

Chief cell

4. Examine the pancreas slide, using low-power magnification. Observe the exocrine (acinar) cells that secrete pancreatic juice. See figure 36.11 in Laboratory Exercise 36 for a micrograph of the pancreas.
5. Complete Part D of the laboratory report.

PROCEDURE E—SMALL AND LARGE INTESTINES

1. Review the sections entitled "Small Intestine" and "Large Intestine" in chapter 17 of the textbook.
2. As a review activity, label figure 47.11.
3. Observe the human torso model, and locate each of the following features:

small intestine
   duodenum
   jejunum
   ileum
mesentery
ileocecal sphincter (valve)
large intestine
   large intestinal wall
      haustra
      teniae coli
      epiploic appendages

   cecum
   vermiform appendix
   ascending colon
   right colic (hepatic) flexure
   transverse colon
   left colic (splenic) flexure
   descending colon
   sigmoid colon
   rectum
   anal canal
   anal columns
anal sphincter muscles
   internal anal sphincter
   external anal sphincter
anus

4. Using low-power magnification, examine a microscopic section of small intestine wall. Identify the mucosa, submucosa, muscular layer, and serosa. Note the villi that extend into the lumen of the tube. Study a single villus, using high-power magnification. Note the core of connective tissue and the covering of simple columnar epithelium that contains some lightly

Figure 47.10 Label the features associated with the liver and pancreas.

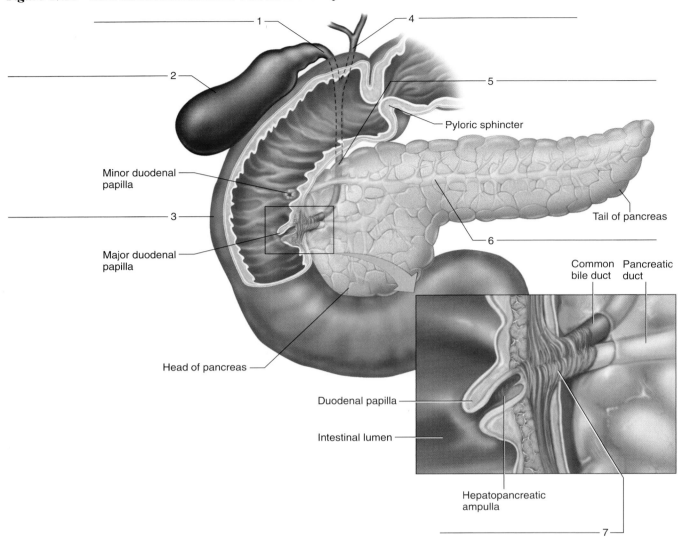

Minor duodenal papilla

Major duodenal papilla

Head of pancreas

Pyloric sphincter

Tail of pancreas

Common bile duct   Pancreatic duct

Duodenal papilla

Intestinal lumen

Hepatopancreatic ampulla

stained goblet cells (fig. 47.12). What is the function of these villi?

_____

_____

_____

5. Prepare a labeled sketch of the wall of the small intestine in Part E of the laboratory report.

6. Examine a microscopic section of large intestine wall. Note the lack of villi. Also note the tubular

mucous glands that open on the surface of the inner lining and the numerous lightly stained goblet cells. Locate the four layers of the wall (fig. 47.13). What is the function of the mucus secreted by these glands?

_____

_____

_____

7. Complete Part F of the laboratory report.

Figure 47.11 Label this diagram of the small and large intestines by placing the correct numbers in the spaces provided.

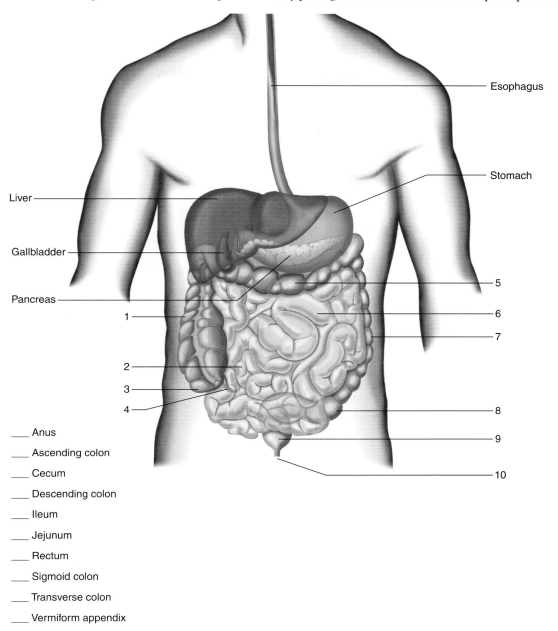

Esophagus

Stomach

Liver

Gallbladder

Pancreas

1

2

3

4

5

6

7

8

9

10

____ Anus

____ Ascending colon

____ Cecum

____ Descending colon

____ Ileum

____ Jejunum

____ Rectum

____ Sigmoid colon

____ Transverse colon

____ Vermiform appendix

Critical Thinking Application

How is the structure of the small intestine better adapted for absorption than the large intestine?

_____

_____

_____

_____

Web Quest

Summarize the functions of the organs of the digestive system. Search these at
www.mhhe.com/shier11
Click on Student Edition. Click on Martin Lab Manual, Web Quest.

Figure 47.12 Micrograph of the small intestine wall (40×).

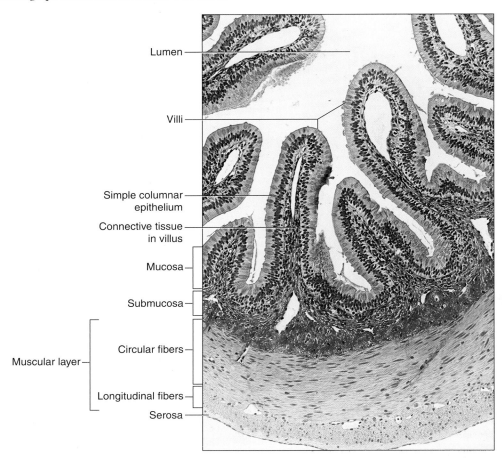

Lumen

Villi

Simple columnar epithelium

Connective tissue in villus

Mucosa

Submucosa

Muscular layer

Circular fibers

Longitudinal fibers

Serosa

Figure 47.13 Micrograph of the large intestine wall (64×).

Lumen

Mucosa with mucous glands

Submucosa

Muscular layer (circular and longitudinal)

Serosa

Name _____

Date _____

Section _____

DIGESTIVE ORGANS

PART A

Match the terms in column A with the descriptions in column B. Place the letter of your choice in the space provided.

Column A	Column B
a. Adenoids (pharyngeal tonsils)	_____ 1. Bonelike substance beneath tooth enamel
b. Crown	_____ 2. Smallest of major salivary glands
c. Dentin	_____ 3. Tooth specialized for grinding
d. Incisor	_____ 4. Chamber between tongue and palate
e. Lingual frenulum	_____ 5. Projections on tongue surface
f. Molar	_____ 6. Cone-shaped projection of soft palate
g. Oral cavity	_____ 7. Attaches tooth to jaw
h. Papillae	_____ 8. Chisel-shaped tooth
i. Periodontal ligament	_____ 9. Space between the teeth, cheeks, and lips
j. Sublingual gland	_____ 10. Anchors tongue to floor of mouth
k. Uvula	_____ 11. Lymphatic tissue in posterior wall of pharynx near auditory tubes
l. Vestibule	_____ 12. Portion of tooth projecting beyond gum

PART B

Complete the following:

1. The part of the pharynx superior to the soft palate is called the _____.

2. The middle part of the pharynx is called the _____.

3. The inferior portion of the pharynx is called the _____.

4. _____ is the main secretion of the esophagus.

5. The esophagus penetrates the diaphragm through an opening called the _____.

6. Summarize the functions of the esophagus. _____

_____

_____

PART C

Complete the following:

1. Name the four regions of the stomach. _____

2. Name the valve that prevents regurgitation of food from the small intestine back into the stomach._____

   _____

3. Name the gastric cells that secrete digestive enzymes._____

4. Name the gastric cells that secrete hydrochloric acid. _____

5. Name the most important digestive enzyme in gastric juice._____

6. Name a substance needed for efficient absorption of vitamin B_{12}. _____

7. Name a hormone secreted by the stomach that stimulates gastric glands to secrete. _____

8. Name the semifluid paste of food particles and gastric juice. _____

9. Summarize the functions of the stomach. _____

   _____

   _____

   _____

PART D

Match the terms in column A with the descriptions in column B. Place the letter of your choice in the space provided.

Column A	Column B
a. Amylase (salivary)	_____ 1. Activates protein-digesting enzyme trypsin
b. Bile salts	_____ 2. Causes emulsification of fats
c. Cholecystokinin	_____ 3. Carries on phagocytosis in liver
d. Enterokinase	_____ 4. Carbohydrate-digesting enzyme
e. Kupffer cells	_____ 5. Fat-digesting enzyme
f. Lipase	_____ 6. Protein-digesting enzyme
g. Nuclease	_____ 7. Stimulates gallbladder to release bile
h. Secretin	_____ 8. Stimulates pancreas to secrete fluids high in bicarbonate ions
i. Trypsin	_____ 9. Nucleic acid-digesting enzyme

402

PART E

Prepare a sketch of a cross section of the small intestine. Label the four layers, villi, and lumen. Indicate the magnification used for your sketch.

PART F

Complete the following:

1. Name the three portions of the small intestine._____

2. Describe the function of the mesentery. _____

3. Name the lymphatic capillary found in an intestinal villus. _____

4. Name five digestive enzymes secreted by the small intestinal mucosa. _____

   _____

5. Name the valve that controls the movement of material between the small and large intestines._____

   _____

6. Name the small projection that contains lymphatic tissue attached to the cecum. _____

7. Summarize the functions of the small intestine. _____

   _____

   _____

   _____

8. Summarize the functions of the large intestine._____

   _____

   _____

NOTES

CAT DISSECTION: DIGESTIVE SYSTEM

MATERIALS NEEDED

Preserved cat
Dissecting tray
Dissecting instruments
Bone cutter
Disposable gloves
Human torso model
Hand lens

 SAFETY

- Wear disposable gloves when working on the cat dissection.
- Dispose of tissue remnants and gloves as instructed.
- Wash the dissecting tray and instruments as instructed.
- Wash your laboratory table.
- Wash your hands before leaving the laboratory.

In this laboratory exercise, you will dissect the major digestive organs of the cat. As you observe these organs, compare them with those of the human by observing the parts of the human torso model; however, keep in mind that the cat is a carnivore (flesh-eating mammal) and that the organs of its digestive system are adapted to capturing, holding, eating, and digesting the bodies of other animals. In contrast, humans are omnivores (eat both plant and animal substances). Because humans are adapted to eating and digesting a greater variety of foods, comparisons of the cat and the human digestive organs may not be precise.

PURPOSE OF THE EXERCISE

To examine the major digestive organs of the cat and to compare these organs with those of the human.

LEARNING OBJECTIVES

After completing this exercise, you should be able to

1. Locate and identify the major digestive organs of the cat.

2. Identify the corresponding organs in the human torso model.
3. Compare the digestive system of the cat with that of the human.

PROCEDURE

1. Place the preserved cat in the dissecting tray with its ventral surface down.
2. Locate the major salivary glands on one side of the head. To do this, follow these steps:
   a. Clear away any remaining fascia and other connective tissue from the region below the ear and near the joint of the mandible.
   b. Identify the *parotid gland,* a relatively large mass of glandular tissue just below the ear. Note the parotid duct (Stensen's duct) that passes over the surface of the masseter muscle and opens into the mouth.
   c. Look for the *submandibular gland* just below the parotid gland, near the angle of the jaw.
   d. Locate the *sublingual gland* that is adjacent and medial to the submandibular gland (fig. 48.1).
3. Open the oral cavity. To do this, follow these steps:
   a. Use scissors to cut through the soft tissues at the angle of the mouth.
   b. When you reach the bone of the jaw, use a bone cutter to cut through the bone, thus freeing the mandible.
   c. Open the mouth wide, and locate the following features:

   cheek
   lip
   vestibule
   palate
       hard palate
       soft palate
   palatine tonsils (small, rounded masses of glandular tissue in the lateral wall of the soft palate)
   tongue
       frenulum
       papillae (examine with a hand lens)

Figure 48.1 Major salivary glands of the cat.

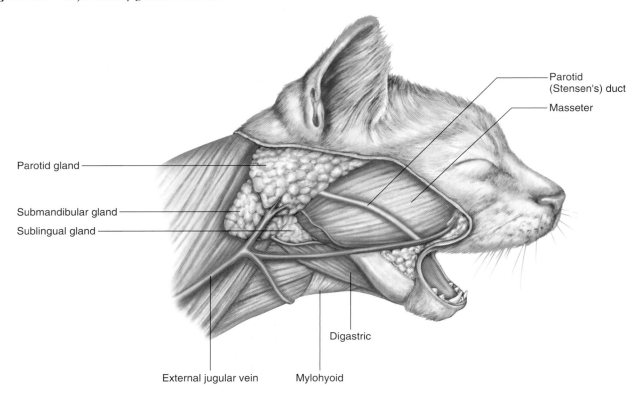

Parotid (Stensen's) duct

Masseter

Parotid gland

Submandibular gland

Sublingual gland

Digastric

External jugular vein

Mylohyoid

4. Examine the teeth of the maxilla. How many incisors, canines (cuspids), bicuspids, and molars are present?

_____

_____

5. Complete Part A of Laboratory Report 48.
6. Examine organs in the abdominal cavity with the cat positioned with its ventral surface up. Review the normal position and function of the greater omentum.
7. Examine the *liver,* which is located just beneath the diaphragm and is attached to the central portion of the diaphragm by the *falciform ligament.* Also, locate the *spleen,* which is posterior to the liver on the left side (fig. 48.2). The liver has five lobes— a right medial, right lateral (which is subdivided into two parts by a deep cleft), left medial, left lateral, and caudate lobe. The caudate lobe is the smallest lobe and is located in the median line, where it projects into the curvature of the stomach. The caudate lobe is covered by a sheet of mesentery, the *lesser omentum,* that connects the liver to the stomach (figs. 48.3 and 48.4). Find the greenish *gallbladder* on the inferior surface of the liver on the right side. Also note the

cystic duct, by which the gallbladder is attached to the *common bile duct,* and the *hepatic duct,* which originates in the liver and attaches to the cystic duct. Trace the common bile duct to its connection with the duodenum.
8. Locate the *stomach* in the left side of the abdominal cavity. At its anterior end, note the union with the *esophagus,* which passes through the diaphragm. Identify the *cardiac, fundic, body,* and *pyloric regions* (listed from entrance to exit) of the stomach. Use scissors to make an incision along the convex border of the stomach from the cardiac region to the pylorus. Note that the lining of the stomach has numerous folds (*rugae*). Examine the *pyloric sphincter,* which creates a constriction between the stomach and small intestine.
9. Locate the *pancreas.* It appears as a grayish, two-lobed elongated mass of glandular tissue. One lobe lies dorsal to the stomach and extends across to the duodenum. The other lobe is enclosed by the *mesentery,* which supports the duodenum (figs. 48.3 and 48.4).
10. Trace the *small intestine,* beginning at the pyloric sphincter. The first portion, the *duodenum,* travels posteriorly for several centimeters. Then it loops back around a lobe of the pancreas. The proximal

Figure 48.2 Ventral view of abdominal organs of the cat.

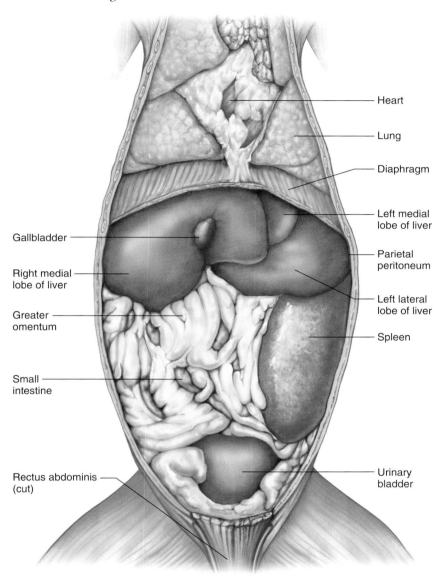

Heart

Lung

Diaphragm

Left medial lobe of liver

Parietal peritoneum

Left lateral lobe of liver

Spleen

Urinary bladder

Gallbladder

Right medial lobe of liver

Greater omentum

Small intestine

Rectus abdominis (cut)

half of the remaining portion of the small intestine is the *jejunum,* and the distal half is the *ileum.* Open the duodenum and note the velvety appearance of the villi. Note how the mesentery supports the small intestine from the dorsal body wall. The small intestine terminates on the right side, where it joins the large intestine.

11. Locate the *large intestine,* and identify the *cecum, ascending colon, transverse colon,* and *descending colon.* Also locate the *rectum,* which extends through the pelvic cavity to the *anus.* Make an incision at the junction between the ileum and cecum, and look for the *ileocecal sphincter.*
12. Complete Part B of the laboratory report.

Figure 48.3 Ventral view of the cat's abdominal organs with intestines reflected to the right side.

Right medial lobe of liver

Common bile duct

Lesser omentum

Right lateral lobe of liver

Duodenum

Pancreas

Transverse colon

Small intestine

Mesentery

Descending colon

Gallbladder

Diaphragm

Left medial lobe of liver

Left lateral lobe of liver

Esophagus

Cardiac
Fundic
Pyloric — Stomach
Body

Spleen

Kidney

Parietal peritoneum

Rectum

Urinary bladder

Figure 48.4 Abdominal organs of the cat with the greater omentum removed. The left liver lobes have been reflected to the right side.

Left lateral lobe of liver

Caudate lobe of liver

Gallbladder

Left medial lobe of liver

Common bile duct

Right medial lobe of liver

Jejunum

Kidney

Ileum

Right horn of uterus

Lesser omentum

Stomach

Duodenum

Pancreas

Spleen

Colon

NOTES

CAT DISSECTION: DIGESTIVE SYSTEM

PART A

Complete the following:

1. Compare the locations of the major salivary glands of the human with those of the cat. _____
   _____
   _____
   _____
   _____

2. Compare the types and numbers of teeth present in the cat's maxilla with those of the human. _____
   _____
   _____
   _____
   _____

3. In what ways do the cat's teeth seem to be adapted to a special diet? _____
   _____
   _____
   _____
   _____

4. What part of the human soft palate is lacking in the cat? _____
5. What do you think is the function of the transverse ridges (rugae) in the hard palate of the cat? _____
   _____
   _____
   _____

6. How do the papillae on the surface of the human tongue compare with those of the cat? _____
   _____
   _____
   _____

PART B

Complete the following:

1. Describe how the peritoneum and mesenteries are associated with the organs in the abdominal cavity. _____

    _____
    _____
    _____
    _____
    _____
    _____

2. Describe the inner lining of the stomach. _____

    _____
    _____
    _____
    _____

3. Compare the structure of the human liver with that of the cat. _____

    _____
    _____
    _____
    _____

4. Compare the structure and location of the human pancreas with those of the cat. _____

    _____
    _____
    _____

5. What feature of the human cecum is lacking in the cat? _____

    _____

LABORATORY EXERCISE 49

ACTION OF A DIGESTIVE ENZYME

MATERIALS NEEDED

0.5% amylase solution*
Beakers (50 and 500 mL)
Distilled water
Funnel
Pipets (1 and 10 mL)
Pipet rubber bulbs
0.5% starch solution
Graduated cylinder
(10 mL)
Test tubes
Test-tube clamps
Wax marker

Iodine-potassium-iodide
solution
Medicine dropper
Ice
Water bath, 37°C (98.6°F)
Porcelain test plate
Benedict's solution
Hot plates
Test-tube rack
Thermometer

*The amylase must be free of sugar. See Appendix 1.

⚠ SAFETY

- Use only a mechanical pipetting device (never your mouth). Use pipets with rubber bulbs or dropping pipets.
- Wear safety glasses when working with acids and when heating test tubes.
- Use test-tube clamps when handling hot test tubes.
- If an open flame is used for heating the test solutions, keep clothes and hair away from the flame.

The digestive enzyme in salivary secretions is called *salivary amylase.* Pancreatic amylase is secreted among several other pancreatic enzymes. A bacterial extraction of amylase is available for laboratory experiments. This enzyme splits starch molecules into sugar (disaccharide) molecules, which is the first step in the digestion of complex carbohydrates.

As in the case of other enzymes, amylase is a protein whose activity is affected by exposure to certain environmental factors, including excessive heat, radiation, electricity, and certain chemicals.

PURPOSE OF THE EXERCISE

To investigate the action of amylase and the effect of heat on its enzymatic activity.

LEARNING OBJECTIVES

After completing this exercise, you should be able to

1. Describe the action of amylase.
2. Test a solution for the presence of starch or the presence of sugar.
3. Test the effects of varying temperatures on the activity of amylase.

PROCEDURE A—AMYLASE ACTIVITY

1. Mark three clean test tubes as *tubes 1, 2,* and *3,* and prepare the tubes as follows:

   Tube 1: **Add 6 mL of amylase solution.**

   Tube 2: **Add 6 mL of starch solution.**

   Tube 3: **Add 5 mL of starch solution and 1 mL of amylase solution.**

2. Shake the tubes well to mix the contents, and place them in a warm water bath, 37°C (98.6°F), for 10 minutes.
3. At the end of the 10 minutes, test the contents of each tube for the presence of starch. To do this, follow these steps:
   a. Place 1 mL of the solution to be tested in a depression of a porcelain test plate.
   b. Next add one drop of iodine-potassium-iodide solution, and note the color of the mixture. If the solution becomes blue-black, starch is present.
   c. Record the results in Part A of Laboratory Report 49.
4. Test the contents of each tube for the presence of sugar (disaccharides in this instance). To do this, follow these steps:
   a. Place 1 mL of the solution to be tested in a clean test tube.
   b. Add 1 mL of Benedict's solution.
   c. Place the test tube with a test-tube clamp in a beaker of boiling water for 2 minutes.

d. Note the color of the liquid. If the solution becomes green, yellow, orange, or red, sugar is present. Blue indicates a negative test, whereas green indicates a positive test with the least amount of sugar, and red indicates the greatest amount of sugar present.

e. Record the results in Part A of the laboratory report.

5. Complete Part A of the laboratory report.

PROCEDURE B—EFFECT OF HEAT

1. Mark three clean test tubes as *tubes 4, 5,* and *6.*

2. Add 1 mL of amylase solution to each of the tubes, and expose each solution to a different test temperature for 3 minutes as follows:

   Tube 4: **Place in beaker of ice water (about 0°C [32°F]).**

   Tube 5: **Place in warm water bath (about 37°C [98.6°F]).**

   Tube 6: **Place in beaker of boiling water (about 100°C [212°F]). Use a test-tube clamp.**

3. Add 5 mL of starch solution to each tube, shake to mix the contents, and return the tubes to their respective test temperatures for 10 minutes. It is important that the 5 mL of starch solution added to tube 4 be at ice-water temperature before it is added to the 1 mL of amylase solution.

4. At the end of the 10 minutes, test the contents of each tube for the presence of starch and the presence of sugar by following the directions in Procedure A.

5. Complete Part B of the laboratory report.

 LEARNING EXTENSION

Devise an experiment to test the effect of some other environmental factor on amylase activity. For example, you might test the effect of a strong acid by adding a few drops of concentrated hydrochloric acid to a mixture of starch and amylase solutions. Be sure to include a control in your experimental plan. That is, include a tube containing everything except the factor you are testing. Then you will have something with which to compare your results. *Carry out your experiment only if it has been approved by the laboratory instructor.*

Name _____

Date _____

Section _____

ACTION OF A DIGESTIVE ENZYME

PART A—AMYLASE ACTIVITY

1. Test results:

Tube	Starch	Sugar
1 Amylase solution		
2 Starch solution		
3 Starch-amylase solution		

2. Complete the following:

   a. Explain the reason for including tube 1 in this experiment. _____
   _____
   _____
   _____

   b. What is the importance of tube 2? _____
   _____
   _____
   _____

   c. What do you conclude from the results of this experiment?_____
   _____
   _____
   _____

PART B—EFFECT OF HEAT

1. Test results:

Tube	Starch	Sugar
4 0°C (32°F)		
5 37°C (98.6°F)		
6 100°C (212°F)		

2. Complete the following:

   a. What do you conclude from the results of this experiment?_____

   _____

   _____

   _____

   _____

   b. If digestion failed to occur in one of the tubes in this experiment, how can you tell if the amylase was destroyed by the factor being tested or if the amylase activity was simply inhibited by the test treatment?

   _____

   _____

   _____

   _____

   _____

Critical Thinking Application

What test result would occur if the amylase you used contained sugar? _____
Would your results be valid? Explain your answer.

_____

_____

_____

RESPIRATORY ORGANS

MATERIALS NEEDED

Textbook
Human skull (sagittal section)
Human torso model
Larynx model
Thoracic organs model
Compound light microscope
Prepared microscope slides of the following:
    Trachea (cross section)
    Lung, human (normal)

For Demonstrations:

Animal lung with trachea (fresh or preserved)
Bicycle pump
Prepared microscope slides of the following:
    Lung tissue (smoker)
    Lung tissue (emphysema)

 SAFETY

- Wear disposable gloves when working on the fresh or preserved animal lung demonstration.
- Wash your hands before leaving the laboratory.

The organs of the respiratory system include the nose, nasal cavity, sinuses, pharynx, larynx, trachea, bronchial tree, and lungs. They mainly function to process incoming air and to transport it to and from the atmosphere outside the body and the air sacs of the lungs.

In the air sacs, gas exchanges take place between the air and the blood of nearby capillaries. The blood, in turn, transports gases to and from the air sacs and the body cells. This entire process of transporting and exchanging gases between the atmosphere and the body cells is called *respiration.*

PURPOSE OF THE EXERCISE

To review the structure and function of the respiratory organs and to examine the tissues of some of these organs microscopically.

LEARNING OBJECTIVES

After completing this exercise, you should be able to

1. Locate the major organs of the respiratory system.
2. Describe the functions of these organs.
3. Recognize tissue sections of the trachea and lung.
4. Identify the major features of these tissue sections.

PROCEDURE A—RESPIRATORY ORGANS

1. Review the section entitled "Organs of the Respiratory System" in chapter 19 of the textbook.
2. As a review activity, label figures 50.1, 50.2, 50.3, and 50.4.
3. Examine the sagittal section of the human skull, and locate the following features:

   nasal cavity
       nasal septum
       nasal conchae
       meatuses
   sinuses
       maxillary sinus
       frontal sinus
       ethmoidal sinus
       sphenoidal sinus

4. Observe the larynx model, the thoracic organs model, and the human torso model. Locate the features listed in step 3. Also locate the following:

   pharynx
       nasopharynx
       oropharynx
       laryngopharynx
   larynx (palpate your own larynx)
       vocal cords
           false vocal cords (vestibular folds)
           true vocal cords (vocal folds)

Figure 50.1 Label the major features of the respiratory system.

Nose — 1
— 7
Sphenoidal sinus
— 8
2
Tongue —
— 9
Lip —
3
4
Esophagus
— 10
5
6
11

thyroid cartilage ("Adam's apple")

cricoid cartilage

epiglottis

epiglottic cartilage

arytenoid cartilages

corniculate cartilages

cuneiform cartilages

glottis

trachea (palpate your own trachea)

bronchi

    primary bronchi

    secondary bronchi

lung

    hilum

    lobes

        superior lobe

        middle lobe (right only)

        inferior lobe

    lobules

visceral pleura

parietal pleura

pleural cavity

5. Complete Part A of Laboratory Report 50.

DEMONSTRATION

Observe the animal lung and the attached trachea. Identify the larynx, major laryngeal cartilages, trachea, and the incomplete cartilaginous rings of the trachea. Open the larynx and locate the vocal folds. Examine the visceral pleura on the surface of a lung. A bicycle pump could be used to demonstrate lung inflation. Section the lung and locate some bronchioles and alveoli. Squeeze a portion of a lung between your fingers. How do you describe the texture of the lung?

_____

_____

_____

Figure 50.2 Label the features of this sagittal section of the upper respiratory tract.

1
2
3
4
5
6
Hyoid bone
7
8
9
10
11
12
13
14
Esophagus

PROCEDURE B—RESPIRATORY TISSUES

1. Obtain a prepared microscope slide of a trachea, and use low-power magnification to examine it. Notice the inner lining of ciliated pseudostratified columnar epithelium and the deep layer of hyaline cartilage, which represents a portion of an incomplete (C-shaped) tracheal ring (fig. 50.5).
2. Use high-power magnification to observe the cilia on the free surface of the epithelial lining. Locate the wineglass-shaped goblet cells, which secrete a protective mucus, in the epithelium (fig. 50.6).
3. Prepare a labeled sketch of a representative portion of the tracheal wall in Part B of the laboratory report.
4. Obtain a prepared microscope slide of human lung tissue. Examine it, using low-power magnification, and note the many open spaces of the air sacs (alveoli). Look for a bronchiole—a tube with a relatively thick wall and a wavy inner lining. Locate the smooth muscle tissue in the wall of this tube (fig. 50.7). You also may see a section of cartilage as part of the bronchiole wall.
5. Use high-power magnification to examine the alveoli (fig. 50.8). Note that their walls are composed of simple squamous epithelium. You also may see sections of blood vessels containing blood cells.
6. Prepare a labeled sketch of a representative portion of the lung in Part B of the laboratory report.
7. Complete Part C of the laboratory report.

Figure 50.3 Label the major features of the larynx: (*a*) anterior view; (*b*) posterior view.

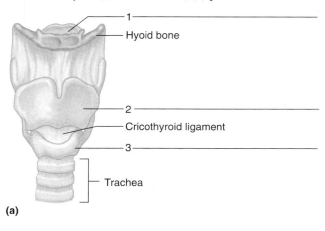

1 _____
— Hyoid bone

2 _____
—Cricothyroid ligament

3 _____
— Trachea

(a)

— Hyoid bone

4 _____

—Corniculate cartilage

5 _____

—Arytenoid cartilage

6 _____

— Trachea

(b)

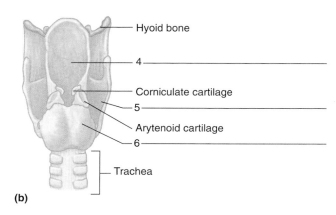

Figure 50.4 Label the features of the superior aspect of the larynx with the glottis closed.

Anterior

Posterior portion
of tongue

_____ 1 _____ 3 _____

_____ 2 _____ 4 _____

Corniculate cartilage

Cuneiform
cartilage

Figure 50.5 Micrograph of a section of the tracheal wall (63×).

Connective tissue

Hyaline cartilage

Connective tissue

Ciliated epithelium

Lumen of trachea

Figure 50.6 Micrograph of ciliated epithelium in the respiratory tract (275×).

Connective tissue

Epithelial cell

Goblet cell

Cilia

Lumen

DEMONSTRATION

Examine the prepared microscope slides of the lung tissue of a smoker and a person with emphysema, using low-power magnification. How does the smoker's lung tissue compare with that of the normal lung tissue that you examined previously?

_____

_____

_____

_____

How does the emphysema patient's lung tissue compare with the normal lung tissue?

_____

_____

_____

_____

Web Quest

Review the structure and function of the respiratory system at

www.mhhe.com/shier11

Click on Student Edition. Click on Martin Lab Manual, Web Quest.

Figure 50.7 Micrograph of human lung tissue (35×).

— Bronchiole

— Blood vessel

— Lumen of bronchiole

— Alveolus

Figure 50.8 Micrograph of human lung tissue (250×).

Lumen of capillary —

Simple squamous epithelial cells —

Alveolus —

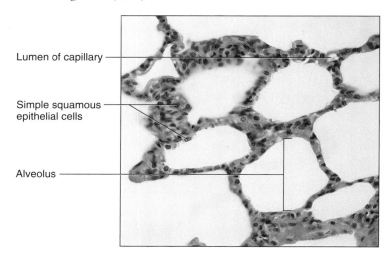

Name _____

Date _____

Section _____

RESPIRATORY ORGANS

PART A

Match the terms in column A with the descriptions in column B. Place the letter of your choice in the space provided.

Column A

a. Alveolus
b. Cricoid cartilage
c. Epiglottis
d. Glottis
e. Lung
f. Nasal concha
g. Pharynx
h. Pleural cavity
i. Sinus (paranasal sinus)
j. Vocal cord (true)

Column B

_____ 1. Potential space between visceral and parietal pleurae

_____ 2. Most inferior portion of larynx

_____ 3. Serves as resonant chamber and reduces weight of skull

_____ 4. Microscopic air sac for gas exchange

_____ 5. Consists of large lobes

_____ 6. Opening between vocal cords

_____ 7. Fold of mucous membrane containing elastic fibers responsible for sounds

_____ 8. Increases surface area of nasal mucous membrane

_____ 9. Passageway for air and food

_____ 10. Partially covers opening of larynx during swallowing

PART B

1. Sketch and label a portion of the tracheal wall.

2. Sketch and label a portion of lung tissue.

PART C

Complete the following:

1. What is the function of the mucus secreted by the goblet cells? _____

_____

_____

2. Describe the function of the cilia in the respiratory tubes. _____

_____

_____

3. How is breathing affected if the smooth muscle of the bronchial tree relaxes? _____

_____

_____

Critical Thinking Application

Why are the alveolar walls so thin?

_____

_____

_____

_____

LABORATORY EXERCISE 51

CAT DISSECTION: RESPIRATORY SYSTEM

MATERIALS NEEDED

Preserved cat
Dissecting tray
Dissecting instruments
Disposable gloves
Human torso model

 SAFETY

- Wear disposable gloves when working on the cat dissection.
- Dispose of tissue remnants and gloves as instructed.
- Wash the dissecting tray and instruments as instructed.
- Wash your laboratory table.
- Wash your hands before leaving the laboratory.

In this laboratory exercise, you will dissect the major respiratory organs of a cat. As you observe these structures in the cat, compare them with those of the human torso model.

PURPOSE OF THE EXERCISE

To examine the major respiratory organs of the cat and to compare these organs with those of the human.

LEARNING OBJECTIVES

After completing this exercise, you should be able to

1. Locate and identify the major respiratory organs of the cat.
2. Identify the corresponding organs in the human torso model.
3. Compare the respiratory system of the human with that of the cat.

PROCEDURE

1. Place the preserved cat in a dissecting tray with its ventral surface up.
2. Examine the *nostrils (external nares)* and *nasal septum.*
3. Open the mouth wide to expose the *soft palate.* Cut through the tissues of the soft palate, and observe the *nasopharynx* above it. Locate the small openings of the *auditory tubes* in the lateral walls of the nasopharynx. Insert a probe into an opening of an auditory tube.
4. Pull the tongue forward, and locate the *epiglottis* near its base. Also identify the *glottis,* which is the opening into the larynx. (In the human, the term *glottis* refers to the opening between the vocal folds within the larynx.) Locate the *esophagus,* which is dorsal to the larynx.
5. Open the thoracic cavity, and expose its contents.
6. Dissect the *trachea* in the neck, and expose the *larynx* at the anterior end near the base of the tongue. Note the *tracheal rings,* and locate the lobes of the *thyroid gland* on each side of the trachea, just posterior to the larynx. Also note the *thymus gland,* a rather diffuse mass of glandular tissue extending along the ventral surface of the trachea into the thorax (see fig. 45.3 and figs. 51.1 and 51.2).
7. Examine the larynx, and identify the *thyroid cartilage* and *cricoid cartilage* in its wall. Make a longitudinal incision through the ventral wall of the larynx, and locate the *vocal cords* inside.
8. Trace the trachea posteriorly to where it divides into *primary bronchi,* which pass into the lungs.
9. Examine the *lungs,* each of which is subdivided into three lobes—an *anterior (cranial),* a *middle,* and a *posterior (caudal) lobe.* The right lung of the cat has a small fourth *accessory (mediastinal; cardiac)* lobe associated with the right posterior lobe. Notice the thin membrane, the *visceral pleura,* on the surface of each lung. Also notice the *parietal pleura,* which forms the inner lining of the thoracic wall, and locate the spaces of the *pleural cavities.*
10. Make an incision through a lobe of a lung, and examine its interior. Note the branches of the smaller air passages.

Figure 51.1 Ventral view of the cat's thoracic cavity.

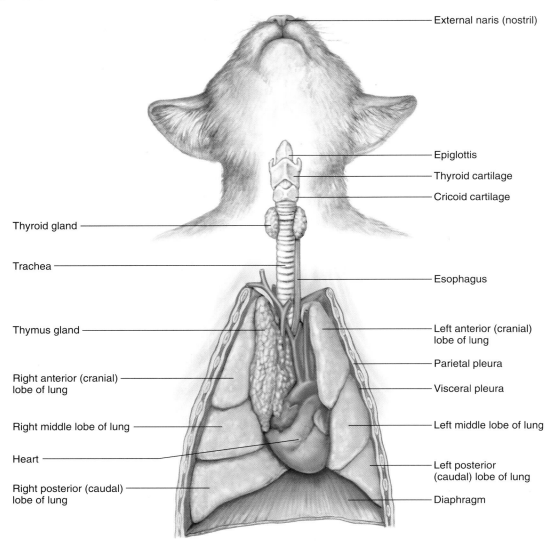

External naris (nostril)

Epiglottis

Thyroid cartilage

Cricoid cartilage

Thyroid gland

Trachea

Esophagus

Thymus gland

Left anterior (cranial) lobe of lung

Parietal pleura

Right anterior (cranial) lobe of lung

Visceral pleura

Right middle lobe of lung

Left middle lobe of lung

Heart

Left posterior (caudal) lobe of lung

Right posterior (caudal) lobe of lung

Diaphragm

11. Examine the *diaphragm,* and note that its central portion is tendinous.

12. Locate the *phrenic nerve.* This nerve appears as a white thread passing along the side of the heart to the diaphragm.

13. Examine the organs located in the *mediastinum.* Note that the mediastinum separates the right and left lungs and pleural cavities within the thorax.

14. Complete Laboratory Report 51.

Figure 51.2 Features of the cat's neck and oral cavity.

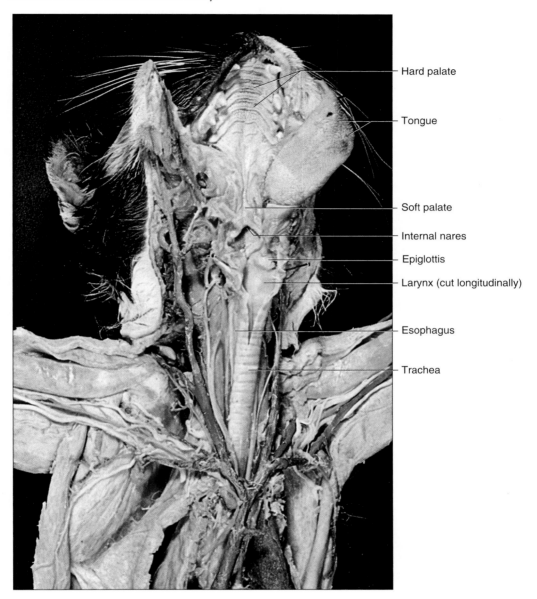

Hard palate

Tongue

Soft palate

Internal nares

Epiglottis

Larynx (cut longitudinally)

Esophagus

Trachea

NOTES

Name _____

Date _____

Section _____

CAT DISSECTION: RESPIRATORY SYSTEM

Complete the following:

1. What is the purpose of the auditory tubes opening into the nasopharynx? _____
   _____
   _____
   _____
   _____

2. Distinguish between the glottis and the epiglottis. _____
   _____
   _____
   _____
   _____

3. Are the tracheal rings of the cat complete or incomplete? _____ How does this feature
   compare with that of the human? _____
   _____
   _____

4. How does the structure of the primary bronchi compare with that of the trachea? _____
   _____
   _____

5. Compare the number of lobes in the human lungs with the number of lobes in the cat._____
   _____
   _____
   _____
   _____

6. Describe the attachments of the diaphragm. _____
   _____
   _____
   _____
   _____

7. What major structures are located within the mediastinum of the cat? _____
   _____ How does this compare to the human mediastinum?_____
   _____

NOTES

LABORATORY EXERCISE 52

BREATHING AND RESPIRATORY VOLUMES AND CAPACITIES

MATERIALS NEEDED

Textbook
Spirometer, handheld (dry portable)
70% alcohol
Cotton
Disposable mouthpieces
Meterstick

For Demonstration:

Lung function model

 SAFETY

- Clean the spirometer with cotton moistened with 70% alcohol before each use.
- Place a new disposable mouthpiece on the stem of the spirometer before each use.
- Dispose of the cotton and mouthpieces according to directions from your laboratory instructor.

Breathing involves the movement of air from outside the body through the bronchial tree and into the alveoli and the reversal of this air movement. These movements are caused by changes in the size of the thoracic cavity that result from skeletal muscle contractions and from the elastic recoil of stretched tissues.

The volumes of air that move in and out of the lungs during various phases of breathing are called *respiratory air volumes* and *capacities*. These volumes can be measured by using an instrument called a *spirometer*. However, the values obtained vary with a person's age, sex, height, weight, and physical fitness. Various respiratory capacities can be calculated by combining two or more of the respiratory volumes.

PURPOSE OF THE EXERCISE

To review the mechanisms of breathing and to measure or calculate certain respiratory air volumes and respiratory capacities.

LEARNING OBJECTIVES

After completing this exercise, you should be able to

1. Describe the mechanisms responsible for inspiration and expiration.
2. Define the respiratory air volumes and respiratory capacities.
3. Measure or calculate the respiratory air volumes and capacities.

PROCEDURE A—BREATHING MECHANISMS

1. Review the sections entitled "Inspiration" and "Expiration" in chapter 19 of the textbook.
2. Complete Part A of Laboratory Report 52.

DEMONSTRATION

Observe the mechanical lung function model. Note that it consists of a heavy plastic bell jar with a rubber sheeting clamped over its wide open end. Its narrow upper opening is plugged with a rubber stopper through which a Y tube is passed. Small rubber balloons are fastened to the arms of the Y (fig. 52.1). What happens to the balloons when the rubber sheeting is pulled downward?

_____

_____

What happens when the sheeting is pushed upward?

_____

_____

_____

How do you explain these changes?

_____

_____

_____

What part of the respiratory system is represented by the rubber sheeting? _____

the bell jar?_____

the Y tube? _____

the balloons? _____

Figure 52.1 A lung function model.

Rubber stopper
Y tube
Bell jar
Rubber balloons
Clamp
Rubber sheeting

WARNING

If the subject begins to feel dizzy or light-headed while performing Procedure B, stop the exercise and breathe normally.

PROCEDURE B—RESPIRATORY AIR VOLUMES AND CAPACITIES

1. Review the section entitled "Respiratory Volumes and Capacities" in chapter 19 of the textbook.
2. Complete Part B of the laboratory report.
3. Get a handheld spirometer (fig. 52.2). Point the needle to zero by rotating the adjustable dial. Before using the instrument, clean it with cotton moistened with 70% alcohol and place a new disposable mouthpiece over its stem. The instrument should be held with the dial upward, and air should be blown only into the disposable mouthpiece (fig. 52.3). Movement of the needle indicates the air volume that leaves the lungs. The exhalation should be slowly and forcefully performed. Too rapid an exhalation could result in erroneous data or damage to the spirometer.
4. *Tidal volume* is the volume of air that enters (or leaves) the lungs during a *respiratory cycle* (one inspiration plus the following expiration). *Resting tidal volume* is the volume of air that enters (or leaves) the lungs during normal, quiet breathing

Figure 52.2 A handheld spirometer can be used to measure respiratory air volumes.

(fig. 52.4). To measure this volume, follow these steps:

a. Sit quietly for a few moments.
b. Position the spirometer dial so that the needle points to zero.
c. Place the mouthpiece between your lips and exhale three ordinary expirations into it after inhaling through the nose each time. *Do not force air out of your lungs; exhale normally.*
d. Divide the total value indicated by the needle by 3, and record this amount as your resting tidal volume on the table in Part C of the laboratory report.

Figure 52.3 Demonstration of proper use of a handheld spirometer. Air should only be blown slowly and forcefully into a disposable mouthpiece.

Figure 52.4 Graphic representation of respiratory volumes and capacities.

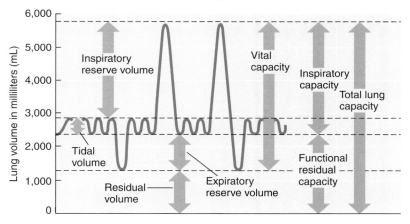

5. *Expiratory reserve volume* is the volume of air in addition to the tidal volume that leaves the lungs during forced expiration. To measure this volume, follow these steps:
   a. Breathe normally for a few moments. Set the needle to zero.
   b. At the end of an ordinary expiration, place the mouthpiece between your lips and exhale all of the air you can force from your lungs through the spirometer.
   c. Record the results as your expiratory reserve volume in Part C.
6. *Vital capacity* is the maximum volume of air that can be exhaled after taking the deepest breath

possible. To measure this volume, follow these steps:
   a. Breathe normally for a few moments. Set the needle at zero.
   b. Breathe in and out deeply a couple of times, then take the deepest breath possible.
   c. Place the mouthpiece between your lips and exhale all the air out of your lungs, slowly and forcefully.
   d. Record the value as your vital capacity in Part C. Compare your result with that expected for a person of your sex, age, and height listed in tables 52.1 and 52.2. Use the meterstick to determine your height in centimeters if

433

Table 52.1 Predicted Vital Capacities (in Milliliters) for Females

Height in Centimeters

Age	146	148	150	152	154	156	158	160	162	164	166	168	170	172	174	176	178	180	182	184	186	188	190	192	194
16	2950	2990	3030	3070	3110	3150	3190	3230	3270	3310	3350	3390	3430	3470	3510	3550	3590	3630	3670	3715	3755	3800	3840	3880	3920
17	2935	2975	3015	3055	3095	3135	3175	3215	3255	3295	3335	3375	3415	3455	3495	3535	3575	3615	3655	3695	3740	3780	3820	3860	3900
18	2920	2960	3000	3040	3080	3120	3160	3200	3240	3280	3320	3360	3400	3440	3480	3520	3560	3600	3640	3680	3720	3760	3800	3840	3880
20	2890	2930	2970	3010	3050	3090	3130	3170	3210	3250	3290	3330	3370	3410	3450	3490	3525	3565	3605	3645	3695	3720	3760	3800	3840
22	2860	2900	2940	2980	3020	3060	3095	3135	3175	3215	3255	3290	3330	3370	3410	3450	3490	3530	3570	3610	3650	3685	3725	3765	3800
24	2830	2870	2910	2950	2985	3025	3065	3100	3140	3180	3220	3260	3300	3335	3375	3415	3455	3490	3530	3570	3610	3650	3685	3725	3765
26	2800	2840	2880	2920	2960	3000	3035	3070	3110	3150	3190	3230	3265	3300	3340	3380	3420	3455	3495	3530	3570	3610	3650	3685	3725
28	2775	2810	2850	2890	2930	2965	3000	3040	3070	3115	3155	3190	3230	3270	3305	3345	3380	3420	3460	3495	3535	3570	3610	3650	3685
30	2745	2780	2820	2860	2895	2935	2970	3010	3045	3085	3120	3160	3195	3235	3270	3310	3345	3385	3420	3460	3495	3535	3570	3610	3645
32	2715	2750	2790	2825	2865	2900	2940	2975	3015	3050	3090	3125	3160	3200	3235	3275	3310	3350	3385	3425	3460	3495	3535	3570	3610
34	2685	2725	2760	2795	2835	2870	2910	2945	2980	3020	3055	3090	3130	3165	3200	3240	3275	3310	3350	3385	3425	3460	3495	3535	3570
36	2655	2695	2730	2765	2805	2840	2875	2910	2950	2985	3020	3060	3095	3130	3165	3205	3240	3275	3310	3350	3385	3420	3460	3495	3530
38	2630	2665	2700	2735	2770	2810	2845	2880	2915	2950	2990	3025	3060	3095	3130	3170	3205	3240	3275	3310	3350	3385	3420	3455	3490
40	2600	2635	2670	2705	2740	2775	2810	2850	2885	2920	2955	2990	3025	3060	3095	3135	3170	3205	3240	3275	3310	3345	3380	3420	3455
42	2570	2605	2640	2675	2710	2745	2780	2815	2850	2885	2920	2955	2990	3025	3060	3100	3135	3170	3205	3240	3275	3310	3345	3380	3415
44	2540	2575	2610	2645	2680	2715	2750	2785	2820	2855	2890	2925	2960	2995	3030	3060	3095	3130	3165	3200	3235	3270	3305	3340	3375
46	2510	2545	2580	2615	2650	2685	2715	2750	2785	2820	2855	2890	2925	2960	2995	3030	3060	3095	3130	3165	3200	3235	3270	3305	3340
48	2480	2515	2550	2585	2620	2650	2685	2715	2750	2785	2820	2855	2890	2925	2960	2995	3030	3060	3095	3130	3160	3195	3230	3265	3300
50	2455	2485	2520	2555	2590	2625	2655	2690	2720	2755	2785	2820	2855	2890	2925	2955	2990	3025	3060	3090	3125	3155	3190	3225	3260
52	2425	2455	2490	2525	2555	2590	2625	2655	2690	2720	2755	2790	2820	2855	2890	2925	2955	2990	3020	3055	3090	3125	3155	3190	3220
54	2395	2425	2460	2495	2530	2560	2590	2625	2655	2690	2720	2755	2790	2820	2855	2885	2920	2950	2985	3020	3050	3085	3115	3150	3180
56	2365	2400	2430	2460	2495	2525	2560	2590	2625	2655	2690	2720	2755	2790	2820	2855	2885	2920	2950	2980	3015	3045	3080	3110	3145
58	2335	2370	2400	2430	2460	2495	2525	2560	2590	2625	2655	2690	2720	2750	2785	2815	2850	2880	2920	2945	2975	3010	3040	3075	3105
60	2305	2340	2370	2400	2430	2460	2495	2525	2560	2590	2625	2655	2685	2720	2750	2780	2810	2845	2875	2915	2940	2970	3000	3035	3065
62	2280	2310	2340	2370	2405	2435	2465	2495	2525	2560	2590	2620	2655	2685	2715	2745	2775	2810	2840	2870	2900	2935	2965	2995	3025
64	2250	2280	2310	2340	2370	2400	2430	2465	2495	2525	2555	2585	2620	2650	2680	2710	2740	2770	2805	2835	2865	2895	2920	2955	2990
66	2220	2250	2280	2310	2340	2370	2400	2430	2460	2490	2525	2555	2585	2615	2645	2675	2705	2735	2765	2800	2825	2860	2890	2920	2950
68	2190	2220	2250	2280	2310	2340	2370	2400	2430	2460	2490	2520	2550	2580	2610	2640	2670	2700	2730	2760	2785	2820	2850	2880	2910
70	2160	2190	2220	2250	2280	2310	2340	2370	2400	2425	2455	2485	2515	2545	2575	2605	2635	2665	2695	2725	2755	2780	2810	2840	2870
72	2130	2160	2190	2220	2250	2280	2310	2335	2365	2395	2425	2455	2480	2510	2540	2570	2600	2630	2660	2685	2715	2745	2775	2805	2830
74	2100	2130	2160	2190	2220	2245	2275	2305	2335	2360	2390	2420	2450	2475	2505	2535	2565	2590	2620	2650	2680	2710	2740	2765	2795

From E. DeF. Baldwin and E. W. Richards, Jr., "Pulmonary Insufficiency 1, Physiologic Classification, Clinical Methods of Analysis, Standard Values in Normal Subjects" in *Medicine* 27:243, © by William & Wilkins. Used by permission.

Table 52.2 Predicted Vital Capacities (in Milliliters) for Males

Height in Centimeters

Age	146	148	150	152	154	156	158	160	162	164	166	168	170	172	174	176	178	180	182	184	186	188	190	192	194
16	3765	3820	3870	3920	3975	4025	4075	4130	4180	4230	4285	4335	4385	4440	4490	4540	4590	4645	4695	4745	4800	4850	4900	4955	5005
18	3740	3790	3840	3890	3940	3995	4045	4095	4145	4200	4250	4300	4350	4405	4455	4505	4555	4610	4660	4710	4760	4815	4865	4915	4965
20	3710	3760	3810	3860	3910	3960	4015	4065	4115	4165	4215	4265	4320	4370	4420	4470	4520	4570	4625	4675	4725	4775	4825	4875	4930
22	3680	3730	3780	3830	3880	3930	3980	4030	4080	4135	4185	4235	4285	4335	4385	4435	4485	4535	4585	4635	4685	4735	4790	4840	4890
24	3635	3685	3735	3785	3835	3885	3935	3985	4035	4085	4135	4185	4235	4285	4330	4380	4430	4480	4530	4580	4630	4680	4730	4780	4830
26	3605	3655	3705	3755	3805	3855	3905	3955	4000	4050	4100	4150	4200	4250	4300	4350	4395	4445	4495	4545	4595	4645	4695	4740	4790
28	3575	3625	3675	3725	3775	3820	3870	3920	3970	4020	4070	4115	4165	4215	4265	4310	4360	4410	4460	4510	4555	4605	4655	4705	4755
30	3550	3595	3645	3695	3740	3790	3840	3890	3935	3985	4035	4080	4130	4180	4230	4275	4325	4375	4425	4470	4520	4570	4615	4665	4715
32	3520	3565	3615	3665	3710	3760	3810	3855	3905	3950	4000	4050	4095	4145	4195	4240	4290	4340	4385	4435	4485	4530	4580	4625	4675
34	3475	3525	3570	3620	3665	3715	3760	3810	3855	3905	3950	4000	4045	4095	4140	4190	4225	4285	4330	4380	4425	4475	4520	4570	4615
36	3445	3495	3540	3585	3635	3680	3730	3775	3825	3870	3920	3965	4010	4060	4105	4155	4200	4250	4295	4340	4390	4435	4485	4530	4580
38	3415	3465	3510	3555	3605	3650	3695	3745	3790	3840	3885	3930	3980	4025	4070	4120	4165	4210	4260	4305	4350	4400	4445	4495	4540
40	3385	3435	3480	3525	3575	3620	3665	3710	3760	3805	3850	3900	3945	3990	4035	4085	4130	4175	4220	4270	4315	4360	4410	4455	4500
42	3360	3405	3450	3495	3540	3590	3635	3680	3725	3770	3820	3865	3910	3955	4000	4050	4095	4140	4185	4230	4280	4325	4370	4415	4460
44	3315	3360	3405	3450	3495	3540	3585	3630	3675	3725	3770	3815	3860	3905	3950	3995	4040	4085	4130	4175	4220	4270	4315	4360	4405
46	3285	3330	3375	3420	3465	3510	3555	3600	3645	3690	3735	3780	3825	3870	3915	3960	4005	4050	4095	4140	4185	4230	4275	4320	4365
48	3255	3300	3345	3390	3435	3480	3525	3570	3615	3655	3700	3745	3790	3835	3880	3925	3970	4015	4060	4105	4150	4190	4235	4280	4325
50	3210	3255	3300	3345	3390	3430	3475	3520	3565	3610	3650	3695	3740	3785	3830	3870	3915	3960	4005	4050	4090	4135	4180	4225	4270
52	3185	3225	3270	3315	3355	3400	3445	3490	3530	3575	3620	3660	3705	3750	3795	3835	3880	3925	3970	4010	4055	4100	4140	4185	4230
54	3155	3195	3240	3285	3325	3370	3415	3455	3500	3540	3585	3630	3670	3715	3760	3800	3845	3890	3930	3975	4020	4060	4105	4145	4190
56	3125	3165	3210	3255	3295	3340	3380	3425	3465	3510	3550	3595	3640	3680	3725	3765	3810	3850	3895	3940	3980	4025	4065	4110	4150
58	3080	3125	3165	3210	3250	3290	3335	3375	3420	3460	3500	3545	3585	3630	3670	3715	3755	3800	3840	3880	3925	3965	4010	4050	4095
60	3050	3095	3135	3175	3220	3260	3300	3345	3385	3430	3470	3500	3555	3595	3635	3680	3720	3760	3805	3845	3885	3930	3970	4015	4055
62	3020	3060	3110	3150	3190	3230	3270	3310	3350	3390	3440	3480	3520	3560	3600	3640	3680	3730	3770	3810	3850	3890	3930	3970	4020
64	2990	3030	3080	3120	3160	3200	3240	3280	3320	3360	3400	3440	3490	3530	3570	3610	3650	3690	3730	3770	3810	3850	3900	3940	3980
66	2950	2990	3030	3070	3110	3150	3190	3230	3270	3310	3350	3390	3430	3470	3510	3550	3600	3640	3680	3720	3760	3800	3840	3880	3920
68	2920	2960	3000	3040	3080	3120	3160	3200	3240	3280	3320	3360	3400	3440	3480	3520	3560	3600	3640	3680	3720	3760	3800	3840	3880
70	2890	2930	2970	3010	3050	3090	3130	3170	3210	3250	3290	3330	3370	3410	3450	3480	3520	3560	3600	3640	3680	3720	3760	3800	3840
72	2860	2900	2940	2980	3020	3060	3100	3140	3180	3210	3250	3290	3330	3370	3410	3450	3490	3530	3570	3610	3650	3680	3720	3760	3800
74	2820	2860	2900	2930	2970	3010	3050	3090	3130	3170	3200	3240	3280	3320	3360	3400	3440	3470	3510	3550	3590	3630	3670	3710	3740

From E. DeF. Baldwin and E. W. Richards, Jr., "Pulmonary Insufficiency 1, Physiologic Classification, Clinical Methods of Analysis, Standard Values in Normal Subjects" in *Medicine* 27:243, © by William & Wilkins. Used by permission.

necessary or multiply your height in inches times 2.54 to calculate your height in centimeters. Considerable individual variations from the expected will be noted due to parameters other than sex, age, and height, which could include physical shape, health, medications, and others.

Critical Thinking Application

It can be noted from the data in tables 52.1 and 52.2 that vital capacities gradually decrease with age. Propose an explanation for this normal correlation.

_____

_____

_____

_____

7. *Inspiratory reserve volume* (IRV) is the volume of air in addition to the tidal volume that enters the lungs during forced inspiration. Calculate your inspiratory reserve volume by subtracting your tidal volume (TV) and your expiratory reserve volume (ERV) from your vital capacity (VC):

$$IRV = VC - (TV + ERV)$$

8. *Inspiratory capacity* (IC) is the maximum volume of air a person can inhale following exhalation of the tidal volume. Calculate your inspiratory capacity by adding your tidal volume (TV) and your inspiratory reserve volume (IRV):

$$IC = TV + IRV$$

9. *Functional residual capacity* (FRC) is the volume of air that remains in the lungs following exhalation of the tidal volume. Calculate your functional residual capacity (FRC) by adding your expiratory reserve volume (ERV) and your residual volume (RV), which you can assume is 1,200 mL:

$$FRC = ERV + 1,200$$

10. Complete Part C of the laboratory report.

LEARNING EXTENSION

Determine your *minute respiratory volume*. To do this, follow these steps:

1. Sit quietly for a while, and then to establish your breathing rate, count the number of times you breathe in 1 minute. This might be inaccurate because conscious awareness of breathing rate can alter the results. You might ask a laboratory partner to record your breathing rate at some time when you are not expecting it to be recorded.
2. Calculate your minute respiratory volume by multiplying your breathing rate by your tidal volume:

_____ × _____ = _____
(breathing   (tidal   (minute respiratory
rate)   volume)   volume)

3. This value indicates the total volume of air that moves into your respiratory passages during each minute of ordinary breathing.

Name _____

Date _____

Section _____

BREATHING AND RESPIRATORY VOLUMES AND CAPACITIES

PART A

Complete the following statements:

1. Breathing also can be called _____.

2. The weight of air causes a force called _____ pressure.

3. The weight of air at sea level is sufficient to support a column of mercury within a tube _____ mm high.

4. If the pressure inside the lungs decreases, outside air is forced into the airways by _____.

5. Nerve impulses are carried to the diaphragm by the _____ nerves.

6. When the diaphragm contracts, the size of the thoracic cavity _____.

7. The ribs are raised by contraction of the _____ muscles, which increases the size of the thoracic cavity.

8. Only a thin film of lubricating serous fluid separates the parietal pleura from the _____ of a lung.

9. A mixture of lipoproteins, called _____, acts to reduce the tendency of alveoli to collapse.

10. The force responsible for normal expiration comes from _____ of tissues and from surface tension.

11. The pressure between the pleural membranes is usually _____ than the atmospheric pressure.

12. Muscles that help to force out more than the normal volume of air by pulling the ribs downward and inward include the _____.

13. The diaphragm can be forced to move higher than normal by contraction of the _____ muscles.

PART B

Match the air volumes in column A with the definitions in column B. Place the letter of your choice in the space provided.

Column A	Column B
a. Expiratory reserve volume	_____ 1. Volume in addition to tidal volume that leaves the lungs during forced expiration
b. Functional residual capacity	
c. Inspiratory capacity	_____ 2. Vital capacity plus residual volume
d. Inspiratory reserve volume	
e. Residual volume	_____ 3. Volume that remains in lungs after the most forceful expiration
f. Tidal volume	
g. Total lung capacity	_____ 4. Volume that enters or leaves lungs during a respiratory cycle
h. Vital capacity	
	_____ 5. Volume in addition to tidal volume that enters lungs during forced inspiration
	_____ 6. Maximum volume a person can exhale after taking the deepest possible breath
	_____ 7. Maximum volume a person can inhale following exhalation of the tidal volume
	_____ 8. Volume of air remaining in the lungs following exhalation of the tidal volume

PART C

1. Test results for respiratory air volumes and capacities:

Respiratory Volume or Capacity	Expected Value* (approximate)	Test Results	Percent of Expected Value (test result/expected value × 100)
Tidal volume (resting) (TV)	500 mL		
Expiratory reserve volume (ERV)	1,100 mL		
Vital capacity (VC)	4,600 mL (or enter yours from the table)		
Inspiratory reserve volume (IRV)	3,000 mL		
Inspiratory capacity (IC)	3,500 mL		
Functional residual capacity (FRC)	2,300 mL		

*The values listed are most characteristic for a tall, young adult.

2. Complete the following:

a. How do your test results compare with the expected values? _____

_____

_____

_____

_____

b. How does your vital capacity compare with the average value for a person of your sex, age, and height?

_____

_____

c. What measurement in addition to vital capacity is needed before you can calculate your total lung capacity?

_____

3. If your experimental results are considerably different than the predicted vital capacities, propose reasons for the differences. As you write this paragraph, consider factors such as smoking, physical fitness, respiratory disorders, and medications. (Your instructor might have you make some class correlations from class data.)

_____

_____

_____

_____

_____

_____

_____

_____

_____

CONTROL OF BREATHING

Normal breathing is controlled from regions of the brainstem called the *respiratory center.* This center initiates and regulates nerve impulses that travel to various breathing muscles, causing rhythmic breathing movements and adjustments to the rate and depth of breathing to meet various cellular needs. The respiratory center includes the *medullary rhythmicity area,* which is composed of two bilateral groups of neurons in the medulla oblongata. They are called the *dorsal respiratory group* and the *ventral respiratory group.* Neurons in another part of the brainstem, the pons, compose the *pontine respiratory group* (formerly the pneumotaxic center and the apneustic center). These neurons make connections with the medullary rhythmicity center, and they may contribute to the basic rhythm of breathing.

Various factors can influence the respiratory center and thus affect the rate and depth of breathing. These factors include stretch of the lung tissues, emotional state, and the presence in the blood of certain chemicals, such as carbon dioxide, hydrogen ions, and oxygen. For example, the breathing rate increases as the blood concentration of carbon dioxide or hydrogen ions increases or as the concentration of oxygen decreases.

PURPOSE OF THE EXERCISE

To review the mechanisms that control breathing and to investigate some of the factors that affect the rate and depth of breathing.

LEARNING OBJECTIVES

After completing this exercise, you should be able to

1. Locate the breathing centers in the brainstem.
2. Describe the mechanisms that control normal breathing.
3. List several factors that influence the breathing center.
4. Test the effect of various factors on the rate and depth of breathing.

PROCEDURE A—CONTROL OF BREATHING

1. Review the section entitled "Control of Breathing" in chapter 19 of the textbook.
2. Study figures 53.1 and 53.2.
3. Complete Part A of Laboratory Report 53.

DEMONSTRATION

When a solution of calcium hydroxide is exposed to carbon dioxide, a chemical reaction occurs and a white precipitate of calcium carbonate is formed as indicated by the following reaction:

$$Ca(OH)_2 + CO_2 \rightarrow CaCO_2 + H_2O$$

Thus, a clear water solution of calcium hydroxide (limewater) can be used to detect the presence of carbon dioxide because the solution becomes cloudy if this gas is bubbled through it.

The laboratory instructor will demonstrate this test for carbon dioxide by drawing some air through limewater in an apparatus such as that shown in figure 53.3. Then the instructor will blow an equal volume of expired air through a similar apparatus. (*Note:* A new sterile mouthpiece should be used each time the apparatus is demonstrated.) Watch for the appearance of a precipitate that causes the limewater to become cloudy. Was there any carbon dioxide in the atmospheric air drawn through the limewater?

_____

If so, how did the amount of carbon dioxide in the atmospheric air compare with the amount in the expired air?

_____
_____
_____

Figure 53.1 The respiratory areas are located in the pons and the medulla oblongata.

- Midbrain
- Fourth ventricle
- Pontine respiratory group
- Pons
- Medulla oblongata
- Ventral respiratory group
- Dorsal respiratory group
- Medullary rhythmicity area
- Phrenic nerve
- Intercostal nerves
- External intercostal muscles
- Internal intercostal muscles
- Diaphragm

Figure 53.2 The medullary rhythmicity area and the pontine respiratory group control breathing.

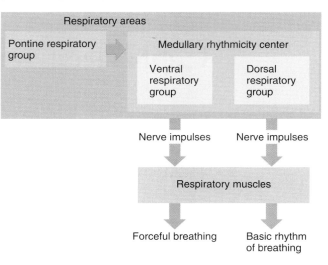

PROCEDURE B—FACTORS AFFECTING BREATHING

Perform each of the following tests, using your laboratory partner as a test subject.

1. *Normal breathing.* To determine the subject's normal breathing rate and depth, follow these steps:
   a. Have the subject sit quietly for a few minutes.
   b. After the rest period, ask the subject to count backwards mentally, beginning with five hundred.
   c. While the subject is distracted by counting, watch the subject's chest movements, and count the breaths taken in a minute. Use this value as the normal breathing rate (breaths per minute).
   d. Note the relative depth of the breathing movements.
   e. Record your observations in the table in Part B of the laboratory report.
2. *Effect of hyperventilation.* To test the effect of hyperventilation on breathing, follow these steps:
   a. Seat the subject and *guard to prevent the possibility of the subject falling over.*
   b. Have the subject breathe rapidly and deeply for a maximum of 1 minute. *If the subject begins to feel dizzy, the hyperventilation should be halted immediately to prevent the subject from fainting from complications of alkalosis. The increased blood pH causes vasoconstriction of cerebral arterioles, which decreases circulation and oxygen to the brain.*

Figure 53.3 Apparatus used to demonstrate the presence of carbon dioxide in air: (*a*) atmospheric air is drawn through limewater; (*b*) expired air is blown through limewater.

(a)

(b)

c. After the period of hyperventilation, determine the subject's breathing rate, and judge the breathing depth as before.
d. Record the results in Part B of the laboratory report.
3. *Effect of rebreathing air.* To test the effect of rebreathing air on breathing, follow these steps:
 a. Have the subject sit quietly (approximately 5 minutes) until the breathing rate returns to normal.

b. Have the subject breathe deeply into a small paper bag that is held tightly over the nose and mouth. *If the subject begins to feel light-headed or like fainting, the rebreathing air should be halted immediately to prevent further acidosis and fainting.*
c. After 2 minutes of rebreathing air, determine the subject's breathing rate, and judge the depth of breathing.
d. Record the results in Part B of the laboratory report.

4. *Effect of breath holding.* To test the effect of breath holding on breathing, follow these steps:
   a. Have the subject sit quietly (approximately 5 minutes) until the breathing rate returns to normal.
   b. Have the subject hold his or her breath as long as possible. *If the subject begins to feel light-headed or like fainting, breath holding should be halted immediately to prevent further acidosis and fainting.*
   c. As the subject begins to breathe again, determine the rate of breathing, and judge the depth of breathing.
   d. Record the results in Part B of the laboratory report.
5. *Effect of exercise.* To test the effect of exercise on breathing, follow these steps:
   a. Have the subject sit quietly (approximately 5 minutes) until breathing rate returns to normal.
   b. Have the subject exercise by moderately running in place for 3–5 minutes. *This exercise should be avoided by anyone with health risks.*
   c. After the exercise, determine the breathing rate, and judge the depth of breathing.
   d. Record the results in Part B of the laboratory report.
6. Complete Part B of the laboratory report.

 LEARNING EXTENSION

A *pneumograph* is a device that can be used together with some type of recording apparatus to record breathing movements. The laboratory instructor will demonstrate the use of this equipment to record various movements, such as those that accompany coughing, laughing, yawning, and speaking.

Devise an experiment to test the effect of some factor, such as hyperventilation, rebreathing air, or exercise, on the length of time a person can hold the breath. *After the laboratory instructor has approved your plan,* carry out the experiment, using the pneumograph and recording equipment. What conclusion can you draw from the results of your experiment?

_____

_____

_____

_____

CONTROL OF BREATHING

PART A

Complete the following statements:

1. The respiratory center is widely scattered throughout the _____ and _____ of the brainstem.

2. The _____ respiratory group primarily stimulates the diaphragm.

3. The _____ respiratory group primarily stimulates the intercostals and abdominal muscles.

4. Chemosensitive areas are stimulated by changes in the blood concentrations of carbon dioxide and _____ ions.

5. As the blood concentration of carbon dioxide increases, the breathing rate _____.

6. _____ combines with water to form carbonic acid.

7. When carbonic acid dissociates, _____ and hydrogen ions are released.

8. As a result of increased breathing, the blood concentration of carbon dioxide is _____.

9. The chemoreceptors that sense low blood oxygen concentration are located in the aortic bodies and the _____ bodies.

10. As the blood concentration of oxygen decreases, the breathing rate _____.

11. The _____ nerve carries sensory impulses from the lungs to the respiratory center.

12. As a result of hyperventilation, breath-holding time is _____.

PART B

1. Record the results of your breathing tests in the table.

Factor Tested	Breathing Rate (breaths/min)	Breathing Depth (+, ++, +++)
Normal		
Hyperventilation		
Rebreathing air		
Breath holding		
Exercise		

2. Briefly explain the reason for the changes in breathing that occurred in each of the following cases:

   a. Hyperventilation

   _____

   _____

   _____

   _____

   b. Rebreathing air

   _____

   _____

   _____

   _____

   c. Breath holding

   _____

   _____

   _____

   _____

   d. Exercise

   _____

   _____

   _____

   _____

3. Complete the following:

   a. Why is it important to distract a person when you are determining the normal rate of breathing?

   _____

   _____

   b. How can the depth of breathing be measured accurately?

   _____

   _____

   _____

Critical Thinking Application

Why is it dangerous for a swimmer to hyperventilate in order to hold the breath for a longer period of time?

_____

_____

_____

_____

KIDNEY STRUCTURE

 SAFETY

- Wear disposable gloves when working on the kidney dissection.
- Dispose of the kidney and gloves as directed by your laboratory instructor.
- Wash the dissecting tray and instruments as instructed.
- Wash your laboratory table.
- Wash your hands before leaving the laboratory.

The two kidneys are the primary organs of the urinary system. They are located in the upper quadrants of the abdominal cavity, against the posterior wall and behind the parietal peritoneum. They perform a variety of complex activities that lead to the production of urine.

The other organs of the urinary system include the ureters, which transport urine away from the kidneys; the urinary bladder, which stores urine; and the urethra, which conveys urine to the outside of the body.

PURPOSE OF THE EXERCISE

To review the structure of the kidney, to dissect a kidney, and to observe the major structures of a nephron microscopically.

LEARNING OBJECTIVES

After completing this exercise, you should be able to

1. Describe the location of the kidneys.
2. Locate and identify the major structures of a kidney.

3. Identify the major structures of a nephron.
4. Trace the path of filtrate through a renal tubule.
5. Trace the path of blood through the renal blood vessels.

PROCEDURE A—KIDNEY STRUCTURE

1. Review the section entitled "Kidney Structure" in chapter 20 of the textbook.
2. As a review activity, label figures 54.1 and 54.2.
3. Complete Part A of Laboratory Report 54.
4. Observe the human torso model and the kidney model. Locate the following:

   kidneys
   ureters
   urinary bladder
   urethra
   renal sinus
   renal pelvis
      major calyces
      minor calyces
   renal papillae
   renal medulla
      renal pyramids
   renal cortex
      renal columns (extensions of renal cortex between renal pyramids)
   nephrons

5. To observe the structure of a kidney, follow these steps:
   a. Obtain a pig or sheep kidney and rinse it with water to remove as much of the preserving fluid as possible.
   b. Carefully remove any adipose tissue from the surface of the specimen.
   c. Locate the following features:

   renal capsule
   hilum
   renal artery

Figure 54.1 Label the major structures of the urinary system.

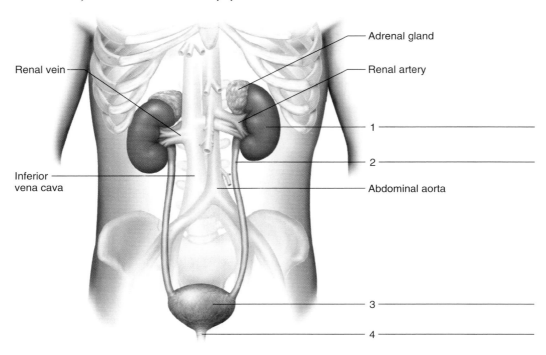

Adrenal gland

Renal artery

Renal vein

1

2

Inferior
vena cava

Abdominal aorta

3

4

Figure 54.2 Label the major structures in the longitudinal section of a kidney.

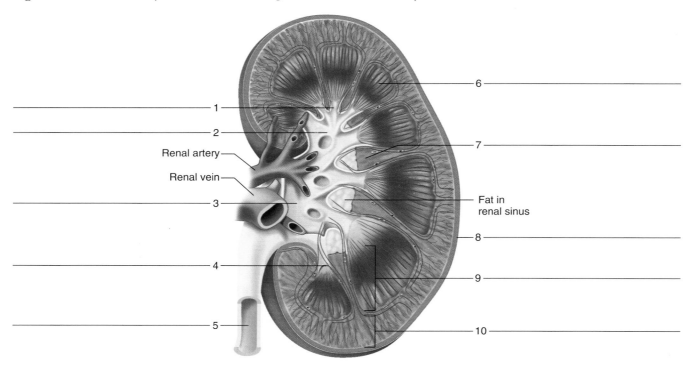

1

2

Renal artery

Renal vein

3

4

5

6

7

Fat in
renal sinus

8

9

10

Figure 54.3 Longitudinal section of a pig kidney that has a triple injection of latex (*red* in the renal artery, *blue* in the renal vein, and *yellow* in the ureter and renal pelvis).

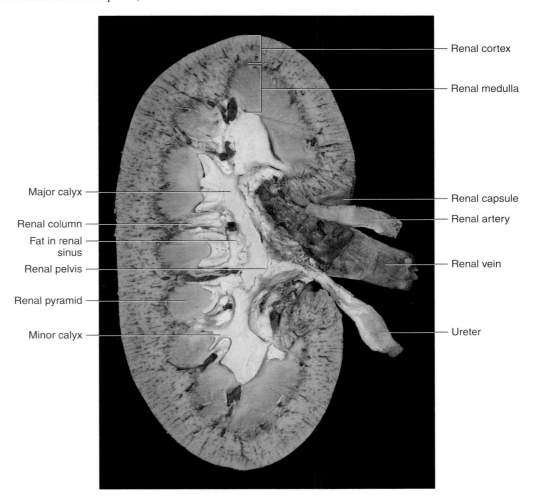

Renal cortex

Renal medulla

Major calyx

Renal capsule

Renal column

Renal artery

Fat in renal sinus

Renal pelvis

Renal vein

Renal pyramid

Minor calyx

Ureter

renal vein

ureter

d. Use a long knife to cut the kidney in half longitudinally along the coronal plane, beginning on the convex border.

e. Rinse the interior of the kidney with water, and using figure 54.3 as a reference, locate the following:

renal pelvis

major calyces

minor calyces

renal cortex

renal columns (extensions of renal cortex between renal pyramids)

renal medulla

renal pyramids

PROCEDURE B—THE RENAL BLOOD VESSELS AND NEPHRONS

1. Review the sections entitled "Renal Blood Vessels" and "Nephrons" in chapter 20 of the textbook.
2. As a review activity, label figure 54.4.
3. Complete Part B of the laboratory report.
4. Obtain a microscope slide of a kidney section and examine it, using low-power magnification. Locate the *renal capsule,* the *renal cortex* (which appears somewhat granular and may be more darkly stained than the other renal tissues,) and the *renal medulla* (fig. 54.5).
5. Examine the renal cortex, using high-power magnification. Locate a *renal corpuscle.* These structures appear as isolated circular areas. Identify the *glomerulus,* which is the capillary cluster inside

Figure 54.4 Label the major structures of the nephron and the blood vessels associated with it, using the terms provided.

Interlobular artery

Renal cortex
Renal medulla

From renal artery

To renal vein

Terms:
Afferent arteriole
Ascending limb of the nephron loop
Collecting duct
Descending limb of the nephron loop
Distal convoluted tubule
Efferent arteriole
Glomerular capsule
Glomerulus
Interlobular vein
Peritubular capillary
Proximal convoluted tubule

the corpuscle, and the *glomerular capsule,* which appears as a clear area surrounding the glomerulus. Also note the numerous sections of renal tubules that occupy the spaces between renal corpuscles (fig. 54.5*a*).

6. Prepare a labeled sketch of a representative section of renal cortex in Part C of the laboratory report.

7. Examine the renal medulla, using high-power magnification. Identify longitudinal and cross sections of various collecting ducts. Note that these ducts are lined with simple epithelial cells, which vary in shape from squamous to cuboidal (fig. 54.5*b*).

8. Prepare a labeled sketch of a representative section of renal medulla in Part D of the laboratory report.

Web Quest

Review the structure and function of the urinary system at
www.mhhe.com/shier11
Click on Student Edition. Click on Martin Lab Manual, Web Quest.

Figure 54.5 (*a*) Micrograph of a section of the renal cortex (220×). (*b*) Micrograph of a section of the renal medulla (80× micrograph enlarged to 200×).

(a)

Glomerulus ⎤
⎬ Renal corpuscle
Glomerular ⎦
capsule

Renal tubules

Collecting duct
(longitudinal section)

Collecting duct
(cross section)

(b)

NOTES

KIDNEY STRUCTURE

PART A

Match the terms in column A with the descriptions in column B. Place the letter of your choice in the space provided.

Column A

a. Calyces
b. Hilum
c. Nephron
d. Renal column
e. Renal cortex
f. Renal papilla
g. Renal pelvis
h. Renal pyramid
i. Renal sinus

Column B

_____ 1. Shell around the renal medulla

_____ 2. Branches of renal pelvis to renal papillae

_____ 3. Conical mass of tissue within renal medulla

_____ 4. Projection with tiny openings into a minor calyx

_____ 5. Hollow chamber within kidney

_____ 6. Microscopic functional unit of kidney

_____ 7. Cortical tissue between renal pyramids

_____ 8. Superior funnel-shaped end of ureter inside the renal sinus

_____ 9. Medial depression for blood vessels and ureter to enter kidney chamber

PART B

Complete the following:

1. Distinguish between a renal corpuscle and a renal tubule. _____

_____

_____

_____

_____

2. Number the following structures to indicate their respective positions in relation to the nephron. Assign the number 1 to the structure attached to the glomerular capsule.

_____ Ascending limb of nephron loop

_____ Collecting duct

_____ Descending limb of nephron loop

_____ Distal convoluted tubule

_____ Proximal convoluted tubule

_____ Renal papilla

3. Number the following structures to indicate their respective positions in the blood pathway within the kidney. Assign the number 1 to the vessel nearest the renal artery.

_____ Afferent arteriole

_____ Efferent arteriole

_____ Glomerulus

_____ Peritubular capillary

_____ Renal vein

4. Explain how the blood vessels associated with the renal corpuscle help to maintain relatively high blood pressure within the glomerulus. _____

_____

_____

_____

_____

_____

_____

5. Describe the *juxtaglomerular apparatus.* _____

_____

_____

_____

_____

_____

PART C

Sketch a representative section of renal cortex. Label the glomerulus, glomerular capsule, and sections of renal tubules.

PART D

Sketch a representative section of renal medulla. Label a longitudinal section and a cross section of a collecting duct.

URINALYSIS

MATERIALS NEEDED

Normal and abnormal simulated urine specimens are
suggested as a substitute for collected urine.
Disposable urine-collecting container
Paper towel
Urinometer cylinder
Urinometer hydrometer
Laboratory thermometer
pH test paper
Reagent strips (individual or combination strips such as
Chemstrip or Multistix) to test for the presence of
the following:
  Glucose
  Protein
  Ketones
  Bilirubin
  Hemoglobin/occult blood
Compound light microscope
Microscope slide
Coverslip
Centrifuge
Centrifuge tube
Graduated cylinder, 10 mL
Medicine dropper
Sedi-stain

 SAFETY

- Consider using simulated urine samples available from
  various laboratory supply houses.
- Wear disposable gloves when working with body
  fluids.
- Work only with your own urine sample.
- Use an appropriate disinfectant to wash the
  laboratory table before and after the procedures.
- Place glassware in a disinfectant when finished.
- Dispose of contaminated items as directed by your
  laboratory instructor.
- Wash your hands before leaving the laboratory.

Urine is the product of kidney functions, which include the removal of various waste substances from
the blood and the maintenance of body fluid and electrolyte balances. Consequently, the composition of
urine varies from time to time because of differences in
dietary intake and physical activity. Also, the volume of

urine produced by the kidneys varies with such factors
as fluid intake, environmental temperature, relative hu-
midity, respiratory rate, and body temperature.

An analysis of urine composition and volume often
is used to evaluate the functions of the kidneys and
other organs. This procedure, called *urinalysis,* involves observing the physical characteristics of a urine
sample, testing for the presence of certain organic and
inorganic substances, and examining the microscopic
solids present in the sample.

PURPOSE OF THE EXERCISE

To perform the observations and tests commonly used
to analyze the characteristics and composition of urine.

LEARNING OBJECTIVES

After completing this exercise, you should be able to

1. Evaluate the color, transparency, and specific
   gravity of a urine sample.
2. Determine the pH of a urine sample.
3. Test a urine sample for the presence of glucose,
   protein, ketones, bilirubin, and hemoglobin.
4. Perform a microscopic study of urine sediment.
5. Evaluate the results of these observations and tests.

WARNING

While performing the following tests, you should
wear disposable latex gloves so that skin contact
with urine is avoided. Observe all safety procedures
listed for this lab. (Normal and abnormal simulated
urine specimens could be used instead of real urine
for this lab.)

PROCEDURE

1. Proceed to the restroom with a clean disposable
   container. The first small volume of urine should not
   be collected because it contains abnormally high
   levels of microorganisms from the urethra. Collect a
   midstream sample of about 50 mL of urine. The best

collections are the first specimen in the morning or one taken 3 hours after a meal. Refrigerate samples if they are not used immediately.

2. Place a sample of urine in a clean, transparent container. Describe the *color* of the urine. Normal urine varies from light yellow to amber, depending on the presence of urochromes, which are end-product pigments produced during the decomposition of hemoglobin. Dark urine indicates a high concentration of pigments.

   Abnormal urine colors include yellow-brown or green, due to elevated concentrations of bile pigments, and red to dark brown, due to the presence of blood. Certain foods, such as beets or carrots, and various drug substances also may cause color changes in urine, but in such cases the colors have no clinical significance. Enter the results of this and the following tests in Part A of Laboratory Report 55.

3. Evaluate the *transparency* of the urine sample (that is, judge whether the urine is clear, slightly cloudy, or very cloudy). Normal urine is clear enough to see through. You can read newsprint through slightly cloudy urine; you can no longer read newsprint through cloudy urine. Cloudy urine indicates the presence of various substances that may include mucus, bacteria, epithelial cells, fat droplets, or inorganic salts.

4. Determine the *specific gravity* of the urine sample. Specific gravity is the ratio of the weight of something to the weight of an equal volume of pure water. For example, mercury (at 15°C) weighs 13.6 times as much as an equal volume of water; thus, it has a specific gravity of 13.6. Although urine is mostly water, it has substances dissolved in it and is slightly heavier than an equal volume of water. Thus, urine has a specific gravity of more than 1.000. Actually, the specific gravity of normal urine varies from 1.003 to 1.035.

   To determine the specific gravity of a urine sample, follow these steps:

   a. Pour enough urine into a clean urinometer cylinder to fill it about three-fourths full. Any foam that appears should be removed with a paper towel.

   b. Use a laboratory thermometer to measure the temperature of the urine.

   c. Gently place the urinometer hydrometer into the urine, and *make sure that the float is not touching the sides or the bottom of the cylinder* (fig. 55.1).

   d. Position your eye at the level of the urine surface. Determine which line on the stem of the hydrometer intersects the lowest level of the concave surface (meniscus) of the urine.

Figure 55.1 Float the hydrometer in the urine, making sure that it does not touch the sides or the bottom of the cylinder.

Hydrometer

Urine in urinometer cylinder

URINE SPECIMEN

   e. Because liquids tend to contract and become denser as they are cooled, or to expand and become less dense as they are heated, it may be necessary to make a temperature correction to obtain an accurate specific gravity measurement. To do this, add 0.001 to the hydrometer reading for each 3 degrees of urine temperature above 25°C or subtract 0.001 for each 3 degrees below 25°C. Enter this calculated value in the table of the laboratory report as the test result.

5. Reagent strips can be used to perform a variety of urine tests. In each case, directions for using the strips are found on the strip container. *Be sure to read them.*

   To perform each test, follow these steps:

   a. Obtain a urine sample and the proper reagent strip.

   b. Read the directions on the strip container.

   c. Dip the strip in the urine sample.

   d. Remove the strip at an angle and let it touch the inside rim of the urine container to remove any excess liquid.

   e. Wait for the length of time indicated by the directions on the container before you compare the color of the test strip with the standard color scale on the side of the container. The value or amount represented by the matching color should be used as the test result and recorded in Part A of the laboratory report.

6. Perform the *pH test.* The pH of normal urine varies from 4.6 to 8.0, but most commonly, it is near 6.0 (slightly acidic). The pH of urine may decrease as a result of a diet high in protein, or it may increase with a vegetarian diet. Significant daily variations within the broad normal range are results of concentrations of excesses from variable diets.

7. Perform the *glucose test.* Normally, there is no glucose in urine. However, glucose may appear in the urine temporarily following a meal high in carbohydrates. Glucose also may appear in the urine as a result of uncontrolled diabetes mellitus.

8. Perform the *protein test.* Normally, proteins of large molecular size are not present in urine. However, those of small molecular sizes, such as albumins, may appear in trace amounts, particularly following strenuous exercise. Increased amounts of proteins also may appear as a result of kidney diseases in which the glomeruli are damaged or as a result of high blood pressure.

9. Perform the *ketone test.* Ketones are products of fat metabolism. Usually they are not present in urine. However, they may appear in the urine if the diet fails to provide adequate carbohydrate, as in the case of prolonged fasting or starvation, or as a result of insulin deficiency (diabetes mellitus).

10. Perform the *bilirubin test.* Bilirubin, which results from hemoglobin decomposition in the liver, normally is absent in urine. It may appear, however, as a result of liver disorders that cause obstructions of the biliary tract. Urochrome, a normal yellow component of urine, is a result of additional breakdown of bilirubin.

11. Perform the *hemoglobin/occult blood test.* Hemoglobin occurs in the red blood cells, and because such cells normally do not pass into the renal tubules, hemoglobin is not found in normal urine. Its presence in urine usually indicates a disease process, a transfusion reaction, or an injury to the urinary organs.

12. Complete Part A of the laboratory report.

13. A urinalysis usually includes a study of urine sediment—the microscopic solids present in a urine sample. This sediment normally includes mucus, certain crystals, and a variety of cells, such as the epithelial cells that line the urinary tubes and an occasional white blood cell. Other types of solids, such as casts or red blood cells, may indicate a disease or injury if they are present in excess. (Casts are cylindrical masses of cells or other substances that form in the renal tubules and are flushed out by the flow of urine.)

    To observe urine sediment, follow these steps:

    a. Thoroughly stir or shake a urine sample to suspend the sediment, which tends to settle to the bottom of the container.

    b. Pour 10 mL of urine into a clean centrifuge tube and centrifuge it for 5 minutes at slow speed (1,500 rpm). Be sure to balance the centrifuge with an even number of tubes filled to the same levels.

    c. Carefully decant 9 mL (leave 1 mL) of the liquid from the sediment in the bottom of the centrifuge tube, as directed by your laboratory instructor. Resuspend the 1 mL of sediment.

    d. Use a medicine dropper to remove some of the sediment and place it on a clean microscope slide.

    e. Add a drop of Sedi-stain to the sample, and add a coverslip.

    f. Examine the sediment with low-power (reduce the light when using low power) and high-power magnifications.

    g. Identify the kinds of solids present with the aid of figure 55.2.

    h. In Part B of the laboratory report, make a sketch of each type of sediment that you observed.

14. Complete Part B of the laboratory report.

Figure 55.2 Types of urine sediment. Healthy individuals lack many of these sediments and possess only occasional to trace amounts of others.

Crystals

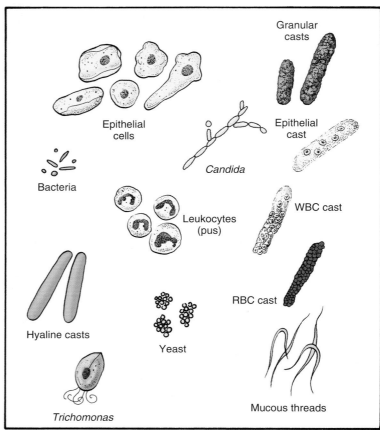

Cells and casts

Name _____

Date _____

Section _____

URINALYSIS

PART A

1. Enter your observations, test results, and evaluations in the following table:

Urine Characteristics	Observations and Test Results	Normal Values	Evaluations
Color		Light yellow to amber	
Transparency		Clear	
Specific gravity (corrected for temperature)		1.003–1.035	
pH		4.6–8.0	
Glucose		0 (negative)	
Protein		0 to trace	
Ketones		0	
Bilirubin		0	
Hemoglobin/occult blood		0	
(Other)			
(Other)			

2. Summarize the results of the urinalysis. _____

_____

_____

_____

_____

_____

_____

Critical Thinking Application

Why do you think it is important to refrigerate a urine sample if an analysis cannot be performed immediately after collecting it?

_____

_____

_____

_____

PART B

1. Make a sketch for each type of sediment you observed. Label any from those shown in figure 55.2.

2. Summarize the results of the urine sediment study. _____

_____

_____

_____

_____

_____

_____

CAT DISSECTION: URINARY SYSTEM

 SAFETY

In this laboratory exercise, you will dissect the urinary organs of the cat. As you observe these structures, compare them with the corresponding human organs by observing the parts of the human torso model.

PURPOSE OF THE EXERCISE

To examine the urinary organs of the cat and to compare them with those of the human.

LEARNING OBJECTIVES

After completing this exercise, you should be able to

1. Locate and identify the urinary organs of the cat.
2. Identify the corresponding organs in the human torso model.
3. Compare the urinary organs of the cat with those of the human.

PROCEDURE

1. Place the preserved cat in a dissecting tray with its ventral surface up.
2. Open the abdominal cavity, and remove the liver, stomach, and spleen.
3. Push the intestines to one side, and locate the *kidneys* in the dorsal abdominal wall on either side of the vertebral column. Note that the kidneys are

located dorsal to the *parietal peritoneum* (retroperitoneal).
4. Carefully remove the parietal peritoneum and the adipose tissue surrounding the kidneys. Locate the following, using figures 45.8 and 56.1 as guides:

ureters
renal arteries
renal veins

5. Locate the *adrenal glands,* which lie medially and above the kidneys and are surrounded by connective tissues. Note that the adrenal glands are attached to blood vessels and are separated by the abdominal aorta and inferior vena cava.
6. Expose the ureters by cleaning away the connective tissues along their lengths. Note that they enter the *urinary bladder* on the dorsal surface.
7. Examine the urinary bladder, and note how it is attached to the abdominal wall by folds of peritoneum that form ligaments. Locate the *medial ligament* on the ventral surface of the bladder that connects it with the linea alba and the *two lateral ligaments* on the dorsal surface.
8. Remove the connective tissue from around the urinary bladder. Use a sharp scalpel to open the bladder, and examine its interior. Locate the openings of the ureters and the urethra on the inside.
9. Expose the *urethra* at the posterior of the urinary bladder.
10. Remove one kidney, and section it longitudinally along the coronal plane (figs. 56.2 and 56.3). Identify the following features:

renal capsule
renal cortex
renal medulla
renal pyramid
renal papilla
renal sinus
renal pelvis

11. Discard the organs and tissues that were removed from the cat, as directed by the laboratory instructor.
12. Complete Laboratory Report 56.

Figure 56.1 The urinary organs of a female cat.

Adrenal
glands

Renal artery

Kidney

Renal vein

Posterior vena cava

Abdominal
aorta

Ureters

Urinary bladder

Rectum

Urethra

Figure 56.2 Longitudinal section of a cat's kidney.

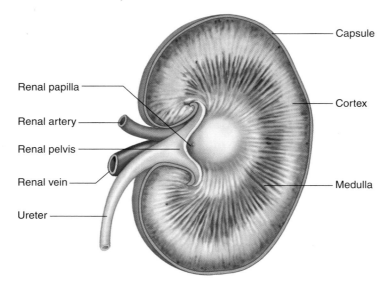

Capsule

Renal papilla

Renal artery

Cortex

Renal pelvis

Renal vein

Medulla

Ureter

Figure 56.3 Female urinary and reproductive systems of a pregnant cat.

Kidney

Renal pelvis

Renal cortex

Renal medulla

Ovary

Ureter

Left uterine horn
(contains embryo)

Body of uterus

Urinary bladder

Vagina

Urethra

NOTES

Name _____

Date _____

Section _____

CAT DISSECTION: URINARY SYSTEM

Complete the following:

1. Compare the positions of the kidneys in the cat with those in the human. _____
   _____
   _____
   _____

2. Compare the locations of the adrenal glands in the cat with those in the human. _____
   _____
   _____
   _____
   _____
   _____

3. What structures of the cat urinary system are retroperitoneal? _____
   _____
   _____
   _____

4. Describe the wall of the urinary bladder of the cat. _____
   _____
   _____
   _____

5. Compare the renal pyramids and renal papillae of the human kidney with those of the cat. _____
   _____
   _____
   _____
   _____

Notes

LABORATORY EXERCISE 57

MALE REPRODUCTIVE SYSTEM

MATERIALS NEEDED

Textbook
Human torso model
Model of the male reproductive system
Anatomical chart of the male reproductive system
Compound light microscope
Prepared microscope slides of the following:
    Testis section
    Epididymis, cross section
    Penis, cross section

The organs of the male reproductive system are specialized to produce and maintain the male sex cells, to transport these cells together with supporting fluids to the female reproductive tract, and to produce and secrete male sex hormones.

These organs include the testes, in which sperm cells and male sex hormones are produced, and sets of internal and external accessory organs. The internal organs include various tubes and glands, whereas the external structures are the scrotum and the penis.

PURPOSE OF THE EXERCISE

To review the structure and functions of the male reproductive organs and to examine some of these organs microscopically.

LEARNING OBJECTIVES

After completing this exercise, you should be able to

1. Locate and identify the organs of the male reproductive system.
2. Describe the functions of these organs.
3. Recognize sections of the testis, epididymis, and penis microscopically.
4. Identify the major features of these microscopic sections.

PROCEDURE A—MALE REPRODUCTIVE ORGANS

1. Review the sections entitled "Testes," "Male Internal Accessory Organs," and "Male External Reproductive Organs" in chapter 22 of the textbook.

2. As a review activity, label figures 57.1 and 57.2.
3. Observe the human torso model, the model of the male reproductive system, and the anatomical chart of the male reproductive system. Locate the following features:

testes
    seminiferous tubules
    interstitial cells (Leydig cells)
inguinal canal
spermatic cord
epididymis
ductus deferens (vas deferens)
ejaculatory duct
seminal vesicles
prostate gland
bulbourethral glands
scrotum
penis
    corpora cavernosa
    corpus spongiosum
    tunica albuginea
    glans penis
    external urethral orifice
    prepuce
    crura
    bulb

4. Complete Part A of Laboratory Report 57.

PROCEDURE B—MICROSCOPIC ANATOMY

1. Obtain a microscope slide of human testis section and examine it, using low-power magnification (fig. 57.3). Locate the thick *fibrous capsule* (tunica albuginea) on the surface and the numerous sections of *seminiferous tubules* inside.
2. Focus on some of the seminiferous tubules, using high-power magnification (fig. 57.4). Locate the *basement membrane* and the layer of *spermatogonia* just beneath the basement membrane. Identify some *sustentacular cells*

465

Figure 57.1 Label the major structures of the male reproductive system in this sagittal view.

Urinary bladder

Superior pubic ramus (cut)

1

2

Corpus cavernosum

Corpus spongiosum

3

4

5

6

7

Ureter

Large intestine

8

Ejaculatory duct

9

10

Anus

11

Figure 57.2 Label the diagram of (*a*) the sagittal section of a testis and (*b*) a cross section of a seminiferous tubule by placing the correct numbers in the spaces provided.

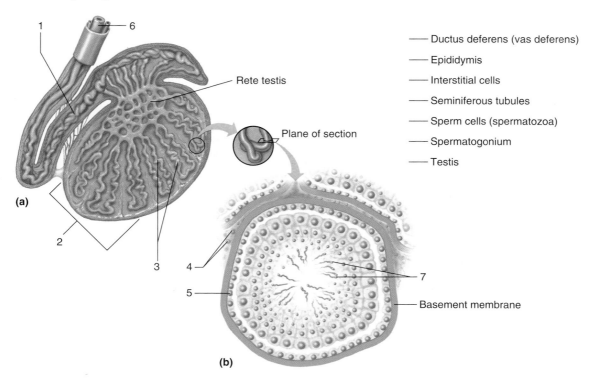

Rete testis

Plane of section

(a)

(b)

——— Ductus deferens (vas deferens)

——— Epididymis

——— Interstitial cells

——— Seminiferous tubules

——— Sperm cells (spermatozoa)

——— Spermatogonium

——— Testis

Basement membrane

Figure 57.3 Micrograph of a human testis (1.7×).

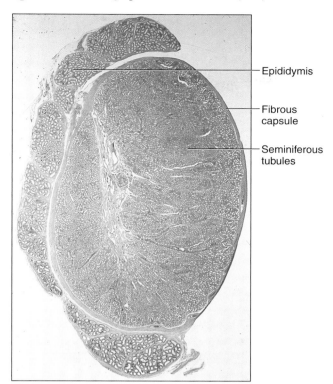

Epididymis

Fibrous capsule

Seminiferous tubules

(supporting cells; Sertoli cells), which have pale, oval-shaped nuclei, and some *spermatogenic cells,* which have smaller, round nuclei. Spermatogonia give rise to spermatogenic cells that are in various stages of spermatogenesis as they are forced toward the lumen. Near the lumen of the tube, find some darkly stained, elongated heads of developing sperm cells. In the spaces between adjacent seminiferous tubules, locate some isolated *interstitial cells* (Leydig cells).

3. Prepare a labeled sketch of a representative section of the testis in Part B of the laboratory report.
4. Obtain a microscope slide of a cross section of *epididymis* (fig. 57.5). Examine its wall, using high-power magnification. Note the elongated, *pseudostratified columnar epithelial cells* that comprise most of the inner lining. These cells have nonmotile stereocilia (microvilli) on their free surfaces. Also note the thin layer of smooth muscle and connective tissue surrounding the tube.
5. Prepare a labeled sketch of the epididymis wall in Part B of the laboratory report.
6. Obtain a microscope slide of a *penis* cross section, and examine it with low-power magnification (fig. 57.6). Identify the following features:

corpora cavernosa

corpus spongiosum

Figure 57.4 Micrograph of seminiferous tubules (50× micrograph enlarged to 135×).

Sperm cell nucleus

Sustentacular cell (supporting cell; Sertoli cell)

Lumen

Spermatogenic cells

Interstitial cells (Leydig cells)

Seminiferous tubule

Spermatogonium

Basement membrane

Figure 57.5 Micrograph of a cross section of a human epididymis (50× micrograph enlarged to 145×).

— Pseudostratified columnar epithelial cells

— Nonmotile cilia

— Sperm cells in lumen

— Smooth muscle cell

— Epididymis (cross section)

Figure 57.6 Micrograph of a cross section of the body of the penis (5×).

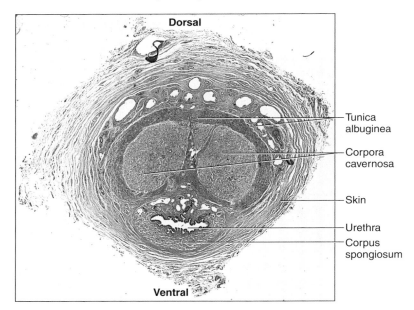

Dorsal

— Tunica albuginea

— Corpora cavernosa

— Skin

— Urethra
— Corpus spongiosum

Ventral

tunica albuginea

urethra

skin

7. Prepare a labeled sketch of a penis cross section in Part B of the laboratory report.
8. Complete Part B of the laboratory report.

Web Quest

Review the structures and functions of the male reproductive system at

www.mhhe.com/shier11

Click on Student Edition. Click on Martin Lab Manual, Web Quest.

Name _____

Date _____

Section _____

MALE REPRODUCTIVE SYSTEM

PART A

Complete the following statements:

1. Each testis is suspended by a (an) _____ within the scrotum.
2. The descent of the testes from near the developing kidneys is stimulated by the male sex hormone _____.
3. The descent of the testes is aided by a fibromuscular cord called the _____.
4. As the testes descend, they pass through the _____ of the abdominal wall into the scrotum.
5. Connective tissue subdivides a testis into many _____, which contain seminiferous tubules.
6. The _____ is a highly coiled tube on the surface of the testis.
7. The _____ cells of the epithelium that line the seminiferous tubule give rise to sperm cells.
8. _____ is the process by which sperm cells are formed.
9. Immature sperm cells formed from secondary spermatocytes during meiosis are called _____.
10. The number of chromosomes normally present in a human sperm cell is _____.
11. The anterior end of a sperm head, called the _____, contains enzymes that aid the penetration of an egg cell at the time of fertilization.
12. Sperm cells undergo maturation while they are stored in the _____.
13. The secretion of the seminal vesicles is rich in the monosaccharide called _____.
14. Prostate gland secretion helps neutralize seminal fluid because the prostate secretion is _____.
15. The secretion of the _____ glands lubricates the end of the penis in preparation for sexual intercourse.
16. The pH of seminal fluid is slightly _____.
17. The dartos muscle is in the subcutaneous tissue in the wall of the _____.
18. The sensitive, cone-shaped end of the penis is called the _____.
19. _____ is the movement of sperm cells and various glandular secretions into the urethra.
20. _____ is the process by which semen is forced out through the urethra.

PART B

1. Sketch and label a representative section of the testis.

2. Sketch and label a region of the epididymis.

3. Sketch and label a penis cross section.

4. Briefly describe the function of each of the following:
   a. sustentacular cell (supporting cell; Sertoli cell)

   _____
   _____
   _____

   b. spermatogenic cell

   _____
   _____
   _____

   c. interstitial cell (Leydig cell)

   _____
   _____
   _____

   d. epididymis

   _____
   _____
   _____

   e. corpora cavernosa and corpus spongiosum

   _____
   _____
   _____

FEMALE REPRODUCTIVE SYSTEM

The organs of the female reproductive system are specialized to produce and maintain the female sex cells, to transport these cells to the site of fertilization, to provide a favorable environment for a developing offspring, to move the offspring to the outside, and to produce female sex hormones.

These organs include the ovaries, which produce the egg cells and female sex hormones, and sets of internal and external accessory organs. The internal accessory organs include the uterine tubes, uterus, and vagina. The external organs are the labia majora, labia minora, clitoris, and vestibular glands.

PURPOSE OF THE EXERCISE

To review the structure and functions of the female reproductive organs and to examine some of their features microscopically.

LEARNING OBJECTIVES

After completing this exercise, you should be able to

1. Locate and identify the organs of the female reproductive system.
2. Describe the functions of these organs.
3. Recognize sections of the ovary, uterine tube, and uterine wall microscopically.
4. Identify the major features of these microscopic sections.

PROCEDURE A—FEMALE REPRODUCTIVE ORGANS

1. Review the sections entitled, "Ovaries," "Female Internal Accessory Organs," "Female External Reproductive Organs," and "Mammary Glands" in chapter 22 of the textbook.
2. As a review activity, label figures 58.1, 58.2, 58.3, 58.4, and 58.5.
3. Observe the human torso model, the model of the female reproductive system, and the anatomical chart of the female reproductive system. Locate the following features:

ovaries
    medulla
    cortex
ligaments
    broad ligament
    suspensory ligament
    ovarian ligament
    round ligament
uterine tubes (oviducts; fallopian tubes)
    infundibulum
    fimbriae
uterus
    fundus
    body
    cervix
    cervical orifice
    endometrium
    myometrium
    perimetrium (serous membrane)
rectouterine pouch
vagina
    fornices
    vaginal orifice
    hymen
    mucosal layer
    muscular layer
    fibrous layer

Figure 58.1 Label the ligaments and other structures associated with the female internal reproductive organs.

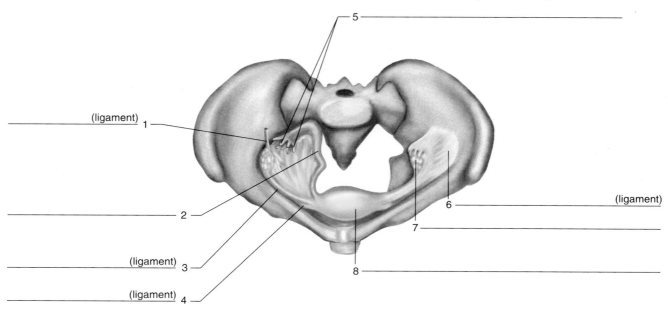

5 _____

(ligament) 1 _____

(ligament) _____ 6

7 _____

_____ 2

(ligament) 3 _____

8 _____

(ligament) 4 _____

Figure 58.2 Label the structures of the female reproductive system in this sagittal view.

8 _____

Perimetrium

Myometrium

Endometrium

Rectouterine pouch

1 _____

2 _____

3 _____

9 _____

Urinary bladder _____

Rectum

Symphysis pubis _____

10 _____

Urethra _____

4 _____

5 _____

Anus

6 _____

7 _____

Figure 58.3 Label the female external reproductive organs and associated structures.

Figure 58.4 Label this ovary by placing the correct numbers in the spaces provided.

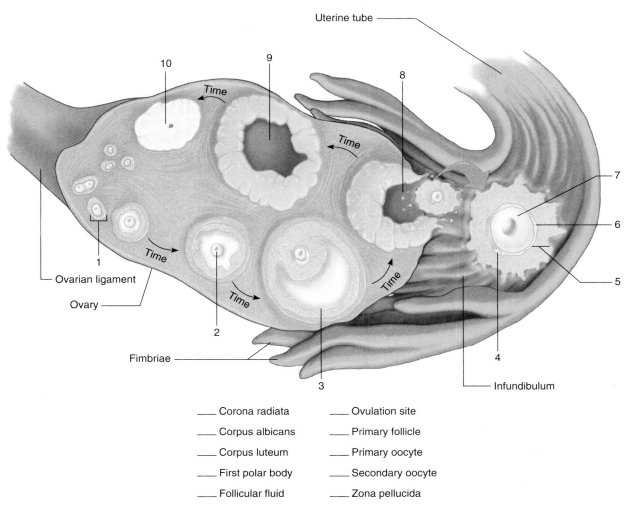

____ Corona radiata   ____ Ovulation site

____ Corpus albicans   ____ Primary follicle

____ Corpus luteum   ____ Primary oocyte

____ First polar body   ____ Secondary oocyte

____ Follicular fluid   ____ Zona pellucida

Figure 58.5 Label the structures of the breast (anterior view), using the terms provided.

Terms:
Adipose tissue
Alveolar glands
Areola
Lactiferous duct
Nipple

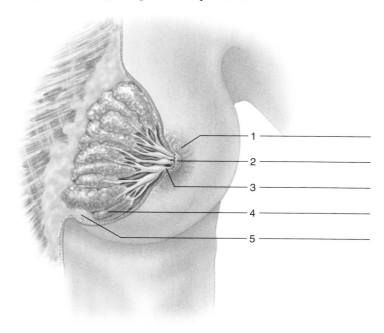

1 _____
2 _____
3 _____
4 _____
5 _____

vulva (external accessory organs)

  mons pubis

  labia majora

  labia minora

  vestibule

  vestibular glands

  clitoris

    corpora cavernosa

    glans

breasts

  nipple

  areola

  alveolar glands (compose milk-producing parts
    of mammary glands)

  lactiferous ducts

  adipose tissue

4. Complete Part A of Laboratory Report 58.

PROCEDURE B—MICROSCOPIC ANATOMY

1. Obtain a microscope slide of an ovary section with maturing follicles, and examine it with low-power magnification (fig. 58.6). Locate the outer layer, or *cortex,* which is composed of densely packed cells, and the inner layer, or *medulla,* which largely consists of loose connective tissue.

2. Focus on the cortex of the ovary, using high-power magnification (fig. 58.7). Note the thin layer of small cuboidal cells on the free surface. These cells comprise the *germinal epithelium.* Also locate

some *primordial follicles* just beneath the germinal epithelium. Note that each follicle consists of a single, relatively large *primary oocyte* with a prominent nucleus and a covering of *follicular cells.*

3. Prepare a labeled sketch of the ovarian cortex in Part B of the laboratory report.

4. Use low-power magnification to search the ovarian cortex for maturing follicles in various stages of development. Prepare three labeled sketches in Part B of the laboratory report to illustrate the changes that occur in a follicle as it matures.

5. Obtain a microscope slide of a cross section of a uterine tube. Examine it, using low-power magnification (fig. 58.8). Note that the shape of the lumen is very irregular.

6. Focus on the inner lining of the uterine tube, using high-power magnification. Note that the lining is composed of *simple columnar epithelium* and that some of the epithelial cells are ciliated on their free surfaces.

7. Prepare a labeled sketch of a representative region of the wall of the uterine tube in Part B of the laboratory report.

8. Obtain a microscope slide of the uterine wall section (fig. 58.9). Examine it, using low-power magnification, and locate the following:

endometrium (inner mucosal layer)

myometrium (middle, thick muscular layer)

perimetrium (outer serosal layer)

Figure 58.6 Micrograph of the ovary (30× micrograph enlarged to 80×).

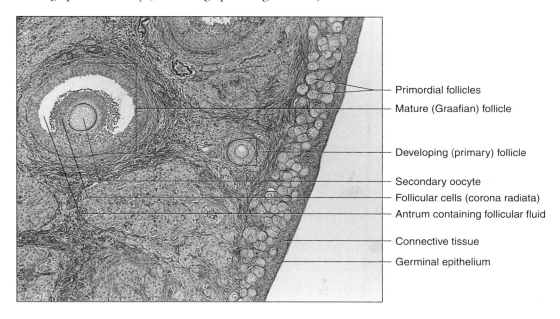

- Primordial follicles
- Mature (Graafian) follicle
- Developing (primary) follicle
- Secondary oocyte
- Follicular cells (corona radiata)
- Antrum containing follicular fluid
- Connective tissue
- Germinal epithelium

Figure 58.7 Micrograph of the ovarian cortex (100× micrograph enlarged to 200×).

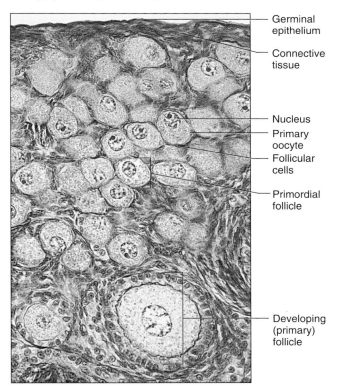

- Germinal epithelium
- Connective tissue
- Nucleus
- Primary oocyte
- Follicular cells
- Primordial follicle
- Developing (primary) follicle

9. Prepare a labeled sketch of a representative section of the uterine wall in Part B of the laboratory report.
10. Complete Part B of the laboratory report.

DEMONSTRATION

Observe the slides in the demonstration microscopes. Each slide contains a section of uterine mucosa taken during a different phase in the reproductive cycle. In the *early proliferative phase,* note the simple columnar epithelium on the free surface of the mucosa and the many sections of tubular uterine glands in the tissues beneath the epithelium. In the *secretory phase,* note that the endometrium is thicker and that the uterine glands appear more extensive and that they are coiled. In the *early menstrual phase,* note that the endometrium is thinner because its surface layer has been lost. Also note that the uterine glands are less apparent and that the spaces between the glands contain many leukocytes. What is the significance of these changes?

_____

_____

_____

Web Quest

Review the structures and functions of the female reproductive system at
www.mhhe.com/shier11
Click on Student Edition. Click on Martin Lab Manual, Web Quest.

Figure 58.8 Micrograph of a cross section of the uterine tube (8×).

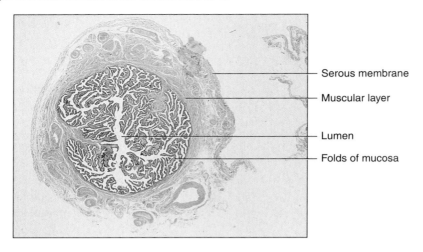

— Serous membrane

— Muscular layer

— Lumen

— Folds of mucosa

Figure 58.9 Micrograph of a section of the uterine wall (10× micrograph enlarged to 35×).

— Lumen

— Endometrium

— Myometrium

FEMALE REPRODUCTIVE SYSTEM

PART A

Complete the following statements:

1. The ovaries are located in the lateral wall of the _____ cavity.

2. The largest of the ovarian attachments is called the _____ ligament.

3. The ovarian cortex appears granular because of the presence of _____.

4. The meiosis of egg formation is called _____.

5. A primary oocyte is closely surrounded by flattened epithelial cells called _____ cells.

6. When a primary oocyte divides, a secondary oocyte and a(an) _____ are produced.

7. Primordial follicles are stimulated to develop into primary follicles by the hormone called _____.

8. _____ is the process by which a secondary oocyte is released from the ovary.

9. Uterine tubes are also called _____.

10. The _____ is the funnel-shaped expansion at the end of a uterine tube.

11. The _____ ligament is a band of tissue within the broad ligament that helps to hold the uterus in proper position.

12. A portion of the uterus called the _____ extends downward into the upper portion of the vagina.

13. The inner mucosal lining of the uterus is called the _____.

14. The myometrium is largely composed of _____ tissue.

15. The vaginal orifice is partially closed by a thin membrane called the _____.

16. The group of external accessory organs that surround the openings of the urethra and vagina comprise the _____ .

17. The rounded mass of fatty tissue overlying the symphysis pubis of the female is called the _____.

18. The female organ that corresponds to the male penis is the _____.

19. The _____ of the female corresponds to the bubourethral glands of the male.

20. Orgasm is accompanied by a series of reflexes involving the lumbar and _____ regions of the spinal cord.

PART B

1. Sketch and label a representative region of the ovarian cortex.

2. Sketch and label a series of three changes to illustrate follicular maturation.

3. Sketch and label a representative section of the wall of a uterine tube.

4. Sketch and label a representative section of uterine wall.

5. Complete the following:
   a. Describe the fate of a mature follicle. _____
   _____
   _____

   b. Describe the function of the cilia in the lining of the uterine tube. _____
   _____
   _____

   c. Briefly describe the changes that occur in the uterine lining during a reproductive cycle. _____
   _____
   _____

LABORATORY EXERCISE 59

CAT DISSECTION: REPRODUCTIVE SYSTEMS

MATERIALS NEEDED

Preserved cat
Dissecting tray
Dissecting instruments
Bone cutters
Disposable gloves
Models of human reproductive systems

 SAFETY

- Wear disposable gloves when working on the cat dissection.
- Dispose of tissue remnants and gloves as instructed.
- Wash the dissecting tray and instruments as instructed.
- Wash your laboratory table.
- Wash your hands before leaving the laboratory.

In this laboratory exercise, you will dissect the reproductive system of the cat. If you have a female cat, begin with Procedure A. If you have a male cat, begin with Procedure B. After completing the dissection, exchange cats with someone who has dissected one of the opposite sex, and examine its reproductive organs.

As you observe the cat reproductive organs, compare them with the corresponding human organs by examining the models of the human reproductive systems.

PURPOSE OF THE EXERCISE

To examine the reproductive organs of the cat and to compare them with the corresponding organs of the human.

LEARNING OBJECTIVES

After completing this exercise, you should be able to

1. Locate and identify the reproductive organs of a cat.
2. Identify the corresponding organs in models of the human reproductive systems.
3. Compare the reproductive organs of the cat with those of the human.

PROCEDURE A—FEMALE REPRODUCTIVE SYSTEM

1. Place the preserved female cat in a dissecting tray with its ventral surface up, and open its abdominal cavity.
2. Locate the small oval ovaries just posterior to the kidneys (figs. 56.3 and 59.1).
3. Examine an ovary, and note that it is suspended from the dorsal body wall by a fold of peritoneum called the *mesovarium.* Another attachment, the *ovarian ligament,* connects the ovary to the tubular *uterine horn* (figs. 56.3 and 59.1).
4. Near the anterior end of the ovary, locate the funnel-shaped *infundibulum,* which is at the end of the *uterine tube,* or *oviduct.* Note the tiny projections, or *fimbriae,* that create a fringe around the edge of the infundibulum. Trace the uterine tube around the ovary to its connection with the uterine horn near the attachment of the ovarian ligament.
5. Examine the uterine horn. Note that it is suspended from the body wall by a fold of peritoneum, the *broad ligament,* that is continuous with the mesovarium of the ovary. Also note the fibrous *round ligament,* which extends from the uterine horn laterally and posteriorly to the body wall (figs. 56.3 and 59.1).
6. To observe the remaining organs of the reproductive system more easily, remove the left hindlimb by severing it near the hip with bone cutters. Then use the bone cutters to remove the left anterior portion of the pelvic girdle. Also remove the necessary muscles and connective tissue to expose the structures shown in figure 59.2.
7. Trace the uterine horns posteriorly, and note that they unite to form the *uterine body,* which is located between the urethra and rectum. The uterine body is continuous with the *vagina,* which leads to the outside.
8. Trace the *urethra* from the urinary bladder posteriorly, and note that it and the vagina open into a common chamber, called the *urogenital sinus.* The opening of this chamber, which is ventral to the anus, is called the *urogenital aperture.* Locate the *labia majora,* which are folds of skin on either side of the urogenital aperture.

Figure 59.1 Ventral view of the female cat's reproductive system.

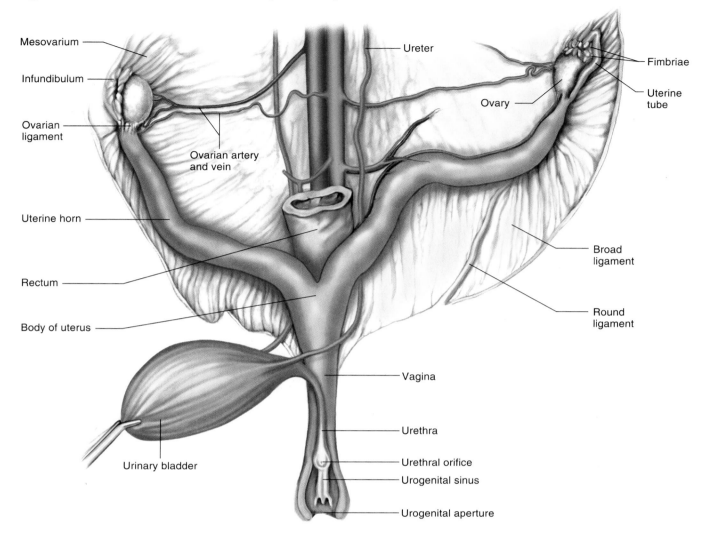

9. Use scissors to open the vagina along its lateral wall, beginning at the urogenital aperture and continuing to the body of the uterus. Note the *urethral orifice* in the ventral wall of the urogenital sinus, and locate the small, rounded *cervix* of the uterus, which projects into the vagina at its deep end. The *clitoris* is located in the ventral wall of the urogenital sinus near its opening to the outside.
10. Complete Part A of Laboratory Report 59.

PROCEDURE B—MALE REPRODUCTIVE SYSTEM

1. Place the preserved male cat in a dissecting tray with its ventral surface up.
2. Locate the *scrotum* between the hindlimbs. Make an incision along the midline of the scrotum, and expose the *testes* inside (fig. 59.3). Note that the testes are separated by a septum and that each testis is enclosed in a sheath of connective tissue.

3. Remove the sheath surrounding the testes, and locate the convoluted *epididymis* on the dorsal surface of each testis (fig. 59.4).
4. Locate the *spermatic cord* on the right side, leading away from the testis. This cord contains the *ductus (vas) deferens,* which is continuous with the epididymis as well as with the nerves and blood vessels that supply the testis on that side. Trace the spermatic cord to the body wall, where its contents pass through the *inguinal canal* and enter the pelvic cavity (fig. 59.4).
5. Locate the *penis,* and identify the *prepuce,* which forms a sheath around the penis. Make an incision through the skin of the prepuce, and expose the *glans* of the penis. Note that the glans has minute spines on its surface.
6. To observe the remaining structures of the reproductive system more easily, remove the left hindlimb by severing it near the hip with bone cutters. Then use the bone cutters to

Figure 59.2 Lateral view of the female cat's reproductive system.

Colon

Urinary bladder

Ureter

Urethra

Vagina

Urogenital sinus

Urogenital aperture

Uterine horn

Uterine body

Rectum

Anal gland

Anus

remove the left anterior portion of the pelvic girdle. Also remove the necessary muscles and connective tissues to expose the organs shown in figure 59.5.

7. Trace the ductus deferens from the inguinal canal to the penis. Note that the ductus deferens loops over the ureter within the pelvic cavity and passes downward behind the urinary bladder to join the urethra. Locate the *prostate gland,* which appears as an enlargement at the junction of the ductus deferens and urethra.

8. Trace the urethra to the penis. Locate the *bulbourethral glands,* which form small swellings on either side at the proximal end of the penis.

9. Use a sharp scalpel to cut a transverse section of the penis. Identify the *corpora cavernosa,* each of which contains many blood spaces surrounded by a sheath of connective tissue.

10. Complete Part B of the laboratory report.

Figure 59.3 Male reproductive system of the cat.

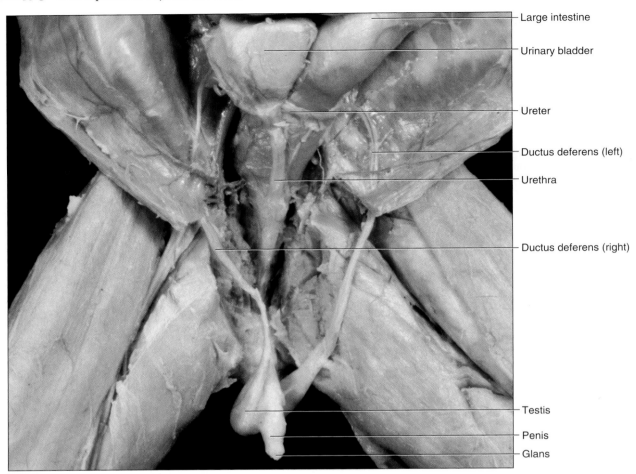

Large intestine

Urinary bladder

Ureter

Ductus deferens (left)

Urethra

Ductus deferens (right)

Testis

Penis

Glans

Figure 59.4 Ventral view of the male cat's reproductive system.

Kidney

Adrenal gland

Ureter

Urinary bladder

Ductus deferens

Inguinal canal

Prostate gland

Rectum

Urethra

Spermatic cord

Crus of penis

Bulbourethral gland

Testis

Epididymis

Penis

Glans penis

Figure 59.5 Lateral view of the male cat's reproductive system.

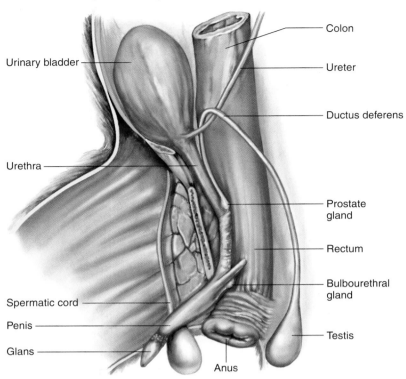

Urinary bladder

Urethra

Spermatic cord

Penis

Glans

Colon

Ureter

Ductus deferens

Prostate gland

Rectum

Bulbourethral gland

Testis

Anus

Laboratory Report **59**

Name _____

Date _____

Section _____

CAT DISSECTION: REPRODUCTIVE SYSTEMS

PART A

Complete the following:

1. Compare the relative lengths and paths of the uterine tubes (oviducts) of the cat and the human. _____
   _____
   _____
   _____
   _____
   _____

2. How do the shape and structure of the uterus of the cat compare with that of the human? _____
   _____
   _____
   _____
   _____
   _____

3. Assess the function of the uterine horns of the cat. _____
   _____
   _____
   _____
   _____
   _____

4. Compare the relationship of the urethra and the vagina in the cat and in the human. _____
   _____
   _____
   _____
   _____
   _____

PART B

Complete the following:

1. Compare the glans of the penis in the cat and in the human. _____

    _____

    _____

    _____

    _____

    _____

2. How do the location and the relative size of the prostate gland of the cat compare with that of the human?_____

    _____

    _____

    _____

    _____

    _____

3. What glands associated with the human ductus deferens are missing in the cat? _____

    _____

    _____

4. Compare the prepuce in the cat and in the human. _____

    _____

    _____

    _____

FERTILIZATION AND EARLY DEVELOPMENT

MATERIALS NEEDED

Textbook
Sea urchin egg suspension*
Sea urchin sperm suspension*
Compound light microscope
Depression microscope slide
Coverslip
Medicine droppers
Prepared microscope slide of the following:
   Sea urchin embryos (early and late cleavage)
Models of human embryos

For Learning Extension:

Vaseline
Toothpick

For Demonstration:

Preserved mammalian embryos

*See the Instructor's Manual for a source of materials.

Fertilization is the process by which the nuclei of an egg and a sperm cell come together and combine their chromosomes, forming a single cell called a zygote.

Ordinarily, before fertilization can occur in a human female, an egg cell must be released from the ovary and must be carried into a uterine tube. Also, semen containing sperm cells must be deposited in the vagina; some of these sperm cells must travel through the uterus and into the uterine tubes. Although many sperm cells may reach an egg cell, only one will participate in the fertilization of the egg.

Shortly after fertilization, the zygote undergoes division (mitosis) to form two cells. These two cells become four, they in turn divide into eight, and so forth. The resulting mass of cells continues to grow and undergoes developmental changes and growth that give rise to an offspring.

PURPOSE OF THE EXERCISE

To review the process of fertilization, to observe sea urchin eggs being fertilized, and to examine embryos in early stages of development.

LEARNING OBJECTIVES

After completing this exercise, you should be able to

1. Describe the process of fertilization.
2. Describe the early developmental stages of a sea urchin.
3. Describe the early developmental stages of a human.
4. Identify the major features of human embryo models.

PROCEDURE A—FERTILIZATION

1. Review the sections entitled "Fertilization" and "Period of Cleavage" in chapter 23 of the textbook.
2. As a review activity, label figure 60.1.
3. Complete Part A of Laboratory Report 60.
4. Although it is difficult to observe fertilization in animals since the process occurs internally, it is possible to view forms of external fertilization. For example, egg and sperm cells can be collected from sea urchins, and the process of fertilization can be observed microscopically. To make this observation, follow these steps:
   a. Place a drop of sea urchin egg-cell suspension in the chamber of a depression slide, and add a coverslip.
   b. Examine the egg cells, using low-power magnification.
   c. Focus on a single egg cell with high-power magnification, and sketch the cell in Part B of the laboratory report.
   d. Remove the coverslip and add a drop of sea urchin sperm-cell suspension to the depression slide. Replace the coverslip, and observe the sperm cells with high-power magnification as they cluster around the egg cells. This attraction is stimulated by gamete secretions.
   e. Observe the egg cells with low-power magnification once again, and watch for the appearance of *fertilization membranes.* Such a membrane forms as soon as an egg cell is penetrated by a sperm cell; it looks like a clear halo surrounding the egg cell.
   f. Focus on a single fertilized egg cell, and sketch it in Part B of the laboratory report.

Figure 60.1 Label the diagram of the stages of early human development.

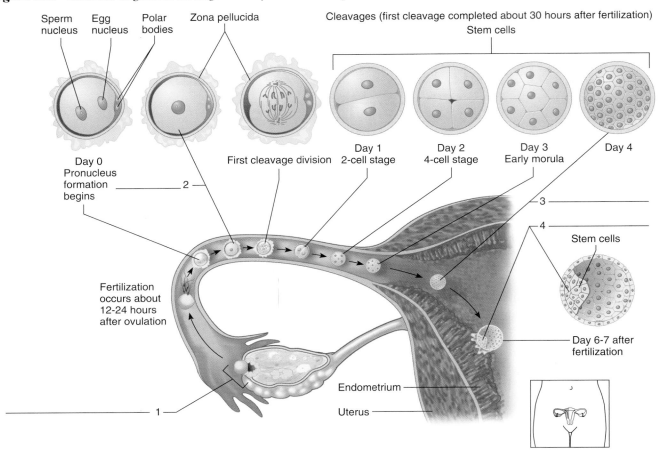

Sperm nucleus

Egg nucleus

Polar bodies

Zona pellucida

Cleavages (first cleavage completed about 30 hours after fertilization)

Stem cells

Day 0 Pronucleus formation begins

2

First cleavage division

Day 1 2-cell stage

Day 2 4-cell stage

Day 3 Early morula

Day 4

3

4

Stem cells

Fertilization occurs about 12-24 hours after ovulation

Day 6-7 after fertilization

Endometrium

Uterus

1

 LEARNING EXTENSION

Use a toothpick to draw a thin line of Vaseline around the chamber of the depression slide containing the fertilized sea urchin egg cells. Place a coverslip over the chamber, and gently press it into the Vaseline to seal the chamber and prevent the liquid inside from evaporating. Keep the slide in a cool place so that the temperature never exceeds 22°C (72°F). Using low-power magnification, examine the slide every 30 minutes, and look for the appearance of two-, four-, and eight-cell stages of developing sea urchin embryos.

PROCEDURE B—SEA URCHIN EARLY DEVELOPMENT

1. Obtain a prepared microscope slide of developing sea urchin embryos. This slide contains embryos in various stages of cleavage. Search the slide, using low-power magnification, and locate embryos in two-, four-, eight-, and sixteen-cell stages. Observe

that cleavage results in an increase of cell numbers; however, the cells get progressively smaller.

2. Prepare a sketch of each stage in Part C of the laboratory report.

PROCEDURE C—HUMAN EARLY DEVELOPMENT

1. Review the sections entitled "Period of Cleavage" and "Embryonic Stage" in chapter 23 of the textbook.
2. As a review activity, study and label figures 60.2 and 60.3.
3. Complete Parts D and E of the laboratory report.
4. Observe the models of human embryos, and identify the following features:

blastomeres

morula

blastocyst

inner cell mass

trophoblast

Figure 60.2 Label the major features of the early embryo and the structures associated with it, using the terms provided.

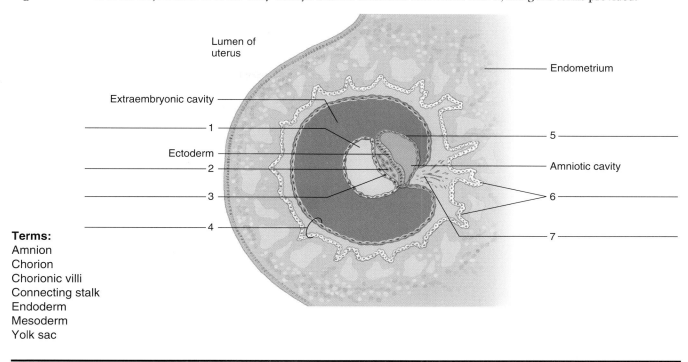

Lumen of uterus

Endometrium

Extraembryonic cavity

1

Ectoderm

2

3

4

5

Amniotic cavity

6

7

Terms:
Amnion
Chorion
Chorionic villi
Connecting stalk
Endoderm
Mesoderm
Yolk sac

Figure 60.3 Label the structures associated with this seven-week-old embryo.

1

2

Amnion

Chorion

3

Developing ear

Developing eye

Umbilical arteries

Umbilical vein

Chorionic villi

Lacuna

Placenta

Chorion

Endometrium

Myometrium

embryonic disc

primary germ layers

    ectoderm

    endoderm

    mesoderm

connecting stalk

chorion

chorionic villi (from trophoblast)

lacunae

amnion

amniotic fluid

umbilical cord

    umbilical arteries

    umbilical vein

yolk sac

allantois

placenta

DEMONSTRATION

Observe the preserved mammalian embryos that are on display. In addition to observing the developing external body structures, identify such features as the chorion, chorionic villi, amnion, yolk sac, umbilical cord, and placenta. What special features provide clues to the types of mammals these embryos represent?

_____

_____

_____

Web Quest

Examine topics of infertility, fetal development, pregnancy, birth, and many more.
www.mhhe.com/shier11

Click on Student Edition. Click on Martin Lab Manual, Web Quest.

Laboratory Report 60

Name _____

Date _____

Section _____

FERTILIZATION AND EARLY DEVELOPMENT

PART A

Complete the following statements:

1. The zona pellucida surrounds the cell membrane of a(an) _____.

2. Enzymes secreted by the _____ of a sperm cell help it to penetrate the zona pellucida.

3. The cell resulting from fertilization is called a(an) _____.

4. The cell resulting from fertilization divides by the process of _____.

5. _____ is the phase of development during which cellular divisions result in smaller and smaller cells.

6. _____ on the inner lining of the uterine tube aid in moving a developing embryo.

7. The trip from the site of fertilization to the uterine cavity takes about _____ days.

8. The hollow ball of cells formed early in development is called a(an) _____.

9. A human offspring is called a(an) _____ until the end of the eighth week of development.

10. After the eighth week, a developing human is called a(an) _____ until the time of birth.

PART B

Prepare sketches of the following:

Single sea urchin egg (___×)	Fertilized sea urchin egg (___×)

PART C

Prepare sketches of the following:

Two-cell sea urchin embryo (____×)	Four-cell sea urchin embryo (____×)
Eight-cell sea urchin embryo (____×)	Sixteen-cell sea urchin embryo (____×)

PART D

Match the terms in column A with the descriptions in column B. Place the letter of your choice in the space provided.

Column A	Column B
a. Blastocyst	_____ 1. Germ layer that gives rise to muscle and bone tissues
b. Chorionic villi	_____ 2. Blastocyst cells that give rise to embryo proper
c. Connecting stalk	_____ 3. Spaces around chorionic villi that become filled with maternal blood
d. Ectoderm	
e. Endoderm	_____ 4. Hollow ball of cells
f. Inner cell mass	_____ 5. Cells forming wall of blastocyst
g. Lacunae	_____ 6. Solid ball of about sixteen cells
h. Mesoderm	_____ 7. Inner germ layer of embryonic disc
i. Morula	_____ 8. Slender extensions that grow out from the trophoblast
j. Trophoblast	_____ 9. Tissue connecting embryo proper to developing placenta
	_____ 10. Outer germ layer of embryonic disc

PART E

Complete the following statements:

1. The thin membrane that separates the embryonic blood from the maternal blood is called the

   _____.

2. The embryonic membrane that is attached to the edge of the embryonic disc and surrounds the developing body

   is called the _____.

3. The umbilical cord contains three blood vessels, two of which are _____.

4. Eventually the amniotic cavity is surrounded by a double-layered membrane called the

   _____.

5. The _____ and allantois function to form blood cells during the early stages

   of development.

6. The _____ gives rise to the cells that later become sex cells.

7. The _____ gives rise to the umbilical blood vessels.

8. The embryonic stage is completed by the end of the _____ week of development.

9. All essential external and internal body parts are formed during the _____ stage

   of development.

10. _____ fluid protects the embryo from jarred movements and provides a watery

    environment for development.

NOTES

GENETICS

MATERIALS NEEDED

Textbook
Pennies (or other coins)
Dice
PTC paper
Astigmatism chart
Ichikawa's or Ishihara's color plates for
    colorblindness test

Many examples of human genetics in this laboratory exercise are basic, external features to observe. Some traits are based upon simple Mendelian genetics. As our knowledge of genetics continues to develop, traits such as tongue roller and free earlobe may no longer be considered examples of simple Mendelian genetics. We may need to continue to abandon some simple Mendelian models. New evidence may involve polygenic inheritance, effects of other genes, or environmental factors as more appropriate explanations. Therefore, the analysis of family genetics is not appropriate nor is it the purpose of this laboratory exercise.

Genetics is the study of the inheritance of characteristics. The genes that transmit this information are coded in segments of DNA in chromosomes. Homologous chromosomes possess the same gene at the same *locus*. These genes may exist in variant forms, called *alleles*. If a person possesses two identical alleles, the condition is *homozygous*. If a person possesses two different alleles, the condition is *heterozygous*. The particular combination of these gene variants (alleles) represents the person's *genotype;* the appearance of the individual that develops as a result of the way the genes are expressed represents the person's *phenotype*.

If one allele determines the phenotype by masking the expression of the other allele in a heterozygous individual, the allele is termed *dominant*. The allele whose expression is masked is termed *recessive*. If the heterozygous condition determines an intermediate phenotype, the inheritance represents *incomplete dominance*. However, different alleles are *codominant* if both are expressed in the heterozygous condition. Some characteristics that are inherited on the sex chromosomes result in phenotype frequencies that

might be more prevalent in males or females. Such characteristics are called sex-linked (X-linked or Y-linked) characteristics.

As a result of meiosis during the formation of eggs and sperm, a mother and father each transmit an equal number of chromosomes (the haploid number 23) to form the zygote (diploid number 46). An offspring will receive one allele from each parent. These gametes combine randomly in the formation of each offspring. Hence, the *laws of probability* can be used to predict possible genotypes and phenotypes of offspring. A genetic tool called a *Punnett square* simulates all possible combinations (probabilities) that can occur in offspring genotypes and resulting phenotypes.

PURPOSE OF THE EXERCISE

To observe some selected human traits, to use pennies and dice to demonstrate laws of probability, and to solve some genetic problems using a Punnett square.

LEARNING OBJECTIVES

After completing this exercise, you should be able to

1. Observe and record twelve genotypes and phenotypes of selected human traits.
2. Demonstrate the laws of probability using tossed pennies and dice.
3. Predict genotypes and phenotypes of complete dominance, codominance, and sex-linked problems using Punnett squares.

PROCEDURE A—HUMAN GENOTYPES AND PHENOTYPES

A complete set of genetic instructions in one human cell constitutes one's *genome*. The human genome contains about 2.9 billion base pairs representing approximately 24,000 protein-encoding genes. These instructions represent our genotypes and are expressed as phenotypes that are sometimes clearly observable on our bodies. Some of these traits are listed in table 61.1 and are discernible in figure 61.1.

Because a dominant trait might be homozygous or heterozygous, only one capital letter is used along with

Table 61.1 Examples of Some Common Human Phenotypes

Dominant Traits and Genotypes	Recessive Traits and Genotypes
Tongue roller (R__)	Nonroller (rr)
Freckles (F__)	No freckles (ff)
Widow's peak (W__)	Straight hairline (ww)
Dimples (D__)	No dimples (dd)
Free earlobe (E__)	Attached earlobe (ee)
Normal skin coloration (M__)	Albinism (mm)
Astigmatism (A__)	Normal vision (aa)
Natural curly hair (C__)	Natural straight hair (cc)
PTC taster (T__)	Nontaster (tt)
Blood type A (I^A __), B (I^B __), or AB ($I^A I^B$)	Blood type O (ii)
Normal color vision ($X^C X^C$), ($X^C X^c$), or ($X^C Y$)	Red-green colorblindness ($X^c X^c$) or ($X^c Y$)

a blank for the possible second dominant or recessive allele. For a recessive trait, two lowercase letters represent the homozygous recessive genotype for that characteristic. It should be noted that dominant does not always correlate with the predominance of the allele in the gene pool; dominant means one allele will determine the appearance of the phenotype.

1. **Tongue roller/nonroller:** The dominant allele (*R*) determines the person's ability to roll the tongue into a U-shaped trough. The homozygous recessive condition (*rr*) prevents this tongue rolling (fig. 61.1). Record your results in the table in Part A of Laboratory Report 61.

2. **Freckles/no freckles:** The dominant allele (*F*) determines the appearance of freckles. The homozygous recessive condition (*ff*) does not produce freckles (fig. 61.1). Record your results in the table in Part A of the laboratory report.

3. **Widow's peak/straight hairline:** The dominant allele (*W*) determines the appearance of a hairline above the forehead that has a distinct downward point in the center, called a widow's peak. The homozygous recessive condition (*ww*) produces a straight hairline (fig. 61.1). A receding hairline would prevent this phenotype determination. Record your results in the table in Part A of the laboratory report.

4. **Dimples/no dimples:** The dominant allele (*D*) determines the appearance of a distinct dimple in one or both cheeks upon smiling. The homozygous recessive condition (*dd*) results in the absence of dimples (fig. 61.1). Record your results in the table in Part A of the laboratory report.

5. **Free earlobe/attached earlobe:** The dominant allele (*E*) codes for the appearance of an inferior earlobe that hangs freely below the attachment to the head. The homozygous recessive condition (*ee*) determines the earlobe attaching directly to the head at its inferior border (fig. 61.1). Record your results in the table in Part A of the laboratory report.

6. **Normal skin coloration/albinism:** The dominant allele (*M*) determines the production of some melanin, producing normal skin coloration. The homozygous recessive condition (*mm*) determines albinism due to the inability to produce or use the enzyme tyrosinase in pigment cells. An albino does not produce melanin in the skin, hair, or the middle tunic (choroid coat, ciliary body, and iris) of the eye. The absence of melanin in the middle tunic allows the pupil to appear slightly red to nearly black. Remember that the pupil is actually an opening in the iris that is filled with transparent aqueous humor. An albino human has pale white skin, flax-white hair, and a pale blue iris. Record your results in the table in Part A of the laboratory report.

7. **Astigmatism/normal vision:** The dominant allele (*A*) results in an abnormal curvature to the cornea or the lens. As a consequence, some portions of the image projected on the retina are sharply focused, and other portions are blurred. The homozygous recessive condition (*aa*) generates normal cornea and lens shapes and normal vision. Use the astigmatism chart and directions to assess this possible defect described in Laboratory Exercise 35. Other eye defects, such as nearsightedness (myopia) and farsightedness (hyperopia), are different genetic traits due to genes at other locations. Record your results in the table in Part A of the laboratory report.

8. **Curly hair/straight hair:** The dominant allele (*C*) determines the appearance of curly hair. Curly hair is somewhat flattened in cross section, as the hair follicle of a similar shape served as a mold for the root of the hair during its formation. The homozygous recessive condition (*cc*) produces straight hair. Straight hair is nearly round in cross section from being molded into this shape in the hair follicle. In some populations (Caucasians) the heterozygous condition (*Cc*) expresses the intermediate wavy hair phenotype (incomplete dominance). This trait determination assumes no permanents or hair straightening procedures have been performed.

Figure 61.1

Representative genetic traits comparing dominant and recessive phenotypes: (*a*) tongue roller; (*b*) nonroller; (*c*) freckles; (*d*) no freckles; (*e*) widow's peak; (*f*) straight hairline; (*g*) dimples; (*h*) no dimples; (*i*) free earlobe; (*j*) attached earlobe.

Dominant Traits   **Recessive Traits**

(a) Tongue roller

(b) Nonroller

(c) Freckles

(d) No freckles

(e) Widow's peak

(f) Straight hairline

Figure 61.1 (Continued).

Dominant Traits

(g) Dimples

(i) Free earlobe

Recessive Traits

(h) No dimples

(j) Attached earlobe

Such hair alterations do not change the hair follicle shape, and future hair growth results in original genetic hair conditions. Record your unaltered hair appearance in the table in Part A of the laboratory report.

9. **PTC taster/nontaster:** The dominant allele (*T*) determines the ability to experience a bitter sensation when PTC paper is placed on the tongue. About 70% of people possess this dominant gene. The homozygous recessive condition (*tt*) makes a person unable to notice the substance. Place a piece of PTC (phenylthiocarbamide) paper on the upper tongue surface and chew it slightly to see if you notice a bitter sensation from this harmless chemical. The nontaster of the PTC paper does not detect any

taste at all from this substance. Record your results in the table in Part A of the laboratory report.

10. **Blood type A, B, or AB/blood type O:** There are three alleles (*I^A*, *I^B*, and *i*) in the human population affecting RBC membrane structure. Because these alleles are located on a single pair of homologous chromosomes, a person could possess either two of the three alleles or two of the same allele. All of the possible combinations of these alleles of genotypes and the resulting phenotypes are depicted in table 61.2. The expression of the blood type AB is a result of both codominant alleles located in the same individual. Possibly you have already determined your blood type in Laboratory Exercise 39 or have it recorded on a blood donor

Table 61.2 Genotypes and Phenotypes (Blood Types)

Genotypes	Phenotypes (Blood Types)
$I^A I^A$ or $I^A i$	A
$I^B I^B$ or $I^B i$	B
$I^A I^B$ (codominant)	AB
ii	O

card. (If simulated blood-typing kits were used for Laboratory Exercise 39, those results would not be valid for your genetic factors.) Record your results in the table in Part A of the laboratory report.

11. **Sex determination:** A person with sex chromosomes XX displays a female phenotype. A person with sex chromosomes XY displays a male phenotype. Record your results in the table in Part A of the laboratory report.

12. **Normal color vision/red-green color-blindness:** This condition is a sex-linked (X-linked) characteristic. The alleles for color vision are also on the X chromosome, but absent on the Y chromosome. As a result, a female might possess both alleles (C and c), one on each of the X chromosomes. The dominant allele (C) determines normal color vision; the homozygous recessive condition (cc) results in red-green colorblindness. However, a male would possess only one of the two alleles for color vision because there is only a single X chromosome in a male. Hence a male with even a single recessive gene for colorblindness possesses the defect. Note all the possible genotypes and phenotypes for this condition (table 61.1). Review the color vision test in Laboratory Exercise 35 using the color plates in figure 35.4 and Ichikawa's or Ishihara's book. Record your results in the table in Part A of the laboratory report.

PROCEDURE B—LAWS OF PROBABILITY

The laws of probability provide a mathematical way to determine the likelihood of events occurring by chance. This prediction is often expressed as a ratio of the number of results from experimental events to the number of results considered possible. For example, when tossing a coin there is an equal chance of the results displaying heads or tails. Hence the probability is one-half of obtaining either a heads or a tails (there are two possibilities for each toss). When all of the probabilities of all possible outcomes are considered for the result, they will always add up to a 1. To predict the probability of two or more events occurring in succession, multiply the probabilities of each individual event. For example, the probability of tossing a die and displaying a 4 two times in a row is $1/6 \times 1/6 = 1/36$ (there are

six possibilities for each toss). Each toss in a sequence is an *independent event* (chance has no memory). The same laws apply when parents have multiple children (each fertilization is an independent event). Perform the following experiments to demonstrate the laws of probability:

1. Use a single penny (or other coin) and toss it 20 times. Predict the number of heads and tails that would occur from the 20 tosses. Record your prediction and the actual results observed in Part B of the laboratory report.

2. Use a single die (*pl.* dice) and toss it 24 times. Predict the number of times a number below 3 (numbers 1 and 2) would occur from the 24 tosses. Record your prediction and the actual results in Part B of the laboratory report.

3. Use two pennies and toss them simultaneously 32 times. Predict the number of times two heads, a heads and a tails, and two tails occur. Record your prediction and the actual results in Part B of the laboratory report.

4. Use a pair of dice and toss them simultaneously 32 times. Predict the number of times for both dice coming up with odd numbers, one die an odd and the other an even number, and both dice coming up with even numbers. Record your prediction and the actual results in Part B of the laboratory report.

5. Obtain class totals for all of the coins and dice tossed by adding your individual results to a class tally location as on the blackboard.

6. A Punnett square can be used for a visual representation to demonstrate the probable results for two pennies tossed simultaneously. For the purpose of a genetic comparison, an *h* (heads) will represent one "allele" on the coin; a *t* (tails) will represent a different "allele" on the coin.

Coin #1 Possibilities

		h	*t*	
Coin #2 Possibilities	*h*	*hh*	*ht*	Possible Combinations of Two Tossed Pennies
	t	*ht*	*tt*	(in Boxes)

7. Complete Part B of the laboratory report.

PROCEDURE C—GENETIC PROBLEMS

1. A Punnett square can be constructed to demonstrate a visual display of the predicted offspring from parents with known genotypes. Recall that in complete dominance, a dominant allele is expressed in the phenotype, as it can mask the other recessive allele on the homologous chromosome pair. Recall also that during meiosis, the homologous chromosomes with their alleles separate (Mendel's Law of Segregation) into different gametes. An example of such a cross

might be a homozygous dominant mother for dimples (*DD*) has offspring with a father homozygous recessive (*dd*) for the same trait. The results of such a cross, according to the laws of probability, would be represented by the following Punnett square:

Female Gametes

		D	D	
Male Gametes	d	Dd	Dd	Possible Genotypes of
	d	Dd	Dd	Offspring (in Boxes)

Results: Genotypes: 100% *Dd* (all heterozygous)

Phenotypes: 100% dimples

In another example, assume that both parents are heterozygous (*Dd*) for dimples. The results of such a cross, according to the laws of probability, would be represented by the following Punnett square:

Female Gametes

		D	d	
Male Gametes	D	DD	Dd	Possible Genotypes
	d	Dd	dd	of Offspring

Results: Genotypes: 25% *DD* (homozygous dominant); 50% *Dd* (heterozygous); 25% *dd* (homozygous recessive) (1:2:1 genotypic ratio)

Phenotypes: 75% dimples; 25% no dimples (3:1 phenotypic ratio)

2. Work the genetic problems 1 and 2 in Part C of the laboratory report.
3. The ABO blood type inheritance represents an example of codominance. Review table 61.2 for the genotypes and phenotypes for the expression of this trait. A similar technique to that used previously can be used to predict the offspring of parents of known genotypes. In this example, assume the genotype of the mother is $I^A I^B$, and the father is *ii*. The results of such a cross would be represented by the following Punnett square:

Female Gametes

		I^A	I^B	
Male Gametes	i	$I^A i$	$I^B i$	Possible Genotypes of
	i	$I^A i$	$I^B i$	Offspring

Results: Genotypes: 50% $I^A i$ (heterozygous for A); 50% $I^B i$ (heterozygous for B) (1:1 genotypic ratio)

Phenotypes: 50% blood type A; 50% blood type B (1:1 phenotypic ratio)

Note: In this particular cross, all of the children would have blood types unlike either parent.

4. Work the genetic problems 3 and 4 in Part C of the laboratory report.
5. Review the inheritance of red-green colorblindness, which is an X-linked characteristic, in table 61.1. A similar technique to that used to identify complete dominance can be used to predict the offspring of parents of known genotypes. In this example, assume the genotype of the mother is heterozygous $X^C X^c$ (normal color vision, but a carrier for the colorblindness defect), and the father is $X^C Y$ (normal color vision; no allele on the Y chromosome). The results of such a cross would be represented by the following Punnett square:

Female Gametes

		X^C	X^c	
Male Gametes	X^C	$X^C X^C$	$X^C X^c$	Possible Genotypes
	Y	$X^C Y$	$X^c Y$	of Offspring

Results: Genotypes: 25% $X^C X^c$; 25% $X^C X^c$; 25% $X^C Y$; 25% $X^c Y$ (1:1:1:1 genotypic ratio)

Phenotypes for sex determination: 50% females; 50% males (1:1 phenotypic ratio)

Phenotypes for color vision: Females 100% normal color vision (however, 50% are heterozygous carriers for colorblindness)

Males 50% normal; 50% with red-green colorblindness (1:1 phenotypic ratio)

Note: In X-linked inheritance the colorblind males received the recessive gene from their mothers.

6. Complete Part C of the laboratory report.

Web Quest

Search this site for additional family genetic information at
www.mhhe.com/shier11
Click on Student Edition. Click on Martin Lab Manual, Web Quest.

Name _____

Date _____

Section _____

GENETICS

PART A

1. Enter your test results for genotypes and phenotypes in the table. Circle your particular phenotype and genotype for each of the twelve traits.

Trait	Dominant Phenotype	Genotype	Recessive Phenotype	Genotype
Tongue movement	Roller	R__	Nonroller	rr
Freckles	Freckles	F__	No freckles	ff
Hairline	Widow's peak	W__	Straight	ww
Dimples	Dimples	D__	No dimples	dd
Earlobe	Free	E__	Attached	ee
Skin coloration	Normal (some melanin)	M__	Albinism	mm
Vision	Astigmatism	A__	Normal	aa
Hair shape*	Curly	C__	Straight	cc
Taste	PTC taster	T__	Nontaster for PTC	tt
Blood type	A, B, or AB	I^A__; I^B__; or $I^A I^B$	O	ii
Sex		XX or XY		
Color vision	Normal	$X^C X$__ or $X^C Y$	Red-green colorblindness	$X^C X^c$ or $X^c Y$

*In some populations (Caucasians) the heterozygous condition (Cc) results in the appearance of wavy hair, which actually represents an example of incomplete dominance for this trait.

2. Analyze all the genotypes that you circled for the dominant phenotypes. If it is feasible to observe your biological parents and siblings for any of these traits, are you able to determine if any of your dominant genotypes are homozygous dominant or heterozygous? _____ If so, which ones? Explain the rationale for your response.

_____

_____

_____

_____

_____

PART B

1. Single penny tossed 20 times and counting heads and tails:

Probability (prediction): ___/20 heads ___/20 tails
(Note: Traditionally, probabilities are converted to the lowest fractional representation.)

Actual results: ____ heads ____ tails

Class totals: ____ heads _____ tails

2. Single die tossed 24 times and counting the number of times a number below 3 occurs:

   Probability: ____/24 number below 3 (numbers 1 and 2)

   Actual results: ____ number below 3

   Class totals: ____ number below 3 ____ total tosses by class members

3. Two pennies tossed simultaneously 32 times and counting the number of two heads, a heads and a tails, and two tails:

   Probability: ____/32 of two heads ____/32 of a heads and a tails ____/32 of two tails

   Actual results: ____two heads ____heads and tails ____two tails

   Class totals: ____two heads ____heads and tails ____two tails

4. Two dice tossed simultaneously 32 times and counting the number of two odd numbers, an odd and an even number, and two even numbers:

   Probability: ____/32 of two odd numbers ____/32 of an odd and an even number ____/32 of two even numbers

   Actual results: ____ two odd numbers ____ an odd and an even number ____ two even numbers

   Class totals: ____ two odd numbers ____ an odd and an even number ____ two even numbers

5. Use the example of the two dice tossed 32 times and construct a Punnett square to represent the possible combinations that could be used to determine the probability (prediction) of odd and even numbers for the resulting tosses. Your construction should be similar to the Punnett square for the two coins tossed that is depicted in Procedure B of the laboratory exercise.

6. Complete the following:

   a. Are the class totals closer to the predicted probabilities than your results? _____ Explain your response.

   _____

   _____

   _____

   _____

   b. Does the first toss of the penny or the first toss of the die have any influence on the next toss? _____ Explain your response.

   _____

   _____

   _____

   _____

   c. Assume a family has two boys or two girls. They wish to have one more child, but hope for the child to be of the opposite sex from the two they already have. What is the probability that the third child will be of the opposite sex? _____ Explain your response.

   _____

   _____

   _____

   _____

d. What is the probability (prediction) that a couple without children will eventually have four children, all girls? _____ Explain your response.

_____

_____

_____

_____

PART C

For each of the genetic problems, (a) determine the parents' genotypes, (b) determine the possible gametes for each parent, (c) construct a Punnett square, and (d) record the resulting genotypes and phenotypes as ratios from the cross. Problems 1 and 2 involve examples of complete dominance; problems 3 and 4 are examples of codominance; problem 5 is an example of sex-linked (X-linked) inheritance.

1. Determine the results from a cross of a mother who is heterozygous (*Rr*) for tongue rolling with a father who is homozygous recessive (*rr*).

2. Determine the results from a cross of a mother and a father who are both heterozygous for freckles.

3. Determine the results from a mother who is heterozygous for blood type B and a father who is homozygous dominant for blood type A.

4. Determine the results from a mother who is heterozygous for blood type A and a father who is heterozygous for blood type B.

5. Colorblindness is an example of X-linked inheritance. Hemophilia is another example of X-linked inheritance, also from a recessive allele (*h*). The dominant allele (*H*) determines whether the person possesses normal blood clotting. A person with hemophilia has a permanent tendency for hemorrhaging due to a deficiency of one of the clotting factors (VIII—antihemophilic factor). Determine the offspring from a cross of a mother who is a carrier (heterozygous) for the disease and a father with normal blood coagulation.

Critical Thinking Application

Assume that the genes for hairline and earlobes are on different pairs of homologous chromosomes. Determine the genotypes and phenotypes of the offspring from a cross if both parents are heterozygous for both traits. (1) First determine the genotypes for each parent. (2) Determine the gametes, but remember each gamete has one allele for each trait (gametes are haploid). (3) Construct a Punnett square with 16 boxes that has four different gametes from each parent along the top and the left edges. (This is an application to demonstrate Mendel's Law of Independent Assortment.) (4) List the results of genotypes and phenotypes as ratios.

APPENDIX 1

PREPARATION OF SOLUTIONS

Amylase solution, 0.5%
Place 0.5 g of bacterial amylase in a graduated cylinder or volumetric flask. Add distilled water to the 100 mL level. Stir until dissolved. See the Instructor's Manual for a supplier of amylase that is free of sugar. (Store amylase powder in a freezer until mixing this solution.)

Benedict's solution
Prepared solution is available from various suppliers.

Caffeine, 0.2%
Place 0.2 g of caffeine in a graduated cylinder or volumetric flask. Add distilled water to the 100 mL level. Stir until dissolved.

Calcium chloride, 2.0%
Place 2.0 g of calcium chloride in a graduated cylinder or volumetric flask. Add distilled water to the 100 mL level. Stir until dissolved.

Calcium hydroxide solution (limewater)
Add an excess of calcium hydroxide to 1 L of distilled water. Stopper the bottle and shake thoroughly. Allow the solution to stand for 24 hours. Pour the supernatant fluid through a filter. Store the clear filtrate in a stoppered container.

Epsom salt solution, 0.1%
Place 0.5 g of Epsom salt in a graduated cylinder or volumetric flask. Add distilled water to the 500 mL level. Stir until dissolved.

Glucose solutions
1. *1.0% solution.* Place 1 g of glucose in a graduated cylinder or volumetric flask. Add distilled water to the 100 mL level. Stir until dissolved.
2. *10% solution.* Place 10 g of glucose in a graduated cylinder or volumetric flask. Add distilled water to the 100 mL level. Stir until dissolved.

Iodine-potassium-iodide (IKI solution)
Add 20 g of potassium iodide to 1 L of distilled water, and stir until dissolved. Then add 4.0 g of iodine, and stir again until dissolved. Solution should be stored in a dark stoppered bottle.

Methylene blue
Dissolve 0.3 g of methylene blue powder in 30 mL of 95% ethyl alcohol. In a separate container, dissolve 0.01 g of potassium hydroxide in 100 mL of distilled water. Mix the two solutions. (Prepared solution is available from various suppliers.)

Physiological saline solution
Place 0.9 g of sodium chloride in a graduated cylinder or volumetric flask. Add distilled water to the 100 mL level. Stir until dissolved.

Potassium chloride, 5%
Place 5.0 g of potassium chloride in a graduated cylinder or volumetric flask. Add distilled water to the 100 mL level. Stir until dissolved.

Quinine sulfate, 0.5%
Place 0.5 g of quinine sulfate in a graduated cylinder or volumetric flask. Add distilled water to the 100 mL level. Stir until dissolved.

Ringer's solution (frog)
Dissolve the following salts in 1 L of distilled water:

> 6.50 g sodium chloride
> 0.20 g sodium bicarbonate
> 0.14 g potassium chloride
> 0.12 g calcium chloride

Sodium chloride solutions
1. *0.9% solution.* Place 0.9 g of sodium chloride in a graduated cylinder or volumetric flask. Add distilled water to the 100 mL level. Stir until dissolved.
2. *1.0% solution.* Place 1.0 g of sodium chloride in a graduated cylinder or volumetric flask. Add distilled water to the 100 mL level. Stir until dissolved.
3. *3.0% solution.* Place 3.0 g of sodium chloride in a graduated cylinder or volumetric flask. Add distilled water to the 100 mL level. Stir until dissolved.
4. *5.0% solution.* Place 5.0 g of sodium chloride in a graduated cylinder or volumetric flask. Add distilled water to the 100 mL level. Stir until dissolved.

Starch solutions
1. *0.5% solution.* Add 5 g of cornstarch to 1 L of distilled water. Heat until the mixture boils. Cool the liquid, and pour it through a filter. Store the filtrate in a refrigerator.
2. *1.0% solution.* Add 10 g of cornstarch to 1 L of distilled water. Heat until the mixture boils. Cool the liquid, and pour it through a filter. Store the filtrate in a refrigerator.
3. *10% solution.* Add 100 g of cornstarch to 1 L of distilled water. Heat until the mixture boils. Cool the liquid, and pour it through a filter. Store the filtrate in a refrigerator.

Sucrose, 5% solution
Place 5.0 g of sucrose in a graduated cylinder or volumetric flask. Add distilled water to the 100 mL level. Stir until dissolved.

Wright's stain
Prepared solution is available from various suppliers.

APPENDIX 2

ASSESSMENTS OF LABORATORY REPORTS

Many assessment models can be used for laboratory reports. A rubric, which can be used for performance assessments, contains a description of the elements (requirements or criteria) of success to various degrees. The term *rubric* originated from *rubrica terra,* which is Latin for the application of red earth to indicate anything of importance. A rubric used for assessment contains elements for judging student performance, with points awarded for varying degrees of success in meeting the objectives. The content and the quality level necessary to attain certain points are indicated in the rubric. It is effective if the assessment tool is shared with the students before the laboratory exercise is performed.

Following are two sample rubrics that could easily be modified to meet the needs of a specific course. Some of the elements for these sample rubrics may not be necessary for every laboratory exercise. The generalized rubric needs to contain the possible assessment points that correspond to objectives for a specific course. The point value for each element may vary. The specific rubric example contains performance levels for laboratory reports. The elements and the point values could easily be altered to meet the value placed on laboratory reports for a specific course.

ASSESSMENT: GENERALIZED LABORATORY REPORT RUBRIC

Element	Assessment Points Possible	Assessment Points Earned
1. Figures are completely and accurately labeled.	_____	_____
2. Sketches are accurate, contain proper labels, and are of sufficient detail.	_____	_____
3. Colored pencils were used extensively to differentiate structures on illustrations.	_____	_____
4. Matching and fill-in-the-blank answers are completed and accurate.	_____	_____
5. Short-answer/discussion questions contain complete, thorough, and accurate answers. Some elaboration is evident for some answers.	_____	_____
6. Data collected are complete, accurately displayed, and contain a valid explanation.	_____	_____
Total Points	_____	_____

ASSESSMENT: SPECIFIC LABORATORY REPORT RUBRIC

Element	Excellent Performance (4 points)	Proficient Performance (3 points)	Marginal Performance (2 points)	Novice Performance (1 point)	Points Earned
Figure labels	Labels completed with ≥90% accuracy.	Labels completed with 80%–89% accuracy.	Labels completed with 70%–79% accuracy.	Labels <70% accurate.	
Sketches	Accurate use of scale, details illustrated, and all structures labeled accurately.	Minor errors in sketches. Missing or inaccurate labels on one or more structures.	Sketch is not realistic. Missing or inaccurate labels on two or more structures.	Several missing or inaccurate labels.	
Matching and fill-in-the-blanks	All completed and accurate.	One to two errors or omissions.	Three to four errors or omissions.	Five or more errors or omissions.	
Short-answer and discussion questions	Answers are complete, valid, and contain some elaboration. No misinterpretations are noted.	Answers are generally complete and valid. Only minor inaccuracies were noted. Minimal elaboration exists.	Marginal answers to the questions and contains inaccurate information.	Many answers are incorrect or fail to address the topic. There may be misinterpretations.	
Data collection and analysis	Data are complete and displayed with a valid interpretation.	Only minor data missing or a slight misinterpretation exists.	Some omissions. Not displayed or interpreted accurately.	Data are incomplete or show serious misinterpretations.	

Total Points Earned _____

PHOTO CREDITS

Preface

Author photo: J. Womack Photography

Lab Exercise 1

1.1, 1.2, 1.3: © McGraw-Hill Companies/J. Womack Photography

Lab Exercise 2

2.3, 2.4: © McGraw-Hill Companies/J. Womack Photography

Lab Exercise 4

4.1–4.3, 4.6: © McGraw-Hill Companies/J. Womack Photography

Lab Exercise 5

5.3: © Ed Reschke; 5.4a–c: Richard Rodewald/Biological Photo Service

Lab Exercise 6

6.1: © McGraw-Hill Companies/J. Womack Photography

Lab Exercise 7

7.1(all) & 7.3: © Ed Reschke; 7.4a,b: Courtesy of the March of Dimes Birth Defects Foundation; 7.5(all): © Ed Reschke

Lab Exercise 8

8.1a,b: © Ed Reschke; 8.1c: © Manfred Kage/Peter Arnold; 8.1d: © Ed Reschke; 8.1e: © Fred Hossler/Visuals Unlimited; 8.1f: © Ed Reschke

Lab Exercise 9

9.1a–c: © Ed Reschke; 9.1d: © John D. Cunningham/Visuals Unlimited; 9.1e: © Ed Reschke/Peter Arnold; 9.1f,g: © Ed Reschke; 9.1i: © Ed Reschke; 9.1j: © Ed Reschke/Peter Arnold

Lab Exercise 10

10.1a,b: © Ed Reschke; 10.1c: © Manfred Kage/Peter Arnold; 10.1d: © Ed Reschke

Lab Exercise 11

11.4a: © Victor B. Eichler, Ph.D; 11.4b: © McGraw-Hill Companies/Carol D. Jacobson, Ph.D, Dept. of Veterinary Anatomy, Iowa State University; 11.4c: © Victor B. Eichler, Ph.D; 11.4d: © Per H. Kjeldsen, University of Michigan, Ann Arbor

Lab Exercise 12

12.3: © Victor B. Eichler; 12.4a,b: © McGraw-Hill Companies/J. Womack Photography; 12.5a,b:

© McGraw-Hill Companies/J. Womack Photography

Lab Exercise 13

13.2: © McGraw-Hill Companies/J. Womack Photography

Lab Exercise 14

14.6–14.11: © McGraw-Hill Companies/J. Womack Photography

Lab Exercise 15

15.2a–15.3c: © McGraw-Hill Companies/J. Womack Photography; 15.6: © Dr. Kent M. Van De Graaff

Lab Exercise 16

16.7: © Martin M. Rotker; 16.8: Courtesy of Eastman Kodak; 16.9: © Martin M. Rotker; 16.10: © McGraw-Hill Companies/J. Womack Photography

Lab Exercise 17

17.7–17.9: © Martin M. Rotker; 17.10: © McGraw-Hill Companies/J. Womack Photography

Lab Exercise 20

20.4a–c: © McGraw-Hill Companies/J. Womack Photography

Lab Exercise 21

21.5a–c: © McGraw-Hill Companies/J. Womack Photography

Lab Exercise 23

23.7a,b: © McGraw-Hill Companies/J. Womack Photography

Lab Exercise 24

24.2–24.22: Courtesy of Dr. Sheril Burton; 24.23: © McGraw-Hill Companies/Photo Ralph W. Stevens III, Ph.D

Lab Exercise 25

25.3–25.7: © Ed Reschke

Lab Exercise 27

27.2(all): © McGraw-Hill Companies/J. Womack Photography

Lab Exercise 28

28.5: © Martin Rogker/Photo Researchers, Inc.

Lab Exercise 29

29.2, 29.6: © McGraw-Hill Companies/J. Womack Photography

Lab Exercise 30

30.1, 30.2: © Ed Reschke

Lab Exercise 31

31.2: © Dwight Kuhn; 31.4: © Ed Reschke

Lab Exercise 32

32.4: © McGraw-Hill Companies/J. Womack Photography; 32.5: © Biophoto Associates/Photo Researchers, Inc.; 32.6a–32.7: © McGraw-Hill Companies/J. Womack Photography; 32.8: © John D. Cunningham/Visuals Unlimited

Lab Exercise 33

33.2: © John D. Cunningham/Visuals Unlimited

Lab Exercise 34

34.4: © Per H. Kjeldsen, University of Michigan, Ann Arbor; 34.5: © McGraw-Hill Companies/J. Womack Photography; 34.7a: © Carroll Weiss/Camera M.D. Studios; 34.9: © McGraw-Hill Companies/J. Womack Photography; 34.10a,b: © Carroll Weiss/Camera M.D. Studios

Lab Exercise 35

35.3: © McGraw-Hill Companies/J. Womack Photography

Lab Exercise 36

36.2: © Biophoto Associates/Photo Researchers, Inc.; 36.3: © Ed Reschke; 36.4: © Biophoto Associates/Photo Researchers, Inc.; 36.5, 36.6: © Ed Reschke; 36.7: © Dr. F. C. Skvara/Visuals Unlimited

Lab Exercise 38

38.2a–d: © McGraw-Hill Companies/Photo by James Shaffer; 38.5: Courtesy of Stuart J. Fox; 38.8: © McGraw-Hill Companies/J. Womack Photography

Lab Exercise 40

40.4, 40.5, 40.6: © McGraw-Hill Companies/J. Womack Photography

Lab Exercise 42

42.3: © Biophoto Associates/Photo Researchers, Inc.

Lab Exercise 45

45.2–45.9: Courtesy of Dr. Sheril Burton

Lab Exercise 46

46.3: © John Watney/Photo Researchers, Inc.; 46.4: © John D. Cunningham/Visuals Unlimited; 46.5: © Biophoto Associates/Photo Researchers, Inc.

Lab Exercise 47

47.4: © Biophoto Associates/Photo Researchers, Inc.; 47.6 & 47.9: © Ed Reschke; 47.12: © Dennis Strete; 47.13: © Ed Reschke/Peter Arnold

Lab Exercise 48

48.4: Courtesy of Dr. Sheril Burton

Lab Exercise 50

50.5: © Ed Reschke; 50.6: © Biophoto Associates/Photo Researchers, Inc.; 50.7: Victor B. Eichler, Ph.D.; 50.8: © Dwight Kuhn

Lab Exercise 51

51.2: Courtesy of Dr. Sheril Burton

Lab Exercise 52

52.1–52.3: © McGraw-Hill Companies/J. Womack Photography

Lab Exercise 54

54.3: © McGraw-Hill Companies/J. Womack Photography; 54.5a: © Biophoto Associates/Photo Researchers, Inc.; 54.5b: © Manfred Kage/Peter Arnold

Lab Exercise 56

56.3: © McGraw-Hill Companies/Photo by Ralph W. Stevens III, Ph.D.

Lab Exercise 57

57.3: © Biophoto Associates/Photo Researchers, Inc.; 57.4, 57.5: © Ed Reschke; 57.6: © 1989 Michael Peres

Lab Exercise 58

58.6: © Ed Reschke/Peter Arnold; 58.7: © Ed Reschke; 58.8, 58.9: © 1989 Michael Peres

Lab Exercise 59

59.3: © McGraw-Hill Companies/Photo Ralph W. Stevens III, Ph.D.

Lab Exercise 61

61.1(all): © McGraw-Hill Companies/J. Womack Photography

*Lab Exercise 62

62.1(both): © 2002 Phipps & Bird, Inc.; 62.2 Narco Bio-Systems Narco Trace® Narco Bio-Systems is a division of International Biomedical Inc.; 62.3: © McGraw-Hill Companies/Richard Pflanzer; 62.5a,b: © McGraw-Hill Companies/J. Womack Photography

*Lab Exercise 63

63.1: © McGraw-Hill Companies/J. Womack Photography

*Lab Exercise 64

64.2: © McGraw-Hill Companies/J. Womack Photography

---

*These laboratory exercises are available at www.mhhe.com/shier11

INDEX

515

urine
    color of, 454
    pH test of, 455
    sediments of, 455, 456
    specific gravity of, 454
    strip tests of, 454-455
    transparency of, 454
urogenital aperture, 479,
    480, 481
urogenital sinus, 479, 480, 481
uterine tube, 471, 472, 477,
    479, 480
uterus, 461, 471, 472, 477, 479,
    480, 481
uvula, 394

V

vagina, 174, 461, 471, 480, 481
vagus nerve, 233, 234, 241,
    242, 374
vas deferens, 465, 466, 480, 482,
    483, 484
vastus intermedius muscle, 204, 207
vastus lateralis muscle, 181, 186,
    204, 205, 207
vastus medialis muscle, 186, 202,
    204, 207
vein(s), 11, 359-360
    abdominal, 359-360, 365
    arm, 359
    of cat, 377-382
    forelimb, 380
    head and neck, 359, 363
    hindlimb, 380, 381
    leg, 360, 366
    neck, 380
    pelvis, 360, 366
    shoulder, 359
    structure of, 345, 346, 347
    thorax, 359, 364, 380
vena cava
    anterior, 375, 377, 380
    inferior, 329, 330, 334, 357, 366,
        369, 446
    posterior, 375, 377, 378, 379,
        380, 381, 382, 460
    superior, 329, 330, 334, 357,
        364, 369
ventral respiratory group neurons,
    439, 440
ventricles
    cardiac, 329, 330, 334, 371, 372,
        374, 375
    cerebral, 231, 237, 242,
        243, 327
vermiform appendix, 399
vertebra prominens (C7), 115,
    116, 122
vertebrae, 10, 115, 116, 117, 118,
    121-122
vertebral arch, 115
vertebral artery, 372
vertebral canal, 115

vertebral column, 115-116,
    121-122
vertebral foramen, 115, 117, 118
vestibular membrane, 264
vestibulocochlear nerve, 233, 234,
    241, 242, 261, 263
villi, chorionic, 489, 490
visceral pericardium, 371
vision. *See also* eye
    tests of, 285-292
visual acuity test, 285
vital capacity, 433, 434, 435
vitreous humor, 278, 279-280, 283
vocal cords, 425
vomer bone, 105, 106, 111, 113, 114
vulva, 474

W

warm receptors, 249
Weber test, 263, 266
wet mount, 35-37
Wharton's duct, 393, 406
white blood cells, 306
    count of, 306, 317-318, 319
    urinary, 456
white matter, 219, 220, 224, 242
white pulp, 388
whitefish blastula, 59, 65
widow's peak/straight hairline,
    496, 497
Wright's stain, 505

X

x ray
    elbow, 130
    foot, 141
    hand, 131
    knee, 140
    pelvis, 140
    shoulder, 130
    vertebra prominens, 122
xiphihumeralis muscle, 192, 193,
    194, 195, 199

Y

yellow marrow, 92
yolk sac, 489, 490

Z

zona fasciculata, 296
zona glomerulosa, 296
zona pellucida, 473
zona reticularis, 296
zygomatic bone, 105, 106, 111,
    112, 113, 114
zygomatic process, 112
zygomaticus major muscle,
    157, 162
zygomaticus minor muscle,
    157, 158